Why Do You Need This New Edition?

As we developed this new third edition, we were committed to strengthening the theme of embracing difference throughout the book. We added cross-cultural examples to help illustrate the importance of understanding difference, and expanded students' opportunities to reflect, practice, and therefore learn about the importance of embracing that difference. As reinforced throughout the book, students become more effective communicators when they understand and appreciate difference, because they can more appropriately respond to complex communication situations.

One of the inspirations for the changes in this edition was the Edward M. Kennedy Serve America Act, which reauthorizes and expands national service programs and was signed by President Barack Obama in April 2009. National initiatives devoted to volunteerism and community involvement, such as Serve.gov and ServiceNation, are inspiring a new era of voluntary citizen service in America. The ideals of service are based on the acceptance of differing values and cultures, and the ethical treatment of neighbors and fellow citizens.

Some of the more important changes in this edition include:

1. a new feature, *Serving Your Community*, which provides students with an opportunity to engage in volunteer activities and service learning, which helps students appreciate the importance of assisting others and provides them with an opportunity to work with people whose life experiences can be very different from their own. In addition to the intrinsic value of service, these activities can lead to potential internships and employment opportunities for students after graduation. Of course, these activities also help students enhance their communication skills.

2. the new component of critical thinking in the *Communication and Ethics* section of each chapter, designed to enhance students' understanding of the importance of ethics. This new dimension provides students with specific questions to reflect upon based on the opening scenarios in each chapter.

3. an updated *Communication and Technology* section in each chapter. As current technology continues to evolve very quickly, students need to understand the role that technology plays when communicating with others. We want to make students aware of what technology can do, as well as make them sensitive to principles of communication etiquette that dictate how they can best use current technology to enhance their communication with each other.

4. strengthening the relevance of the Public Communication section. By including examples of rhetoric from the historic 2008 presidential election throughout these sections, we have made the text more current and relevant.

5. politically diverse examples of rhetoric for students to read and dissect, further emphasizing the importance of embracing difference. Examples of speeches delivered from different political perspectives gives students the opportunity to reflect upon the rhetoric generated from different political positions which, in turn, potentially helps them understand multiple political views.

6. the addition of a key concepts list at the end of each chapter, which highlights the themes that are critical to students' learning and understanding.

Communication
Embracing Difference

Third Edition

Daniel M. Dunn
Purdue University Calumet

Lisa J. Goodnight
Purdue University Calumet

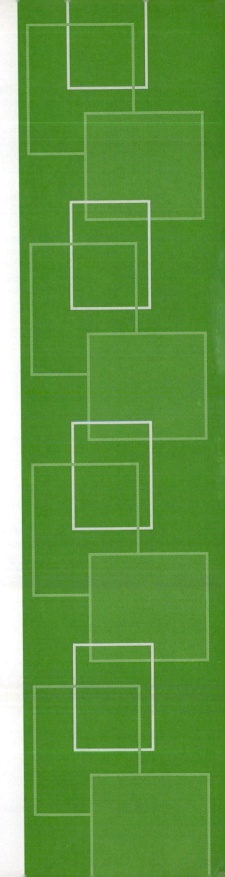

Allyn & Bacon

Boston   Columbus   Indianapolis   New York   San Francisco   Upper Saddle River
Amsterdam   Cape Town   Dubai   London   Madrid   Milan   Munich   Paris   Montreal   Toronto
Delhi   Mexico City   São Paulo   Sydney   Hong Kong   Seoul   Singapore   Taipei   Tokyo

Editor in Chief, Communication: Karon Bowers
Editorial Assistant: Stephanie Chaisson
Marketing Manager: Blair Tuckman
Project Manager: Barbara Mack
Managing Editor: Linda Mihatov Behrens
Development Assistant: Patrick Barb
Media Producer: Megan Higginbotham
Project Coordination, Text Design, and Electronic Page
    Makeup: Electronic Publishing Services Inc., NYC
Senior Operations Specialist: Nick Sklitsis
Operations Specialist: Mary Ann Gloriande
Art Director, Cover: Anne Nieglos
Cover Designer: Kathryn Foot
Creative Director: Leslie Osher
Cover Image: © Lisa Henderling/CORBIS All Rights Reserved
Manager, Photo Rights and Permissions: Zina Arabia
Manager, Visual Research: Beth Brenzel
Image Permission Coordinator: Silvana Attanasio
Photo Researcher: Kathy Ringrose

Library of Congress Cataloging-in-Publication Data

Dunn, Daniel M.
    Communication : embracing difference / Daniel M. Dunn ; Lisa J. Goodnight. — 3rd ed.
        p. cm.
    Includes bibliographical references and index.
    ISBN-13: 978-0-205-68812-8 (paperbound)
    ISBN-10: 0-205-68812-8
    1.   Oral communication.   I.   Goodnight, Lisa J. II. Title.
    P95.D86 2010
    302.2'242—dc22

                                                        2009038208

10   9   8   7   6   5   4   3   2   1   EDW   13   12   11   10

Photo credits appear on page 351, which constitutes an extension of the copyright page.

Allyn & Bacon
is an imprint of

www.pearsonhighered.com

ISBN-13: 978-0-205-68812-8
ISBN-10:   0-205-68812-8

For Linda and Laura
—D. M. D.

For Lee and Hannah
—L. J. G.

Contents

9 Communicating in Small Groups   168

10 Solving Problems Using Small Groups   187

UNIT III   PUBLIC COMMUNICATION

11 Selecting a Speech Topic and Adapting to the Audience   202

Sample Student Persuasive Speech   334

Preface

We teach a very diverse population of students. Our students range widely in age, ethnicity, race, religion, sexual orientation, social role, and socioeconomic status. Many are first-generation college students and often attend our colleges or universities part-time while holding a full-time job. They are mothers, fathers, grandparents, and teenagers. *Communication: Embracing Difference* is written for them. It is also written for you, teachers of all different types of students. It reflects the full lives of our students in their work, family life, community, and here at school. This text is a tool that will help you provide students with opportunities to explore and celebrate the richness of difference and diversity in society.

PERSPECTIVE OF THE BOOK

Humans approach communication from diverse and unique positions. Because communication is an interdependent process that involves at least two people, multiple approaches to communication situations exist. Understanding the diversity of communication approaches can lead to a greater overall understanding of others.

In our view, valuing diversity goes beyond simply focusing on race, gender, or ethnicity. Embracing difference is a way of viewing the world in which differences among people are valued. When we embrace difference we learn to appreciate multiple approaches to communicating with others. This worldview provides us with diverse approaches to learning, problem solving and working with people.

Embracing difference promotes learning from diverse perspectives and increases our ability to successfully respond to a wider variety of communication solutions. Thus the theme of embracing difference is integrated throughout the entire text.

Once students have been exposed to a wide variety of communication options, it is the practical application of communication skills that helps them formulate appropriate responses to new situations. Practicing these skills in a variety of settings, including interpersonal, small-group and public communication, helps students become more confident and successful communicators.

One of the inspirations for this third edition was the Edward M. Kennedy Serve America Act, which reauthorizes and expands national service programs and was signed by President Barack Obama in April 2009. National initiatives devoted to volunteerism and community involvement, such as Serve.gov and ServiceNation, are inspiring a new era of voluntary citizen service in America. The ideals of service are based on the acceptance of differing values and cultures, and the ethical treatment of neighbors and fellow citizens.

ORGANIZATION OF THE BOOK

Communication: Embracing Difference is comprised of three units containing sixteen chapters. Unit One, The Process of Communication, includes chapters on perception, language, nonverbal behavior, and listening. Unit Two, Interpersonal Communication, emphasizes theories and skills of interpersonal communication including self-disclosure, conflict, and an entire chapter on communication climate. A chapter on interviewing covers the principles and practices of interviewing with special attention to informative and employment interviewing. The unit also includes an overview of small-group communication, small-group decision making, and leadership. Unit Three, Public Communication, discusses the process and practice of public speaking in six chapters. Subjects such as speech topic selection, research, audience analysis, delivery, presentational aids, informative speaking, and persuasive speaking are covered in depth.

PEDAGOGICAL FEATURES RETAINED FROM THE SECOND EDITION

The theme of embracing difference is integrated into every aspect of the text. The following pedagogical features will help students to reflect on, apply, and critically think about communication.

■ Chapter Opening Scenarios

Each chapter begins with a scenario that describes a real-life communication situation faced by our students. These stories not only resonate with our students' lives at work, home, and school, they also highlight the increasing diversity of student populations across the country.

■ Ethics in Communication

This feature brings students back to the situation presented at the beginning of the chapter, following up on the ethical dilemmas suggested there. It helps students to see and understand the ethical choices people make in a variety of real-life circumstances. The feature may be used as a starting point for class discussion or for a reflection assignment such as a journal.

■ Communication and Technology

This feature discusses how technological advances have changed the way we communicate. Topics such as email and computer-mediated communication, blogs, iPods, the use of the Internet for research, the role of presentational software in public speaking, and working in virtual teams are discussed.

STUDENT-ORIENTED PEDAGOGY

Generously sprinkled throughout each chapter are activities designed to help students think about and practice effective communication. These include:

"Embracing Difference", a new feature that provides students with the opportunity to reflect on the importance of diversity. Each chapter contains an application activity that demonstrates how embracing difference can enhance communication and strengthen confidence.

"Communication in Action", a series of activities that provide students with the opportunity to see communication theories "in action" as they apply the concepts outlined in the text to real life situations.

"Skill Building", another feature that provides opportunities for students to develop and practice the skills taught in the text and apply them to real life or hypothetical situations by themselves or with others.

Learning Objectives that help students focus on the overall concepts, theories, and skills discussed in the different chapters. To help students understand the relationship between concepts and skills, the objectives are divided into two lists: (1) concepts students should know at the end of the chapter, and (2) skills students should practice at the end of the chapter.

Chapter Summaries for students to review the main themes of each chapter.

Review Questions that help students reflect on the chapter material and can also be used for study guides, quizzes, or exams.

A Glossary of Terms that serve as a helpful reference tool at the end of the text.

NEW FEATURES IN THE THIRD EDITION

In this new third edition we were committed to strengthening the theme of embracing difference throughout the book. We added cross-cultural examples to help illustrate the importance of understanding the different chapters in the book. We also expanded students' opportunities to reflect, practice, and therefore learn about the importance of embracing difference. As reinforced throughout the book, students become more effective communicators when they understand and appreciate difference, because they can more appropriately respond to complex communication situations.

◾ Serving Your Community

This new feature provides students with an opportunity to engage in service learning. We believe that engaging in service learning helps students appreciate the importance of assisting others and, in turn, provides them with an opportunity to work with people whose life experiences can be very different from their own. Service learning is also a component of experiential learning, and experiential learning potentially helps students test some of the theories that they studied in their classes. In addition to the intrinsic value of serving others, this activity can lead to potential internships that can provide students with employment opportunities when they graduate.

◾ Expanding Ethics and Communication

In an effort to enhance students' understanding of the importance of ethics, we have added the component of critical thinking in the Communication and Ethics section of each chapter. This new dimension provides students with specific questions to reflect upon based on the opening scenarios in each chapter.

◾ Communication and Technology

We have upgraded the Communication and Technology section in each chapter. This is significant because we want students to understand the role that technology plays when communicating with others. Also, we want to expose students to the most current technology as well as to make them sensitive to principles of communication etiquette that dictate how we use technology to enhance their communication with each other.

◾ Revision of the Public Communication Section

In an effort to strengthen the relevance of the public communication section, we upgraded the public speaking chapters. Specifically, we strengthened examples of rhetoric from the historic 2008 presidential election throughout the public speaking chapters. To support our effort to embrace difference, we highlighted politically diverse examples of rhetoric for students to read and dissect. Examples of speeches delivered from politically diverse perspectives give students the opportunity to reflect upon the rhetoric generated from different political positions, which, in turn, potentially help them understand multiple political perspectives.

◾ New Student–Oriented Pedagogy

In an effort to help students grasp critical themes throughout the book, we added a key concepts list at the end of each chapter. We hope students will review the list, reread the chapter, and highlight the themes identified as critical to their learning. A list of key concepts at the end of each chapter helps students focus on major concepts covered in the book.

AVAILABLE SUPPLEMENTS

NAME OF THE SUPPLEMENT	AVAILABLE IN PRINT	AVAILABLE ONLINE	INSTRUCTOR OR STUDENT SUPPLEMENT	DESCRIPTION
Instructor's Manual and Test Bank (ISBN: 0205791565)		✓	Instructor Supplement	Available for download at www.pearsonhighered.com/irc (access code required), this text-specific instructor resource, prepared by Patricia Mellon of Purdue University Calumet, is organized into two parts: *Part 1: Instructor's Manual* contains sample syllabi, chapter summaries, learning objectives, overviews, lecture outlines, and discussion topics. *Part 2: Test Bank* contains more than 1000 questions blending multiple-choice, true/false, short-answer, matching, and essay, organized by chapter. Each question is referenced by page number.
MyTest (ISBN: 0205781357)		✓	Instructor Supplement	This flexible, online test generating software includes all questions found in the Test Bank section of the Instructor's Manual and Test Bank. Available at www.pearsonmytest.com (access code required).
PowerPoint™ Presentation (ISBN: 0205791573)		✓	Instructor Supplement	Available for download at www.pearsonhighered.com/irc (access code required), this text-specific package, prepared by Patricia Mellon of Purdue University Calumet, provides a basis for your lecture with PowerPoint™ slides for each chapter of the book.

(continued)

NAME OF THE SUPPLEMENT	AVAILABLE IN PRINT	AVAILABLE ONLINE	INSTRUCTOR OR STUDENT SUPPLEMENT	DESCRIPTION
MyCommunicationKit for *Communication: Embracing Difference,* 3rd edition (Instructor Access Code ISBN: 0205593720; Standalone Student Access Code ISBN: 020567416X; and Text + MyCommunicationKit access code ISBN: 0205799000)		✓	Instructor & Student Supplement	Prepared by Christine Camadeca of Purdue University Calumet, the MyCommunicationKit for *Communication: Embracing Difference,* 3rd edition, is a book-specific, dynamic, interactive study tool for students. Offerings are organized by chapter and include practice exams (with page references), relevant media, learning objectives, and weblinks. www.mycommunicationkit.com (access code required).
A Guide for New Teachers of Introduction to Communication: Interactive Strategies for Teaching Communication, 4th edition. (ISBN: 0205750001)	✓	✓	Instructor Supplement	Prepared by Susanna G. Porter, Kennesaw State University, and Heather Dillon, Urbana, Illinois, this guide is designed to help new teachers effectively teach the introductory communication course. It is full of first-day-of-class tips, great teaching ideas, outside and Pearson resources, and sample activities and assignments.
Pearson Allyn & Bacon Introduction to Communication Video Library	✓		Instructor Supplement	Pearson Allyn & Bacon's Introduction to Communication Video Library contains a range of videos from which adopters can choose. Videos cover a variety of topics and scenarios for communication foundations, interpersonal communication, small group communication, and public speaking. Please contact your Pearson representative for details and a complete list of videos and their contents to choose which would be most useful in your class. Some restrictions apply.
Allyn & Bacon Digital Media Archive for Communication, Version 3.0 (ISBN: 0205437095)	✓		Instructor Supplement	The Digital Media Archive CD-ROM contains electronic images of charts, graphs, tables, and figures, along with media elements such as video and related web links. These media assets are fully customizable to use with our pre-formatted PowerPoint™ outlines or to import into your own lectures. (Windows and Mac.)

NAME OF THE SUPPLEMENT	AVAILABLE IN PRINT	AVAILABLE ONLINE	INSTRUCTOR OR STUDENT SUPPLEMENT	DESCRIPTION
Preparing Visual Aids for Presentations, 5th edition (ISBN: 020561115X)	✓		Student Supplement	Prepared by Dan Cavanaugh, this 32-page visual guide provides a host of ideas for using today's multimedia tools to improve presentations, including suggestions for planning a presentation, guidelines for designing visual aids and storyboarding, and a walkthrough that shows how to prepare a visual display using PowerPoint™ Available for purchase.
Public Speaking in the Multicultural Environment, 2nd edition. (ISBN: 0205265111)	✓		Student Supplement	Prepared by Devorah A. Lieberman, Portland State University, this booklet helps students learn to analyze cultural diversity within their audiences and adapt their presentations accordingly. Available for purchase.
Speech Preparation Workbook (ISBN: 013559569X)	✓		Student Supplement	Prepared by Jennifer Dreyer, San Diego State University, and Gregory H. Patton, San Diego State University, this workbook takes students through the stages of speech creation—from audience analysis to writing the speech—and includes guidelines, tips, and easy-to-fill-in pages. Available for purchase.
The Speech Outline: Outlining to Plan, Organize, and Deliver a Speech (ISBN: 032108702X)	✓		Student Supplement	Prepared by Reeze L. Hanson and Sharon Condon, Haskell Indian Nations University, this outlining book includes activities, exercises, and answers to help students develop and master the critical skill of outlining. Available for purchase.
Pearson Allyn & Bacon Introduction to Communication Study Site (open access)		✓	Student Supplement	The Pearson Allyn & Bacon Introduction to Communication Study Site features practice tests, learning objectives, and weblinks. The site is organized around the major topics typically covered in the Introduction to Communication course. Available at www.abintrocommunication.com.

ACKNOWLEDGMENTS

We are indebted to many people for their help with this third edition. First, we thank the Purdue University Calumet community for its support for this project especially our colleagues in the Department of Communication and Creative Arts. We also want to thank our students for providing us with the inspiration for writing this book and for sharing their real-life experiences with us. We thank our colleague Rebecca House Stankowski for her assistance. A special thanks goes to all the past and present graduate teaching assistants in Communication and Creative Arts at Purdue University Calumet for their ideas, inspiration, and assistance, especially Patricia Mellon, Christine Camadeca, Shelly Robinson, Diane Mead-Seabolt, Paul Whitten, and Lindsay Hingst.

We also thank the reviewers for the third edition who provided many helpful ideas and suggestions:

Mark G. Henderson, Jackson State University

Nancy Henschel, Lakeshore Technical College

Rhonda Jackson, Mountain View College, Cedar Valley College

Bonnie Jefferis, St. Petersburg College

William Proctor, Lipscomb University

Carol Roark, Edison State College

Dan Rogers, Cedar Valley College

Chris Smejkal, St. Louis Community College at Meramec

Denise Sperruzza, St. Louis Community College at Meramec

Ruth Spillberg, Curry College

Of course, this third edition would not have been completed without the editors and support staff at Pearson Allyn & Bacon. We are indebted to Karon Bowers, Editor in Chief of Communication, for her support and encouragement. We thank Susan Brilling for her help in the beginning of the revision process. Finally, we thank our families. Their overall support and encouragement inspired us as we completed this third edition. Linda and Laura Dunn, Lee and Hannah Rademacher, and Nancy and Joseph Goodnight, this book is dedicated to you.

An Overview of Communication

AFTER STUDYING THIS CHAPTER, YOU SHOULD

understand

- the definition of communication.
- the functions of communication.
- the significance of intrapersonal communication to both interpersonal and public communication.

be able to

- explain the various components of the communication process.
- describe the difference between dyadic communication and small-group communication.

Sue, Jose, Alicia, and Cory are sitting in a classroom waiting for class to begin. They have been in their communication class together for two weeks and tonight the first journal assignment is due.

Sue is a mother of two small children and can come to campus only two nights a week. Her husband does shift work in the steel mill, so Sue must schedule her classes around his work schedule. She has enjoyed interacting with her fellow classmates and is excited about learning new ideas. Sue's younger daughter had an ear infection this week, so Sue was not able to finish the assignment.

Jose is an older returning student. He works all day as a construction worker and is taking classes with the hopes of getting a promotion to supervisor. By the time he gets to campus, he is tired and would rather not interact with other students. He likes the class sessions when he can just listen and take notes. Jose completed his assignment, but fears he has not done it correctly.

Alicia just graduated from high school and is excited about attending the local university. She and her parents have been saving for her education for several years, and she will be the first one in her family to attend college. Alicia was an honor student in high school and hopes to major in biology and eventually go to medical school. She is working part-time on campus in the financial aid office and has already joined several student organizations. She is a bit anxious about giving speeches but is looking forward to learning about communication. Her journal assignment has been done since the day after it was assigned. She has revised it twice but is still nervous about turning it in.

Cory also just graduated from high school and doesn't know what he wants to do. He has been unable to find a well-paying job, so his parents are forcing him to take classes. He works part-time for a computer company repairing hardware. Cory is shy and does not want to interact with others. He would rather be at home surfing the Internet or texting with friends. So far the class hasn't been too boring, but Cory thinks the assignments require too much work. He did not do the journal assignment due tonight.

■ ■ ■ ■ ■

All of these students are looking for something different from this communication course, and each has approached the first assignment differently. Each will approach learning in a unique and different way. Obviously, Sue, Jose, Alicia, and Cory will send and receive messages differently. This chapter discusses how diversity in age, gender, ethnicity, family roles, learning styles, religion, and approach affect the communication process.

THE COMMUNICATION PROCESS

It takes a significant amount of work and energy to communicate effectively with others. One measure of our effectiveness stems from our understanding of ourselves and of others, a subject that is treated at length in the following chapter. Several factors contribute to our effectiveness as communicators, namely, our ability to listen, our verbal communication skills, our nonverbal communication skills, our understanding of our relationships with others, our ability to analyze an audience, and our knowledge of the way to research, prepare, and deliver a public speech. All these topics (and more) are covered in subsequent chapters. **Communicating effectively, more broadly, stems from an overall understanding that people are simultaneously different and similar**. We approach communication and each communication situation from diverse perspectives. In the beginning of the chapter we see four different people who have diverse expectations about their communication course experience. Sue, for example, is anxious to meet new people and wants to learn new ideas. Cory, on the other hand, is shy and not at all excited at the prospect of having to meet his fellow students. Yet, these two seemingly different people share some things in common. They are in the same communication class and live in the same geographic area. These two things alone can form the basis for common ground and the foundation for effective communication. The theme of "difference" will be explored throughout the text. First, however, to pave the way for these discussions, we must understand the nature of the communication process.

We used to think of communication as a one-way process. This was called the **linear model** of communication. The linear model argued that communication can move in only one direction, from the sender to the receiver. The receiver played a passive role in the overall process. Over the years, scholars have added to and revised the linear model. We now describe communication as an ongoing, dynamic process. The **transactional model** describes communication as an interdependent process whereby the speaker and receiver are simultaneously sending and receiving messages. With this in mind, let's turn to a more detailed definition of communication.

Communication is the interdependent process of sending, receiving, and understanding messages. This definition implies that the components of the communication process (discussed later in this section) cannot be examined separately. Rather, the relationship that exists between the sender and the receiver, as well as the environment of the communication event, must be viewed as a whole. According to this perspective, if any of the components or circumstances change (that is, the number of individuals involved in the interaction, the seating arrangements, or the time of day), the communication event is altered.

Each person in this family has a unique approach to the communication process.

Communication is an ongoing process; we never stop sending and receiving messages. In fact, we do both simultaneously. For example, when we tell our supervisor about how all our overtime is hurting our grades, we also observe the supervisor's reaction to what we are saying—we simultaneously send a message *and* receive the supervisor's message (that is, his or her concern, or surprise, or apparent lack of concentration on what we are saying).

Even though we may not deliberately or directly communicate with another person, we constantly send out information about ourselves. Our clothing, our behavior toward others (children, spouses, lovers, colleagues, and so on), and the amount of eye contact we establish all communicate information about ourselves. People make inferences about our behavior, just as we interpret what we observe about others.

As you will discover, communication is a dynamic process, a process that changes from one communication setting to the next. Although it is difficult to predict the ways your ideas will be interpreted by others, certain components are always present in the communication process: people, a message, encoding, decoding, the channel, feedback, the context, and noise (Figure 1.1). Understanding these components will give you both an awareness of the communication process and a working vocabulary to help you formulate and analyze messages.

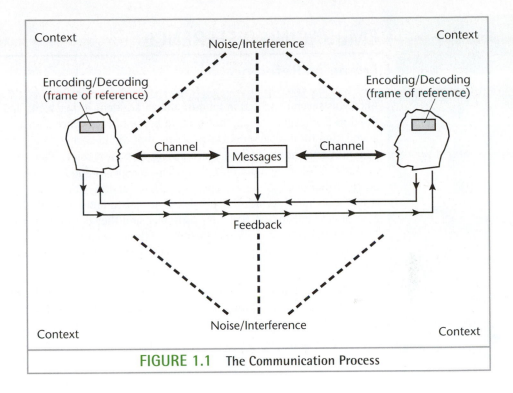

FIGURE 1.1   The Communication Process

■People

People are an integral part of the communication process. Today's technology offers sophisticated means of sending and receiving messages. Yet this technology simply facilitates human communication, which includes conversations between individuals, public speeches delivered to an audience, employee interviews, small-group discussions, knowing glances between friends or partners, and so on. None of these situations is possible without the involvement of people.

Each of us is unique in many ways. Our ethnicity, race, sexual orientation, gender, socioeconomic status, age, values, and many other characteristics make up who we are, how we feel, and, more importantly, how we approach communication. These aspects together create our frame of reference. **Frame of reference** allows us to create and interpret messages. It is our unique view of the world and everything in it. Think about the other students in your class. What characteristics do you share with them? Are you all the same age? How many men and women are in the class? How about ethnicity and race? Paying close attention to the frames of reference of your classmates will help you become a more effective communicator this semester.

Human interaction places the individual in two roles: the source and the receiver. The **source** is the person who creates and sends a message, whereas the **receiver** is the individual to whom the message is sent. The receiver also sends messages back to the source, so the entire process bounces back and forth. For example, Joan (the receiver) listens to Karl (the source) explain how his overtime on the job is affecting his grades at school. She remarks, "I understand, and let's try to

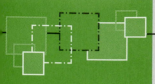

EMBRACING DIFFERENCE

Frame of Reference

Alice was severely injured in an automobile accident in her teens and has been confined to a wheelchair since that time. In her political science course, she is constantly advocating for disability reform to ensure that disabled citizens are accorded their full constitutional rights. Several times during class discussions Paul expresses his impatience with Alice by rolling his eyes when she speaks about disability rights. Jennifer, on the other hand, is more supportive of Alice and her cause. After the first few class sessions, Jennifer decides that she wants to get to know Alice better and asks if they can form a study group. She talks with Alice and they decide to share their class notes to make the class load easier for both of them. Jennifer realizes that even though Alice is different from her, she has a position that Jennifer can learn from and gain a new perspective.

1. Describe the differences between Jennifer's and Paul's frames of reference? How do their frames of reference affect how they interact with Alice?

2. How can Jennifer's appreciation of difference contribute to her effectiveness as a communicator? How can we use Jennifer's approach to communication as a model for our own communication?

work something out with your schedule for next week." What she has done, momentarily, is send a message of her own. For that instant, Karl becomes the receiver. When people communicate with each other, messages are sent and received simultaneously.

■ Message

The **message** is the thought, feeling, or action that is sent from the source to the receiver with the use of symbols. When we create messages, we have a choice of code systems, such as verbal or nonverbal and oral or nonoral (see Chapters 4 and 5). Thus, messages can be communicated either verbally or nonverbally, intentionally or unintentionally. Verbal messages are composed of words: "I was so offended by Larry's comments that I thought I was going to scream at him!" Nonverbal messages are composed of gestures, facial expressions, vocal inflection, touch, and so on. Nonverbally, we might communicate our anger at Larry's comments by glaring at him or turning red. The content of our messages can reflect a great deal of preparation or structure (as in public speeches), a casualness (as in a conversation with a good friend), or no forethought at all (as in many of our nonverbal messages).

We can also strategically alter our message to be better understood by the receiver. For example, a speaker will want to do extensive audience analysis before giving a public speech to ensure that the audience understands the message. We can alter our message through language choice, delivery style, and many other variables we will discuss in later chapters.

SKILL BUILDING

Your Frame of Reference

Listed below are some items that are components of your frame of reference and, consequently, you as a communicator. Take a few moments to reflect on your frame of reference by answering the following questions.

1. What is your family like? Do you have sisters and brothers? Are you married? Do you have children? Are you part of a step-family?

2. What education or special skills do you have? How long have you been attending college? Do other members of your family have a college degree or graduate degree? Do you have specialized training?

3. Where do you call home? What is the neighborhood like? Is your family's original home in another country? Is your neighborhood dominated by one ethnic background?

4. What is your religious background? Are you affiliated with a religious group? Were you raised in this religion? What are the major beliefs of your religious group?

5. Are you interested in local, national, or world politics? What is your party affiliation, if any? Have you taken an active part in campaigning for a cause or a candidate?

6. What is your work experience? What is your current job, if any? If you could have any job, what would it be? If you have decided on a major, what most influenced you in making that choice?

7. What is your ethnic background? How much contact with other ethnic groups or races have you had in your community? How do you celebrate holidays? What are some of the stereotypes about your ethnic group?

8. Are you male or female? How does gender affect your communication? What is the gender of most of your friends? What is your sexual orientation?

9. How old are you? How does your age affect your communication? Is it more difficult to communicate with those older or younger than you?

10. What special interests do you have? How do you spend your free time? Do you have any hobbies? Do you play or watch sports? What kind of music do you listen to?

■ Encoding

Encoding is the process of putting thoughts, ideas, or feelings into meaningful symbols that another person can understand. Symbols represent things—our feelings, names for the objects around us, explanations for behaviors, and so on. We are most familiar with the concept of words (language) as our primary symbol system (more about this in Chapter 4). When we want to send a message, we rely on our frame of reference to choose the appropriate symbol. For example, the words chosen for this message would be easily understood by the receiver: "I'm really glad to see you. I've missed you so much these past two weeks." Nonverbal symbols also convey our messages effectively. A hug, for example, symbolizes an expression of warmth toward another person. In both these examples, the symbols used to convey the message (verbal expression using words, nonverbal expression using a hug) are easily discerned by the receiver.

■ Decoding

Decoding is the process of interpreting or attaching meaning to another person's message. Communication often stops because people decode messages differently based on their frame of reference. Because of diverse attitudes, knowledge, and past experiences, receivers often interpret messages differently from the way they were intended by the senders. Take the example of Shelly and Tom:

> Shelly and Tom have been dating for the past two years. They are ready to go off to different colleges this fall. Shelly will be attending the large state university several hours away, while Tom is staying home to attend the local college and work part-time. Shelly feels it is time to see other people and wants to break off their relationship. She calls Tom and says she has something important to talk to him about and they set up a place and time to meet. Tom, however, believes that he will do better in school because he is in a committed and loving relationship with Shelly and knows they will be able to visit one another on the weekends, exchange daily emails, and phone calls. When Shelly called to say she had something important to discuss, Tom assumed they would discuss when they would announce their engagement to their families. Obviously, Tom has decoded the meaning of Shelly's message differently than she intended.

■ Channel

The **channel** is the vehicle by which the message is communicated from the source to the receiver. Familiar channels include the various types of media—television, radio, movies, newspapers, magazines, computer chat rooms, and social networking sites like Facebook—as well as letters, reports, email, and our voices.

Sight and sound are the primary channels we use to communicate with others. We can see people's facial expressions and read the written word. The sound of our voices can travel thousands of miles by telephone, can be recorded on tape, or can be broadcast via radio or television. Another one of our senses, touch, also can act as the channel. We might place our hand on a friend's shoulder to communicate our concern for the loss of a loved one. At such times the use of touch can communicate much more than words.

■ Feedback

Another important component in the communication process is feedback. **Feedback** is the receiver's response to the sender's message; it provides information about the way the message is being interpreted. For example:

> Tameka is working with several of her colleagues on a new procedure to order office supplies. There have been several instances of overordering and it has cost the company thousands of dollars. Tameka and her team have been asked to determine the best way to control office supply ordering. After many weeks of discussion, each team member presents his or her idea to the group. The group discusses each idea and then decides on the best procedure to recommend to their supervisor.

The group's discussion of each idea is an example of feedback.

Often we are unaware of the feedback we send to others. For instance, Candi may tell Jorge that she is interested in hearing about his trip to Cincinnati, but she may be nonverbally communicating her boredom by glancing at the clock or stifling a yawn. In this example, the verbal feedback and the nonverbal feedback differ; Candi's verbal expression of interest is not supported by her nonverbal yawn. At other times, what we say is supported by our nonverbal response. For example, Glen might tell Kevin that he understands Kevin's instructions, and he reinforces this verbal feedback by nodding his head.

As senders we sometimes have difficulty interpreting the feedback we get from a receiver. For instance, we might interpret the feedback from an audience as being negative, when in reality it is positive. Consider the following:

> Cathy is a student who likes to sit in the front row. She feels this helps her stay involved in the class. She never misses class and also enjoys listening to speeches; however, because she finds direct eye contact difficult, she looks down at her class notes frequently. When Sean gives his speech, he may misinterpret her behavior as a negative response to his message.

Cathy's behavior toward the speaker is motivated by her own discomfort, not by her disapproval of the presentation. Now consider another student:

> James sits in the front row for a different reason. He hopes to make a positive impression on both his instructor and his peers. He consistently gives Sean nonverbal approval by nodding his head after the presentation of each idea. Occasionally as he nods, he is daydreaming about the upcoming weekend. So, even though James is providing Sean with positive feedback, he is not really listening.

Listening is covered in Chapter 3.

ZITS © *ZITS* Partnership. King Features Syndicate. Used by permission.

The preceding examples illustrate the difficulty we can face when attempting to interpret the feedback given by receivers. Because we use feedback to alter our subsequent messages, problems can arise when our interpretations are incorrect. Remember, we are using our frame of reference to encode a message, and the receiver is using his or her different frame of reference to decode the message. If, for example, the speaker interprets Cathy's lack of eye contact as disapproval of his or her presentation, then his or her future interactions with Cathy might be less than friendly. The importance of interpreting messages accurately is stressed throughout this book.

■ Context

The conditions surrounding communication with others are referred to as the **context** of the interaction. What types of conditions are there? The **physical setting** in which the communication occurs can have a substantial impact on communication. Consider the difference between discussing a business proposal with a few clients over lunch at a posh restaurant and discussing the same proposal with the same clients in your firm's conference room. The location influences the degree of formality in the interaction. Such factors as seating arrangements, time of day, degree of privacy, room size, temperature, and lighting affect how people communicate with each other.

A second aspect of context is the **psychological climate** of the interaction. This refers to the attitudes and feelings we have about ourselves and the other people involved in the communication. These feelings can affect how we respond to others. For example:

> Savannah is an engineering major and has a difficult time in Professor Anderson's course. Savannah feels very uncomfortable interacting with her professor because he walks with a cane due to a disability. Professor Anderson has multiple sclerosis. Savannah brings these negative feelings about Professor Anderson to every class meeting. She does not ask questions when material is unclear and she does not participate in class. The psychological climate during each class is very tense for Savannah.

COMMUNICATION IN ACTION

Understanding the Communication Process

1. Try to explain your last difficult encounter with someone by using the following terms:

   a. Source   e. Channel   i. Decoding
   b. Frame of Reference   f. Feedback   j. Noise
   c. Receiver   g. Context
   d. Message   h. Encoding

2. How do the source's and receiver's different approaches to communication affect the outcome of the interaction?

3. How can your understanding of frame of reference enhance your confidence as a communicator?

A positive psychological climate, on the other hand, can contribute immensely to the interaction between people. Consider the following:

> Beth, a student in the communication class, is terrified of public speaking. Because her instructor offers encouragement to all the students, Beth gradually feels a genuine warmth develop within the class. After several weeks Beth gains confidence and actually looks forward to coming to class. She notices changes in her classmates as well. As the semester progresses, Beth's speeches, as well as those of her classmates, show significant improvement.

Chapter 7 includes a more detailed discussion of communication climates, both supportive and defensive.

■ Noise and Interference

Noise, any intended or unintended stimulus that affects the fidelity of a sender's message, disrupts the communication process. Noise is often thought of as **interference** to the communication process. Noise can be external or internal, and it can influence our ability to process information. **External noise** includes sounds or visual stimuli that draw our attention away from the intended message. Imagine how difficult it would be to deliver a speech with construction workers drilling outside the classroom; it would be equally difficult for the audience to concentrate on the speaker's message.

Internal noise includes our own thoughts or feelings that prevent us from processing a sender's message—such thoughts as our plans for the upcoming weekend, bills that need to be paid and mailed, the fact that we have not had anything to eat since we woke up this morning, the fact that we really dislike the campus newspaper, and so on. When we find ourselves concentrating on such stimuli instead of devoting our full attention to the sender's message, we say that noise is interfering with the communication process. In Chapter 3 we will tackle the subject of listening interference in greater detail.

FUNCTIONS OF COMMUNICATION

Why do we communicate? By nature, we are social beings who need others to survive and thrive in our society. Communication allows us to form societies, create our identities, and accomplish a variety of tasks. Most importantly, we use communication to bridge the gap between people and to form common ground. Communication functions in five specific ways.

1. *Communication creates and maintains our sense of self or our identity.* From the moment we were born, we were engaged in the communication process. Our parents talked to us, read books to us, and played games with us. It is through communication that we learned our name and gender; we learned about love, frustration, and fear; and we learned how to be part of a family. Specifically, communicating with others helped us to create who we are. For example, what does it mean to be a girl in our society? Well, that all depends on who you ask. In some families, it means to take care of all the household chores like cooking, cleaning, and laundry. Although social expectations are changing and some families share all the household responsibilities, in many homes, gender stereotypes dictate who does what. What else does it mean to be a girl? One study shows that even at birth, gender expectations shape who we become. Baby congratulations cards for girls are pink, show bunnies or birds, and portray the baby as sleeping or immobile. Boy cards are primarily blue, show cars and sports equipment, and portray the baby as active in play (Willer 2001). These stereotypes are subtle and we may hardly notice them, but they play a role in what is expected of us and how we create our identity.

2. *Communication helps us create communities.* Of course, we all live in a community of some kind just by virtue of living in a house, apartment, or dorm. But communities are more than geographic locations. Communities are also created by shared meanings for symbols. These shared meanings bind people together in support or work networks. So, someone who lives hundreds or thousands of miles from you could be part of your social community because you both share a similar language or symbol system. For example, people who text share meanings for special symbols, and if you don't know what the symbols mean, you can't communicate. Do you know what LOL means? Laughing Out Loud. How about TMI? Too Much Information. These are examples of how shared meanings allow us to communicate and thus create communities.

3. *Communication forms and strengthens relationships.* Through communication, we form human bonds that, in turn, form our friendships, families, and work

ETHICS in Communication
Different Approaches

In the beginning of the chapter, we learned about four students in a communication course. Sue, Jose, Alicia, and Cory have been in class together for two weeks, and their first assignment is due tonight. Each has taken a different approach to the assignment and to how each communicates about the assignment to the instructor.

Sue has been taking care of her daughter this week. Her daughter had an ear infection and Sue spent hours in the doctor's office and then standing in line at the pharmacy. Her daughter has not slept through the night for several days, and Sue is exhausted. She did not have time to complete her journal assignment.

Jose has been working overtime, but he completed his journal assignment. He was somewhat confused by the assignment, so he emailed the instructor, as the syllabus suggested he do. Alicia is concerned about her first assignment. As a matter of fact, she has revised it twice and is still not sure if she has done it correctly. Alicia has created a "time management" study schedule so that she can have enough time to work and study. She thought about stopping by the instructor's office hours to clarify the assignment but decided to "just finish it" and hope it is done correctly.

Finally, Cory has taken a very different approach to the assignment. Feeling forced into taking college classes, Cory is not motivated to complete the assignment. He believes that the assignment requires too much work, and he would rather be doing anything else but studying.

When we communicate, we have many choices to make. Whom we talk to and what we talk about are two important considerations. Sometimes the choices are easy, and other times we must overcome our uneasiness or fear and share our feelings and thoughts. Sometimes it is better not to share information. If we intentionally do not communicate when we know we should, we maybe acting unethically. Each of us communicates differently and each communication situation involves a question of ethics. As you think about Sue, Jose, Alicia, and Cory, answer the following questions:

1. Describe each student's dilemma.

2. What should each student do to communicate effectively and ethically?

3. Have you ever been in their situation? What did you do and why? Describe your communication behavior.

relationships. We fall in love using communication. We solve problems at work by communicating with our co-workers, and we create lasting friendships by sharing stories, experiencing new things, and being supportive of one another. It is through communication that we share our emotions and feelings.

4. *Part of being in a relationship is the ability to influence the other person.* Communication is how we do this. Communication allows us to sell products, campaign for an issue or candidate, debate a topic in class, or get the television remote from our significant other. Persuasion is an integral part of our lives because we are not only the sources of persuasive communication but are also the receivers of over thousands of persuasive messages per day.

5. *Communication conveys and creates information.* How many times a day do you check the Internet for some form of information like the weather report, sports score, or

Through communication, this couple has formed a strong and lasting relationship.

late-breaking news? Communication allows us to find information that will help us fulfill our needs. For example:

> Alex was planning her vacation to Michigan. Alex's family will be spending a week at a cottage on Lake Michigan, and Alex wants to know several things before they go. What is the weather forecast (do I need a jacket, jeans, umbrella)? What is the fastest route to the cottage (should we take the toll road or the expressway)? What kind of restaurants are nearby (fast food or more formal)? What kind of shopping is available (grocery, clothing, sports)? These are all questions Alex needs answered before she packs her suitcase and leaves for her vacation.

Communication also helps us create information and knowledge. Have you ever worked in a group and found that you were coming up with new ideas and concepts as your discussion progressed? Through communication, we create information and knowledge. We learn from one another and use that information to develop new ideas and concepts.

Serving Your COMMUNITY   Understanding Frame of Reference

In an effort to increase your understanding of others and your frame of reference, do the following:

- Contact the Director of Student Services on your campus and offer to volunteer your services.
- Interact and spend time with students with special needs over a two-week period. After each day of volunteering record your feelings relating to the experience.
- Take time to share your observations with the Director of Student Services.

How did this experience help you recognize and appreciate difference? How has your frame of reference changed after your interaction with fellow students you might not have had the opportunity to know before this experience?

TYPES OF COMMUNICATION

■ Intrapersonal

Communication takes place when we interact with one other person, when we interact with a small group, and when we speak to an audience. A special type of communication, intrapersonal communication, is an integral part of any communication event. **Intrapersonal communication** is communication with ourselves; it is an ongoing process that includes such activities as evaluating ourselves and our relationships with others, planning for the future, and doing some internal problem solving. We engage in intrapersonal communication all the time—as we get ready for work or school, during our three-mile jog, as we prepare dinner for ourselves, and before our presentation at a business meeting. The following sections discuss two other types of communication: interpersonal communication and public communication.

■ Interpersonal

Interpersonal communication is the informal exchange that occurs between two or more people. It usually occurs on two levels: dyads (groups of two) and small groups.

Dyadic communication is the interaction between two people. It can focus on safe topics, such as our day at the office, or on highly sensitive issues, such as our love for a particular person. Dyadic communication tends to be informal, and therefore requires little or no preplanning. Interviews are the exception; they are generally

Rick Warren, Pastor of Saddleback Church, engages in public communication at the Presidential Inaugural Ceremony in 2009.

formal in nature. (Chapter 8 is devoted to this topic.) Through dyadic communication we can learn a great deal about ourselves and our relationships with others.

■ Small Group

Small-group communication includes those interactions with three to eight people present. In most instances, small-group communication is less intimate than dyadic communication and less formal than public speaking. Small-group communication can occur as an informal discussion of such social issues as gun violence or shelters for runaway adolescents or serve as a vehicle for problem solving in organizations. Small-group communication is discussed in more detail in Chapters 9 and 10.

■ Public

Public communication involves having an individual share information with a large group; the usual structure has a speaker presenting ideas to an audience. Public communication is more formal than interpersonal communication; it therefore requires more preparation on the sender's part. Usually, speakers have a limited amount of time in which to share their ideas; this forces them to plan and organize what they want to say in advance. Chapters 11 to 16 treat the area of public communication in depth, addressing such subjects as topic selection and researching, organizing, and delivering a public speech.

UNDERSTANDING DIFFERENCE, DIVERSITY, AND COMMUNICATION

For many people, the primary goal of a communication course is to broaden their understanding of the communication process and to become better at something they have been doing since birth: communicating with others. If we reflect for a moment about our communication with others, we realize that some encounters are easier for us than others. For instance, we might feel relaxed talking with a close friend or spouse, but we are self-conscious and nervous when we are introduced to someone new, especially someone who is different from us in some way. This anxiety is familiar to all of us—who among us has not been in a situation in which we have felt uncomfortable and wished that we could be more at ease?

The intent of this book is to help you become a confident, effective communicator by teaching you about the complex nature of communication and by presenting a variety of skills that can help you improve your communication. The application of these skills in both your interpersonal and public communication encounters can transform you into a competent communicator.

Humans approach communication and communication situations from diverse and unique positions. The differences we have should be understood and celebrated because they lead to greater understanding and thus more effective communication. As we learned earlier in the chapter, our frame of reference is made up of

Communication and TECHNOLOGY
Changing the Way We Communicate

Technology has changed the way we communicate with one another. An explosion of technological advances has made communication cheap, easy, and immediate. Mobile phones and computers have become an integral part of our daily lives. These statistics tell the story.

Mobile Phones

- Three billion people use mobile phones in the world today (Plunket Research, 2008).

- U.S. mobile phone users make or receive about 204 calls a month while teens 13 to 17 make 231 calls per month (Reardon, 2008).

- Wireless users send 48 billion text messages per month worldwide (Plunket Research, 2008) with teens 13 to 17 in the United States sending and receiving about 1740 text message per month (Reardon, 2008).

Computers (according to the Pew Internet and American Life Project, 2008)

- 74% of all adults use the Internet.

- 93% of 12- to 17-year-olds use the Internet.

- 80% of 33- to 44-year-olds shop online (the most of any age group).

- People between 33 and 72 years old look for information online from government websites and for religious information.

The advent of these technological advances has made communicating easier, but it has also created new communication problems.

Nomophobia is the fear of being out of mobile phone contact, and about 53% of the general public has this fear (Rocca, 2008). Are we afraid of being alone? According to this study, our main reason for using mobile communication devices is to stay in touch with family and friends.

The Internet and email create another set of problems for communicators. Email lends itself to "bad manners." Using all capital letters indicating that the sender is yelling or not using emoticons or smileys (see Chapter 4) to indicate the tone of the message are two common mistakes made by email users. Also, we are more likely to send a message with negative comments than we are to actually say them to the person's face (see Chapter 7). Lastly, most of us think of email as being a form of private communication. Not so, according to a 2000 study by the American Management Association. "Nearly three fourths of the country's largest corporations eavesdrop on their employee's email use" (Davich, 2001). According to Brian Krebs, 33% of companies pay staff to read outgoing and incoming email and instant messages and one-third of employees have been fired for misuse of their companies' technology (2006).

We can enhance our relationships and overall communication with the use of technology. We just need to be careful about how and when we decide to use our mobile phone or send an email.

---

many different variables, including our age, gender, ethnicity, race, religion, family roles, work experience, geographic location, sexual orientation, learning style, and socioeconomic status. Our frame of reference is unique and thus makes us different from others. We may look different, sound different, and think and feel differently. The variables that create our frame of reference affect the communication process.

For example, when we see someone who looks or sounds different from us, we may become defensive and close ourselves off from any interaction with this person. But if we instead value the differences and strive to understand this person, then we can have a greater understanding and more effective communication. Specifically:

> During the first week, students in a communication class are placed in study groups. Noelle, an 18-year-old first-year student who is African American is grouped with Mo (short for Mohamed), also 18 years old and in his first year. Katie, who is 25, is close to graduation, white, and is a working single mother. Cathy, who is 55, is a junior, Hispanic, and a returning student who works full-time. Cathy's youngest son just left home and so she is an "empty nester." Noelle thinks to herself, "How am I going to be able to work and study with this group? I don't have anything in common with them." When the group begins to work together, Noelle discovers that she and Katie live in the same town, that Mo knows Cathy's son, and they are all nervous about doing presentations in front of the class.

At first Noelle saw only the differences between herself and her group members. But after taking the time to get to know them, Noelle found they all had much in common.

The first part of this chapter discussed the nature and components of the communication process. Building on this foundation, future chapters will explore the numerous aspects of both interpersonal and public communication, including our perceptions of ourselves and others, listening, nonverbal communication, improving the communication climate, selecting speech topics, analyzing the audience, and organizing speeches.

Each chapter presents an explanation of the topic and then suggests specific skills that can be used to improve your effectiveness as a communicator. By embracing our differences, your confidence, and ultimately your effectiveness, will be enhanced as a communicator. For example, after reading Chapter 7 on improving the communication climate, you will be better acquainted with the subject of supportive climates; as a result, you will be better able to see how you can play an active role in creating this type of climate. At the same time, you will be able to recognize when you and others act defensively.

In each chapter both the discussion of the topic and the suggested skills will help you to become an active participant in the communication process. Your involvement in a particular activity (Embracing Difference, Communication in Action, Skill Building, or Service Learning), whether it is gathering evidence for a persuasive speech or observing nonverbal behavior of an interviewer, has the potential to strengthen your confidence because it forces you to practice what you have learned. We hope this text will help you to enhance your ability to interpret, adjust, and respond to others in a variety of communication situations with people who are just like you and, more importantly, with people who are different from you.

SUMMARY

Communication is the interdependent process of sending, receiving, and understanding messages. Although it is an ongoing, dynamic process that changes from one communication setting to the next, there are certain components that are always present: people, a message, encoding, decoding, the channel, feedback, the context, and noise.

Communication functions in several ways. It can create our sense of self, form relationships and communities, be used to persuade, and convey and create information.

Communication can take place when we interact with one other person, when we interact with a small group, and when we speak to an audience. In all these situations, intrapersonal communication (communication with ourselves) can be expected. Interpersonal communication is the informal exchange that occurs between two or more people; the interaction between two people is called dyadic communication, whereas an interaction involving three to eight people is called small-group communication. A final type of communication, public communication, involves having an individual share information with a large group.

The last section of this introductory chapter included a discussion of difference and diversity and their relationship to communication. First encounters with new people and public speaking are two common causes of anxiety, yet there are ways for us to become better, more effective communicators. Most importantly, we must celebrate and appreciate the different approaches to communication we all have as a means of improving our communication effectiveness. Throughout this book specific techniques for improving our communication will accompany the discussions of each communication topic.

REVIEW QUESTIONS

1. Define communication.
2. Explain the difference between encoding and decoding.
3. How can people use nonverbal communication to give a sender feedback?
4. Differentiate between external and internal noise.
5. How does communication create our sense of self?
6. Describe the different types of communication.

KEY CONCEPTS

linear model
transactional model
communication
frame of reference
source
receiver
message

encoding
decoding
channel
feedback
context
physical setting
psychological climate

noise: internal and external interference
intrapersonal communication
interpersonal communication
dyadic communication
small-group communication
public communication

CHAPTER 2

Perception

AFTER STUDYING THIS CHAPTER, YOU SHOULD

understand

- the three steps involved in processing information.
- definitions of self-concept and self-esteem.
- the factors that influence our perception of others.
- the two forms of stereotyping: "allness" and "halo and horns."

be able to

- use feedback from others to help shape your self-concept.
- develop accurate perceptions of yourself and others.

The Border Tool and Dye Company employs 50 people. It is a small company, and everyone seems to work well together. A vice president's position has opened up, and the company's four managers are being considered for the promotion. The four managers include the following:

Tony, who is in his mid-thirties, has worked for the company since high school. Although he has been promoted several times in the past few years, this year he did not receive a merit raise. He comes from a traditional family and attends church regularly with his wife and five children. Amy, Tony's wife, stays home to take care of their children.

Connie, who is single and in her early forties, has lived with her partner for the past three years. They adopted a child last year and share all the parenting responsibilities. Connie earned her college degree several years ago after attending classes at night. She was promoted to manager after receiving her degree in management.

Anita, who is a recent immigrant from the Middle East, is in her late twenties. She has a college degree in manufacturing and has worked at the company for only a few months. In her short time in this country, she has had difficulty adjusting to the different communication styles of her co-workers and to the culture overall. She lives alone in a studio apartment and works more hours than any of the other managers.

Tom, who is over 50 years old, has been a manager the longest. He earned his degree in communication almost 30 years ago and was hired as a manager when the company opened 10 years ago. He is divorced from his wife but sees his two daughters every weekend.

■ ■ ■ ■ ■

Each of these people has his or her own view of himself or herself and of the other managers. These views, or perceptions, affect the way in which each communicates. How do you think each of these managers views himself or herself? How do you think each views the others? In this chapter, we will discuss how our differences affect our perceptions of others and self and, ultimately, how these perceptions effect our interpersonal communication and public communication.

As we learned in Chapter 1, people are very different. Look at the people described in the beginning of this chapter. They are certainly different in many ways. Our past experiences, age, gender, societal roles, and many other characteristics make each of us unique. These differences need to be understood and accepted in order for us to become more effective communicators. One important result of our differences is the unique way each of us views the world around us. This is called perception. **Perception** is the process of assigning meaning to stimuli. The way we select stimuli from the environment, organize them, and eventually interpret their meaning play an important role in the way we communicate in relationships and in public-speaking situations. In this chapter we shall learn more about the process of perception, how we perceive ourselves, and how we perceive others. Finally, we shall look at some strategies for developing accurate perceptions about ourselves and others.

THE PROCESS OF PERCEPTION

None of us perceives the world objectively. Our perception of each new situation is tempered by our preconceived ideas, our current physiological and psychological states, our interest or attention, and our goals. This is called our frame of reference (see Chapter 1). Essentially, all our perceptions are subjective and unique. Understanding that each of us operates from such a base is the first step in making our communication more effective. Let's discuss the way we select, organize, and interpret the stimuli in our environment—that is, the process of perception.

■ Selective Attention

We are constantly bombarded by stimuli. Since we cannot respond to all the information we are exposed to, we are forced to exercise a degree of selectivity. The process of determining what we pay attention to and what we ignore is called **selective attention.** Of the dozens of shows broadcast on television at any given hour, we are likely to respond to only a few; this is an example of selective attention. Specifically, think about how you watch TV. Do you "flip" through the channels looking for something interesting to watch? What determines what channels you watch and what channels you ignore? How we select stimuli from our environment is a uniquely personal phenomenon that depends on our interests and needs.

One important factor in selecting stimuli is our level of interest in it. We are often drawn to topics that directly affect us. For instance, we would probably pay particular attention to student gossip regarding a tuition increase because such a change would have an immediate impact on us. Similarly, the more intriguing we

Selective attention is the process of determining what we pay attention to and what we ignore.

find a topic, the more likely we will be motivated to select it and focus our attention on it. For instance, if Erin is very interested in political communication, she is likely to stop on channels such as CSPAN, MSNBC, or CNN. The content of these channels stimulates Erin's interest enough to make her want to listen to the shows' ideas. On the other hand, if Charles has very little interest in government or politics, it will take more than the political content of the shows to keep him involved. Other factors, such as Charles's desire to see how his stocks are doing or to get the latest score for the Chicago Cubs baseball game, might encourage him to pay attention to those channels.

Needs, physical or emotional desires that grow out of circumstances in our immediate environment, also motivate us to select and assign meaning to certain stimuli, as reflected in the preceding example of Charles. Consider this example as well: If our secondhand car completely "dies," we suddenly find ourselves paying particular attention to television advertisements for good "buys." Our need for reliable transportation motivates us to look for a new vehicle.

Needs are triggered by all sorts of circumstances—hunger, security, longing to be part of a group, desire for recognition, self-fulfillment. Abraham Maslow's hierarchy of needs, discussed more thoroughly in Chapter 11, can be used as a framework for understanding needs shared by all of us. We are especially sensitive to those stimuli in our environment that we perceive as having the potential to satisfy our needs. For example, until we purchase another used car, we will continue to read the ads in the local newspaper. After the purchase, however, we no longer have either the need or interest to scan the classified section of the paper (assuming, of course, that the car we bought is satisfactory).

■ Organization

Before we can begin to interpret the stimuli we have selected from our environment, we must be able to place them in a structure that allows us to make sense of them. **Organization** is simply another phase of the perception process; in other words, we perceive that certain items belong together, and we therefore tend to organize them that way. Consider the organization found in any grocery store. We expect that all types of cereal will be stocked in the same aisle, and nearly without exception, they are. How frustrated we would be if this were not the case; we would need to wander from aisle to aisle in search of our favorite kind. Similarly, stimuli can be organized into patterns that make sense. Three elements of organization aid this process: similarity, proximity, and closure.

SKILL BUILDING

Selective Attention

Pay close attention to what you attend to for 24 hours. Keep a log.

1. What television channels do you watch the most? Describe the kinds of shows that you seek out.
2. When you read a newspaper, what section of the paper do you read first? Second? Third?
3. What radio stations do you listen to? Describe the content.
4. Why do you think you pay attention to these things? How do these reflect your frame of reference?

Similarity

Stimuli that resemble one another are commonly grouped together. Their **similarity** dictates that they be treated in this way. The preceding description of a grocery store's organization demonstrates the idea of similarity. So too does the organization of a library's book collection. Specifically, cookbooks are shelved in one section, biographies in another, photography books in another, and so on. The arrangement is by subject; therefore, books about similar topics are likely to be cataloged and shelved in the same area.

Proximity

Stimuli also can be organized according to their **proximity,** or closeness to one another (Figure 2.1). When we group two events together because of the closeness of their occurrence, we are applying the principle of proximity. For example, we can probably recall someone talking about the significance of a particular event because it happened "right after my grandfather died" or "the night my daughter was born." We also might recall when a newspaper account of an automobile accident caught our attention because the accident happened next to the high school we attended. Such associations help to organize the stimuli we have selected from our environment.

Eight shoes or four pairs

FIGURE 2.1   **Example of Proximity**

Closure

Finally, the element of **closure** contributes to the way we organize stimuli. That is, when we are familiar with an idea or topic, we tend to "fill in the gaps" when pieces are missing. In formulating an opinion about someone, for example, we sometimes make assumptions based on our observations. For instance, if we see an elegantly dressed woman step out of a shiny Mercedes, we assume that this person is wealthy. Closure also affects how we listen to a speaker. Sometimes we inadvertently fill in a speaker's words before he or she actually articulates them; we are so familiar with a phrase that we know what the speaker will say even though he or she has not completed the thought. For instance, many of us could complete a reference to Patrick Henry's famous words, "Give me liberty. . . ."

A number of potential problems can develop as we attempt to organize information as described so far. For example, referring to people's similarities can lead to stereotyping, a concept discussed at length later in this chapter. With closure, our inclination to "fill in the gaps" or "fill in the missing words" might actually cause us to make false assumptions about a person or that person's message. For example:

> Chantel's father has always been a strong supporter of conservative candidates and causes. She has heard him go on and on about the need for less government spending and reduced taxes. Recently at dinner, Chantel's father began to talk about President Obama's policies to stimulate the economy. Chantel, thinking that she knew exactly what her father was going to say, tuned him out and thought about the meeting she had that day with a potential client. On the contrary, Chantel's father was arguing for Obama's stimulus plan, which would increase government spending.

Chantel used closure to fill in the gaps of her father's message and assumed she knew what he was going to say. Thus, Chantel missed the meaning of her father's message.

Finally, because individuals perceive things differently, the way they organize information is likely to be widely varied too. The uniqueness of our perception can result in a breakdown in communication/understanding between people. This phenomenon is discussed more thoroughly in the next subsection.

■ Interpretation

It is during the interpretation phase of the perception process that we communicate our perceptions to others. As we discussed in Chapter 1, during the encoding and decoding process, we use our frame of reference to make sense of the stimuli. Several factors affect how we interpret what we have perceived: our past experiences, our attitudes, personal constructs and prototypes, and attribution.

Our past experiences play a fundamental role in the way we **interpret** information, especially since it can determine how we look at both the present and the future. Joan, hearing the meteorologist announce that a snowstorm is beginning to hit the city, decides to phone the babysitter to let her know that both Joan and her husband will probably reach home later than usual because of slow traffic. Joan's past experience driving in snow enables her to anticipate these conditions.

Unlike the positive effect of Joan's past experience in the preceding example, clinging to the past can create problems for an individual who cannot seem to let go of a negative experience. Consider this example:

> Keisha, a skilled and competent civil engineer, is scheduled to have an interview with a new engineering firm. She is quite nervous, in part because it has been four years since her last employment interviewing experience. She landed her present job after earning her engineering degree, but she still recalls one miserable interview in which she fumbled her responses and did not get the job she wanted most. Although she comes to this interview with four years of experience, she cannot seem to shake her fear of repeating her previous performance. These thoughts prevent her from interpreting the present interview more positively.

Past experience often shapes our attitude about a particular subject. Certainly Keisha's case is an example of this phenomenon. **Attitude,** a predetermined position regarding a person, event, concept, or object, affects the way we interpret data. For instance, our attitude toward a speaker can determine the way we respond to that person's speech. If we like the speaker's voice or admire his or her confidence, we may interpret the presentation as more powerful. Likewise, our attitude toward the speaker's topic may play a significant role in the way we assess its treatment. Someone who works for Greenpeace, for instance, is likely to be critical of a speech that praises the oil industry, even if the speech is well organized and well presented.

Our attitude concerning a stimulus can change with time. This transformation occurs when we reinterpret the meaning of information because of changed circumstances. Consider the following example:

> Alison has just graduated from high school and is really looking forward to attending the local university. In high school, Alison was a cross-country and track star. She lettered in both sports and was a finalist at the state cross-country tournament. Alison never really socialized with the "theater" people and thought they were strange because of the way they dressed and talked. Upon entering her communication class on the first day, Alison sees several people who look like the theater people she knew in high school. She decides to avoid them and sit next to students who look more like her. As the class progresses and Alison is forced to interact with all the students in her class, she realizes that the theater people are really creative, intelligent, and fun. She is thrilled when she gets a chance to work with Dennis and Cynthia, two students involved in the arts program on campus, on their group project for class.

Altered circumstances forced Alison to reinterpret her thoughts and attitudes about her fellow students.

Connected to personal experiences and attitudes, personal constructs and prototypes guide our interpretation of people. **Personal constructs** are the characteristics we use to judge others. We form our interpretation of them and their behavior by assessing specific qualities such as appearance, intelligence, or friendliness on a continuum from positive to negative. For example, we might see someone as fitting somewhere between pretty and ugly or smart and dumb or warm and cold. **Prototypes** are representatives of our ideal. We use this ideal as a means of comparison. We have an image of the "perfect" boss or the best basketball player. When we interpret someone or someone's behavior, we judge them against our ideal image. This comparison helps us to make judgments about people.

Attribution can also play a significant role in our interpretation of behavior. **Attribution** involves assigning causation to our behavior and the behavior of others. We use our frame of reference to interpret human action. How we perceive the cause for an action will affect our overall perception of self or others. Specifically, if an important task at work is not completed, we can blame a specific person by interpreting the incomplete work as a sign of laziness. Or, we may blame the incomplete work on the poor computer software program. These are examples of external attribution (outside forces or influences such as computer software, the weather, and poor management) and internal attribution (inside forces or influences such as personal characteristics, including laziness, meanness, and incompetence). **Self-serving bias** is a form of attribution. Self-serving bias occurs when we see ourselves in a positive light by blaming others or external forces for problems. But, when the same problem happens to others, we perceive the reason for the problem as internal, or some type of personal flaw. For example:

> Sue and Lynda work in the same office as assistants to the Director of Personnel. Andrew, the Director of Personnel, asked Sue to book his air travel to the national meeting last month. Sue booked the wrong flight, which resulted in a three-hour layover for Andrew and several others in their department. Lynda told her husband, "Sue is just so sloppy and careless. She just didn't pay attention to the flights she booked." Last week, Andrew asked Lynda to book his flight for another trip. She also booked the wrong flight with a long layover. This time, however, Lynda said to her husband, "Andrew did not give me all the information I needed to book the trip. If he had been specific about his meeting schedule, I would have booked the correct flight."

Lynda's perception of Sue's behavior and her own is an example of self-serving bias. While she blames Sue's mistake on some flaw in Sue's work habits, Lynda blames Andrew for her mistake.

Table 2.1, The Process of Perception, summarizes the three steps of perception: selective attention, organization, and interpretation.

TABLE 2.1	The Process of Perception
Selective attention	Determining what we pay attention to and what we ignore
Organization	Categorizing stimuli into patterns
Interpretation	Making sense of the stimuli with the use of our frame of reference

PERCEPTIONS OF OURSELVES

Our discussion so far has focused on the process of perception. We have learned that perception is highly selective and that it affects the way we organize and interpret the stimuli in our environment. How does this process of perception relate to the way we see ourselves?

■ Self-Concept

Central to the way we perceive the world is the way we see ourselves. Our perception of ourselves dictates the way we send and receive messages. **Self-concept** is our perception of ourselves, or how we picture ourselves in a very broad sense. In other words, how you would "define" yourself. For example, Andrea might define herself this way: "I am a daughter, partner, friend, student in business management, president of my church council, and avid runner." All the roles Andrea plays help to define who she is and help her to understand her self-concept. Self-concept is a complex phenomenon that has significant implications for communication. Its key role in the communication process can be attributed to the fact that much of the way we interact with others stems from our self-concept. This example clarifies this point:

> As an attorney, Victor considers himself to be a specialist in the area of wills and estates. His self-confidence is reflected in his communication with those clients who seek his professional help in such matters. He is forceful, knowledgeable, and dynamic. However, when Victor agrees to handle a divorce settlement for his neighbor, his communication with his client is less effective. He speaks softly and often uses "tag" questions such as "That's right, isn't it?" This can be attributed to his decreased feeling of confidence in the area of divorce law.

The way in which we send and receive messages, then, is affected by our own beliefs about ourselves. Since we all have different experiences, knowledge, and attitudes, we possess different strengths and weaknesses that provide the basis for our unique self-concept. Our self-concept is also situational; that is, there are certain situations in which we feel comfortable with the role that we play, while other situations present a greater challenge for us. The preceding example of Victor is a case in point. Here is another: Dan, one of the authors, feels comfortable teaching a basic communication class but finds it threatening to take his car into the garage for service. This is a result of his level of competence in one area and lack of confidence in another.

■ Self-Esteem

Self-esteem is our measure of self-worth; as such, it is the evaluative dimension of our self-concept. For example:

> Deena's grandmother was a nurse, and Deena believes that nursing is a noble profession. So, when Deena decided to go back to college, she

chose nursing as her major. Deena feels great about her decision to attend college part-time while working and about choosing nursing as a career. Deena's positive feelings about herself help to elevate her self-concept.

While not actually a part of our self-concept or self-esteem, the feedback we receive from others significantly affects how we see and feel about ourselves. Moreover, it is the way we perceive that feedback that will have the greatest impact on our self-concept and self-esteem. For instance, if we receive large doses of positive feedback from our family, we are likely to perceive ourselves in a positive light. This, in turn, affects the way we present ourselves to others.

Because we all have different strengths and weaknesses, it is important not to judge others according to our own positive and negative points. Two factors that affect our self-concept are the self-fulfilling prophecy and significant others. Both are discussed in the following section.

By permission of Tony Cochran and Creators Syndicate.

■ Self-Fulfilling Prophecy

Self-fulfilling prophecy occurs when our behavior matches someone else's expectations. For example, when an individual perceives us to be a certain way, he or she begins to treat us according to that preconceived notion, and eventually we act out or fulfill the way we are being perceived. The following example demonstrates how the self-fulfilling prophecy operates:

John comes from a highly critical home environment. His parents have difficulty expressing positive feelings toward him, which reinforces his feelings of inadequacy. Moreover, they constantly push him to take on new challenges. The same theme is reinforced on the job; John's boss frequently gives him challenging assignments, but in the same breath communicates his doubts about John's ability to complete the tasks.

As John begins to internalize the image that others have of him, his confidence diminishes. Inevitably, his behavior reflects that loss of self-esteem. He stops sharing his ideas with others and reevaluates his goals for the future. His communication becomes guarded; he avoids interaction with others.

COMMUNICATION IN ACTION

Understanding Your Self-Concept

Describe your self-concept using the following categories:

- your role within your family
- your career goals
- your relationships with your school peers
- your ethnicity, gender, and age
- your physical traits
- your personality traits.

Now, evaluate your self-concept in each of the preceding categories. In other words, how do you feel about your self (self-esteem) concerning each of the categories? How can your understanding of your self-concept enhance your confidence as a communicator?

Although usually thought of in negative terms, the self-fulfilling prophecy also can have a positive effect on our self-concept. This happens when we are exposed to positive feedback from others. Such feedback suggests that we are capable, talented, and admired. If this feedback is reinforced over a period of time, we naturally begin to believe it.

■ Significant Others

The development of our self-concept is also influenced by **significant others,** those individuals whom we allow to influence our lives. We often feel that it is necessary to gain acceptance from these people because we think their approval will enhance our self-concept. At times we place greater importance on the opinions and advice of our significant others than we do on our own:

> During high school, Martie envisioned herself becoming a great chef. She even gathered information about various cooking schools, both in the United States and abroad. However, instead of filling out applications for these schools, Martie mailed applications to several liberal arts colleges and universities. The reason? Martie's father wanted her to become a medical doctor, and Martie eventually decided not to disappoint her dad.

■ Reflective Appraisal

The overall image of ourselves is based on our view of how we believe others' see us. This image is called a **reflective appraisal** (Sullivan, 1953). Reflective appraisals are also called the "looking-glass self" because we see ourselves through other people's eyes (Cooley, 1912). For example:

> Edwina always wanted to be a teacher, but was convinced she was not smart enough to finish the required course work and student teaching to

EMBRACING DIFFERENCE

The Self-Fulfilling Prophecy

Kathy is the supervisor of the Accounting Department at Midwestern Electronics' Minneapolis Division. Avery has just been transferred to her unit. In reviewing Avery's personnel file, Kathy discovered that Avery has a history of difficulty in communicating with his supervisors. Although prior supervisors commented favorably about his capabilities as an accountant, they also noted his inability to follow specific supervisor directions. Other company employees have also discussed Avery's reputation with Kathy. Kathy is an experienced supervisor who understands that she cannot prejudge Avery or his pattern of behavior may continue. She knows that Avery is aware of what other supervisors have said about him and is just behaving the way everyone expects.

1. How will Kathy's appreciation of difference strengthen her ability to work with Avery? How might this affect Avery and his communication?

2. Describe how the self-fulfilling prophecy has operated in one of your own relationships.

3. How can Kathy's experience help you understand the importance of embracing difference?

receive her teaching license. During her sophomore year, Edwina was selected to do an internship with an elementary school, helping students with learning disabilities to read. The students at Homan Elementary School loved Edwina and encouraged her to pursue her dream of being a teacher. Edwina began to see herself through her students' eyes and felt confident enough about her abilities to change her major to education.

Families and peers are two groups of significant others that have a strong effect on the development of our self-concept.

■ Family

During our childhood and adolescence we are in constant contact with **family** members. Consequently, parents play an overwhelming role in the development of our self-concept. The example of Martie and her father illustrates this point. As youngsters, we are dependent on our parents; this relationship is likely to change as we grow older and begin to challenge and question our parents' judgments and values.

In some cases, family influence can be devastating to our self-concept. If we grow up in a home where little warmth and love are demonstrated, we may believe that we are not lovable; if our parent's scream and shout to vent their frustrations, we may grow up thinking we are the cause of their problems.

Of course, the opposite also can occur. We may grow up in a family environment that is overprotective, one in which individuals are not given the opportunity to explore and take risks. Parents often want to protect their children from the outside world, hence their love is overly possessive. The children, in turn, may feel guilty when they do not want to return the smothering affection shown by their parents. In both these family environments the feedback received from the parents is likely to have a negative impact on the self-concepts of the children involved.

Under ideal circumstances, our families can represent a highly constructive influence on the development of our self-concept. When our home life is warm and the environment is conducive to expressing and sharing feelings, our self-concept is positive. Furthermore, when problems arise and the necessary time is taken to discuss them openly, this also can have a positive impact on our self-concept.

■ Peers

Peers, another group of significant others, also can profoundly influence our self-concept. Some people go out of their way to gain the acceptance of their peers in order to boost their own self-concept; however, we sometimes let our peers play a disproportionate role in our lives because we feel it is vital to be accepted as part of the group.

A by-product of peer pressure can be the exhibition of counterproductive behavior. For example, a young teenager might join a violent street gang in order to be accepted by his or her peers. In this case, the peer pressure is potentially detrimental to the teen's self-concept, because he or she will look to others for self-esteem. In fact, the tension he or she feels from a diminished self-concept may motivate him or her to seek a group that shares his or her insecurities.

Interactions with our friends greatly influence the development of our self-concept.

Communication and TECHNOLOGY
Presenting Your "Self" and Finding a Mate on the Internet

Many of us turn to the Internet to find a date or even a lifelong mate. Over 20 million people use an online dating site each month, according to the *Dating Online Newsletter*. Websites such as Match.com, eHarmony.com, and Chemistry.com and more specific dating sites like SingleC.com (Christians), SingleParentMeet .com (single parents), Datemypet.com (for pet lovers), Gay.com (gay and lesbians), and Jdate.com (Jewish singles) connect people locally and from around the world. As part of the dating process, each person creates a personal ad about him- or herself. The ad lists likes, dislikes, education level, income, and hobbies. In addition, a description of the person is included. Characteristics such as age, weight, height, hair and eye color, and overall "looks" are described. The ad also describes the kind of person one is looking to meet.

According to Sherry Turkle in her book *Life on the Screen*, when we enter cyberspace, we create *virtual* identities (1995). In other words, we can reconstruct our "self" or "selves" as we communicate on the World Wide Web in chat rooms, on bulletin boards, through email, and on personal web pages. She says, "Many more people experience identity as a set of roles that can be mixed and matched, whose diverse demands need to be negotiated" (1995, 180). Thus, our email "style" is different when sending a memo to our boss than it is when we send a joke to our best friend. We have always adjusted our "self" or image to more effectively communicate. Now, because of the nature of technology, however, we can create or reconstruct our image and identity specifically for cyberspace. Many of us "adjust" our weight or age or upload old pictures of ourselves. Is this lying? "Those studying impression management online have found that when people misrepresent themselves, it is often because they are attempting to express an idealized or future version of themselves" (Rosenbloom, 2008).

So, whether writing your own personal ad or reading someone else's, be aware that on the Internet, we are a presenting a version of self and that self is constantly changing and adapting to the ever-changing technological world.

On the other hand, peers, like families, can be a positive force in shaping self-concept. Associations with people who are capable of providing support and positive feedback help to boost self-esteem. For example, a friend may encourage you to apply for a job by giving you a "pep" talk: "Your experience as a welder gives you an edge over the other candidates. What better qualification is there for selling and demonstrating how welding equipment works than the experience you have acquired during the past four years?"

PERCEPTIONS OF OTHERS

The same factors (discussed earlier) that apply to the process of perception also apply to our perceptions of others. In other words, certain aspects of another person either draw our attention or are ignored, depending on our own interests and needs. We sort out these facts and then make an effort to interpret them based on our past experience, attitudes, personal constructs, and prototypes. During the process, we develop a perception of this person that subsequently affects our communication with him or her.

Whether our perception of another person is generally positive (he or she is friendly, attractive, talented, knowledgeable, kind, and so on), negative (he or she is overbearing, critical, stubborn, stupid, grouchy, and so on), or neutral (he or she is okay), we react to that perception. It is this reaction that affects our communication with the person. In sum, our perceptions of others could serve to filter messages so we what hear only we want to hear. Attribution can play a significant role in our interpretation of others and their behavior.

Attribution involves assigning causation to our behavior and the behavior of others. We use our frame of reference to interpret our actions. How we perceive the cause for an action will affect our overall perception of ourselves or others.

■ Stereotyping

Stereotyping, placing or categorizing people, places, objects, or events into groups based on generalized characteristics, also contributes to the way we perceive others. Although stereotyping helps us "order" stimuli, it can distort reality because it fails to recognize individual differences among people and objects. Our perception of others is commonly the result of "allness" stereotyping or "halo and horns" stereotyping. We shall take a look at each of these practices next.

With **allness stereotyping,** we attribute a particular characteristic to a group of people; for the purpose of this discussion, we shall use bankers as our select group. Based on our limited contact with bankers, we generalize that this group is conservative. When we find out that someone we have just met is a banker, we then make the assumption (frequently wrong) that this person is also conservative. By superficially categorizing people into groups, we severely diminish the possibility of perceiving the unique differences among people.

The following situation aptly demonstrates the narrow-mindedness that commonly results from allness stereotyping:

> Years ago, Vernon worked for one summer as a construction laborer building garages. He liked interacting with the other workers but found most of them "pretty dumb." Now he and his wife are having a deck built on the back of their home. Every day before he leaves for work, Vernon says hello to the construction workers but does not engage them in any substantive conversation. After a few days, a member of the crew, Marshall, asks Vernon if he or someone on the crew has done something to offend Vernon because Vernon seems to ignore them. Vernon is surprised at how articulate Marshall is and through their conversation learns that Marshall and several other members of the crew all studied engineering in college.

Vernon used allness stereotyping and assumed that all construction workers are "pretty dumb." Obviously, he was mistaken and had to revise his perceptions of the crew.

How many times have you heard someone pass judgment on another person without first interacting with that individual? We have all made judgments about a person's behavior by placing that person in a racial, ethnic, or social group without knowing much, if anything, about the actual person. The tendency to place people in a group and make generalizations about their behavior because of their group membership illustrates how allness stereotyping can distort reality. A related form of stereotyping, **halo and horns stereotyping,** happens this way: Based on our observations of an individual in a particular situation or setting, we develop either a positive or negative perception about that person; we then allow our initial perception to transfer to other situations. The significance of halo and horns stereotyping is that we see an individual in either a consistently positive or consistently negative light, which effectively eliminates the sounder practice of assessing the individual's other characteristics on their own merits. Consider the following:

> Tamara loves yoga. She has been taking a class for the past year and has just been asked to join the advanced class by Stan, the supervising yoga instructor. Stan also asks Tamara if she might be interested in teaching a class for beginners on Saturday mornings. "You have mastered all the techniques and are my best student, Tamara," Stan tells her. "I think you would make an excellent teacher."

What's wrong with Stan's logic in this example? Is he making an objective assessment of Tamara's potential as a teacher? Would Tamara have the patience to teach others? How might she interact with students who don't take yoga seriously? Making positive or negative judgments about a person's behavior based on limited information often hinders the communication process.

DEVELOPING ACCURATE PERCEPTIONS OF OURSELVES AND OTHERS

Accurate perceptions of both ourselves and others mean better communication and understanding between individuals, something all of us desire. In other words, we want to match our perceptions with those of others to ensure we share the same meanings. In previous sections of this chapter we discussed not only the process of perception, but also specific factors that influence our perception of ourselves and our perceptions of others. Some of these factors, such as self-esteem and stereotyping, actually cause us to form perceptions that are different from our partner's. In this final section we shall suggest how to develop accurate perceptions of ourselves and others.

Our perception of ourselves is strongly tied to the notion of self-concept. As defined earlier, self-esteem is a reflection of the way we view our worth or value. For instance, our work with the Meals-On-Wheels program raises our self-esteem because we view our efforts as worthwhile. On the other hand, our self-esteem diminishes when we judge ourselves to be clumsy in athletics. What should be apparent to us (but frequently is not) is that our self-concept is situational—our estimate of ourselves varies according to the circumstances of the particular situation. To perceive ourselves accurately, then, we must realistically evaluate our behavior in a given situation and take into account the feedback we receive from others. Our perceptions become blurred when we begin to generalize that we behave or communicate a particular way "all the time." This estimation is usually inaccurate.

◼ Impression Management

How we want others to perceive us is called **impression management.** Our self-concept and self-esteem greatly effect how we present ourselves to our friends, family, and work colleagues. Depending on the situation, we take on roles just as actors do, and we then interact with others to create an image of ourselves. For example, when Lisa, one of the authors, teaches, she wears "professional" clothes and answers her phone by saying, "This is Dr. Goodnight." She does this because she wants to project an image of professionalism and competence. At home, Lisa wears jeans and answers the phone, "Hello." In each situation, she is playing a different role and projecting a different kind of image.

Accurate perceptions of others are sometimes hindered by clinging to first impressions and by stereotyping. In order to develop accurate perceptions of others, we must avoid relying on first impressions and stereotypes; instead, we should be open to altering our perceptions when new information about a person warrants such a change.

We sometimes form an initial impression of someone and then stick to it. Because many people feel uncomfortable when they first meet someone, and therefore may act shy or nervous, a first impression may not be an accurate one. This means that distortion and misunderstanding of the other person's behavior can easily occur. Consider the following:

> Bob's behavior is loud and obnoxious at the party where Cristy first meets him. His crude jokes call a great deal of attention to him. After several minutes, people start to whisper about his inappropriate behavior and try to avoid him. Cristy decides that he is a jerk.
>
> At another party two weeks later, Cristy runs into Bob again. This time he behaves much differently. He is more natural and does not try to "put on a show." Instead, he appears relaxed and is easy to talk to. In fact, Cristy is comfortable enough to ask him why he behaved the way he did at the first party. He tells her that he gets so nervous about meeting and talking to new people that he feels he has to impress everyone.

Luckily, Cristy did not adhere to her initial impression of Bob, whose earlier communication behavior grew out of his own discomfort. It took a second encounter and asking questions of Bob for Cristy to realize that her first impression had, indeed, been unfair. Armed with additional information, she was ready to alter her former perception of Bob.

The public-speaking situation is another area where we must be careful about clinging to first impressions. As people get more confident about making speeches, there are undoubtedly significant changes in the way they present themselves. Consider the case of Natalie:

> Natalie has just been hired as the new director of the local YWCA. Part of her job includes soliciting contributions from various businesses in the

community. Her initial fund-raising effort involves talking to officials of the town's largest bank. She is nervous about her presentation, and consequently, she does not make a particularly strong impression on the bank trustees. A few of these individuals, however, recognize the importance of the agency's service to the community and subsequently show their support with monetary gifts.

Four months later Natalie is serving on a community task force with two bank officers. In the intervening months she has gained confidence in her new position, which is evidenced by her effective participation on this committee. The bank trustees note the changes in Natalie's public image and dismiss their earlier doubts about her capabilities.

Once again, first impressions proved to be inaccurate.

Stereotypes, much like first impressions, are the result of having either too little or inaccurate information about someone. Based on brief observations and insufficient information, we think we know how another person will behave. Is our perception likely to be accurate? Probably not. For example, it is illogical to think that because Sam is single, he is also shy. We must get to know him better before we can make such a statement (while it is possible that Sam is shy, there is an equal chance that he is not). Our communication with others depends, to a large degree, on the way we perceive them. When our perceptions are inaccurate, the possibility of misunderstandings between ourselves and others increases. We must always realize that we are all different in many ways, and as a competent communicator, our job is to verify our perceptions and strive to understand the other person. In order to do this, we can use perception checking.

■ Perception Checking

Using questions to clarify our understanding of the message is called **perception checking.** To do this, we must assume that our first impression is not always correct and we need further clarification. Your perception is based on your frame of reference, so your perception may be different from the perception of the person you are communicating with. We can reach mutual understanding with perception checking. Here are a few guidelines for asking questions.

1. State your observations as clearly as possible. Be descriptive about what you have seen or heard. Example: "You seem pretty upset about your math quiz grade. You sat through class without taking any notes or participating in the discussion after we received our grades."

2. Ask if the other person sees or hears the same thing. Example: "Are you upset?"

3. Offer a few possible interpretations. Example: "Is it your grade, or is something else bothering you?"

Be sure to perception check in a nonthreatening way to minimize defensiveness. The goal of perception checking is to clarify meaning, not put the other person on the spot. We will discuss more about perception checking in Chapter 3.

In the chapters that follow we shall see that perception plays a key role in nearly all aspects of the communication process: in listening, in verbal communication, in nonverbal communication, in our relationships with others, and in public speaking.

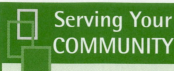

Serving Your COMMUNITY

Accurate Perception of Others

In an effort to achieve accurate perceptions of others, do the following:

- Identify a community group that you do not belong to and that has different views than you. Contact the leadership of this organization.
- Ask if you can attend at least two meetings as part of a school project to observe the behaviors and interactions of the people at the meeting.
- Interview people at the meeting to clarify why they are part of this organization and what the organization means to them.
- When observing the organization and interviewing the members, please be aware of the following components:
  - Avoid relying on first impression and stereotypes.
  - Practice perception checking.

Reflect on how your initial perception compared to and differed from your observations and the information you obtained from the interviews. How did this process help you recognize and appreciate difference?

ETHICS in Communication

Understanding Self-Concept and Self-Esteem

In Chapter 1, we discussed how our differences sometimes enrich and sometimes deter effective communication. Let's look at how the managers in the beginning of this chapter may view themselves. They are certainly different from one another and have their own unique way of seeing themselves and the world around them. Their self-concepts and levels of self-esteem will have an impact on how they communication intrapersonally and interpersonally.

Tony is a father, husband, church member, and manager. He receives positive support and feedback from his wife, children, and friends. He communicates freely with his family and friends about his dreams, ambitions, fears, and feelings. At work, however, despite his past promotions, Tony feels a bit insecure. The lack of merit raise this year was seen by Tony as negative feedback on his job performance. He finds himself more and more hesitant to speak up at meetings, for example, because he feels intimidated by his college-educated colleagues.

Connie is a mother, partner, college graduate, and manager. Like Tony, she receives love and support from her family and friends. She and her partner have developed and nurtured and egalitarian relationship where they share in all the joys and responsibilities of their family's life. After completing her college degree, Connie was promoted and given a large pay raise. She worked hard for her degree by attending classes at night, part-time, for six years.

Anita is single, a recent immigrant, college graduate, and manager. At work, Anita is self-assured and assertive. She was at the top of her graduating class and is confident about her knowledge and expertise in manufacturing technology. Anita is dedicated to her job and works long hours to ensure that her division is the most productive. Like Connie, Anita is not shy about voicing her ideas and concerns, but this was not always the case. When Anita first joined the company, she was intimidated by her co-workers' "aggressive" communication styles and hesitated to offer her opinions. After several weeks, however, Anita received positive feedback on her ideas and overall work performance from her colleagues and superiors. In her personal life, however, she has not received much positive feedback.

Tom is a father, divorcee, college graduate, and manager. He is older than the other managers and has been at the company the longest. At work, Tom is intimidated by the younger managers because he fears they may know more than he does about technology. Unlike Tony, who is quiet, Tom is loud and aggressive in meetings. At home, Tom is adjusting to living alone. He misses his daughters and the companionship of a partner.

These four managers have been affected greatly by the feedback of others. Colleagues and superiors at work as well as their families and friends have impacted the perceptions each has about himself or herself. They also illustrate that self-concept is situational. At home and at work, we can feel quite differently about ourselves. Ethical communication begins with accurately and realistically evaluating our behavior in any given situation while taking into account the feedback of significant others. We need to be honest with ourselves and with others about our perceptions and be willing to adjust our first impressions. As you think about Tony, Connie, Anita, and Tom, answer the following questions:

1. Describe the self-esteem of each person.

2. How do the different situations (home and work) affect their self-esteem?

3. Describe how each person's self-esteem affects their ability to communicate effectively and ethically.

4. Have you ever felt like any of these people? When and where? Describe your communication behavior.

SUMMARY

Perception is a dynamic process in which we assign meaning to stimuli. This process involves three critical stages: selective attention, organization, and interpretation.

We first select stimuli from the environment through a process called selective attention. What we pay attention to is generally determined by our interests and needs. Next, we attempt to organize the information we have selected from the environment. To make the stimuli more understandable, we can group them according to similarity or proximity. In addition, the element of closure contributes to the way we organize stimuli. Finally, we are ready to interpret the stimuli. Factors that affect how we interpret what we have perceived include our past experiences, attitudes, personal constructs, prototypes, and attribution.

A key ingredient in the way we perceive the world is the way we see ourselves. Self-concept is the total perception we have of ourselves. Self-esteem is the way we measure our self-worth. Furthermore, the way we perceive feedback from others greatly affects our self-concept and self-esteem. Factors such as the self-fulfilling prophecy and significant others (including families and peers) contribute to the development of our self-concept.

Our perception of others affects how we communicate with them. Factors such as power and stereotyping (including allness stereotyping and halo and horns stereotyping) play a major role in the way we see other people.

Improving the accuracy of our perceptions requires that we avoid such practices as clinging to first impressions and stereotyping. The degree to which we are successful can be measured by our improved communication with others.

REVIEW QUESTIONS

1. Describe the three-stage process of perception.
2. What is attribution?
3. Define self-concept and self-esteem.
4. How does feedback from others affect the way we view ourselves?
5. What is self-fulfilling prophecy?
6. How does stereotyping distort reality?
7. How can we ensure our perceptions of self and others are accurate?

KEY CONCEPTS

perception
selective attention
needs
organization
similarity
proximity
closure
interpretation
attitude

personal constructs
prototypes
attribution
self-serving bias
self-concept
self-esteem
self-fulfilling prophecy
significant others

reflective appraisals
family
peers
stereotyping
allness stereotyping
halo/horns stereotyping
impression management
perception checking

Listening

AFTER STUDYING THIS CHAPTER, YOU SHOULD

understand

- the differences between hearing and listening.
- how noise interferes with listening.
- how delivery interferes with listening.
- how language interferes with listening.
- how perceptions interfere with listening.
- the types of listening.

be able to

- use the skill of questioning to be a more effective listener.
- use the skill of paraphrasing to be a more effective listener.
- use the skill of interpreting to be a more effective listener.

At a local electronics store, two customers were attempting to return the same defective color printer. William and Olga bought their printers on sale but found that digital photos did not print clearly. Each wants a refund.

William enters the store and quickly goes to the Customer Service counter. He is dressed professionally, in a suit and tie, since he is coming home from a long day at the office. Jamal, the clerk on duty, informs William that he can only exchange the printer for a new one because William does not have the receipt. William asks to speak to the manager. When the manager, Angela, arrives, she listens intently to William's description of the photos he tried to print and the additional money spent on replacement cartridges. She asks him to repeat the details so she can take careful notes. Angela empathizes with his story and issues him a full refund. She offers him an apology and hopes he will shop again at the store.

Just as William leaves the counter, Olga approaches with the printer. Olga is in her late seventies and is recovering from a stroke she had a few months ago. Due to the stroke, Olga has difficulty speaking clearly and walking is also difficult because she is slightly paralyzed on her right side. She tries to explain to Jamal that she would like a refund for the printer because it is defective. He interrupts her in the middle of her explanation and states she cannot have a refund without the receipt. Olga, like William before her, asks to speak with the manager. When Angela arrives, she tries to listen to Olga but is distracted. She should have left for her dinner break 20 minutes ago and is anxious to leave the store. In addition, another customer is waiting to talk to her on the phone about another problem. Angela gets short with her when Olga struggles to clearly articulate the words to explain the problem with the printer. Angela reluctantly offers only to exchange the printer. She does not take notes and offers no apology or offer to shop again at the store as she picks up the phone to talk to the waiting customer.

■ ■ ■ ■ ■

Why is Angela treating these two customers with the same problem differently? She appears to listen intently to William but interrupts Olga. In this chapter, we will discuss the communication skill of listening and how our frame of reference can affect our ability to listen. We will also discuss how we can improve our listening skills in order to improve our overall communication.

One part of the communication process that we take for granted is listening. Perhaps the reason for this is the attention we so often place on sending messages. Mention that you are taking a communication class to someone, and his or her response is apt to be, "Oh, aren't you scared to death to give a speech in front of a class? I dread getting up in front of others." You are not likely to hear, "Don't you worry about being an effective listener?" While you may chuckle over this illustration, the fact is that listening needs to be taken seriously. Remember, communication is an interdependent process that requires both the sender (speaker) and receiver (listener) to be engaged in the interaction. In this chapter, we focus on the skill of listening and ways to improve our listening skills.

In recent years, both the business community and numerous professions have recognized the importance of effective listening. According to the International Listening Association, more than 35 business studies have indicated that listening is the "top skill needed for success in business." Because of this, listening workshops are commonplace in business and industry today. This effort seems entirely appropriate when we consider how much time we spend each day listening to colleagues, friends, family, television, radio, and so on. In fact, we spend about between 24 and 55 percent of our day listening, according to the International Listening Association.

Becoming an effective communicator begins with listening. As we discussed in Chapter 1, effective communicators value diverse approaches to communication. Thus, valuing diversity begins with effective listening skills. As a skilled listener, you can better understand your audience and his or her message and offer appropriate feedback.

HEARING AND LISTENING

What is the difference between hearing and listening? **Hearing** is one's physical ability to perceive sounds; listening is the process of giving thoughtful attention to what we hear. **Listening** is more complex than hearing because it demands that we concentrate on what others say to us. To listen effectively, we must take the focus off ourselves and focus on the other person. This is difficult to do. We sometimes assume that when we send a message, the other party will listen to it and understand its meaning. If this were true, we would not have conflict or misunderstandings when we communicate with others. Clearly, we don't always listen, and even when we do, we may not understand the meaning of the message.

Listening takes more than just the use of our ears. We must also listen with our eyes and heart. The Chinese symbol for listening includes the ears, eyes, and heart (Figure 3.1). Effective communicators are able to take the focus off themselves and

FIGURE 3.1   The Chinese Character That Symbolizes the Verb "to listen"

use their frame of reference to listen to the message. Manny is an example of an effective listener:

> Manny has been working as an emergency room nurse for five years. He is very close to finishing his bachelor's degree in nursing. One of the skills that makes Manny an excellent nurse is his listening skills. He is able to focus on the patient's message but also pays close attention to the patient's body movement, clothing, and other nonverbal messages. Recently, a woman with a broken wrist was brought into the emergency room by her boyfriend. The patient said she fell down the stairs. Manny asked her to tell him the story of how it happened. As she spoke, Manny noticed that her voice was shaking and her lip was cut. She also did not make eye contact with her boyfriend. Manny deduced that the woman had not just fallen but was probably pushed by her boyfriend. He informed the doctor, and they were able to find help for the patient from the local battered women's shelter. Had Manny not used his effective listening skills, he would not have been able to help his patient.

In order to be an effective listener, Manny had to focus on his patient and not himself. He had to ignore all the internal and external noise. Many factors influence our ability to be effective listeners.

FACTORS THAT INTERFERE WITH LISTENING

An important part of being an effective communicator is to develop skills in the area of listening. These skills help us to understand the messages others send and ensure that our responses to these messages are appropriate. Later in this chapter we discuss specific skills for effective listening. First, however, we shall consider a

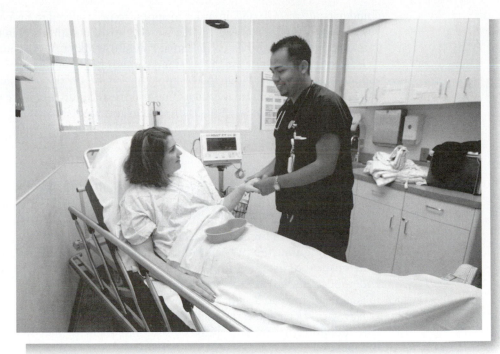

We listen not only with our ears, but with our ears and heart, as well.

number of variables that can interfere with our ability to listen: noise, delivery, language, message overload, and perceptions. A basic understanding of these obstacles will help us to implement the skills described later in this chapter.

■ Noise

Noise can interfere with our ability to listen because it prohibits us from actually hearing the message, and it can be intentional or unintentional. Incidents of noise fall into two categories: external and internal. **External noise** consists of sounds or visual stimuli that draw our attention away from an intended message. For example, if a road crew is repairing the street directly below the lecture hall where your class is underway, you and your fellow students may have difficulty hearing the professor because of the noisy equipment. Eventually, you all may give up the struggle and simply quit listening to the message.

Internal noise consists of our own thoughts or feelings that prevent us from listening to someone else's message. In the weekly progress meeting, you are thinking about last night's dinner conversation with your spouse about whether to take a vacation this summer or the half-written report sitting on your desk at work. In either case, you are thinking about something other than your supervisor and her message.

Similarly, internal noise can hinder our interactions or conversations with others. For example, Professor Shelley is so absorbed in his own thoughts about his daughter going away to college that he resorts to pat verbal responses, like "Yes,

I understand" or "Go on," in order to appear to be involved in his conversation with his student Kamal. Professor Shelley's preoccupation with his own thoughts makes it impossible for him to listen to Kamal's questions about the upcoming unit exam.

In order to become effective listeners, we must do our best to ignore all external and internal noise. Our focus should always be on the speaking situation and especially the speaker and message. This is difficult to do, but if we pay attention to noise, we will undoubtedly miss the speaker's message.

■ Delivery

Another factor that affects our ability to listen is the speaker's delivery style. Many times we can be distracted by the speaker's voice, bodily movement, dress, or appearance. We fail to listen to the message and instead focus on the delivery, good or bad, of the message. Take the speaker who uses "ums," "ya knows," or "like" throughout the presentation. You may find yourself listening for the next "um" instead of listening for the main ideas. Or, you may find the speaker's voice and appearance so credible and authentic that you do not critically listen to the message but instead accept it because of the speaker's delivery style. Either way, you are not focusing on the message, but the speaker's delivery style. Competent listeners don't ignore the speaker's style but focus primarily on the content of the message.

■ Language

Have you ever tried to discuss a problem with a colleague or friend, but his or her choice of words only resulted in you becoming angry, not solving the problem? This is an example of language interfering with the listening process. Messages that include words or phrases that offend us, such as ethnic or racist slurs, slanderous comments, sexist and homophobic comments, profanity, or condescending references, often trigger a negative reaction that actually prevents us from listening to the sender's complete message.

In addition to offending listeners, language can alienate, frustrate, or annoy listeners, and by doing so, diminish our ability or desire to listen. For instance, **jargon**—highly specialized words used and understood by specific groups of people—might intimidate or frustrate listeners unfamiliar with the profession or activity associated with such language. Bankers talk about "Fanny-Maes," "balloon versus fixed rates," and "negative amortizations" when describing loans; however, to those who have never applied for a home or business loan, these terms may be intimidating. Feeling like an outsider can affect how we listen: "I'll never be able to understand what they're talking about. Why should I listen?"

When we are faced with this kind of interference, we should strive to understand the message by taking detailed notes (discussed later in the chapter) so that we can ask questions of the speaker later. We can also confront the speaker about his or her use of phrases or words that offend us. Perhaps the speaker never intended to offend us and perceives the meaning of a specific word or phrase differently.

■ Message Overload

Message overload can also hinder us from becoming effective listeners. **Message overload** refers to our attention to details instead of the main ideas of the message. The extent to which we concentrate on the details of the message, instead of the major points, can actually interfere with our ability to listen. Consider the following situation:

> Adel's manager has mandated that all employees become proficient in all company software, including PowerPoint, Word, and Excel. Adel decides to attend the beginner's workshop on word processing, primarily because he feels intimidated by the prospect of working with computers. As soon as the instructor begins her introduction, Adel starts taking copious notes. By doing so, he fails to listen for her main ideas, which form the foundation of word processing. At the end of the workshop, Adel's notes are filled with details, yet his understanding of word processing remains sketchy.

Adel is experiencing message overload. He needs to listen for the central ideas of the presentation and the connections between the ideas to discern the major theme.

■ Perceptions

How does our self-perception act as a barrier to listening? In simple terms, if we find the communication setting or the message threatening in some way, we may become defensive, which, in turn, causes us to do a poor job of listening. Defensive communication is our response to threatening interpersonal or public-speaking situations. (The subject of defensive communication is treated in detail in Chapter 7.) These threatening situations can take many forms, but a common factor is that we

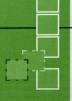

SKILL BUILDING

Avoiding Message Overload

Pick a class in which you take extensive notes.

1. During the next lecture, make an effort to listen for the instructor's major points. Record these in your notes, along with any important subpoints.

2. After class, review your notes. Rewrite the major themes.

3. Before the next class, review the major themes to help plant the ideas in your head.

4. How does focusing on the overall themes help you to avoid the practice of listening only for details?

Communication and TECHNOLOGY
iPods and Social Isolation?

Apple has sold about 175 million iPods as of late 2008 (Muller, 2009). More likely than not, you own one and may even be listening to it as you read this textbook. White "ear buds" (the label for the headphones) are everywhere: at the grocery store, on the treadmill at the gym, in line at the post office, on the bus or plane, and in the college classroom.

Professors at universities and colleges around the country are making their lectures available for podcast. Course-casting allows students to listen to and review the day's lecture. It is reinforcement of the content, not a substitute for attending the class session, according to Karen Bragg, director of university relations at Pick-A-Prof, a company that provides podcasting services to universities (Fox, 2006). But, there have been reports at several universities that student attendance is lower when course-casting is available.

Experts warn us that iPods can create social isolation. We are spending our time listening to music or watching a video instead of communicating with others. Jacqueline Whitmore states, "Some people think this technology can make us more productive. But it's not helping us with social skills. It's alienating us from other people," (Shrieves, 2006). Furthermore, according to Richard Lachmann, a sociology professor, "The danger is that we start losing touch with the people in our lives—even if it's just the cashier because we won't get off the phone or take off headphones to exchange pleasantries" (Shrieves, 2006). In other words, we walk around "in a kind of fog of technological insulation" (Burke quoted in Shrieves, 2006). Yet, one study found that iPod use actually increases the productivity of some workers. Spherion, an employment agency, found that "80 percent of workers listening to iPods reported increased job satisfaction and productivity as a result of listening to their music. So, how can iPods cause both increased distraction and productivity? By cutting people off from what they perceive as their main distraction: their co-workers" (Starr, 2008).

ZITS © ZITS Partnership. King Features Syndicate. Used by permission.

feel insecure or inadequate. When these feelings surface, they affect our ability to listen. For an example, let's go back to the issue of jargon, a form of language interference. Nearly all of us have been in situations where others used jargon, whether it is doctors spouting medical terms, lawyers talking "legalese," or actors critiquing a performance in their own special language, and we have felt like an outsider.

COMMUNICATION IN ACTION

Perception and Listening

1. Identify an individual with whom you feel uncomfortable.
2. How do you react when this person speaks to you?
3. Evaluate how you listen to this person. Do you interrupt this person? Do you let your mind drift?
4. Name someone whom you admire.
5. How do you react when this person speaks to you?
6. Evaluate how you listen to this person.
7. Describe the differences in how you listen to this person and to the individual identified in #1.
8. What accounts for the difference in the way you listen?
9. How can understanding the relationship between perception and listening enhance your confidence as a communicator?

What sometimes accompanies this feeling of being on the outside are feelings of frustration or intimidation, which may trigger self-doubt or a lowered self-esteem. "I'm not as smart as these doctors. I'll never understand what they're talking about or feel comfortable around them." If we dwell on our lowered self-esteem, we may drift from the conversation or speech and stop listening.

In addition, the way we perceive others affects our desire to listen to them. Simply stated, if our perception of someone is basically a positive one, we are likely to want to listen to that person; a negative perception hampers our desire to listen. Rick Warren, pastor of the Saddleback Church in California, for example, is perceived by many liberals as very conservative because of some of his stands on social issues. Thus, when President-elect Barack Obama chose Warren to give the invocation at the Inaugural ceremony, many liberals were angry because they thought they "knew exactly what he's going to say." In fact, Warren's prayer was much more embracing of difference than expected. Conversely, if we respect a professor, we are more likely to listen to him or her and act on his or her advice to read a particular book or to pursue an advanced degree.

EFFECTIVE LISTENING

Despite the stumbling blocks to effective listening we have discussed so far—noise, delivery, language, message overload, and our perceptions of ourselves and others—it is possible to become a good listener. What is necessary is an understanding of the factors that contribute to effective listening, accompanied by our

In our significant relationships, we use active listening.

commitment to develop the ability to listen effectively. These factors include recognizing the importance of active listening and implementing responsive listening skills. First, let's discuss the types of listening: active and passive.

■ Active and Passive Listening

Active listening is listening with a sense of purpose and involvement. This is a sharp contrast to **passive listening,** in which the only party involved in the message is the sender. Watching television, for example, requires no more of you than that you be a passive listener; there is no need to provide feedback regarding the message being televised. With active listening, you decide in advance that it is important for you to focus on the sender's message; you therefore make every effort to stay involved in the interaction. For example:

> Paul is beginning his new job today as an internal sales representative for a pipefitting firm. Part of his first day includes extensive orientations from personnel (to discuss employee benefits), the safety marshall (to discuss emergency operations), and the office manager (to discuss office procedures and regulations). Paul comes to the orientation with a large three-ring binder, legal pad, and several pens. As each speaker presents his or her material, Paul takes careful notes, asks questions, and files all the handouts in his binder.

ETHICS in Communication
The Skill of Listening

In the beginning of the chapter, we read about Angela, the store manager, and her interactions with two customers, William and Olga. Each wanted to return a color printer and asked for a full refund. Angela gives William his money back but only offers to exchange Olga's printer.

Angela's frame of reference influences how she listens and responds to these two customers with the same problem. She sees only the differences between William and Olga, such as their outward appearance (age and gender) and ability to articulate their problem. Angela fails to see the similarities and lets their differences dictate how she communicates with them. Ethical listening requires that we strive to understand the other, despite their differences, and actively participate in the interaction by ignoring distractions and using our responsive listening skills. As you think about Angela, William, and Olga, answer these questions:

1. What makes Angela an effective listener during her interaction with William? How does her perception of William affect her listening skills?

2. What interferes with Angela's ability to listen carefully to Olga? How does her perception of Olga affect her listening skills?

3. Have you even been in Angela, William, or Olga's situation? Describe your communication behavior.

Paul knows that he must stay focused on the message by taking notes and staying organized. There are three specific types of active listening. They are informative, critical, and empathetic. We will discuss each in some detail.

■ Informational Listening

One of the primary reasons we engage in communication (as we learned in Chapter 1) is to learn new ideas or to transmit information. In these situations, we use informational listening. **Informational listening** allows us to focus on the content of the message in order to gain knowledge. We use this kind of listening in the classroom, for example. Paul, in the preceding example, is using informational listening in his orientations from personnel, the safety marshall, and the office manager. Informational listening requires that we keep an open mind while we listen to the entire message. This can be difficult, especially if a message argues against something we feel strongly about. Another difficulty with informational listening, as we discussed earlier in the chapter, is message overload. Be sure to focus on the main ideas or arguments of the message.

■ Critical Listening

Critical listening begins with informational listening. Before we listen to evaluate, we must first listen to the message. **Critical listening** asks us to evaluate the speaker's message or intent. For example:

Wendy has been selected to sit on her first jury. Wendy is nervous about the idea of making a final judgment of guilt or innocence. As the lawyers present their opening arguments, Wendy listens carefully to each presentation, paying close attention to the facts and arguments. Although she thinks the defendant may be guilty, she forces herself to suspend judgment until all the facts have been presented.

With critical listening, you may also be asked to offer constructive feedback to the speaker. Like Wendy, be sure to postpone judgment until you've heard the entire message. Also, be sure that your feedback is focused and will ultimately be helpful to the speaker. As you listen to evaluate, pay close attention to your frame of reference and your perceptions of the speaker and his or her message. Your biases could cloud your judgment. As with informational listening, try to keep an open mind and suspend your judgment until you have heard the entire message.

■ Empathetic Listening and Being Supportive

Empathy, the ability to understand what someone else is feeling, involves looking at a situation from the other person's perspective. Empathetic listeners strive to take the focus off themselves, to avoid being judgmental, and to display sensitivity to the sender's nonverbal communication. As empathetic listeners, our utmost concern is to understand the sender's message, even though our efforts might dictate that we hold in check our own feelings about a topic. Consider the following:

> Sarah has just found out that her 18-month-old son, Michael, has autism (a neurological disorder). She is devastated by the news and fears that her son will never have a full and normal life. She calls her best friend, Darla, to share her news. Darla listens intently and tries to imagine herself in Sarah's position.

In this example, Darla's ability to take the focus off herself enables her to listen carefully to Sarah.

Part of empathy involves being nonjudgmental. As empathetic listeners, we try to avoid judging the statements of others; instead, we strive to keep an open mind while the other party is speaking (there is always time afterward to evaluate the entire message). If we mentally criticize what the other person is saying, we risk missing part of the message.

Listening with empathy also demands that we pay attention to the sender's nonverbal communication. Nonverbal communication is communication without words (this topic is discussed in Chapter 5). Active listeners look for nonverbal messages that support verbal statements. Such efforts help them get to the heart of the sender's message. For example:

> Libby is telling her neighbor, Elana, about a job performance appraisal she has scheduled for tomorrow with her supervisor. Elana can see that Libby is nervous about the appraisal not only by listening to what she says about her supervisor and about the job she has done, but also by the fact that she is talking faster than usual and she keeps jumping up from the kitchen table where they are having a cup of coffee.

By taking into account nonverbal as well as verbal communication, the active listener can construct a more accurate picture of the sender's message.

Supportive behavior is communication designed to assist or encourage speakers to express their feelings. It communicates to them that we are involved in the interaction and that we are making an effort to understand their position. In fact, according to Wendy Samter (1994), supportive or comforting communication is considered one of the most important interpersonal communication skills.

On the other hand, according to Brant Burleson (2003), insensitive, but well-meaning messages of support can be harmful to the receiver because the messages intensify the receiver's hurt and undermine his or her ability to cope with the problem.

Supportive listeners are involved verbally and nonverbally. Additionally, they avoid making judgments about the sender's feelings; instead, supportive listeners communicate a sense of caring or empathy. For instance, the remark, "I understand why you acted the way you did" lends support to the person who has just finished telling you why she broke up with her boyfriend. This statement does not judge the other person's actions.

We also can offer support to others through the use of nonverbal communication. Appropriate nonverbal communication demonstrates our involvement in the listening process. One way to show that we care about another person's message is to use direct eye contact. Along with a supportive nod, direct eye contact demonstrates our support and communicates to others that we are listening.

■ Remembering: An Essential Part of Active Listening

Active listening requires that we take the focus off of ourselves and pay attention to the message and the speaker. With effective listening, we hope to gain knowledge, evaluate a message, or offer support to a friend. In each situation, it is necessary for us to retain the message for later use. According to the International Listening Association, we may remember only 20 percent of what we hear and can only recall 50 percent of what has been said immediately after the interaction. Taking notes can help us to remember a speaker's message. Although this may not be practical with empathetic listening, note taking is a useful tool in other listening situations. Whether you are listening to a professor's lecture, a supervisor's report about company profits, or sitting on a jury, note taking can increase your ability to remember information. Note taking requires that you become an active participant in the process. It also helps you to stay focused on the speaking situation and avoid internal noises. Here are some guidelines for effective note taking:

1. Write down any words or terms you don't understand.

2. Try to determine the speaker's argument or thesis statement. In other words, what does the speaker want you to remember?

3. Determine the speaker's main ideas.

4. Write down anything the speaker repeats several times or has on a visual aid. Repetition signals that something is important.

5. Formulate questions about the message that you could ask the speaker later.

6. Don't get caught up in all the details. Look for the overall message (Rademacher, 2001).

■ Responsive Listening Skills and Checking Our Perceptions

We have just concluded a section that described active listening and the techniques to accomplish this skill. There are other skills that can enhance your listening effectiveness. These are known collectively as responsive listening skills and require us to interact with the sender. In other words, as listeners, we provide the sender with feedback about the message by questioning, paraphrasing, and interpreting his or her statements and by offering support that encourages the sender to speak. In addition, these skills help us to check our own perceptions of the meaning of the speaker's message (see Chapter 2).

Questioning

Questioning is a communication skill designed to help us understand another person's message. It also keeps us involved in the interaction. Questions should be specific about the speaker's message. Consider the following situation:

> Carlos is a mortgage loan officer at First American Savings and Loan. He is scheduled to speak at this month's library program, "Refinancing Your

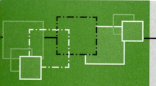

EMBRACING DIFFERENCE

Listening with Empathy

Erica has a strong belief about reproductive freedom for women. She has always felt that a woman should have control over her body. The Right to Life group on campus invited Father Jones, a conservative priest for the Catholic Church, to give a lecture on the belief that life begins at the time of conception. Erica felt that she needed to hear a different point of view so she attended the lecture. In order to really listen to a different perspective, she engaged in the following behaviors:

a. She attempted to listen without judgment.

b. She listened to the message from the perspective of the speaker.

c. She focused on the nonverbal behavior of the speaker.

While Erica did not change her position, she did gain an appreciation for the Right to Life perspective.

1. By embracing difference, how has Erica enhanced her ability as a communicator?

2. How can listening with empathy enhance your confidence as a communicator?

3. How can Erica's experience help you understand the importance of embracing difference?

Home." In his talk he explains the different types of mortgages—fixed rate and adjustable—and points out the advantages and disadvantages of each. Taylor has done her best to avoid message overload and has listened for all the central ideas, but she still is confused by some of the terminology. At the conclusion of the presentation, Taylor asks Carlos a few questions: "How does the lending institution determine the points charged to the buyer?" "Under what circumstances is an adjustable mortgage most advantageous?"

The questions asked by Taylor help her to clarify the information in Carlos's presentation. In addition, the feedback provided by Taylor's questions indicates to Carlos how well the material is understood by the audience.

Paraphrasing

Paraphrasing means restating another person's message in our own words. Paraphrasing forces us to digest the sender's message and then ask for confirmation that we have understood that message. The benefit of this skill is that we receive immediate feedback from the other person—either we have understood or misunderstood the message. This process gives us a better understanding of the sender's message. Consider the following interaction between Dave and Kevin. Kevin is Dave's supervisor at a large engineering firm. They are meeting to discuss Kevin's recent evaluation of Dave.

> **Dave:** I have a question about this evaluation.
>
> **Kevin:** O.K. (pause). Is there a problem?
>
> **Dave:** I don't understand what you mean by this comment, "I am concerned about Dave's attitude." Are you saying I have an attitude problem?
>
> **Kevin:** No, not at all. I think you are a very dedicated worker.
>
> **Dave:** Then are you saying that I'm too focused on the work and not enough on my relationships with my colleagues in the office?
>
> **Kevin:** No. I'm saying that we need to stop spreading you so thin; we need to give you an opportunity to focus more on your work, instead of trying to handle so many other responsibilities.
>
> **Dave:** So you are saying that the company realizes the stress I've been under and wants to help me reduce the stress?
>
> **Kevin:** Yes. It's the company's responsibility to hire additional employees so that you can work in your area of expertise.
>
> **Dave:** Gotcha. I had interpreted your comment as a criticism. I'm sure glad I asked you about it. Thanks.

In this interaction, both parties paraphrased the other's questions and concerns. By doing so, they were able to listen more effectively and understand each other better.

Interpreting

Interpreting a message is similar to paraphrasing. Interpreting requires that you clarify the meaning of a message but also allows you to offer an alternative perception. Because we all view things differently, an interpretation could help the speaker see things from your point of view. For example:

> Shaunna and her best friend Tasha are sitting in the campus cafeteria discussing their computer class and their instructor Professor Howard. Shaunna says, "I know he doesn't like me. I have stayed after class the last two sessions to ask him a question about using PowerPoint, and he just blows me off and tells me to stop by during his office hours. He really doesn't want to help me." Tasha responds, "I heard you two talking, and I also noticed that he was looking at his watch. It did seem as if he was in a hurry and couldn't spend the time helping you. But, don't you remember he told us on the first day that he teaches two classes back to back and the classes are in different buildings? He's probably not able to help you because he had to run to his next class. Why don't you go during his office hours and see if he can help you then?"

Tasha is offering an alternative view of the situation to Shaunna. Tasha's interpretation may help Shaunna to see her interaction with Professor Howard differently.

All the responsive listening skills just discussed increase our understanding of another person's message by directly involving us in the communication process. The opportunity to express our understanding communicates to the sender that we have been attentive listeners. We are able to check our perceptions of the message and clarify any misunderstandings. Furthermore, as listeners through questioning, paraphrasing, and interpreting, speakers find out how effectively they have communicated their message.

Serving Your COMMUNITY   Effective Listening Skills

In an effort to improve your listening skills please engage in the following activity:

- Interview someone who volunteers at an organization such as a hospital, daycare, Habitat for Humanity, or Red Cross. The purpose of the interview is to find out his or her motivation for volunteering and the specific values or goals of the organization.

- Using the listening skills of questioning, paraphrasing, and interpreting, respond to this person using language to show that you are listening and trying to understand his or her position.

- How did this process help you recognize the importance of effective listening? What parts of your frames of reference did you find you have in common with the person you interviewed? How did you overcome your differences in order to effectively listen?

SUMMARY

Listening is the process of giving thoughtful attention to what we hear. It goes beyond hearing, which is our ability to perceive sounds. Poor listening skills can create a lack of understanding between the sender and receiver. Variables that interfere with our ability to listen effectively include noise, delivery, language, message overload, and perceptions of self and others.

Despite the barriers discussed in the first part of the chapter, it is possible to become an effective listener. One way to achieve this is by becoming an active listener, which means listening with a sense of purpose and involvement. Passive listening requires nothing from the receiver. There are three types of active listening: informational, critical, and empathetic. Informational listening is used to gain knowledge. Critical listening requires us to evaluate the speaker's message or intent. Empathetic listening requires that we take the focus off of ourselves, avoid being judgmental, and display sensitivity to the sender's verbal and nonverbal communication. It is essential to all active listening that we listen to remember the message for later use. Note taking can help us do this.

Responsive listening skills help us to become effective listeners. These skills include questioning, paraphrasing, and interpreting and require listeners to interact with the sender.

REVIEW QUESTIONS

1. What are the differences between hearing and listening?
2. Describe the factors that interfere with our ability to listen?
3. Why is remembering the message an essential part of active listening?
4. What is the goal of informational listening?
5. Why is it important to listen to the entire message before passing judgment?
6. List some ways you can be an empathetic listener and offer support to another.
7. Define paraphrasing and interpreting. How are they similar? Different?

KEY CONCEPTS

hearing
listening
external noise
internal noise
jargon

message overload
active listening
passive listening
informational listening
critical listening

empathy
questioning
paraphrasing
interpreting

CHAPTER 4

Verbal Communication

AFTER STUDYING THIS CHAPTER, YOU SHOULD

understand

- why language is symbolic.
- the relationships between words, thoughts, and objects.
- how language communicates power.
- the difference between connotation and denotation.
- how such cultural influences as ethnic background, race, and geographic regions affect the meanings of words.
- the relationship between perception and language.
- the problems with language.

be able to

- use descriptive language to improve verbal communication.
- use dating to improve verbal communication.
- use indexing to improve verbal communication.
- avoid profanity and generic language.
- show respect for others through language.

One of the requirements for April's communication course is to observe and critique a public speech by Dr. Calvin Smith, a well-known expert in philosophy. Dr. Smith's presentation will take place in the campus auditorium, and the campus and local communities are invited to attend. April is excited about the speech because she loved her introductory philosophy course, in which she read some of Dr. Smith's work. She loved the way the class challenged her to think about her identity and the way we all choose to present ourselves to the outside world.

Five minutes before the presentation was to begin, the auditorium was almost full. April found a seat near the back. She saw several of her classmates and thought she might catch some of them at the end to compare notes and discuss the overall speech. At six o'clock, Dr. Moriarity, the Dean of Liberal Arts, introduced Dr. Smith. The dean read a long list of the books Dr. Smith had written and distinguished awards he had received. April was even more excited to hear what Dr. Smith had to say after such an impressive introduction. After the applause died down, Dr. Smith began to speak. He said:

> The title of my presentation is "Living the Human Life: A Philosophical Exploration." I hope we can explore the philosophical implications of the examined life. To begin, let me pose a question. What is the epistemological position of a subjective relativist? If we consider the ontological or cosmological construction of such a being, we can understand that this person has no epistemological stance, from a philosophical standpoint, of course. Furthermore, let us juxtapose the essence of this person by understanding the binary opposition of being and not being. In order to do this, however, we must first understand, as Sartre said, the phenomenological journey of praxis and consciousness.

April was completely lost. She continued to listen for another hour and still did not understand anything Dr. Smith had said. None of her classmates were able to understand the presentation. In her critique of his presentation, April wrote that she did not know what many of his words meant. She had never heard them before, and Dr. Smith did not define them during his presentation.

■ ■ ■ ■ ■

Clearly, Dr. Smith was not able to communicate his ideas to April or any of her classmates. In this chapter, we will discuss how language can hinder and enhance our communication. We will also discuss how our differences—such as gender, age, ability, ethnicity, culture, and approach—can make communication difficult. Finally, we will offer some suggestions on how to improve communication by being aware of our language choices.

Our word choices can make a tremendous difference in how successfully we convey our thoughts and emotions. The more precise and vivid our language is, both in interpersonal and in public communication settings, the greater impact our messages will have. Consider the following responses Latisha gives when asked by her friend Amy, "What's wrong?"

Response A: Oh, I'm just really depressed.

Response B: John and I are both distraught over the layoff notice he received yesterday. We just don't know if he'll be able to find a job with comparable pay. We're worried about paying our bills and about what this is going to do to our lives, especially for the kids.

After listening to the second response, Amy feels great compassion for her friend. Latisha's use of precise language in the second response does a better job of communicating her thoughts and concerns. In public speaking, messages are communicated more effectively when the language is vivid and precise. A few days after the terrorist attacks on the World Trade Center in New York and the Pentagon in Arlington, VA., former President Bush addressed the nation. His vivid language helped to make his message powerful and effective:

We have seen the state of our Union in the endurance of rescuers, working past exhaustion. We have seen the unfurling of flags, the lighting of candles, the giving of blood, the saying of prayers—in English, Hebrew, and Arabic. We have see the decency of a loving and giving people who have made the grief of strangers their own. (2001a)

As we discussed in Chapter 1, we are all unique, and our differences sometimes make it difficult to communicate effectively. Many communication misunderstandings begin with our choice of language or our interpretation of language. In this chapter, we first discuss the nature of language and meaning, and then move to a description of the problems with language. Finally, we offer some suggestions about how to improve our use of language in order to more effectively communicate with our partners, co-workers, and audiences.

THE NATURE OF LANGUAGE AND MEANING

One of the chief ways we express our thoughts, feelings, and attitudes is through verbal communication. Verbal messages are constructed first by selecting words and then by sending them. Words are **symbols** that represent things—our feelings, names for the objects around us, and explanations for behaviors. Words collected together and understood by a large group form a language. Knowledge of this language makes it possible for us to recognize the symbols (words) others use to send their messages. **Language** is an arbitrary system of symbols that is governed by rules and conveys power.

■ Language Is Symbolic

Symbols represent something else. As we learned in Chapter 1, nonverbal messages are symbolic even though they may not contain words. Words are symbols that represent our thoughts, feelings, and ideas in a specific context or relationship. How do you tell someone you love about your feelings? You could send the message nonverbally (see Chapter 5) through a kiss, hug, or tender touch. Verbally, you could just say, "I love you." Sometimes, however, this seems like such a dramatic statement, especially the first time you say it. Thus, we can communicate our feelings with other symbols such as "I care about you" or "I missed you while you were away." Depending on the relationship and the context, these symbols could certainly communicate "love."

Words help us to communicate effectively because they represent both abstract and concrete things. In our society, we have *freedom*, *democracy*, and *justice*. These words represent abstract principles. Words such as *school*, *computer*, and *dog* represent concrete things that we can actually see, touch, or hear.

■ Language Is an Arbitrary System of Symbols

Language is arbitrary because its meaning can change depending on the speaker, audience, and context. The meanings for words are constantly changing and evolving. In addition, new words are created every day. In fact, according to *Oxford Dictionaries*, there are 250,000 distinct English words and each year, new words are added. For example, in 2008, *Merriam-Webster's Collegiate Dictionary* added the following*: **dirty bomb,** a bomb designed to release radioactive material; **mental health day,** a day that an employee takes off from work in order to relieve stress or renew vitality; **netroots,** the grassroots political activisits who communicate via the Internet especially by blogs; **subprime,** having or being an interest rate that is higher than a prime rate and is extended especially to low-income borrowers; and **webinar,** a live online educational presentation during which participating viewers can submit questions and comments. Furthermore, we can choose to alter the meanings of words. Let's look at Professor Nadesan's class.

> Professor Nadesan pointed to a table at the front of the room and asked, "What is this?" The students said, "It's a table," "It's a desk." Professor Nadesan sat on the table and said, "Now what is it?" A student replied, "It's a chair." Then she stood on it as if to change a light bulb and the class said, "Now it's a step stool." Professor Nadesan said, "Okay, which label is the right one?" The class was stumped. All the labels seemed like the right one. "Correct," she said. "All the labels are correct. It just depends on the context."

*By permission. From *Merriam-Webster's Collegiate® Dictionary, 11th Edition* © 2008 by Merriam-Webster, Incorporated (www.Merriam-Webster.com).

Communication and TECHNOLOGY
Communicating on the Internet

New words are created every day. We create words and symbols to adapt to our changing society. In the past decade, we have developed a whole new language for communicating via email and in chatrooms. Two specific kinds of language have been created to make our communication on the Internet more effective. These are called acronyms and email shorthand, and smileys and emoticons. According to Netlingo.com, acronyms and email shorthand are used "because it's quicker and easier to type out a few letters, rather than typing out the full expression." A smiley is "a sequence of characters on your computer keyboard" and tells the receiver "what you really mean when you make an offhand remark," according to Netlingo.com. Smileys are also called emoticons because they convey emotions that might not be known through the use of just words. Here are a few examples of acronyms and emoticons:

Acronyms and Text Messaging Shorthand

182	I hate you	ILU/ILY	I love you
2G2B4G	To good to be forgotten	IMS	I'm sorry
2nite	Tonight	J4F	Just for fun
2more	Tomorrow	M4C	Meet for coffee
9	Parent watching	NOYB	None of your business
99	Parent no longer watching	OMG	Oh my god
AATK	Always at the keyboard	P-ZA	Pizza
AWGTHTGTTA	Are we going to have to go through this again?	P911/PA	Parent alert
BWL	Bursting with laughter	SMIM	Send me an instant message
CM	Call me	SYT	See you tomorrow
CUOL	See you online	THX/TX/THKS	Thanks
F2F	Face to face	UOK	You okay?
GFN	Gone for now	XOXO	Hugs and kisses
GMAB	Give me a break	Y	Why?

Smileys or Emoticons

:-Z	angry	:-V	shouting
:'(	crying	:-@	screaming
%)	confused	:-/	undecided
:-}	embarrassed	(:(	very unhappy
:O	hungry	:-"	whistling
:-*	kiss on the cheek	'-)	winking
:->	sarcastic	I-o	yawning

Meanings for words have changed over the years and within groups. For example, think about the words *cool* and *bad*. *Cool* once only meant a type of temperature. One might say, "This soup is supposed to be hot, but it is cool." Now, however, *cool* means something we like, and we might say, "The new Pink CD is cool." The meaning for *bad* also has evolved. Once we might have said, "This soup tastes bad. There is too much salt in it." Now, you might hear, "This soup tastes bad. Can I have some more?" Each use of the word means something different depending on the sender, the receiver, and the context.

■ Language Is Rule Governed

We learn how to use language by watching and listening to our parents or care-givers from the day we are born. Rules guide our use of language. We learn rules about how to pronounce words and how to spell words. Do you remember learning that the "e" is silent at the end of words such as *cake, ate,* and *kite?* Do you recall learning that "i comes before e except after c"? These rules govern the way we write and speak every day.

There are also rules about how to use language in particular contexts. When is it okay to interrupt your boss? When can you raise your voice to your spouse? What topics can we discuss? These unspoken rules guide our use of language and are called **regulative rules.** For example:

> Tyrone was hired two weeks ago to deliver internal mail throughout a large law firm. He delivers the mail twice a day to all the secretaries in the building. Within the first week, Tyrone learned that he was to be "seen, not heard" by the partners of the firm. He noticed that only the other lawyers and specific secretaries were "allowed" to initiate conversation with the partners. Also, Tyrone learned that he should leave his personal life out of the office. When two secretaries were discussing a family illness, one of the lawyers ordered them back to work and to "discuss your personal problems at lunch."

■ Language Communicates Power

We will learn in Chapter 6 that power is the ability to influence others and that power is a perception. Someone's perception of us is often based on the language we use, and that perception can have an effect on the overall communication process. Power can be communicated through language. Powerless language is characterized by disclaimers such as "I don't think this is the right answer, but . . ." and tag questions such as "I really like this class, don't you?" These statements communicate a sense of uncertainty and tentativeness. The speaker appears more uncertain than assertive (Grob, Meyers, & Schuh, 1997, p. 287). Powerful language, on the other hand, is characterized by assertive statements and certainty. In our society, "powerful language is perceived as more persuasive and credible than powerless language" (Burrell & Koper, 1994, p. 252). Thus, a person using powerful language will be perceived as credible, believable, and more capable.

We form our perceptions of others based, in part, on their language usage.

Studies have shown that in dyadic or interpersonal situations, women tend to use more powerless language, while men use more powerful language. But in a study on small-group interaction, men and women used similar language choices: both used powerful and powerless language (Grob, Meyers, & Schuh, 1997).

THE MEANING OF WORDS

An important theory that explores the relationship between our thoughts and the words we choose to convey those thoughts was developed by C.K. Ogden and I.A. Richards (1923). They maintain that words are symbols and that these symbols are given meaning when they are placed together to make statements. For example, when we ask someone seated at the same table to "pass the salt," that person is likely to respond by picking up the salt shaker and handing it to us. He or she would not in all likelihood toss it down to our end of the table as if it were a football being passed for a touchdown.

According to Ogden and Richards, our thought process is the direct link between the object and the word; consequently, if the word for a particular object is not part of our personal vocabulary, then the word for that object will have no meaning to us. This very thing happens all the time with small children (who are still busy acquiring language). For example, if you were to ask your three-year-old daughter to bring you the dictionary from the kitchen table, she would likely be stumped by your request. You would need to describe and define the term for her, using words that she already understands; that is, "It's the large book that has small holes on one side, by the pages. Each one has a letter of the alphabet on it to help people look up the words they want quickly and easily."

Of course, adults also encounter this type of situation. For instance, Alice, Majia's grandmother, might recognize the term *CD*, having heard it before, yet she might think it refers to a "certified deposit" from a bank or credit union. Because of this, she would not understand Majia when she says, "I would really like some new CDs for Christmas this year, Grandma." Alice would need to ask Majia for an explanation or try to figure out what Majia is talking about by listening to her subsequent comments. There can be no true understanding of a message if the words that compose that message are not a part of our symbol system. In this example, Alice did not understand Majia's statement regarding CDs (compact discs) because the word *CD* was not part of her symbol system (Figure 4.1).

Denotative meaning is the specific reference of a word; it is what we would find if we looked in a dictionary. Denotative meanings are usually shared or understood within a given culture. For instance, most individuals would define *book* as something that is read, and most dictionaries would offer a similar definition for this word.

Multiple meanings occur with denotation on occasion, and these can cause confusion. Take, for example, the word *aggressive*. *Webster's New Collegiate Dictionary* offers the following definitions: "1 a: tending toward or practicing

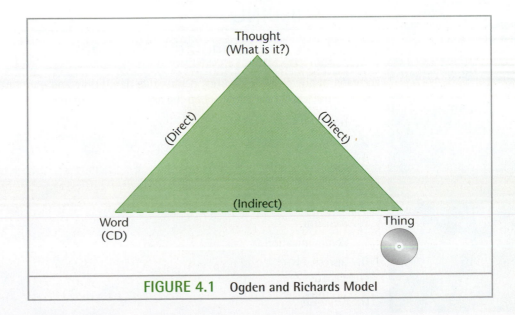

FIGURE 4.1   **Ogden and Richards Model**

aggression <aggressive behavior> b: marked by combative readiness <an aggressive fighter> 2 a: marked by driving forceful energy or initiative: ENTERPRISING <an aggressive salesman> b: marked by obtrusive energy." After hearing the comment, "Nancy is aggressive," we might wonder which definition of *aggressive* the person had in mind. Is Nancy someone who shows a lot of initiative in her work? Or is Nancy the type of person who displays her aggression by trying to dominate or lash out at others? It is easy to see how we might be confused.

A word's **connotative meaning** is that which is determined by someone's experiences, values, and culture. It is the personalized definition we assign to a word. *Aggressive*, for example, is a word used to describe someone's personality or behavior. This description may mean something entirely different to different people. For instance, a positive connotation for *aggressive* might indicate a person who is enterprising, a go-getter; a negative connotation would indicate one who is overbearing or who tries to dominate others. Our individual experiences determine the way we use and interpret the word *aggressive*.

In our examination of verbal communication, we also will discover that our thought processes are central to our choice of words. More precisely, our choice of words grows out of our environment, that is, our cultural background, experiences, knowledge, and attitudes. Our differences make communication a complicated process when choosing words as the sender and when interpreting words as the receiver. In the next section, we shall explore how cultural influences, ethnic/racial/social influences, geographic location, and our perceptions affect our choice of words and the ways in which we interpret the words of others.

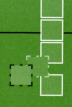

SKILL BUILDING

Denotative and Connotative Meanings

For each of the following words, describe its denotative and connotative meanings. You may use a dictionary to develop the denotative meanings.

1. Home
2. Baby
3. School
4. Table
5. Love
6. Freedom
7. Communication
8. Disrespect
9. Family
10. Feminism

FACTORS THAT INFLUENCE OUR LANGUAGE USE

■ Cultural Influences

Cultural studies routinely include language as one area of research. By **culture** we mean the customary beliefs and attitudes of a racial, religious, or social group. The customs practiced by a group help shape the language used to communicate with others. Furthermore, the language used by a particular culture has its own set of meanings and often sets the group apart from others. According to Lustig and Koester (2010), language is the very essence of a culture and if a language dies, so will the culture. In addition, they argue that people who rarely speak the language of their culture find their ethnic or cultural identity diminished. "Their ability to use the language results in lost opportunities to express their identification with the culture that it symbolizes" (2010, p. 186).

■ Ethnic, Racial, and Social Influences

A country such as the United States is composed of many subcultures. The dozens of groups can be defined as ethnic (Polish Americans, Italian Americans, Irish Americans), racial (African Americans, Hispanics or Latinos, Native Americans), and social (fraternities, steel workers, Goths). The identities of these groups is in some measure maintained by the language they speak. For instance, one would expect to hear Polish spoken in a neighborhood populated predominantly by first-generation Polish Americans. Their language binds them together as a group, but at the same time, their language can act as an insulator. In order for them to be understood outside the confines of their homes, they need to be able to speak the same language as the majority of the population. If they cannot understand a news program broadcast in English, they must rely on others to translate the information for them. And, if their children choose to remain in the neighborhood and speak only Polish, they too will become part of the group.

Some speakers deliberately use language to appeal to a particular group. Stokely Carmichael, during the 1960s, for example, attempted to explain the meaning of *Black Power* to different audiences. When describing the meaning of the term to a primarily white audience, he highlighted the sociological implications this way:

> Traditionally, for each new ethnic group, the route to social and political integration into America's pluralistic society has been through the organization of their own institutions with which to present their communal needs within the larger society. This is simply stating what the advocates of Black Power are saying. The strident outcry, particularly from the liberal community, that has been evoked by this proposal can only be understood by examining the historic relationship between Negro and white power in this country (1969b, p. 102).

The language Carmichael used in his explanation was intentionally analytical, clinical, and academic. He wanted to communicate that Negroes (a deliberate word

Our culture greatly influences the meanings we have for symbols.

choice) had to take the same steps as other ethnic groups trying to legitimately establish themselves in this country.

On the other hand, when describing *Black Power* to a primarily black audience, Carmichael adopted a more emotional language style:

> Now we've got to talk about this thing called the serious coalition. You know what that's all about? That says that black folks and their white liberal friends can get together and overcome. We have to examine our white liberal friends. And I'm going to call names this time around. We've got to examine our white liberal friends who come to Mississippi and march with us and can afford to march because our mothers, who are their maids, are taking care of their house and their children; we got to examine them [applause]. Yeah; I'm going to speak the truth tonight. I'm going to tell you what a white liberal is. You are talking about a white college kid joining hands with a black man in the ghetto, that college kid is fighting for the right to wear a beard and smoke pot, and we fighting for our lives [cheers and applause]. We fighting for our lives [continued applause] (1969a, p. 91).

In explaining the term to supporters of the movement, Carmichael used a particular type of language to rally the audience. His language served to keep the members focused as a group, separate from the white liberals he alluded to. The meaning derived from Carmichael's messages to these racially different audiences was vastly different because of his choice of words and his language style.

■ Geographic Influences

Geographic location often accounts for language differences. For instance, you are probably familiar with the regional variations for carbonated beverages; *soda* is spoken along the East Coast, whereas *pop* is the term used by Midwesterners. The first time Jill heard her cousin order a soda while visiting her in Baltimore, she was surprised to see a glass of cola served by the waitress instead of a drink with ice cream in it. Although her understanding of *soda* was something different from her

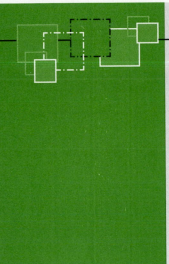

EMBRACING DIFFERENCE

The Meaning of Words

1. List as many dirty words as you can.
2. Name two clean parts of a body.
3. Name three good people.
4. Name three bad foods.
5. What do the words dirty, clean, good, and bad mean to you?
6. Share your list with a classmate.
7. Why are there differences on each list?
8. What factors contribute to these differences?
9. How can an appreciation and understanding of your different answers enhance your ability as a communicator?

cousin's, obviously the waitress spoke the same language. This simple example of geographic influence demonstrates how easily language affects understanding between communicators. When the meaning of words is different for the parties involved, understanding is not complete.

■ Perceptions

Our perceptions are defined by the language we acquire as a result of our cultural background—our education, our family environment, our neighborhood, the geographic area where we grow up, and the social groups we belong to. All these factors shape how we look at the world and at the same time provide us with a language to express what we see as reality.

A theory developed by Edward Sapir (1921) and Benjamin Whorf (1956) suggests that our perception of reality is dependent on the language system that supports our thought processes. Specifically, our language is the tool by which we assign meaning to events we encounter. We tell the doctor in the hospital emergency room, for example, that we think we broke a finger playing racquetball. She responds by telling us that an x-ray will determine whether the injury is a skeletal, comminuted, or compound fracture. Her medical training accounts for the difference in her perception of the situation. Her language, acquired as part of her medical education, reflects her perception. Her superior knowledge of this subject is reflected by a more sophisticated vocabulary.

Here's another example of this hypothesis in action: Ralph invites his friend Charlie over for a couple of beers. Ralph turns on the television set and begins to watch a baseball game. Although Charlie has no interest in the sport and has never learned much about the game, he watches along with his friend. Charlie makes the following comment midway through the third inning: "Too bad that ball was caught. It almost went into the stands." Ralph responds by saying, "Charlie, that player hit a perfectly executed sacrifice fly, which advanced the runner from second to third." Ralph's heightened knowledge about baseball dictates that he describe the "out" this way.

The significance of the Sapir-Whorf hypothesis is that people both perceive and describe events differently, in part because of their language. As communicators, we must realize that the understanding of our verbal messages (and the verbal messages of others) depends on the language system of the listener.

PROBLEMS WITH LANGUAGE

Language itself is often problematic for communicators. The preceding section pointed out that language is dependent on the way we perceive situations. Additionally, problems of understanding arise because others do not perceive our words in the way we intend for them to be understood. Something that is clear to you, for instance, may be "clear as mud" to someone else. To better explain this idea, six general problems of language will be discussed: vague language, abstraction, generalizations multiple meanings, technical language or jargon, and slang.

■ Vague Language

Vague language is language that lacks directness and specificity; it is void of details. Responses spoken in vague terms can leave the other person wondering what you mean. Consider this interaction between Marge and Pamela at the grocery store:

Marge: When did you get back from your vacation?
Pamela: Last Thursday.
Marge: Did you enjoy it?
Pamela: We were rather disappointed; so were the kids.

Unless Marge pursued her questioning (that is, "What was disappointing about the trip?"), she would probably wonder about her neighbor's vacation.

■ Abstraction

Abstraction is the use of broad terms to explain ideas or concepts. For example, if you simply mentioned someone's generosity, you would be talking in an abstract sense; to be more definite, you could mention the large donation that person makes annually to the American Cancer Society. Abstraction becomes a problem when the receiver or audience does not comprehend the sender's message because of the language used. Most students, for example, have experienced walking out of a classroom with absolutely no idea of what the instructor was trying to communicate. If he or she had attempted to more clearly define the terms used, the ideas might have been better understood.

■ Generalization

Similar to the problem that occurs when abstract language is used to define concepts is the problem of **generalization:** the use of nonspecific language to describe objects, events, and feelings. It is easier for misunderstandings to occur when others listen to us speak in generalities. Conversely, specific language forces us to be more clearly focused on our subject. Consider the following conversation between Phillip and his supervisor at the hardware store. In it, the supervisor's comments lack directness:

Supervisor: I need to talk to you.

Phillip: Sure. About what?

Supervisor: I think you're having a difficult time with your work. I'm not really satisfied with your performance.

Phillip: What do you mean?

Supervisor: It seems to me that you don't enjoy your work.

Phillip: What makes you say that?

Supervisor: I think you need to be friendlier to the customers.

Phillip: How do I do that?

Supervisor: Well, I just think you need to be more outgoing. Spend more time around them.

Phillip: What do you mean, talk to them more?

Supervisor: Well, yes, that would be a start.

■ Multiple Meanings

If someone you have just met says to you, "I have an interest in the city's downtown renovation project," does he mean that he has a financial interest in the enterprise or that he is concerned about the project's chances of revitalizing an area that he

COMMUNICATION IN ACTION

Vague Language

Use the example of Phillip and his supervisor to answer the following questions:

1. What would your response be to the supervisor's feedback?
2. Can you clearly understand the position taken by the supervisor?
3. Identify the vague language in the preceding dialogue.
4. Rewrite the dialogue between Phillip and his supervisor, eliminating the vague language.
5. How does vague language hinder communication with others?
6. How can the knowledge gained in this activity enhance your confidence as a communicator?

considers his home? In this example, use of the word *interest* is confusing. In order to determine precisely what the speaker meant by *interest*, either you would have to know the individual well enough to realize what he was implying, or you would need to ask him an additional question or two to better understand the comment. Some words have special meanings to individuals; therefore, it is not always easy to discern what someone else's message means. On the other hand, there are many words that have universal meaning. These make it easier for us to communicate with others.

■ Technical Language or Jargon

Technical language or jargon, the specialized terms associated with a particular discipline, skill, or career, is another factor that contributes to a lack of understanding between people. Technical language is most effective when used with people who are familiar with the terminology. Refer back to the opening story about April and Dr. Smith. Dr. Smith's use of jargon and technical language created a communication barrier that prohibited April from understanding his presentation. Technical language, in addition to contributing to increased difficulty in understanding, also can be intimidating. Frank, who recently retired from his job as a construction worker, received a new laptop computer from his children and grandchildren so he can stay in touch with family members who live all around the country. Frank has never really worked on computers before, so when his daughter asks, "Dad, did you download the pictures I sent you of the kids? I sent them as an attachment to my email. Be sure to back up your hard drive after you save the photos to your pictures file," Frank has no idea what his daughter is talking about. In fact, the computer and the language used to explain how it works is so intimidating and producing so much stress for Frank, that he decides to just stop using it. While the language Frank's daughter used is very common and an effective way to communicate for those of us who use computers every day, for Ralph, it is just confusing and frustrating.

■ Slang

Like technical language, **slang** is used by a specific group. It is used by a co-culture and can be geographic or generational. Are there any specific terms that relate to where you live and are really only understood by those who live there? In Northwest Indiana, we often refer to ourselves as "da region," and the people who live here are called "region rats." These terms reflect our geographic location as the Northwest Indiana region (as the rest of the state refers to us) and our ability to live and thrive in a dirty and polluted environment (close to the steel mills) like rodents. People who visit here generally do not refer to us as region rats. It is a term we have adopted for ourselves as a form of our identity.

Every generation has its own terms and meanings for those terms. Teen culture in the United States has always had its own language. Words like *groovy* or *hip* meant something desirable to the teens that used them 30 years ago. Today, teens have new words or phrases.

Here are some examples from SlangSite.com

Warez	Pirated software, music, movie or game downloaded from the Internet "My computer is loaded with warez from that website."
Props	Recognition or respect "Gotta give him props, he got an A on that test."
Off the hinges	Something that is great or outstanding "This new video game is off the hinges."
B-team	A sarcastic way to put someone down "I am so unimpressed. You should be on the B-team."
Scarf	To eat very quickly
Sammich	Sandwich
	"You scarfed that sammich in two minutes."

If you do not belong to the group, you may not know what the words mean. In this case, slang is used as a way for those of the same group to communicate with one another without "outsiders" understanding the meaning. In the preceding example, teens can use slang to exclude their parents and teachers from the conversation.

■ Euphemisms

Euphemisms are words that substitute for other words because they are more pleasant. For example, we call older people "senior citizens" or we refer to larger sizes of clothes as "plus size." Euphemisms are used to spare someone's feelings or to lessen the impact of the words. When someone dies, for example, we may say that the person has "passed away" or "is no longer with us."

Euphemisms, however, may be confusing and, at times, misleading. When politicians call for "revenue enhancement" or "increased revenue," they are calling for a tax increase. The nuclear industry calls nuclear waste "spent fuel" as a way to make us less fearful. Even though euphemisms can be helpful as a way to spare someone's feelings, be aware that they also can confuse or even mislead the listener.

The Boondocks © 2005, Aaron McGruder. Distributed by Universal Press Syndicate. Reprinted with permission. All rights reserved.

■ Doublespeak

Language can be used to misrepresent ideas or to mislead the listener. William Lutz, a professor from Rutgers University, was one of the first scholars to point out the dangers of using **doublespeak**. He defines doublespeak as "the language that avoids responsibility, that makes the bad seem good, the negative appear positive, something unpleasant appear attractive, language that only appears to communicate" (1999). There are four specific types of doublespeak; two were discussed earlier in this chapter, euphemism and jargon. Lutz adds gobbledygook (words piled on top of one another until there is no meaning at all) and inflated language (used to make something appear better than it really is). Some examples of doublespeak include

"poorly buffered precipitation"—acid rain according to the Environmental Protection Agency.

"effective delivery of ordnance"—a bomb, according to the Department of Defense.

"nutritional avoidance therapy"—a diet.

"chronologically experienced citizen"—an older person.

"negative advancement"—a job demotion.

"negative employment growth"—unemployment.

"awarded a nonpassing grade"—to fail an assignment.

"improperly dependent on a source"—plagiarism.

■ Racist, Sexist, and Other Insensitive Language

Effective communicators need to be aware that our language choices might offend our partner, group members, or audience. Racist and sexist statements are the most obvious language choices that will certainly offend your listener, but there are others we need to avoid. We must also be aware of comments that are ageist (degrading of someone's age), for example, "That old man could never run a marathon"; homophobic (degrading comments about someone's sexual orientation), as in "She looks like a dyke in that leather jacket"; and comments about someone's abilities, like "She's handicapped since the car accident."

These comments not only serve to insult and alienate your audience, but also encourage others to see the person in a negative way. So, when you call someone a "fag," "spic," "gimp," or "old geezer," you are not just using a label, you are showing how little you value the person. These terms are a sign of disrespect and will certainly put an end to the interaction.

IMPROVING VERBAL SKILLS

In the preceding section we identified specific problems concerning language and our communication with others. How do we combat the potential problems associated with vague language, abstraction, generalization, multiple meanings, technical language, and slang?

First and foremost, we need to always be aware of the context in which a message is presented. By *context*, we mean the environment or conditions surrounding the communication between two parties. For instance, the responses of two athletes to a sportscaster's question, "What do you think was the key play of the game?" are bound to be tempered by whether or not the players were on the winning or losing side. Knowledge of the circumstances surrounding the interaction gives us a more complete understanding of the message.

In addition, we can learn specific techniques to help diminish language barriers. These techniques include being descriptive, dating, indexing, avoiding profanity and vulgar language, eliminating sexist language, and showing respect for others.

■ Being Descriptive

Descriptive language employs specific words that represent observable behavior or phenomena. Being descriptive directs our communication to actions that are observable, and at the same time it avoids drawing inferences or making judgments about those actions.

For example, consider the difference between these two statements:

> **Statement A:** Heather doesn't look directly at me when we speak.
>
> **Statement B:** Heather avoids direct eye contact with me because she does not like me.

Statement A is simply an observation made by the individual who is speaking. Statement B goes beyond description; it tries to offer an explanation for Heather's behavior. By doing so, the individual is confronted with a problem addressed earlier in this chapter—making generalizations. In fact, Heather's lack of direct eye contact may be attributed to other factors: Perhaps she is shy, or perhaps she actually likes this person and is too nervous to establish direct eye contact.

Being descriptive helps us communicate more clearly and accurately, and it reduces the misunderstandings that occur between people. At the same time, being descriptive can make our speech more interesting.

■ Dating

Dating is the use of a specific time reference to clarify a message. By interjecting a specific date, we make a statement that is based on fact. The following set of statements illustrates the difference between a general comment and one that is more specific as a result of dating:

> **Russell:** I don't get along with my in-laws.
>
> **Russell:** I didn't get along with my in-laws at Thanksgiving last year.

The first statement is very general; it does not take into account that the situation may have changed at some point. By dating the second statement, Russell avoids making a generalization about the relationship he has with his in-laws.

Without dating, statements made by one party can cause confusion or hard feelings for both parties. Consider this dialogue between Sheila and Jim (dating is not used):

Sheila: I just bought a two-bedroom house in Highland.

Jim: What section of town is the house located in?

Sheila: It's just a few blocks west of the downtown area.

Jim: I've heard that that area of town has a bad flooding problem.

Sheila: You're kidding! The realtor never mentioned that problem to me!

What Jim failed to do in the preceding exchange was to tell Sheila that the flooding problem happened over three years ago. By including this date in his conversation with Sheila, Jim would not be making a misleading statement, and in this case, his comments certainly would not be as upsetting. Dating lends accuracy to our communication with others.

■ Indexing

Indexing is a technique that takes into account the individual differences among people, objects, and places. The use of indexing helps us to focus on the unique qualities of each person or thing. For example, to say that car sales representatives are dishonest would be generalizing or stereotyping. To prevent making such an irresponsible statement, it would be better to say, "The sales representative at Downtown Automotive failed to honor the price he quoted me two days ago, but the sales representative at Suburban Auto came up with the same figures when I went back to put a deposit on a car." This is a more accurate statement because it points out the individual differences between the sales representatives; in this case, one was dishonest, but the other was not. Since language and perception are interconnected, the use of indexing can more accurately reflect our perceptions of people, events, or objects.

■ Avoiding Vulgar Language and Profanity

We have all heard or used "four-letter words." Most of the time, these words are used inappropriately and alienate our audience or partner. Profanity and vulgar language are commonplace and we hear them all the time. Like all other language, profanity is learned by watching and listening to others. One father told this story about his daughter's use of profanity:

Clara was about two years old and we were riding in the car. I was in a hurry to get home after a long day at work and was not being very patient. When a car cut in front of us and we missed a long stop light, I said, "S_ _t!!" A few moments later, Clara repeated the word and laughed. I was horrified.

Profanity and vulgar language can be used to convey strong emotions or to make a point. It is also used to "shock" audiences, as Howard Stern and other "shock jocks" have illustrated. For us, however, profanity and vulgar language can cause more damage than it can help to clarify your message.

■ Eliminating Generic Language

We once agreed that "he" referred to any person or that "man" referred to all people. This is called generic language. Fortunately, this is no longer the case, and dictionaries, newspapers, and textbooks do not use the generic "he" or "man" to refer to men and women. **Generic language** is a problem because it only pretends to include women, when in fact it only refers to men. Language must be inclusive when it is referring to an entire population. Specifically:

1. Avoid the generic "he" when you want to talk about all people. "*A person taking a prescription medication should be sure* **he** *knows the side effects before taking the first dose.*" This sentence is sexist because it refers to only one sex. Think for a moment . . . when you heard this sentence, how did you visualize the person? Was the person a man or woman? Most of us would answer a man because the use of "he" leads us to that picture. The masculine pronoun "he" does not refer to women and men. Instead, try to use a plural ("**People** *taking a prescription medication should be sure* **they** *know the side effects before taking the first dose*"), or use both the male and female pronouns ("*A person taking a prescription medication should be sure* **he** *or* **she** *knows the side effects before taking the first dose*").

2. Avoid using words with "man" when you want to talk about men and women or when you are referring to a woman. Think about all the words that include "man." *Mankind, man-made, policeman, fireman,* and *chairman* are just a few examples. How can a woman be a policeman? She certainly can be a police officer, but calling her a policeman seems silly. Find alternative words for sexist labels as we have done with *policeman* and *police officer.*

Avoiding generic language will help you to relate to the receivers of your message and will ensure that you do not alienate them.

ETHICS in Communication
Appropriate Language Use

In the chapter-opening story, April can't understand a word of Dr. Smith's speech. His presentation to the campus community was confusing and almost everyone in the audience failed to understand his message. Of course, some of the faculty members understood the presentation, but the students and community members could not.

Dr. Smith's speech failed before it began. His language choices were clearly ineffective and unethical. Although the language may have been appropriate for the small audience of faculty members in the audience, it alienated everyone else. Dr. Smith intentionally used language that was inappropriate for his overall audience. As you think about Dr. Smith and his speech, answer the following elements:

1. Describe the problems with his language choices.

2. How could he have improved his speech so that it was effective and ethical?

3. Have you ever been in a situation like April or Dr. Smith? How did the sender's language choices or your own language choices hinder the overall communication process?

Serving Your COMMUNITY   Effective Language Use

In an effort to recognize how language choice creates community, please engage in the following activity:

1. Attend a meeting of a campus or community organization that is unfamiliar to you.
2. Identify a leader or leaders of the group.
3. Listen to the messages articulated by the leader(s).
4. Schedule a time when you can meet with the leader(s) to discuss your observations.
5. Share your observations with the leader(s) to explain how the language used creates community. Practice the following skills when discussing your feedback:
   a. Being descriptive
   b. Dating
   c. Indexing
   d. Avoiding vulgar language and profanity
   e. Eliminating generic language
6. How did this activity help you appreciate differences in language?

SUMMARY

This chapter explored the role of language in the communication process. Words are symbols that represent such things as our feelings, names for the objects around us, and explanations for behaviors. Language is an arbitrary system of symbols and is rule governed. Language also communicates power.

C.K. Ogden and I.A. Richards (1923) developed a theory to explain the relationship between our thoughts and the words we select to express those thoughts. Cultural influences, including ethnic/racial/social groups and geography, and perception are factors that affect our choice of words and our interpretations of others' words. The Sapir-Whorf hypothesis maintains that our perception of reality is dependent on the language system that supports our thought process.

Problems of understanding sometimes arise because others do not perceive our words as we intend for them to be understood. These problems stem from the use of vague language, including abstraction and generalization, the use of words having multiple meanings, and the use of technical language or jargon, and the use of slang.

We can improve our verbal communication by using such techniques as being descriptive, dating, and indexing. We should also avoid profanity and generic forms of language to ensure we don't offend or alienate our listeners. Lastly, we should show respect for others through our language choices.

REVIEW QUESTIONS

1. What is the relationship between the word, the thought, and the thing?
2. Describe how ethnic/racial/social influences and geographic influences affect the meanings of words.
3. Describe powerful and powerless language.
4. What is the relationship between perception and language?
5. Explain the difference between connotation and denotation.
6. Describe ways to improve your verbal communication.
7. How can dating lead to more accurate verbal communication?
8. How can indexing help you avoid stereotyping?
9. Why should we avoid profanity and generic language?
10. How can we show respect for our audiences through our language choices?

KEY CONCEPTS

symbols
language
regulative rules
denotative meaning
connotative meaning
culture

vague language
abstraction
generalization
technical language
jargon
slang

euphemism
doublespeak
descriptive language
dating
indexing
generic language

CHAPTER 5

Nonverbal Communication

AFTER STUDYING THIS CHAPTER, YOU SHOULD

understand

- the nature of nonverbal communication.
- why people react differently to touch.
- how paralanguage operates in nonverbal communication.
- how our silence can send a message.
- the four levels of personal space.
- the significance of territory in nonverbal communication.

be able to

- compare and contrast five types of bodily movements.
- use time to send messages.
- create an image using personal appearance and clothing.
- apply four techniques to improve interpretation and use of nonverbal messages.

Carla, a biology lab instructor, watches her students as they arrive. One by one they enter the room and take a seat at one of the many lab stations. Several students who are dressed like Carla smile and say "hello" as they take their seats. Carla smiles back. A young woman in her early twenties in medical scrubs arrives. Carla says to herself, "Well, at least there will be one smart student in the class. She can help me with some of the slower students."

Right behind the "nurse," a very well dressed woman in her late thirties enters the classroom. She is carrying a briefcase and the course textbook. "I bet she's good at business, but I'll be anxious to see what she does with the labs."

A very young man dressed in ragged jeans and a t-shirt hurries into the classroom. He has several earrings in both ears and a nose ring. Several tattoos cover his forearms and hands. "A loser," says Carla. "He will surely need help with every aspect of the course. Maybe he can be lab partners with the 'nurse' and she can help him get through the course: that is, if he is motivated to do so. I doubt he is!"

The last student to enter, five minutes late, is a man in his forties dressed in a mechanic's uniform that is very soiled from the day's work. Carla says to herself, "He could at least get to class on time. He doesn't care very much. Obviously he works with his hands all day, which will be helpful with the lab equipment, but I know I'll have to spend time with him on the lab reports. Maybe I can partner him with the 'business' woman. She will need help with the labs, and she can help the mechanic with the reports."

■ ■ ■ ■ ■

Carla is making several assumptions about her students' knowledge, motivation, and ability before she really knows anything about them. How is the students' dress affecting Carla's perception of the students? What messages are the students sending by the way they are dressed? Do you think these messages are intentional? Do you think they realize they are sending these messages? In this chapter, we look at nonverbal communication and how we communicate without using language or symbols. Specifically, we will see how our differences affect our sending and interpreting nonverbal messages.

Nonverbal communication encompasses the broad spectrum of messages we send without verbalizing our thoughts or feelings. Included in this definition are bodily movements, space, touch, personal appearance, paralanguage, silence, and time. We communicate nonverbally in our interpersonal relationships, within small groups, and in public-speaking situations. In addition, part of our listening includes nonverbal responses. When we consider the widespread use of nonverbal communication, it becomes evident that this subject warrants further study.

Nonverbal messages are an integral part of our communication. In fact many estimate that as much as 93 percent of the meaning of our message is delivered nonverbally through our tone of voice, facial expressions, and bodily movements while 7 percent is through the actual words or symbols used. That means that when you are talking to your friend about the difficult test you just took, your friend is getting most of the meaning of your message nonverbally. Thus, nonverbal messages work with verbal messages to communicate our thoughts and feelings. Effective communicators understand and appreciate the unique and different ways we use nonverbal messages in every communication situation. In this chapter, we will discuss the nature of nonverbal communication, the types and functions of nonverbal behavior, and finally, ways to improve our use of nonverbal communication.

THE NATURE OF NONVERBAL COMMUNICATION

We have just learned how important nonverbal messages are to the overall communication process. Nonverbal communication is also intentional and unintentional, ambiguous, multichanneled, and culturally bound.

Nonverbal communication can be **intentional** or **unintentional**. In other words, we can decide to send a message using our body, voice, or use of time. Or we can send messages we are unaware we are sending or don't mean to send. For example, when a mother yells at a child because the child ran into the street, she intentionally uses her voice to emphasize the verbal message, "Don't go into the street." But when she tells the story a few minutes later to her husband, her voice shakes. This is unintentional use of voice to convey the message that she was afraid their child would be hit by an oncoming car.

Nonverbal messages are **ambiguous**. It is very difficult for anyone to accurately interpret the meaning of nonverbal communication. Does a wave mean hello or good-bye? What do two hands in the formation of a T mean? A time-out? A technical foul? To understand the meaning, we need to know the context of the communication and the relationship between the sender and receivers. Of course, nonverbal behavior that indicates our emotional state is somewhat easier to interpret accurately. For example, we know that someone crying and sobbing is in some kind of pain or that someone laughing loudly is happy. Well, most of the time. Take the example of Sarah. Sarah was sitting in her hospital bed crying and sobbing almost uncontrollably. When her friend Kristen entered the room, she rushed to her side and said, "Oh my goodness, what has happened? I thought you and the baby were okay." Sarah said, "We are really great. I am just so happy our new little girl is healthy, and I am relieved that the delivery went well." Sarah was not crying because she was sad or in pain, but because she felt intense relief and joy at the birth of her daughter.

We send nonverbal messages through many different channels. Unlike language (see Chapter 4), which provides us with only one channel (symbols), nonverbal communication is **multichanneled.** We can use our body, voice, and appearance to convey the same message. For example:

> Mike is getting ready for his first date with Allyssa. They are going to a movie and then out for pizza. He decides to wear his favorite Abercrombie & Fitch sweater and jeans (he bought at the outlet mall). He takes great care to carefully shave his chin (to avoid any cuts) and brush his teeth. He leaves several minutes before he needs to, to be sure he isn't late. On the way to Allyssa's apartment, he picks up a bouquet of flowers. When he arrives at her door, five minutes early, he greets her with a big smile and the flowers.

What message has Mike sent by his dress, use of time, and facial expression? Obviously, Mike wants Allyssa to know he cares about her and wants her to like him. Mike did not have to say this with words; he used several channels to convey his message.

As we learned in Chapter 1, each of us is unique and different in many ways. Our use of nonverbal communication is one aspect that makes us unique and different because nonverbal behavior is **culturally bound.** In other words, the meanings and functions of nonverbal communication are derived from our culture. According to Lustig and Koester (2010), cultures differ in their nonverbal communication in three ways. First, the norms for *display rules* vary across cultures. Display rules govern when and where different nonverbal behaviors are appropriate, required, or prohibited. Second, cultures have different *repertoire* or range of nonverbal behaviors. Each culture has its own set of behaviors to enact. Finally, cultures have their own *interpretations* for nonverbal behaviors. For example, in Asian cultures, waving an index finger to call a person or hail a taxi is very rude and quite inappropriate. In the United States, this nonverbal behavior is not only acceptable, but widely used.

Each culture has its own set of nonverbal behaviors and meanings. Some cultures have unwritten rules that dictate when touching behavior is appropriate. In European societies, for example, it is commonplace for men to embrace in public as a way of greeting each other, whereas in the United States greetings are usually done with a handshake. Public embraces are less common. How we use time or touch, what is considered beautiful, and how far apart we stand all communicate our culture.

Culture dictates the appropriate use of nonverbal behaviors.

TYPES AND FUNCTIONS OF NONVERBAL COMMUNICATION

We have learned about the nature of nonverbal communication, and now we turn to a discussion about the specific types of nonverbal behavior and their functions as a part of the overall communication process. Specifically, we will discuss bodily movement, touch, paralanguage, silence, space, personal appearance, and the use of time.

■ Bodily Movement

Kinesics is the study of bodily movements. As mentioned at the beginning of this chapter, we communicate a great deal about how we feel in a given situation by our nonverbal actions. Our bodily movements can enhance our ability to communicate effectively. For example, the U.S. Defense Department has begun teaching soldiers stationed in Afghanistan and Iraq how to use gestures to communicate with local populations. Meadow, a professor of psychology, says, "Gesturing is not merely hand-waving. It conveys substantive information and thoughts that often are not conveyed in words" (Bridges, 2006a). Soldiers are trained to include specific gestures like placing theirs hand over their hearts as part of the greeting. Paul Ekman and Wallace V. Friesen developed a classification system that helps us understand our nonverbal communication (1969). Their system identifies the different types of kinesic behaviors: emblems, illustrators, affect displays, regulators, and adaptors. A definition and a discussion of each will help us see how bodily movements affect our communication.

Emblems

Emblems, according to Ekman and Friesen, are body motions that take the place of words (1975). For instance, holding up your hand, palm flattened, signals "stop" to someone standing across the room from you. Likewise, a basketball coach motioning "time-out" with his hands communicates to a player on the court that the player should signal the referee to stop play so that the team can discuss a new strategy. In order for emblems to be an effective form of nonverbal communication, both parties must readily understand the motions being used. A spectator unfamiliar with sports might not understand the "time-out" motion used by those involved in the game and therefore might question why the referee officially signaled time out. Emblems also can be used effectively when there are obstacles to verbal communication. The example of the basketball game applies here as well; the coach may signal to a player to call for time out because the crowd is generating too much noise for the coach to be heard by the player.

Illustrators

Illustrators are nonverbal symbols that reinforce a verbal message. While emblems take the place of a verbal message, illustrators enhance the verbal message. A tight squeeze that accompanies your saying, "I missed you so much these past two weeks," illustrates the sincerity of your verbal message. Similarly, after screaming at your boyfriend or girlfriend, "I never want to see you again," slamming the door further demonstrates your anger. Illustrators must be natural in order to be effective. Consider the effect of slamming a door 10 minutes after you have concluded an argument with someone—the effect would be rather hollow. Effective public speakers frequently use illustrators to emphasize their points. For them it is a natural behavior to raise an arm or point a finger when they become passionate or emphatic about their topic.

Affect Displays

Affect displays are nonverbal signs of our emotional state. Giving someone a cold stare, for example, would indicate that we are angry or displeased. Conversely, a smile would indicate that we are happy or pleased with our immediate environment. According to Ekman and Friesen, facial expressions are used as affect displays (1975). Emotions such as sadness, happiness, fear, surprise, anger, and disgust can be communicated using our faces.

In many cases, we are unaware of the affect displays we use; they tend to be automatic. For instance, Sherry does not realize that she is twisting her hair as she delivers her speech, yet her behavior belies the nervousness she is experiencing.

On the other hand, there are times when we deliberately control our affect displays in order to hide our feelings. What does this mean for the person who observes our behavior? Basically, affect displays can be misleading because they do not always portray how we feel. For example, we might smile after a prospective employer informs us that we were not selected for the position; despite our disappointment, we do not want to let the other person know how much we had hoped to get the job. Perhaps the situation has made us feel self-conscious; we perceive that our image will suffer, so we behave accordingly. Other factors that influence the way we use affect displays include the upbringing we received from our family (for example, some children are taught to display little emotion in public) and gender expectations (for example, men should always appear strong).

Regulators

Regulators are nonverbal behaviors used to control, or regulate, communication between people. These cues indicate whether or not it is appropriate for the sender to continue his or her message. For instance, if you maintain eye contact with the speaker, you will be a more effective listener. Furthermore, if we notice someone smiling at us or nodding his or her head in agreement, we might be encouraged to continue speaking. Catching someone glancing at his or her watch or gazing across the room, however, might indicate that we are not holding the attention of our listeners. As public speakers, we can benefit from reading audience regulators. Often these regulators indicate when adjustments need to be made: whether it is time to move on to the next point or whether we should conclude our speech.

As receivers, we may wish to control the direction or focus of a conversation. One way to achieve this is by using regulators. If we approve of what is being said, we can demonstrate our support by nodding our heads. This communicates to the sender, "Yes, that's right. Please continue." If we wish to change the direction of the communication, we might shake our heads or pound our fists on the table in an attempt to say, "I disagree" or "You're mistaken. Let me tell you how it really is!"

Who uses regulators? Both people with acknowledged influence, such as company executives, parents, or clergy, and individuals who feel uncomfortable expressing themselves verbally. They might effectively control a discussion by using such nonverbal cues. For example, a student listening to an instructor lecture about Chaucer's *Canterbury Tales* may be totally uninterested in the subject, but she realizes that it would be unacceptable to tell the instructor how bored she is. Instead, she can effectively communicate her sentiments by thumbing the pages of a book, yawning, or glancing at the clock on the wall. These regulators represent the student's effort to control the instructor's communication.

Adaptors

Adaptors are nonverbal behaviors individuals use to adjust to or cope with uncomfortable communication situations. They help us relieve the tension we may be feeling. For example, Dean is extremely anxious about his upcoming job interview. What he would really like to do is bound out of his chair, make a mad dash for the elevator, and forget about the whole thing. Instead, he taps his feet nervously on the tile floor, waiting to be called.

Use of Bodily Movements

Watch one of your favorite television dramas (*House, CSI: Crime Scene Investigation, Law and Order*) without the sound on.

- Focus your attention on the characters' use of their bodies to communicate. List their use of emblems, illustrators, regulators, affect displays, and adaptors.
- Could you determine the entire meaning of their messages without the verbal part of the message? Why or why not?
- What parts of the message could you determine?
- How did the characters' use of bodily movement clarify their message? Provide examples.

Although adaptors are meant to help us through stressful situations, they can pose problems for public speakers. An audience who notices a public speaker wringing his or her hands or twisting a strand of hair can easily be distracted by this behavior; their attention shifts from the speaker's message to watching the nonverbal behavior. Once the speaker is made aware of the problem, he or she can practice controlling the distracting behavior during the delivery. The speaker can work at incorporating natural gestures into the delivery to take the place of adaptors. Repeated efforts should result in the speaker actually feeling more comfortable before the audience and in delivering a more effective speech.

■ Touch

Touch is a form of nonverbal communication that conveys a wide range of emotions. Usually, spontaneous touching behavior communicates such emotions as tenderness (a caress), concern (a hand on someone's shoulder, joy (a hug), anger (a slap or punch), or passion (a kiss). Sometimes it is easier to convey our feelings by touching someone than by finding the appropriate words to express our feelings. In such instances, touching is just as effective as a verbal message.

People react differently to touch. Many people respond positively to physical affection because it communicates concern and offers security. Others feel uncomfortable or nervous when touched—to them it is a question of having their personal space violated. As communicators, we need to be sensitive to these differences in people and to respect the feelings of others. Culture has much to do with the way we interpret someone's touch. For example, in April 2009, First Lady Michelle Obama met with Queen Elizabeth of Great Britain. Much was made of their nonverbal behavior because Obama and the Queen each put their arm around the other in a quick embrace. In the United States, politicians embrace all the time, but in Great Britain, the Queen rarely touches anyone in public.

EMBRACING DIFFERENCE

Touch

Avi, an orthodox Jew, is a sales respresentative for Lynn Laboratories. He has a scheduled sales appointment with Dr. Ann James, a local allergist. Ann knows that Avi is a knowledgeable sales representative and is comfortable with his judgment about the drugs she could prescribe to her patients. Ann is also aware of the cultural boundaries in their relationship. Avi, due to his religious convictions, cannot touch Ann—not even a handshake. While Ann is a very demonstrative individual, she knows she cannot violate Avi's personal space. Therefore, when Avi enters Ann's office, she acknowledges Avi without touching him.

1. How has Ann's understanding of difference enhanced her communication and her relationship with Avi?

2. How can Ann's experience help you understand the importance of embracing difference?

Two variables play a role in the way touching is interpreted: our socialization and the context of the situation. Our socialization affects the way we respond to touch because we will react more positively to touch if we have been exposed to touching behavior during our upbringing. On the other hand, if our childhood included minimal touching, we are likely to be more uncertain or uncomfortable with touching as adults.

The context of the communication situation also can affect the way we use touch. For instance, a person may outwardly display affectionate touching behavior to an individual in private, yet the same behavior would be an intrusion of that person's privacy if done in public. Consider, too, that in a work environment intimate touching rarely occurs between colleagues. Under different circumstances, however, these same employees might embrace each other: A wedding or an announcement of a child's birth are two such occasions.

Table 5.1 summarizes the types of bodily movements.

TABLE 5.1 Types of Bodily Movements

Emblems	Body motions that take the place of words
Illustrators	Nonverbal symbols that reinforce a verbal message
Affect displays	Signs of our emotional state
Regulators	Nonverbal behaviors that attempt to control communication
Adaptors	Nonverbal behaviors that grow out of our discomfort

■ Paralanguage and Silence

Paralanguage is the vocal aspect of delivery that accompanies speech and other nonverbal utterances. It can include pitch (tone), volume (loudness), rate (speed), and quality (richness of one's voice), all of which work in conjunction with the spoken word. Chapter 14 presents a more detailed discussion of these factors.

What can we learn about someone from this special form of nonverbal communication? Pitch can bring with it certain associations. We sometimes associate youth or immaturity with a high-pitched voice. Of course, this is not necessarily the case; certain people maintain a high-pitched voice throughout their lives. A deep, resonant voice often communicates just the opposite, the image of someone who has a mature, steady, or dramatic nature.

The *volume* of a message communicates something extra. For example, when we desire to speak to someone on an intimate level, we often use a soft voice. Conversely, we use a loud voice to say "I want your undivided attention" or simply to ensure that our voice is heard in a noisy, crowded room.

The *rate* of our speech can convey our emotional state. When we feel nervous, for example, we tend to speak more rapidly. This happens in both interpersonal and public-speaking situations. Have you ever phoned someone you do not know very well and blurted out the purpose of your call in the first 10 seconds? The interaction goes this way because you are nervous. Contrast this behavior with the normal speed at which we talk. A normal pace communicates that we are more comfortable with our surroundings.

The *quality* of one's voice is highly subjective. Generally speaking, someone with a nasal or grating voice is more annoying to listen to than someone who has a resonant voice.

One aspect of paralanguage that people universally find annoying is the use of **fillers** or **vocal interruptions,** sounds used to fill in the gaps between the words that comprise our messages. Words such as *you know, like, uh, uh,* or *um* are examples of commonly used fillers. It is more effective to pause between ideas than to repeatedly use fillers.

We have discussed the use of voice as a type of nonverbal behavior. Not using your voice is also paralanguage. **Silence** is the absence of using your voice. When we choose not to speak, we are sending a strong message to others. Silence can communicate anger, disappointment, embarrassment, and even affection. We often think of the "silent treatment" when our partner, a family member, or friend refuses to talk because of a disagreement. By refusing to talk, we take control of the communication and assert our power (see Chapter 6). Silence can also communicate uneasiness or discomfort. For example, during Albert's visit to his partner Steve's parents' home, it was clear that Steve's parents were not very comfortable meeting Albert, even though they said they were happy to meet him. During his short visit, several minutes were spent in silence as each tried to think of something to say.

But silence can also send a positive message. We can listen intently to show respect. Or, have you ever sat with someone you love and just held hands? The silence between you can be comforting and affirming.

■ Space

What is your reaction when someone you have just been introduced to moves within a few inches of you to begin a conversation? Do you take a step back? If you are feeling uncomfortable, you might wonder, "Why is this person invading my space?" Factors such as your cultural upbringing play a part in how you respond to someone else's communication. **Proxemics** is the study of physical space as it relates to human interaction. This section discusses two types of space: personal space and territory.

Personal Space

Personal space is the area that exists between ourselves and others. While we are not always conscious of the amount of personal space we need, our communication behavior is likely to change in response to fluctuations in that space. When we feel that someone has infringed on our personal space, for example, we will likely display defensive behavior. In his book *The Hidden Dimension*, Edward Hall (1969) discusses how people use space to insulate and protect themselves. He identifies four distances that correlate with the levels of space that people need in various communication settings. These include intimate distance, personal distance, social distance, and public distance.

Intimate distance is that distance at which it is appropriate for highly personal communication encounters to occur. This area ranges from actual touching to a distance of approximately 18 inches. These encounters are usually private and are reserved for communicating very special feelings. When we put an arm around the shoulder of a friend whose sister has just died, we are within the area known as intimate distance. The nature of this relationship dictates the appropriateness of our behavior. When a stranger stands within a few inches of us on a crowded bus during rush hour, however, we are likely to feel that our personal space has been invaded. To us it seems inappropriate for a stranger to be within this intimate distance.

According to Hall, **personal distance** is that area most appropriate for interpersonal interactions dealing with personal matters, that is, approximately 18 inches to 4 feet. In interpersonal relationships, the closer the parties remain, the more private is the discussion. As people move farther apart physically, the likelihood is greater that the dialogue is becoming less personal. For example, during a small group activity in their history class, Alberto and Sylvia are sitting next to one another. Sylvia, who is visually impaired, begins the discussion and tries to get the other members of her group involved. Each member follows her lead and joins in, except for Alberto. Alberto not only fails to offer any comments, but also slowly moves his chair away from Sylvia. Alberto increases the personal space between himself and his group because he feels uncomfortable and uneasy with Sylvia's disability.

Social distance is that distance most appropriate for communication of a nonpersonal nature. A boardroom business meeting, a family picnic, a literature study group meeting in a member's home, or four couples enjoying an evening together playing bridge are all examples of situations where communication occurs at a social distance, that is, from approximately 4 to 12 feet. Social distance is the one category that cuts across both interpersonal and public communication. Of the examples just listed, the communication at a family picnic is purely interpersonal, yet it is entirely possible for a public presentation to be made by someone at a meeting of company executives.

Public distance, a distance exceeding 12 feet, is most appropriate for public communication. Situations involving public distance are usually more formal or

When waiting to use an ATM machine, we try to maintain social or public distance.

defined by an audience and a speaker. For instance, when we purchase tickets for the performance of a popular comedian, we expect to watch his or her act as part of the audience. If, however, the comedian were to come down off the stage and mingle with the audience and even single out individual members to use in a few jokes, we might feel that the comedian has taken advantage of the personal space we perceive to be appropriate for this situation. We feel uncomfortable because the comedian has acted differently than we expected.

Territory

Territory is the space we stake out as our own. At home, we may have a special chair in the den or family room that we think of as our own; at work, our desk and the area immediately surrounding it are part of our territory. Because we often attach a special significance to territory, it is not uncommon for us to become protective of it. Whether it is a teenager communicating that her bedroom is off limits to other family members;

COMMUNICATION IN ACTION

Territory

- Do you or any members of your family have a particular chair, room of the house, and so on, that you or he or she consider special?
- How do you or he or she communicate to others that the territory is special?
- What happens when someone invades this space? Be specific.
- What does this say about the importance of territory in our communication with others?

an employee who defines his territory by specially arranging his desk, posters, pictures, and plants; or a vice president who furnishes her office in order to convey a particular level of status or power, territory is an expression of our feelings and attitudes.

■ Physical Appearance and Clothing

In our Western culture, appearance matters. People's perceptions of our outward appearance make a big difference in our opportunities to establish relationships, find jobs, and succeed in school. Studies have shown that we care about appearance, and attractive people, overall, find it easier to make friends, gain employment, and earn good grades. What messages are you sending by wearing several earrings or piercing your nose or belly button? In some social groups, this is a sign of being cool or stylish. How might a future employer at a bank, for example, perceive the body piercings? Our physical appearance matters, and we need to be aware that others may view us differently because of it.

The way we dress becomes part of the message we send to others, whether we intend it to or not. Our clothes and style of dress contribute to the way we see ourselves and the way others perceive us. Our style of clothing also reflects our ability or willingness to adjust to a variety of social situations. In other words, what we choose to wear can reflect our desire to gain acceptance within a given social situation. For instance, if we want to "fit in" among the other guests at a formal dinner party, we would wear a tuxedo or an appropriate evening dress. Moreover, our choice of dress reveals information about ourselves and affects our impact in both interpersonal and public communication settings.

What specifically does our clothing communicate? One thing it can indicate is our age or an age we wish to project. If, for example, we want to appear youthful, we would dress according to the latest styles or trends. Beware, however, that we can inadvertently give away our age by wearing clothes considered to be out of date.

Certain types of dress identify individuals as members of particular groups or professions. When we see someone dressed in a blue uniform, we presume (usually correctly) that he or she is a member of a police department. Other examples include black collars worn by priests, military uniforms worn by men and women in the armed forces, uniforms representing different sports, leather jackets worn by members of motorcycle gangs, and native dress representing foreign nations (saris worn by Indian women, for example).

Sometimes we wear clothing specially selected to project an image that is different from the one we have ourselves. Consider these examples: (1) Ken, a college student, copies the style of a popular TV star in order to appear sexy; (2) Fred, a recent graduate, wears a three-piece suit to his interview with a prestigious law firm in order to project an air of maturity and professionalism; and (3) Nicole, a career woman, dresses in a business suit and carries a leather briefcase to her training seminar for local bank managers.

In selecting our clothing, we should keep the following in mind: Our clothes should not draw negative attention to ourselves. Whether we are speaking before an audience or interacting with only one or two other people, we should dress appropriately for the occasion. If we wear something outlandish, no one will pay attention to our message; they will be too busy studying our attire.

A business suit projects an image of competence and professionalism.

■ Time

The study of how we use time is called **chronemics.** In our culture, we use a mono-chromic time system (Lustig & Koester, 2010). This means that we measure time in small increments and things need to be done one at a time. In this kind of sys-tem, we perceive time as a commodity and any time not used appropriately is wasted. We view tardiness as a personal insult, for example. Think about the words we use to describe time: we *save* time by taking a shortcut; we *budget* our time by working longer hours on Thursday so we can leave work early on Friday; and, our group *invested* so much time in this project.

Think about the messages we send with our use of time. What does being prompt or on time mean? What about being late? If you are consistently late for class, what might the instructor think about you and your attitude toward the course? Probably not very positively. We value promptness because it communicates professionalism, caring, and respect. Spending a lot of time with someone is also considered a sign of caring and respect. In one study, the amount of time spent with someone was the leading predictor of relational satisfaction and understanding (Stelzner & Egland, 1995).

Time can communicate status. Think about the people who can keep you wait-ing. We often wait 30 minutes to an hour to see a physician. We accept that our supervisor, instructor, or other authority figure can and will make us wait because their time is perceived as more valuable.

Communication and TECHNOLOGY

Are You a Terrorist? Using Technology to Detect Nonverbal Cues

Researchers at the University at Buffalo in New York are working on a computer that can detect nonverbal communication that might indicate an intent to harm. Specifically, computer and behavioral scientists are working together to identify people who might commit terrorist acts based upon their nonverbal cues. In fact, we already know that many nonverbal cues indicate deceit.

This program will "track faces, voices, bodies, and other biometrics against scientifically tested behavioral indicators to provide a numerical score of the likelihood that an individual may be about to commit a terrorist act," said Venu Govidaraju, professor of computer science and engineering at the University at Buffalo (Goldbaum, 2007). Govidaraju is working with Mark Frank, a social psychologist who has studied human nonverbal communication. Frank said, "No behavior always guarantees that someone is lying, but behaviors do predict emotions or thinking that can help the security officer decide who to watch more carefully." The goal of the research is to use technology to "identify the perpetrator in a security setting before he or she has the chance to carry out the attack," said Govidaraju. The researchers are cautious, however. They warn that "no technology is a substitute for human judgment."

IMPROVING NONVERBAL COMMUNICATION

As you have discovered throughout this chapter, the chief difficulty associated with nonverbal communication is its interpretation by others. It is easy to misunderstand the nonverbal cues you receive, yet it is more difficult to question these behaviors than it is to ask questions about particular verbal statements. As a result, you need to proceed cautiously when drawing conclusions about nonverbal communication. By using the following suggestions, you can increase your ability to accurately interpret nonverbal messages.

■ Explore All Possible Meanings of Nonverbal Messages

Because nonverbal messages can have a variety of meanings, it is easy to misinterpret them. This is one of the difficulties of nonverbal communication. To combat that problem, we should strive for greater accuracy in our interpretation of messages.

How do we achieve this? One way is to try to remain open minded about the different meanings nonverbal behavior can suggest. For instance, if someone fails to establish direct eye contact with us, this might mean (1) that the person is extremely shy, (2) that the person is distracted because he or she has something else on his mind, (3) that the person is not interested in the conversation, or (4) that the person is showing respect as taught in his or her culture (a more detailed discussion of eye contact appears in Chapter 14). Before an accurate conclusion can be reached, all the possibilities should be explored.

■ Look for Nonverbal Messages That Are Consistent with Verbal Statements

Nonverbal communication that supports verbal statements helps confirm the validity of the verbal message. Since nonverbal messages are more spontaneous than verbal messages, they more accurately reflect our feelings. Thus, if the verbal message is supported by the nonverbal behavior, we are probably interpreting the sender's message correctly. However, when the verbal and nonverbal messages are inconsistent, it is generally wiser to check your perception and ask for clarification.

Serving Your COMMUNITY   Nonverbal Communication and Difference

To be able to recognize the different meanings and uses of nonverbal communication, please do the following:

1. Please visit the International Student Services office on your campus.
2. Schedule a meeting with the Director or Assistant Director of International Student Services.
3. Offer to volunteer two hours a week for a month to work with students in the English as a Second Language program.
4. Make sure you are working with students from at least two different countries.
5. Observe the way the international students engage in the nonverbal communication by focusing on the following components:
   a. Bodily movement
   b. Touch
   c. Paralanguage
   d. Space
   e. Territory
   f. Physical appearance and attire
   g. Time
6. Compare and contrast the behavior of the students you observed.
7. Interview these students about your observations and please focus on the following:
   a. Explore all the possible meanings of their nonverbal messages.
   b. Look for nonverbal messages that are consistent with verbal statements.
   c. Use questions and descriptive feedback to achieve accuracy.
   d. Monitor your own use of nonverbal messages.
8. How did this process increase your understanding of difference in nonverbal communication?

ETHICS in Communication
Nonverbal Communication

Review the story at the beginning of the chapter about Carla, the biology lab instructor, and her students. This story is a clear example of what we discussed in Chapter 2. People make judgments about others based on their own perception, and our perception is based on our frame of reference.

In the scenario, Carla is obviously judging her students and their ability to succeed in her class based solely on their nonverbal behavior. For example, because a student is wearing medical scrubs, Carla assumes she will excel in the biology lab. Carla goes on to assume that the student in ragged jeans and a t-shirt is "a loser" and will need help in the class. Lastly, the student who arrives five minutes late and is dressed like a mechanic is judged as unmotivated and unable to write, according to Carla. Based on Carla's frame of reference, she has judged these students and may have acted unethically. Her ability to effectively communicate and teach these students will be greatly affected by her perceptions.

The students, too, must also realize that their nonverbal behavior sends messages. Although these messages may be unintentional, they impact the overall communication process. As you think about Carla and her students, answer the following questions:

1. How can Carla be an ethical and effective communicator and teacher?

2. What can the students do to be more effective communicators nonverbally?

3. Have you ever been in as situation like that of Carla and her students? Describe your communication behaviors.

■ Use Questions and Descriptive Feedback to Achieve Accuracy

We will be able to communicate more effectively if we learn to focus on the behaviors of others and accurately describe what is observable without making unwarranted inferences. Asking questions about observable behavior may help us to avoid the trap of prematurely evaluating others. This process is known as perception checking. Perception checking is a verbal statement that reflects our understanding of a nonverbal message (see Chapters 2 and 3). If we can confront nonverbal behavior by asking specific questions about that behavior, we may find it easier to clear up misinterpretations and avoid unnecessary conflict. Look at the following example of Bob and Nancy on their first date:

Bob: I've noticed that you keep looking at your watch. You must be really bored!

Nancy: No, I'm not. It's just a habit of mine. I'm having a good time, but I'm just a little nervous.

Bob: Me too, I want to get to know you better, but it's always so hard in the beginning. That's probably why I'm rambling so much!

In this example we can see how perception checking helped clarify the communication between Bob and Nancy. Bob's comments focused on the behavior he observed without being critical.

■ Monitor Your Own Use of Nonverbal Communication

Self-reflection is always the first step to understanding and practicing effective communication. Think about what messages you may be sending intentionally or unintentionally with your bodily movement and paralanguage, use of space and time, and your appearance and clothing. Keep in mind that others may interpret your nonverbal messages differently from the way you had intended. Also, be aware that your verbal and nonverbal messages may be inconsistent. Strive to have your nonverbal communication complement and enhance your verbal messages.

SUMMARY

Nonverbal communication is that area of communication in which messages are sent without the use of words. This area includes kinesics, touch, paralanguage, silence, space, personal appearance and clothing, and time.

Ekman and Friesen developed a classification system that divides bodily movements into five categories: (1) emblems (motions that take the place of words); (2) illustrators (nonverbal symbols that reinforce a verbal message); (3) affect displays (nonverbal signs of our emotional state); (4) regulators (nonverbal behaviors used to control or regulate communication between people); and (5) adaptors (nonverbal behaviors used to adjust to or cope with uncomfortable communication situations).

Through touch we communicate a wide range of emotions, including such feelings as tenderness, concern, and anger. How we use touch to communicate nonverbally and how we respond to touch depends on several variables, including our socialization and the context of the communication situation.

Paralanguage, another component of nonverbal communication, is the vocal aspect of delivery that accompanies speech. It can include pitch, volume, rate, and quality, all of which work together with the spoken word. Silence is the absence of using your voice, and it communicates such emotions as anger or contentment.

Proxemics is the study of physical space as it relates to human interaction. We need varying degrees of personal space, the area that exists between ourselves and others, for different communication encounters. Edward Hall identifies four distances that correspond to the levels of space people require: intimate distance, personal distance, social distance, and public distance. In addition to personal space, territory (the space we stake out as our own) is a factor in our nonverbal communication.

How we look and dress become part of the message we send to others. Our clothing can reveal such things as our age, our profession or membership in a particular group, or an image we wish to project.

Our use of time sends a nonverbal message. In our culture, time is viewed as a commodity like money. Time can also communicate our status and power.

Most problems with nonverbal communication center around misinterpretation. There are a number of techniques, however, that can increase our ability to accurately interpret nonverbal messages: explore all possible meanings of nonverbal messages, look for nonverbal messages that are consistent with verbal statements, and use questions and descriptive feedback to achieve accuracy. We should also monitor our own use of nonverbal communication in order to send clear and consistent messages.

REVIEW QUESTIONS

1. Explain why nonverbal communication is ambiguous.
2. Why is nonverbal communication culturally bound? Give an example.
3. Describe the five types of bodily movement.
4. Describe two instances in which you have touched a person and gotten different responses. What might account for the difference?
5. How does paralanguage reveal our feelings about a given situation?
6. List and describe the four categories of personal space.
7. How does clothing contribute to an individual's efforts to create a public image?
8. List and describe the four skills that help us improve our interpretation and use of nonverbal communication.

KEY CONCEPTS

nonverbal communication
intentional/unintentional
    communication
ambiguous nonverbal
    messages
multichanneled
    communication
culturally bound
kinesics

emblems
illustrators
affect displays
regulators
adaptors
touch
paralanguage
fillers or vocal
        interruptions

silence
proxemics
personal space
intimate distance
personal distance
social distance
public distance
territory
chronemics

Understanding Ourselves and Others

AFTER STUDYING THIS CHAPTER, YOU SHOULD

understand

- the definition of interpersonal communication.
- the importance of intimacy and power in relationships.
- the stages of a relationship.
- the four quadrants of the Johari window.
- the benefits of self-disclosure.
- the cautions associated with self-disclosure.
- the three interpersonal needs.
- the four problems associated with interpersonal conflicts.

be able to

- apply cost-benefit theory to one of your own interpersonal relationships.
- apply four techniques to improve your ability to resolve conflicts.

Cara and Emma are students at Morris University. Cara is a junior in nursing and hopes to work in a pediatric ward when she graduates next year. Emma, also a junior, is a sociology major who is interested in social work and wants to work with families experiencing financial and other traumatic stress in their lives. To fulfill a graduation requirement for service learning, Cara and Emma are volunteering at Safe House, a shelter for women and their children.

Tanya, their supervisor, has asked them to work together to develop several activities for the children who will be staying at the shelter during the holiday season. Conflict between Cara and Emma begins immediately. Each has strong opinions about how to make the children's holidays brighter and comforting. Emma wants to develop programs that teach the children about how the holidays are celebrated around the world and in their community. She wants to bring in ethnic holiday food and play ethnic holiday games. Cara, on the other hand, wants the children to just enjoy Christmas. Her idea is to bring in a friend to play Santa Claus who will give gifts to all the children. She thinks spending the holidays in a shelter is not the time or place for "education." She wants the children just to have fun. Emma argues that the kids can have fun and learn something new. Besides, she says, how does Cara know how all the children celebrate Christmas?

■ ■ ■ ■ ■

In this chapter, we discuss how our self-concept affects our ability to see how others view us. We all have interpersonal needs that manifest themselves in our communication with others. Remember, each of us approaches each and every communication situation differently. It is this diversity in approach that makes communication fulfilling, and sometimes frustrating.

If given the option of living in complete isolation or living in the company of others, the majority of us would choose a life that is shared with others. This selection does not imply that such a life would be easy; on the contrary, communicating with others demands considerable time, energy, and understanding.

In the preceding chapters we explored several fundamental components of the communication process. Each of these plays a significant role in our communication behavior with others. Chapter 2 focused, in part, on our self-concept—how it affects our perception of others and how it affects the way we send and receive messages. In Chapter 3 we discovered skills to help us become effective listeners, including such techniques as listening with empathy, questioning, and being supportive. After focusing our attention on the meaning of words and some of the problems we encounter with language, Chapter 4 went on to discuss skills for improving our verbal communication. Finally, in Chapter 5 we explored the complex nature of nonverbal communication, including such topics as nonverbal behaviors; how such factors as space, touch, clothing, time, and paralanguage affect our nonverbal messages; and what we can do to become more skillful at interpreting nonverbal messages.

Taken as a whole, we have amassed a strong foundation of principles and skills that can now be used to assess our relationships with others. In this chapter we shall explore ways to improve our relationships by increasing our understanding of ourselves and the way we interact with others, by becoming aware of the benefits and risks of sharing with others, and by exploring ways to confront conflict within our relationships.

THE NATURE OF INTERPERSONAL RELATIONSHIPS

As we learned in Chapter 1, interpersonal communication is the informal exchange that occurs between two or more people. This can occur in dyads (two people) or in small groups. We will discuss small-group communication in Chapters 9 and 10. Through dyadic communication, we can learn about ourselves and about our relationships with others. Specifically, we will discuss four elements of dyadic relationships: content and relational messages, intimacy, power, and the stages of development and dissolution of relationships. Let's begin with a look at content and relational messages.

■ Content and Relational Messages

When we communicate, we are sending two types of messages. The **content message** is the obvious message. It is the words or language we use. For example, the question "What time will you be home tonight?" asks the receiver to answer with a specific time reference, such as "Five o'clock." There is also a more hidden message embedded in the question. This is called the relational message. These **relational messages** are usually sent nonverbally through tone of voice, body language, or use of space (see Chapter 5). Let's look at the above question again. If I emphasize the word *time* and use a sarcastic tone when I ask my partner, "What *time* will you be home tonight?" I would certainly be sending the message that I am angry or annoyed. This may be due to past behavior (my partner's coming home late) and my feeling neglected or jealous. But, if I use a very soft tone of voice and whisper in my partner's ear, "What time will you be *home* tonight?" I am certainly sending a different kind of message. In this instance, I want my partner to come home and I want him or her to know I will eagerly await his or her return.

We send messages intentionally and unintentionally. As we discussed in Chapter 1, our frame of reference will help us decode our partner's message. As senders, we may not even be aware of the relational messages we send. As effective communicators, we must pay close attention to our content and relational messages, keeping in mind that others may decode our messages differently than the way we intended.

■ Intimacy

When two people share a special private bond, they have intimacy. **Intimacy** is characterized by a sense of closeness and trust we share with another. In our society, we immediately think of physical intimacy, but there are other types of intimacy as well. *Physical intimacy* is not strictly limited to sexual activity. Anytime we share a physical closeness with another (mother and child, close friends, or athletes, for example), we can have intimacy. Emotional intimacy is created through self-disclosure. When we share our feelings for one another and they are returned, we create intimacy. *Intellectual intimacy* is shared when abstract concepts or other intellectually challenging ideas are discussed. Jo and Doug illustrate intellectual intimacy.

> Jo and Doug are both graduate students and love to read. On their first dates, they shared ideas about the meaning of life, religion, music, art, and politics. They loaned each other books and would later debate the theories and ideas embedded in the authors' arguments. Although they often disagreed, Jo and Doug were energized by their conversations and looked forward to their time together.

Lastly, two people can share *spiritual intimacy*. People can share their strong faith in God or other higher powers. The partners may attend religious services, study groups, meditations, or other activities to share their spiritual intimacy.

Intimacy is a necessary component of interpersonal relationships. Through communication, namely self-disclosure (discussed later in this chapter), we form private bonds with others.

Athletes share physical intimacy.

■ Power

When we perceive that a person has **power,** control, authority, or influence over others, our perception dictates how we will communicate with that person. Each relationship we enter has some dimension of power in it. The significance of power rests with one person's ability to influence another's behavior. In interpersonal situations, the person's perceived power motivates others to communicate or behave in a specific way. For example, because certain professional athletes are admired by thousands of children, organizations believe that children will pay close attention to what these athletes say; hence, on television, we hear them telling kids to stay off drugs and stay in school.

Adults also react positively to those people they consider role models or mentors. For example, consider the following:

> Yvonne is completing an internship at a public relations firm where Sharon is her boss. She has observed how Sharon takes charge of an advertising campaign and is amazed at Sharon's many talents, such as her ability to conceptualize the entire campaign, her skillful interactions with clients, her directions to the production staff, and so on. Yvonne's perception of Sharon's abilities is overwhelmingly positive. As their relationship grows, Yvonne finds that she wants to be like Sharon, and Sharon encourages Yvonne to choose a career in public relations.

These examples illustrate positive influences of power. Power can also be intimidating or threatening. Consider the following:

> Mary has been working at Shear Magic for two years. She loves her job as a hair stylist but dislikes the pressure from the owners to attend out-of-town workshops to develop her skills. Mary has attended all the local workshops, but the owners now want her to attend a weekend seminar two hours away from her home. Mary is very uncomfortable about leaving her 18-month-old son Ryan. But Mary also feels uncomfortable about talking to the owners about her feelings because she is afraid they may fire her or cut her hours. She suffers in silence, fearful of losing her job, but also uneasy about leaving her son.

Social power is the "potential for changing attitudes, beliefs, and behaviors of others" (Verderber & Verderber, 1995, p. 284). Each of us has some power, whether we are aware of it or not. French and Raven (1968) have described for us the different types of social power that affect our interpersonal communication. **Coercive power** is derived from one's perceived ability to control another person's behavior through negative reinforcement and intimidation. Coercive power can be communicated through threats or nonverbally by tone of voice, invasion of personal space, or even physical contact. **Reward power** is one's perceived ability to provide things such as money, objects, or love and affection. **Legitimate power** is derived from one's position of authority. People with legitimate power have been given the responsibility (by election or appointment) to assert influence over others.

Communication and TECHNOLOGY
Blogging and Self-Disclosure

A web log, or blog, is a means of self-expression. We can post our deepest thoughts, desires, and dreams anonymously. More than 12 million people keep an online diary or blog (Hart, 2006). People under 30 are the most frequent users of blogs, according to a Pew Internet and American Life report (Hart, 2006). Young adults share their creative projects like drawings, photos, or stories and remix content into their own creative creations. Even more important, bloggers share their most personal thoughts and feelings. Why do so many of us use the Internet to self-disclose information that anyone in the world could access and read?

First, the ability to create and post messages is easy. Free services like Blogger, LiveJournal, Xanga, and MySpace offer space to share content. Just create a blog and creating messages is as easy as sending an email or instant message. Friends can have access to the postings at any time.

Second, self-disclosure is healthy. Sometimes, we just want to "talk" about an issue and not have anyone respond immediately. We just want to let out our feelings. James Hamilton, an associate professor of psychology at the University of Alabama says, "There is ample research to suggest that disclosing secrets or talking about strong emotions improves physical and psychological health. Teenagers are typically very concerned about appearance and reputation, and these blogs and online discussions allow teenagers and children a sort of intimacy in conversation and communication with others that preserves their anonymity in ways that face to face conversations can't" (Seabol, 2005). In other words, the Internet gives us a space to share information without having to provide our identity (see Chapter 2).

Finally, blogs offer opportunities to create relationships and communities with people who share things in common. Readers can make comments and offer feedback to the writer. According to Anne Grossman, blogging can create online group therapy. In fact, people blog about many medical and personal challenges like overeating, depression, cancer, alcoholism, and parenting (2008).

A major concern for parents, however, is that too much personal information is provided. According to Huffaker and Calvert, "on the Internet, where virtuality provides a sense of freedom from physical harm, people may feel less afraid of the online stranger. At the same time, the Internet's anonymity makes it an attractive medium for sexual predators and cyberstalkers, as sexual predators can deceive online adolescents by pretending to be younger than they are" (2005).

For college students, a concern should be their future career aspirations. According to the *Chicago Tribune*, "High Schools, colleges and businesses have begun to use social networking sites such as MySpace, Xanga, and Facebook to keep tabs on students and employees" (Greenfield & Haugh, 2006). Furthermore, "Job recruiters say students' lack of discretion online will catch up to them in their professional lives. A 2005 study conducted by executive job-search agency ExecuNet found that 75% of recruiters already use Web searching as part of the applicant screening process, according to a Columbia News Service report" (Greenfield & Haugh, 2006). Of those job candidates, some 25% were eliminated because of content found on the Web.

Keeping a blog can be a useful way of self-disclosing information. Millions of us do it everyday. Blogging helps us relieve the stress of everyday life by "venting" and it can help us find others who share our interests.

ZITS © *ZITS* Partnership. King Features Syndicate. Used by permission.

Legitimate power is seen in the use of space, for example. The CEO of a company has the largest office, biggest desk, and a beautiful view from the window. These indicate that the person has legitimate power over others in the company. **Expert power** is one's superior knowledge in a particular field. Expert power is influential when the person has a skill or information that you need. Many experts communicate their power through titles such as Doctor or Reverend. We can easily be intimated by expert power and therefore fail to ask questions, for example. Lastly, **referent power** is derived from one's feelings of identification with another. Someone's image or personality may influence us. In the preceding example, Sharon has referent power in her relationship with Yvonne. Yvonne identifies with Sharon and wants to be like her. Table 6.1 describes the five different types of social power.

Each relationship has some level of power that affects the communication between the two friends, lovers, or co-workers. Many times, we may feel powerless in a relationship. **Powerlessness** means that we feel as if we have no say in the relationship or that the other is making all the decisions. We may feel as if we are not in control. No one wants to feel this way. In all relationships, we need to strive to be empowered and to empower our partner. **Empowerment** is the ability to make choices. We want to be able to choose even small things such as what movie to see or where to eat dinner. More importantly, in each relationship we want to choose a partner, to choose whether or not to stay in the relationship, and to create a relationship

TABLE 6.1 Types of Social Power

Coercive power	One's ability to control another person's behavior through negative reinforcement
Reward power	One's ability to provide things such as money, objects, or love
Legitimate power	One's position of authority
Expert power	One's superior knowledge in a particular field
Referent power	One's feelings of identification with another

COMMUNICATION IN ACTION

Types of Power

1. Each of the following statements communicates a type of social power. Identify each statement as coercive, reward, legitimate, expert, or referent power.

   a. If you are not here on time tomorrow, you'll be looking for a new job.

   b. I have been studying this phenomenon for ten years. I know I'm right.

   c. As manager, I want to improve the morale of all employees by offering a workshop on positive mental attitude.

   d. I want to be just like my mother. She is smart, assertive, and caring.

   e. If you go to bed right now, I'll make you pancakes in the morning for breakfast.

2. How can understanding the types of social power enhance your confidence as a communicator?

that is based on mutual respect and equality. When both partners are empowered, our self-concept and self-esteem are higher and we feel more confident and secure in the relationship. Let's look at Miguel and Samantha:

> Miguel and Samantha will be graduating from college this spring. Miguel is looking for a job in journalism, while Samantha is seeking a position in human relations. Each has his or her own set of friends and socializes without his or her partner at least once a week. Miguel and Samantha both work while attending college and share the costs of all their activities, such as eating out or listening to music at the local coffeehouse. Although they are independent, Miguel and Samantha are dependent on one another for intimacy and support. Recently, Miguel failed an exam in his senior seminar in journalism. He was very upset, but Samantha was able to comfort him and together they developed new study strategies for Miguel's next exam. They compromise often in order to ensure that each has his or her needs met in their relationship.

■ Stages of Relationship Development

Romantic relationships and close friendships develop in a similar fashion. Mark Knapp and Anita Vangelisti (1992) created a model for the development of these relationships and the type of communication that takes place between the two people characterizes each stage (Figure 6.1). Relationships you have with family members and work colleagues may evolve and dissolve differently than this model shows.

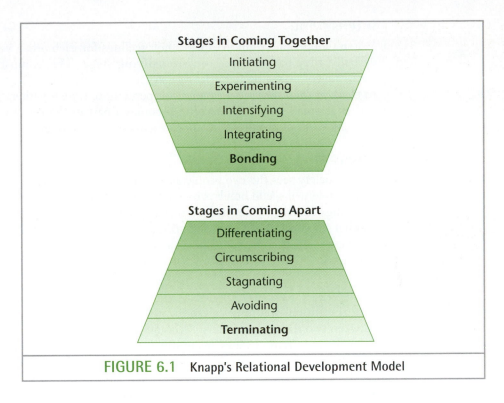

Stages in Coming Together

Initiating
Experimenting
Intensifying
Integrating
Bonding

Stages in Coming Apart

Differentiating
Circumscribing
Stagnating
Avoiding
Terminating

FIGURE 6.1   Knapp's Relational Development Model

Initiating

The first stage is called the initiating stage because the relationship begins with one person making "first contact" or initiating the interaction. **Initiating** is characterized by safe, surface topics such as, "How about this weather?" or "Isn't this a great party?" The most important part of this phase is the first impressions we have about the other. Obviously, if our first impression is not favorable, the relationship may not progress.

Experimenting

Experimenting, the second stage, allows the two people to get better acquainted. We may discuss topics more in-depth, but the topics would still be considered "small talk." This stage could last a few minutes but could also last the length of the relationship. Some relationships just don't progress any further. For example:

> Every year at Christmas time, Rebecca and her husband Andrew must attend Rebecca's company's holiday party. Although they always enjoy the dinner and dancing, Andrew does not like having to make small talk with the other spouses. One husband in particular, Randy, always corners Andrew and wants to discuss the stock market and politics. During the first holiday party several years ago, Andrew sat and talked with Randy for over an hour and decided he did not want to become friends. So, every year at this party, Andrew just exchanges small talk with Randy.

Intensifying

When two people begin to express their feelings for each other, verbally and non-verbally, they have entered the **intensifying** stage. This is most clearly seen in romantic couples, although friends also can enter this stage. The two people begin to think of themselves as a couple and spend more time together. The couple may exchange small gifts, and touching becomes a part of the relationship. They may even address one another with endearments such as "Honey" or "Sweetheart."

Integrating

When society sees the two people as a couple, the **integrating** stage has occurred. The couple will spend holidays together, meet each other's families, and begin buying things together. They may even live together. The two begin to depend on one another for comfort, support, and intimacy. The integration with the other helps us to change and become someone new. We may change our attitude about life, we may become better listeners, or we may even change the way we look.

Bonding

The traditional wedding ceremony is the most popular way to seal the bond between two romantic partners. Although gay couples do not have the opportunity to legally wed in most states, many still have weddings or commitment ceremonies. This stage is the most public of the stages as the couple promises to stay together and love one another in front of friends and family. The couple's **bonding** generates support from their family and friends. The commitment can put new pressure on the relationship, and it certainly changes the nature of the relationship.

Differentiating

The **differentiating** stage is characterized by the need for independence and autonomy. Now that the two people have become a committed couple, each will feel the need to regain their independence. Thus, each person finds ways to differentiate himself or herself from the other. The partners may find hobbies to pursue alone, such as playing softball, taking an aerobics class, or just going out with friends. This stage can cause tension, as one partner may feel threatened by the other's need to be independent. Partners must walk a thin line between staying committed to the relationship and finding autonomy.

Circumscribing

Not all relationships will last a lifetime. Most romantic relationships fail, and in the **circumscribing** stage, partners communicate less and less. Defense mechanisms (see Chapter 7) characterize the communication as the partners avoid discussing problems or become overly critical of each other. The couple is less interested in maintaining the relationship. For example:

> Heather and Lydia have been a couple for two years. They have lived together for the last 18 months. Heather and Lydia are both lawyers and share many of the same interests, such as civil rights law, traveling, and training their golden retriever Chestnut. Lately, however, Lydia has been

A wedding ceremony is an example of the bonding stage in relationship development.

working longer hours and has canceled their planned trip to India. When Heather asks, "Is there something wrong? Have I done something to make you angry?" Lydia just says, "No, of course not. I'm just overloaded at work and feel under stress." Lydia does not verbalize how her feelings have changed toward Heather and believes it is better to just not talk about their relationship.

Stagnating

When a relationship stops growing, it is in the **stagnating** stage. The partners "go through the motions" without much feeling or enthusiasm. The couple may not love one another anymore and are staying together out of convenience, fear, or for others, such as their children. The intimacy of the past is gone, and self-disclosure has stopped.

Avoiding

The **avoiding** stage is characterized by aloofness. The partners spend little time together, and almost all communication has ceased. It is just too difficult and uncomfortable to be together. Some people will make excuses to not see one another: "I have to study for my biology exam" or "I need to spend time with my friends," or one may just say, "I don't think we should see one another for a while."

Terminating

Relationships end. The **terminating** stage includes ending the relationship sometimes very quickly or perhaps over weeks or months. The ending of the relationship does not have to be painful or negative. Some relationships do not work and only bring pain to the partners. It is much better for both people to find other partners. The terminating stage is not inevitable. Some couples can communicate their feelings and problems and return to the intimacy of the past.

SELF-DISCLOSURE WITHIN RELATIONSHIPS

As we assess our relationships with others, we might ask ourselves, "Where is this relationship headed?" Are we involved in a growth relationship, or is the relationship going to remain at a superficial level? If we think we are in a blossoming relationship, we are likely to share increased information about ourselves. At the same time, we are interested in the other person's feedback.

We can improve the quality of relationships through self-disclosure. **Self-disclosure** is the conscious decision to share personal information about ourselves. Its purpose is to help others get to know and understand us better. What we disclose about ourselves can be of little or high risk, or somewhere in between. For example, voicing an opinion about the weather would probably be nonthreatening for us, whereas telling a friend that you don't particularly like her new boyfriend would involve some degree of risk. Likewise, revealing to a spouse that our emotional needs are not being met is certainly a more difficult task. The degree to which we self-disclose depends on how we feel both about ourselves and our relationship with the other person.

■Johari Window

One way to illustrate the ways we communicate with others is the **Johari window.** Joseph Luft and Harry Ingham developed this model, which is designed to be a visual presentation of the self (Luft, 1970). It can be used to explain our communication behaviors with others. Specifically, our interactions are classified as being (1) open, (2) blind, (3) hidden, or (4) unknown (see Figure 6.2). Each of these behaviors represents part of the self, yet in any given interaction one of these behaviors outweighs the others. For example, Antonia openly discloses her career plans with her parents, yet she chooses to hide the seriousness of her relationship with Mike when her parents raise the question. In the first situation, Antonia willingly shares her feelings; in the second, the opposite is true. The way we communicate, then, depends on our relationship with the other party. By assessing our Johari window, we can gain a better understanding of the way we present ourselves to others.

Of the four quadrants that comprise the Johari window, the **open quadrant** represents that aspect of our self that we knowingly share with others and that others can readily determine about us. Information we are willing to divulge to others, such as our feelings about a political candidate, a piece of artwork, our job, or a movie we saw last week, comprises this open side of our self.

The **blind quadrant** of the Johari window represents that part of our self that we either unconsciously reveal to others or are actually unaware of, yet others have

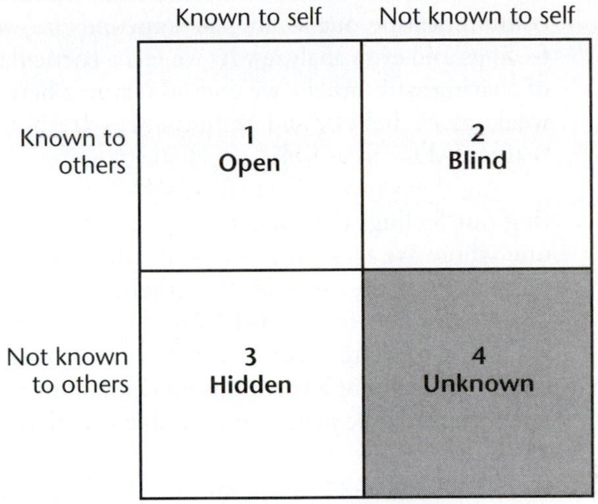

	Known to self	Not known to self
Known to others	1 **Open**	2 **Blind**
Not known to others	3 **Hidden**	4 **Unknown**

FIGURE 6.2   Johari Window

Source: "The Johari Window" from *Group Processes: An Introduction to Group Dynamics,* third edition, by Joseph Luft. Copyright © 1984. Reprinted with permission of The McGraw-Hill Companies, Inc.

knowledge about. In social interactions, for example, our unconscious behavior can sometimes be annoying or distracting. Traci drums her fingers and sways from side to side when she delivers a speech. These unconscious gestures reveal her nervousness to members of the audience. Luther does not know that he is adopted, yet everyone else assembled for the family reunion is aware of the fact. If either Traci or Luther were made aware of the "unknown factors," the information would move from the blind to the open part of the self.

The third quadrant of the Johari window represents the hidden self. The **hidden quadrant** represents the part of us that we are aware of but do not want to share or have not yet shared with others. This may include our dislike of Mexican food, our discomfort over participating in any athletic activity, our fear of being asked a question during class, or our fear of confronting a loved one about wanting to dissolve a relationship.

The last **quadrant** of the Johari window is that part of us that is **unknown** to both ourselves and to everyone else. We can think of this area as including our untapped potential or hidden talents, or simply that part of our self that remains unexplored. For example, we may not realize that we have an aptitude for speaking foreign languages, a special talent for gardening, or the agility to be a good tennis player because we have never pursued these areas.

■ Benefits of Self-Disclosure

The process of self-disclosure has a number of benefits, namely, an increased understanding of ourselves, the ability to express our feelings, and an increased likelihood that others will be more open with us. The end result is that our understanding of our interpersonal relationships grows.

One benefit of self-disclosure is an increased understanding of ourselves. By communicating our feelings to someone else, we are forced to acknowledge these feelings and even analyze why we feel a particular way. Simply stated, in the process of sharing with others, we end up taking a better look at ourselves. Our strengths, weaknesses, beliefs, and ambivalences are not only shared with others, they are reaffirmed for us as well.

Another potential benefit of self-disclosure is the relief we experience from letting our feelings out. In general, we are more inclined to self-disclose with someone whom we trust or know well. After doing so, we generally feel better about ourselves and the possible strengthening of our relationship.

A third benefit of self-disclosure is the increased likelihood that the other party will begin to share his or her feelings and concerns with us. When both parties feel comfortable enough to do this, understanding between individuals is strengthened and intimacy is achieved. An example will clarify this point:

> Stephanie and her neighbor Linda are discussing their three-year-old sons, Chad and Ian. During the course of their conversation, Linda reveals that she sometimes has tremendous feelings of guilt because she works full-time and therefore has less time to spend with Ian. She worries that he is being denied a "full-time" mother. Linda is surprised by Stephanie's response. Stephanie, too, doubts how good a job she is doing as a mother. Although she does not have a job outside her home, Stephanie wonders if her influence is too controlling or smothering. She also admits that she often feels that she would have a better attitude about motherhood if she had some outside activity, such as a job.

By sharing with each other, each woman sees that she is not alone in her concerns; both have similar feelings of guilt over not being the "perfect" mother. Their understanding of each other is increased because of this shared information.

■ Cautions of Self-Disclosure

Trust is a prerequisite for self-disclosure in relationships. We would not consider an open discussion of our feelings with someone we barely know, nor would we expect an acquaintance to disclose something highly personal or sensitive to us.

It is conceivable to trust someone, yet not feel comfortable enough with this person to reveal private feelings. Basically, we look for someone whom we believe will be both a good listener and responsive to our needs. Empathy is often a key ingredient in these interactions. We want the other party to be an uncritical listener who shows support and understanding for our position and ultimately feels comfortable enough to share some of his or her own feelings with us. This give and take between two individuals promotes better understanding of each other and improves communication.

Finally, in order for self-disclosure to be a meaningful process, it should occur in an environment or setting that is natural. For example, if we want to discuss our

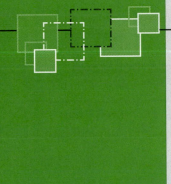

EMBRACING DIFFERENCE

Sharing Feelings

Herlinda and Dave have been friends since they were classmates in their communication course during their first year. Dave grew up in a family where emotions were not easily expressed. Herlinda's family, on the other hand, is very expressive of their emotions. Dave communicates to Herlinda how difficult it is for him to express his feelings. Herlinda is aware of Dave's feelings and it has helped her to understand the difficulty that Dave experiences with self-disclosure. Even though Herlinda's experience with self-disclosure is different than Dave's, she does understand his perspective.

1. How does Herlinda's appreciation of difference enhance her skill as a communicator? How does it increase the intimacy between Herlinda and Dave?

2. How can Herlinda's experience help you understand the importance of embracing difference?

anger over the way our daughter's teacher handled a situation at school, we would make an appointment with the teacher. We would not bring up the subject if we saw the teacher waiting in line with her husband at a crowded restaurant; the time and place would be all wrong. Instead of resolving the problem, we would likely put the teacher on the defensive and create a potentially more uncomfortable situation. Consider the individual and the communication climate (discussed in Chapter 7) before making a decision about self-disclosure.

THEORETICAL EXPLANATIONS OF INTERPERSONAL COMMUNICATION

Several communication theories help to explain the dynamics of our interpersonal relationships. In this part of the chapter we shall discuss two of them. First, Schutz's theory of interpersonal needs outlines our needs and explains the varying degrees of fulfillment; second, cost-benefit theory assesses why we choose either to remain in a relationship or to exit from it.

■ Interpersonal Needs Theory

William Schutz (1966) developed a theory based on the nature of our interpersonal needs. His theory argues that people have certain needs that affect their communication in interpersonal relationships: the need for inclusion, the need for control, and the need for affection.

Inclusion

Inclusion needs, according to Schutz, deal with our desire to be part of a group and lead to a division of people into three categories: undersocial individuals, oversocial individuals, and ideal individuals. *Undersocial individuals* find it difficult to participate in groups, usually because they believe they are not capable of effective social interaction. Among the members of this group are those individuals who consider themselves to be shy, those who fear they will appear to be inarticulate or boring, and those who see themselves as significantly different from other members of the group. In order to cope with their lack of confidence, such individuals communicate by avoiding or retreating from group interactions.

Surprisingly, *oversocial individuals* also feel extremely uncomfortable in social interactions. Rather than shy away from social interaction, however, these individuals push full-speed ahead as a means of compensating for their anxiety. Many of us, for example, know a person like Sabrina, whose social calendar rivals that of a corporate executive. She is a member of several political organizations and three church committees, and she volunteers each Saturday morning at the hospital gift shop. Typically, such excessive group participation indicates an attempt to prove that we are capable of functioning comfortably in these situations.

Ideal individuals, according to Schutz, feel comfortable enough to participate in social groups but do not feel a need to participate in all groups. More important, these individuals are comfortable with themselves in social interactions. They are likely to be skilled at presenting ideas to others and at the same time eager to listen to the ideas of others.

Control

Control needs refer to our desire to have power, influence, or responsibility for our social environment. In terms of control, we may be characterized as abdicrats, autocrats, or democrats. *Abdicrats* find it extremely difficult to participate in the decision-making process because they are afraid of the possible consequences that accompany some decisions. They lack confidence, so they try to refrain from making either definitive or controversial decisions. For example, Edward is a classic "fence sitter"; he waits until others communicate their positions before he shares his. His reluctance encompasses a variety of decision-making situations. Internally, he may question his ability to make appropriate or wise decisions, so he avoids all kinds of decisions. Edward exhibits the communication pattern associated with the abdicrat.

At the other end of the scale is the *autocrat*, an individual who also may feel uncomfortable with decision making, but whose anxiety manifests itself in the opposite way. Instead of retreating from decision making, autocrats attempt to dominate the process. In an effort to camouflage their true feelings, autocrats believe that by making numerous decisions they will prove that they can be influential. Unfortunately, this type of behavior has an extremely negative effect on others. Autocrats do not listen to the ideas of others because they are too absorbed in their role of trying to be influential in the discussion. Many of us have encountered autocrats, perhaps at work or in our own families. These individuals seem obsessed with "having the final say" when making decisions, which, according to Schutz, stems from their efforts to prove that they are really capable of making decisions.

The ideal manifestation of control needs is displayed by the democrat. *Democrats* can cope with the responsibilities of decision making, yet they do not feel the need to have the final say in every decision-making session. They can assume a leadership role when necessary, but they also can function in a less active role without difficulty. These individuals are generally open to a variety of alternatives; they are receptive to ideas that differ from their own and are comfortable with having others participate in the process.

Affection

The third interpersonal need identified by Schutz is the desire for intimacy (see the related discussion earlier in this chapter). An *underpersonal individual*, according to Schutz, will shy away from developing close, intimate relationships with others. Underpersonal individuals may avoid personal discussions or steer conversations to "safe" topics. They frequently have poor self-concepts and believe that they are not capable of sustaining intimate relationships. Consider the following:

> Many consider Kim to be someone who is difficult to get to know. When individuals attempt to get close to her, an invisible wall is erected that communicates "stay away." This pattern of communication surfaces in a variety of situations. At work, she spends very little time socializing with people. When she does socialize with others, she keeps the conversation at a safe level, being cautious not to reveal much about herself.

Kim's desire to protect herself suggests a fear of intimacy. She engages in little sharing with others because she may not feel that she is capable of participating in close relationships.

The fear of intimacy also can cause another type of behavior, exemplified by the *overpersonal individual*. Overpersonal individuals try to compensate for their anxiety by establishing many relationships. In an effort to feel better about themselves, they try to be closely involved with several people. In addition, these individuals are typically possessive of their relationships, which is often stifling and aggravating for all parties involved. A phone call to ask "Why haven't you called lately?" represents the sort of behavior caused by such anxiety. These individuals have an excessive need for support that is both draining and seemingly unending.

Personal individuals feel comfortable with their ability to handle close personal relationships. They realize that relationships are constantly changing and can adjust to this fact. As relationships grow more distant, well-adjusted individuals can, in time, let go without guilt. That is, they will not blame the other person, and more important, they will not feel guilty when the nature of a particular relationship changes. Such individuals realize that sometimes people grow closer together, but at other times people grow apart, and that change is a function of the dynamics of the relationship, not the result of a guilty party's actions. Individuals whose needs for affection are neither deficient nor excessive are better equipped to cope with intimacy.

Schutz's theory of interpersonal needs can contribute to our understanding of the ways people's needs dictate their behavior within different communication situations. Our ability to recognize both deficient communication (*deficient* meaning either undersocial, abdicratic, or underpersonal) and excessive communication (*excessive* meaning oversocial, autocratic, or overpersonal) enables us to better understand the dynamics of a particular relationship. Furthermore, such understanding allows us to step back and analyze the communication of others. Being able to explain another person's communication behavior helps us to avoid personalizing the unmet needs of that person. Accordingly, our responses to interpersonal communication situations are likely to be more sensitive.

■ Cost–Benefit Theory

A theory developed by John Thibaut and Harold Kelley attempts to explain how people assess their relationships (1959). **Cost-benefit theory** (also called *cost-reward theory* or *exchange theory*) suggests that people choose to maintain or exit relationships based on the rewards they receive within those relationships. If the rewards (which may be either emotional, psychological, financial, or physical) are perceived to outweigh the costs (which can include emotional stress, financial expense, amount of time spent in the relationship, or physical abuse), then an individual will likely remain in the relationship. If the costs are perceived to outweigh the rewards, he or she will probably leave the relationship. Consider the following:

> Judd examines the rewards versus the costs in working for his father-in-law. He acknowledges that the salary he receives constitutes the chief reward in the relationship, yet he is bothered by the costs and drawbacks: lack of independence, the social stigma associated with working for a relative, and the tension that it sometimes creates in his marriage to Elaine.

According to Thibaut and Kelley's theory, if Judd believes the costs outweigh the benefits, he will sever the relationship. Conversely, if Judd determines that the benefits (in this case, financial security) outweigh the costs, he will probably decide to remain in his father-in-law's employ. Furthermore, he may work to increase his involvement in the business, perhaps by assuming a greater role in decision making or by striving to become a partner.

Relationships are seldom as simple as the one just outlined. There are times, for example, when we choose to remain in uncomfortable relationships because the alternative is even less desirable. Judd's decision to remain in his father-in-law's firm, despite his frustrations over feeling financially dependent, may be colored by the fact that the employment outlook for architects is bleak in the city where he lives. In this case, the alternative is less appealing than remaining in the relationship.

Cost-benefit theory can be a valuable tool in understanding how we assess relationships. When we feel frustrated in a relationship, we may choose to leave the relationship, or we may try to discuss the problem in an effort to improve the relationship. For example, Judd might attempt to change the dynamics of his working relationship with his father-in-law if his goal is to reap additional rewards. After discussing the situation with his father-in-law, he might be able to identify an area of the business that needs developing and then concentrate his efforts in that direction. If he is successful, he will have achieved a measure of independence that he desired all along. By doing so, Judd has improved his relationship with his father-in-law.

Although cost-benefit theory cannot explain all the complexities of human relationships, applying it to relationships may help us understand some of our relationships more fully, why they are satisfying or dissatisfying to us, and whether or not they are worth trying to improve.

CONFLICT WITHIN RELATIONSHIPS

Conflict is a natural and common occurrence within relationships, but by its very nature it produces discomfort for the parties involved. An area that builds on several of the communication skills discussed in this and previous chapters is *conflict resolution*. According to Joyce H. Frost and William W. Wilmot, **interpersonal conflict** is "an expressed struggle between at least two interdependent parties who perceive incompatible goals, scarce rewards, and interference from the other parties in achieving their goals" (1978, pp. 9–14). In this definition, *expressed struggle* refers to the fact that both parties acknowledge that a problem exists; by contrast, there is no conflict if only one party perceives that there is a problem. Consider the following: Simon is angry with Althea because she did not phone him; however, because Althea is unaware of his frustration, she does not perceive that there is a conflict.

In expressing feelings, people send either verbal or nonverbal messages. Laura, for example, raises her voice when she is upset about something, whereas Jayne shows her discontent by "glaring" at others. When Laura and Jayne express their feelings to each other, the conflict is brought out into the open and they can attempt to resolve it.

What is meant by *incompatible goals?* Basically, in order for one party to gain, there is a perceived loss to the other party. In other words, one party gains at the other party's expense. If your neighbor announces, for example, that he plans to erect a 5-foot fence along your adjoining properties, you might tell him that you are against such a proposal. Your neighbor may want privacy, but you would like the neighborhood to remain open so the children can run between the houses when they play. However, if the neighbor succeeds in getting the necessary papers to allow this action, you might perceive yourself to be the loser, while your neighbor perceives himself to be the winner.

Frequently, conflicts arise over scarce rewards. You and your partner may only have one night out per month. You would like to have an elegant dinner and go dancing. Your partner would rather go to the local bar and grill to eat chicken wings and play Internet trivia. Both of you cannot have your "reward" of a night out. Look again at the story in the beginning of the chapter. Cara and Emma have a conflict over the activities for the shelter. A holiday theme must be chosen soon and someone will lose.

Several factors contribute to the difficulties people experience when involved in conflicts, such as denial, suppression, aggression, passive aggression, and status. These factors inhibit our attempts to resolve conflicts because they stifle open communication between parties.

■ Denial

Denial is our refusal to acknowledge that a problem exists. When we refuse to see a problem, it generally creates tremendous frustration on the part of the second party, who may wish to resolve the problem. For example:

> Martina usually resorts to yelling when she and her husband Eric disagree over an issue. Eric has a serious problem accepting Martina's communication style (that is, her yelling), yet he cannot convince Martina that she has a problem; she contends that venting emotions by yelling is a perfectly natural and acceptable behavior. By denying the problem, Martina makes it difficult for Eric to take any further steps to resolve their differences.

■ Suppression

With **suppression,** we acknowledge that a problem exists, but we attempt to minimize its importance. We fear that confronting the problem may result in consequences that are too difficult or painful for us to address. Like denial, the amount of frustration experienced by the other person can be substantial. For example, Gloria's anger increases each time Joel's mother criticizes their home and Joel fails to talk to his mother about it. Instead, Joel tries to make light of the problem with Gloria.

■ Aggression

Aggression is a problem in conflicts because we are hostile toward the other party and try to intimidate him or her into a resolution that is clearly more advantageous to us. Consider the following:

> Alec and his wife Audrey discuss on a daily basis Alec's desire to move from their current neighborhood to a suburb populated predominantly by successful young professionals. Despite Audrey's pleas that she will not feel comfortable living in the more affluent suburb, Alec insists that the move is right for them. After four months of these persuasive talks, Audrey finally consents to give it a try. The resolution of Alec and Audrey's conflict is only temporary, because from Audrey's point of view, Alec pressured her into something she genuinely opposed. Furthermore, if her discontent about the move persists, she will continue to harbor angry sentiments toward her husband, and the underlying conflict will go unresolved.

Another problem related to aggression is passive aggression. **Passive aggression** is a subtle and covert form of aggression. On the surface, it may appear that the person is complying with a request, compromising, or offering a compliment, but upon closer examination, he or she is acting aggressively. For example, a co-worker will agree to a meeting and then stand you up, or your roommate may "forget" to give you a phone message. Each of these people is angry or upset about something. But instead of discussing the problem, they choose to act in a subtle, covert aggressive manner.

TABLE 6.2	Factors That Contribute to Conflicts
Denial	We refuse to acknowledge that a problem exists.
Suppression	We acknowledge a problem, but we minimize its importance.
Aggression	We are hostile toward the other party and try to intimidate him or her into a resolution.
Passive aggression	We appear to be agreeable but then act in a subtle, covert, aggressive manner.
Status	Either we or the other party uses status to intimidate.

■ Status

A final problem that interferes with conflict resolution is **status.** Status is the relative standing of one party in relation to the other. An individual's status can be either achieved or dictated by society. In interpersonal conflicts, status can act as an inhibitor in two ways: (1) We can use our perceived status to intimidate others, or (2) we can feel intimidated by others who use their status to control interactions. For example:

> Kammi is extremely upset over her principal's decision to cut funds for the remedial reading program she supervises at the middle school yet feels too intimidated by the principal's superior status to strongly voice her objections. The principal, on the other hand, sensing that he will have a difficult battle over the issue, firmly announces that he has given the matter considerable thought and will not reverse his decision to cut the program. He uses his status to prevent an open discussion of the conflict with Kammi.

As with denial, suppression, aggression, and passive aggression, the problem with status is that conflicts are left unsatisfactorily resolved.

The factors that contribute to interpersonal conflict are summarized in Table 6.2.

IMPROVING OUR EFFORTS TO RESOLVE CONFLICTS

After learning about the problems that impede conflict resolution, it is natural to wonder how we can best approach the area of conflict resolution. While no simple formula exists, primarily because each relationship has unique characteristics, several skills can help us deal with conflict in our relationships. These skills include dealing with feelings, keeping the discussion focused on the problem, being a sensitive listener, and being flexible.

ETHICS in Communication
Resolving Conflicts

Conflicts occur in every relationship. When we resolve our conflicts, our relationships can be enhanced by increased trust and intimacy. In the beginning of the chapter, Emma and Cara are in the midst of a conflict about which activities to plan for the children staying at the Safe House shelter during the holiday season. Using what we know about communication, how can Emma and Cara resolve this conflict?

1. Describe the ineffective and unethical communication used by Emma and Cara.

2. Why should each first deal with her feelings before trying to resolve this conflict?

3. Could empathetic listening help them resolve their conflict? How?

4. It appears that there is some common ground in Emma and Cara's ideas. How can they focus their discussion on this?

5. Have you ever been in a situation like Emma or Cara's? How did you resolve the conflict?

■ Deal with Feelings

When we suspect we are having a conflict with someone, the first step is to examine our own feelings concerning the problem. This self-examination helps us better understand exactly what it is that is making us angry, hurt, or frustrated. Once we have acknowledged our feelings, we can more effectively express what is bothering us to the other person. Let us examine the following situation:

> Lorna is furious with her son Adam for staying out past midnight. Initially, she decides to "let him have it" when he comes walking through the front door; then she reconsiders this tactic. She decides that her chief feeling is not anger, but concern for his safety. When Lorna realizes this, she pledges that she will calmly express her feelings to Adam rather than yell at him for being late.

Adam arrives home 10 minutes later and finds his mother waiting for him just inside the front door. He begins to apologize for being so late, but he allows his mother to speak instead. In getting her feelings out, Lorna is surprised and pleased with herself for not turning the situation into a shouting match. By remaining calm, she succeeds in having an open discussion with Adam. Furthermore, they are able to resolve this conflict together.

■ Find a Special Time to Meet

Have you ever felt like you were "attacked" by your significant other? You walked in the door and were confronted by an angry parent, spouse, partner, or roommate. Adam probably thought that's what he was going to face when he came home late. Of course, the natural posture we take is to become defensive and either avoid the situation or feel angry, too. Making a special time to meet or making a "date" to solve the

Serving Your COMMUNITY — Communication and Interpersonal Conflict

In an effort to understand ways to resolve conflict, please engage in the following activity:

1. Please contact your local nursing home and offer to volunteer for three hours.
2. Spend time assisting the residents.
3. Observe the behavior of the residents when they are engaged in a conflict.
4. Schedule a meeting with the director of the nursing home.
5. When meeting with the director, ask how she or he attempts to help the residents resolve their conflicts. Specifically, ask the director:
   a. How do you help the residents deal with their feelings?
   b. How do you schedule time to meet with the people engaged in a conflict?
   c. How do you keep the discussion focused on the problem?
   d. What role does flexibility play in helping the residents resolve their conflict?

problem can significantly improve the chances of resolving the conflict. Both partners should have a chance to think about the problem and then agree to set time aside to discuss it.

■ Keep the Discussion Focused on the Problem

We must try to describe our feelings about the other person's behavior and how it hurts our feelings, annoys us, or angers us. We need to avoid attacking our partner, friend, or co-worker personally and try to focus on the observable behavior that is bothering us. By doing this, we can avoid the pitfall of getting too personal and hurting their feelings, which can only serve to make the matter worse.

■ Use Perception Checking and Empathetic Listening

As we discussed in Chapter 2, we perceive based on our frames of reference. It is essential to check our perceptions of the other person's messages (content and relational) by using questioning, interpreting, and paraphrasing (Chapter 3). Also, looking at a conflict from the other person's perspective can lead to greater understanding of the problem. As indicated in Chapter 3, **empathy** means being able to look at something from someone else's viewpoint. In our attempt to understand the other person's position, we can use the skills associated with effective listening, such as paraphrasing, listening without being judgmental, and being supportive.

Empathy also can help diffuse a conflict. When we take the time to reconstruct the other person's position, we gain insight into why that person communicates the

SKILL BUILDING

Conflict Resolution

1. Discuss the interaction between Dave and Herlinda on page 113 with a partner.
2. When you are discussing their situation, please focus on Dave's behavior.
   a. Is Dave's response realistic?
   b. How does expressing feelings impact their relationship?
3. How can Herlinda help Dave share his feelings? Discuss how she should:
   a. identify her feelings.
   b. keep the discussion focused on the problem.
   c. use perception checking and empathetic listening.
   d. be flexible as she searches for a solution.

way he or she does. A by-product is that we take a better look at our own reactions to this person's communication. The overall effect is to have a more positive understanding of each other.

Finally, by being a sensitive, supportive listener, we encourage the other party to express his or her feelings more freely. This is a desirable way to get at the core of a conflict. If anger, resentment, doubts, or pain remain unspoken, the conflict cannot be resolved and the communication between the individuals will continue to be strained.

■ Find a Solution for Both Parties: Be Flexible

Interpersonal conflicts are more easily resolved when the individuals involved are flexible. Being flexible means having the ability to adapt to a variety of situations. Flexibility suggests that there is more than one way to work through a conflict. Consider the following:

> Claire and her son Jonathon disagree over the type of punishment Jonathon should receive for denting the family car. Claire would like to bar him from driving for one month, particularly because he took the car without her knowledge and permission, whereas Jonathon argues that no punishment is warranted because the accident was the other driver's fault. Realizing that their individual stands are narrow minded, they decide to openly discuss the matter in order to arrive at a better solution. In this case, Claire and Jonathon reach a compromise: Claire agrees to let Jonathon continue to drive the car, and Jonathon agrees to get his mother's okay before taking the car in the future.

This is an ideal situation, because both parties walk away from the conflict having "won" something. Their willingness to talk about the problem and cooperate with each other by collaborating on the solution demonstrates their flexibility.

SUMMARY

People need people—for sharing feelings, for support, for confirmation of their beliefs. Our interpersonal relationships teach us much about ourselves and the way others communicate. Four elements characterize dyadic relationships. Content messages are the words or language we use, and relational messages are the intentional or unintentional nonverbal messages. Intimacy is the sense of closeness and trust shared with another. Power is the perceived control or authority over others. There are several types of social power, including coercive, reward, legitimate, expert, and referent. We should also strive to empower our partners and to feel empowered in our relationships. Romantic relationships develop in stages, according to Mark Knapp and Anita Vangelisti. Each stage of the relationship is characterized by the communication behavior of the two partners.

Self-disclosure, the conscious decision to share personal information, is one way to improve the quality of our relationships. Its benefits include an increased understanding of ourselves, the ability to express our feelings, and an increased likelihood that others will be more open with us. Despite these benefits, a few cautions exist; namely, (1) we need to be selective with whom we share, and (2) self-disclosure should occur under natural conditions. The Johari window, developed by Joseph Luft and Harry Ingham, classifies our interactions as either open, blind, hidden, or unknown. This theory represents a visual presentation of self.

Two interpersonal theories help us understand our communication in dyads: Schutz's theory of interpersonal needs and cost-benefit theory. William Schutz's theory of interpersonal needs argues that our needs for inclusion, control, and affection have an impact on our communication in interpersonal relationships. Finally, John Thibaut and Harold Kelley's cost-benefit theory explains how we assess our satisfaction within a given relationship.

Conflict is an integral part of interpersonal relationships. A number of factors inhibit our attempts to resolve conflicts, including denial, suppression, aggression, and status. In order to improve our efforts in this area, the following skills are recommended: Deal with feelings, find a special time to meet, keep the discussion focused on the problem, use perception checking and empathetic listening, and find a solution for both parties by being flexible.

REVIEW QUESTIONS

1. Define interpersonal communication.
2. What are content and relational messages?
3. List the four types of intimacy and provide an example of each.
4. What role does power play in relationships?
5. Why is it important for both partners to feel empowered?
6. What causes tension in the differentiating stage?
7. What is the most public stage of a relationship?
8. Describe the benefits of self-disclosure.
9. Why is it important to be selective when engaging in self-disclosure?
10. Distinguish among the four quadrants of the Johari window: open, blind, hidden, and unknown.
11. What are the similarities between undersocial and oversocial behavior?
12. Apply cost-benefit theory to one of your current relationships.
13. Differentiate between denial and suppression.
14. How does being an empathetic listener help resolve an interpersonal conflict?

KEY CONCEPTS

content message
relational messages
intimacy
power
social power
coercive power
reward power
legitimate power
expert power
referent power
powerlessness
empowerment
initiating
experimenting

intensifying
integrating
bonding
differentiating
circumscribing
stagnating
avoiding
terminating
self-disclosure
Johari window
open quadrant
blind quadrant
hidden quadrant
quadrant

unknown
interpersonal needs theory
inclusion needs
control needs
affection
cost-benefit theory
interpersonal conflict
denial
suppression
aggression
passive aggression
status
empathy

Creating a Positive Communication Climate

AFTER STUDYING THIS CHAPTER, YOU SHOULD

understand

- why people communicate defensively.
- the eight types of defensive communication.
- the six pairs of communication behaviors in the Gibb study.

be able to

- alter a defensive climate to improve our communication with others.
- compare and contrast the six pairs of communication behaviors in the Gibb study.
- step back from defensiveness to create a supportive communication climate.

Duri ng a meeting with Tanya, their supervisor, Cara and Emma explain their ideas about the upcoming holiday activities for the children staying at Safe House, a shelter for women and their children (from Chapter 6). They have come to an impasse. Cara wants to focus the activities around Christmas traditions like Santa Claus, cookie making, and gift giving. Emma, on the other hand, wants to plan activities celebrating multicultural holidays such as Hanukkah, Kwanzaa, Winter Solstice, and Christmas.

Emma aggressively argues for her ideas and begins to verbally attack Cara. She says that Cara is insensitive to cultural differences and just isn't that smart. Cara responds, not by attacking Emma, but by withdrawing from the conversation. She does not attempt to defend herself and when asked for her opinion, she declines the invitation to participate. Tanya tries to mediate the discussion but is unsuccessful because everyone is tense and uncomfortable. The meeting ends with no resolution.

Afterward, Cara tells the other students volunteering at the shelter that Emma is "out of control" with power and Tanya just doesn't care enough to do anything about it. Furthermore, she says that Emma is forcing her religious beliefs on the children in the shelter and denying them a chance to celebrate a "real" Christmas.

■ ■ ■ ■ ■

In this chapter, we discuss the kinds of communication behaviors exhibited by Emma and Cara. We also discuss some strategies for improving interpersonal communication.

Have you ever felt the way Emma and Cara do? It is difficult to know how to react in a communication setting where you feel threatened. When feelings of self-doubt or insecurity surface, people attempt to protect themselves. This self-protection often manifests itself in the form of defensive communication. **Defensive communication** is a person's reaction, either verbal or nonverbal, to a communication situation in which he or she feels personally threatened or uncomfortable. Many times we feel threatened or insecure when we must communicate with others who are different from us in some way. Instead of taking the focus off of ourselves, we focus on the other person and how he or she may not look or talk like we do. The differences between us can be scary and cause us to communicate defensively. But, as we have discussed in earlier chapters, in order to communicate effectively, we need to focus on the similarities we share with others and begin to value our differences.

The people in our story focused only on themselves and failed to value the others in the room. Likewise, a public speaker who exhibits "forced" humor in front of an audience is also reacting defensively to the fact that he or she is uncomfortable in the situation. The communication we use to protect our "public" self places a shield between ourselves and others. This protective shield, however, creates a number of problems that affect our communication, including an inability to effectively confront problems. Consider, too, that it requires a tremendous amount of energy to simply maintain these protective walls.

Although defensiveness is an understandable reaction to an uncomfortable situation, learning how to cope with defensive communication, both our own and that of others, can lead to greater confidence as a communicator. Becoming aware of the different defense mechanisms is a major step toward self-improvement. One important lesson is learning not to take personally the defensiveness of others. Equally important is learning how to implement a positive communication climate, which may lead to a reduction of defensiveness and an improvement of our communication with others. These objectives are the subject of this chapter.

UNDERSTANDING DEFENSE MECHANISMS

When we feel threatened by a situation or by another person, we often engage in defensive communication, which is simply our effort to protect ourselves. We can exhibit a variety of defensive communication behaviors, and these are called defense mechanisms. Developing an understanding of the different **defense mechanisms** people use should help us to recognize the types of feedback we receive from others. Several defense mechanisms are explained in this section: avoidance, psychological withdrawal, distancing, reaction formation, sarcasm, outdoing others, overly critical communication, and formula communication.

■ Avoidance

Avoidance occurs when we retreat from a problem in a relationship. We are troubled about something, but we decide not to confront the problem or the person associated with the problem. Instead, we convince ourselves that the problem will go away. Avoidance is evident in the following example:

Jasmine and Raphael have been married for five years. Both are in their mid-twenties and were raised by very traditional working-class families. Raphael is a postal carrier and is the primary financial supporter of the family. Jasmine is a full-time server at a local restaurant but attended the local community college part-time before they were married. Raphael, feeling some pressure from his parents, is ready to start a family. Jasmine, however, wants to return to college full-time in order to finish her degree in psychology. Last week, Jasmine made an appointment to meet with an academic counselor to schedule her classes. Raphael is very upset that Jasmine, in his opinion, has put her desire to finish school before his desire to have a child. Raphael chooses not to discuss this with Jasmine and avoids any discussion of Jasmine's enrollment in college and his disappointment.

A satisfactory resolution to the problem is not achieved because this couple will not discuss the resentment Raphael feels toward Jasmine and Jasmine's desire to finish her degree.

In significant relationships, avoidance also can pose a problem. In some work environments or in families, for example, problems are never worked through because the individual members are unwilling to discuss their feelings. Minor incidents are seen as insignificant events and are dismissed or repressed. The frustration associated with these minor episodes may build over the years, resulting in bad feelings among co-workers or family members. When these feelings finally surface, the interaction is often a heated shouting match, the result of buried frustrations.

■ Psychological Withdrawal

Closely related to avoidance is the defense mechanism known as psychological withdrawal. **Psychological withdrawal** occurs when we feel terribly uncomfortable in a particular situation but at the same time feel forced to be physically present. Because we are unable to leave the social setting, we mentally attempt to escape from it. This type of behavior is different from daydreaming during a lecture. Daydreaming can be attributed to boredom or preoccupation with other thoughts; psychological withdrawal can be attributed to uncomfortable feelings. For example:

> Donald and Regina have been separated for eight months. After a year of marriage counseling, they realized that their marriage was over, and Donald moved out of their apartment. Donald is Jewish while Regina is Catholic, and their inability to resolve their religious differences is the primary reason for their separation. Donald had always been close to Regina's brother Thomas, and when Thomas asked a few months ago if Donald would be an usher at his upcoming wedding, Donald accepted. Now that he and Regina have separated, Donald feels uncomfortable seeing Regina and his soon-to-be-ex-relatives at the wedding. Donald keeps his commitment and acts as usher, but he withdraws psychologically, not mingling or socializing at the wedding.

■ Distancing

Distancing is a defensive response that communicates "Do not get close to me." It is our way of shielding or hiding our perceived weaknesses from others. Adjectives sometimes used to describe such people include *conceited*, *cold*, and *aloof*. In reality, people who use distancing are often shy and afraid of opening themselves up to criticism. Distancing communicates that we do not wish to be approached. Dominique is a good example:

> Dominique has just been promoted to a managerial position in the purchasing department she has worked in the past five years as a data entry operator. A single mother of a small daughter, Dominique went to college at night and weekends in order to earn her degree in business

When we are uncomfortable in social situations, we might escape by using psychological withdrawal.

administration. She worked hard for her degree and is well qualified for the promotion. Because she feels unsure of herself in her new role with the same people she once worked with, she decides to make herself inaccessible to those employees she now supervises. She explains in an email that her new responsibilities will keep her busy for the next several weeks and that all requests to see her should be cleared with her secretary.

Dominique's actions communicate to her employees that she wishes to distance herself from them. At the same time, her behavior reveals her lack of confidence in her new position.

■ Reaction Formation

In **reaction formation,** we behave contrary to the way we really feel. This behavior grows out of our need to present an image that is completely different from the one we believe is true. For example, an individual who exhibits reaction formation may feel uncomfortable in certain situations but will put on an act to appear confident. Consider the case of the class clown. This person actually feels uncomfortable in a group setting; however, in order to compensate for that feeling, he or she strives to "prove" to everyone else that he or she enjoys being the center of attention:

> Richard is the oldest member of his computer class. He is married with an adult autistic son who lives at home. Richard is attending college to update his computer skills in hopes of a promotion at work. As president of his local support group for parents of autistic children, Richard is confident and very self-assured. He is a strong community activist for people with disabilities. In this class, however, Richard feels insecure and uncomfortable. To cover his feelings, Richard behaves like the class clown. He consistently tries to get the instructor's attention and his daily efforts at humor are contrived and predictable.

Richard's communication is not intended to be annoying; rather, it represents an effort to be accepted by others. He believes that his instructor and fellow class-mates will not like the "real" Richard and that he must pretend to be someone else while he is in class.

■ Sarcasm

Sarcasm is the use of a biting sense of humor designed to keep people at a distance and to maintain control in a situation. Humor is meant to be spontaneous and non-malicious. The sarcastic person, however, often plans his or her next retort, intent on making others uncomfortable or simply putting them down. The sarcasm is intended to hurt the other person. Initially, we may find the sarcastic person to be humorous or witty; after repeated contact with this person, however, we may feel on guard or tentative. Consider the following:

> **Deneen:** Can you clarify the difference between interpersonal and intrap-ersonal communication?
>
> **Professor Casey:** Were you vacationing? What do you think I have been lecturing about for the past five days?

Professor Casey's remarks in this example demonstrate how sarcasm can play a detrimental role in communication. Because the professor is in a position of authority, Deneen may take his remarks personally and begin to question her own intelligence. Moreover, the professor's sarcastic remarks can adversely affect other class members.

In general, the sarcastic person appears unapproachable. As a result, other people tend to avoid interactions with that person. Let us take another look at the effects of Professor Casey's defensive communication. Danielle, an extremely quiet student, may decide never to speak up in class after the preceding incident, reasoning that she will again be put down. If other class members develop a similar attitude and stop asking questions, what has Professor Casey been able to accomplish? The use of sarcasm allows the professor to place a shield around himself and at the same time makes it difficult for students to question and challenge him. This technique enables the professor to maintain distance between himself and his students; he stays in control by remaining unapproachable.

Outdoing Others

Outdoing others happens when we feel the need to constantly top the achievements of others. We tend to define our self-worth in relation to others. When we try to top someone else, we rarely listen to the communication we receive, because we are too busy worrying about our role in the interaction. Thus, we communicate superficial information instead of communicating important information about our feelings. Despite an inability to take the focus off ourselves, we are not self-centered; rather, our discomfort in interactions causes us to see only how things personally affect us. For example:

> Lorraine had a difficult time with math in high school, and her grades reflected this. Now that she is in college, Lorraine is struggling with a math course that is required for all elementary education majors. She works two nights a week with a tutor because she is motivated to be the first one in her family to earn a college degree. For Amanda, math is easy, but English is very difficult. Amanda's difficulty with English has begun to erode her self-confidence in all her school work. The following dialogue illustrates this point.

> **Lorraine:** I studied the entire weekend for my math test, and I think it was worth it because I received 82 percent on the exam. I finally think I understand what we've been learning this past semester.
>
> **Amanda:** I got 91 percent on the test. I'm really pleased because I didn't have to stay home over the weekend to study. I'm glad math comes so easily to me.

While Lorraine was attempting to share her good news, Amanda felt the need to overshadow her friend's achievement. The dialogue started out by focusing on Lorraine, but it transferred to Amanda in the end. No real self-disclosure took place, and Lorraine is left feeling defeated and uncomfortable.

Overly Critical Communication

Overly critical individuals judge the behavior of others; they compare the accomplishments of others to their own feelings of inadequacy and believe that by criticizing others, their own self-esteem will be enhanced. Their style of communication reflects their own critical nature. Consider the following:

> Serina's mother never worked outside the home because she gave up her dream to become a writer when she met Serina's father, married, and had three children. She resents her choice, although she loves her husband and Serina. Serina put herself through school by working full-time at a local bank while attending college at night. Both Serina and her husband work full-time and their sons go to day care. Serina tries to see her mother at least once a week and often invites her to dinner with her children. Despite Serina's efforts, her mother is overly critical with her communication.

Serina: I'm going to apply for the position in management that just opened up. I see it as a significant advancement for my career.

Serina's mother: Do you really think you are talented enough to be promoted? I think you would be better off keeping your present position. You haven't been terribly successful as a supervisor, so how do you expect to be a capable manager?

Serina's mother is critical because her self-esteem is weak. If Serina's mother is repeatedly critical in her communication with others, it is probably the result of a negative self-concept. Her critical communication in this example would explain her attempt to boost her self-esteem. Clearly, Serina's mother does not value Serina or her siblings for who they are and what they have accomplished as adults.

■ Formula Communication

Formula communication is safe, nonthreatening communication that involves little or no risk on the part of the communicator. It is often evident in the superficial dialogue that people exchange. There is the potential for greater depth in these relationships, but the people involved are hesitant to share their feelings. Consequently, the barriers remain and the communication stays at a superficial level. For example:

> Bob and Emily have been married for six years. Emily has never lived up to her mother-in-law Beth's expectations. Their home was never clean enough or decorated correctly. The meals she prepared for herself and her husband were not nutritious enough and "not what Bob likes," according to Beth. For the first year of Bob and Emily's marriage, Emily tried to please Beth, to no avail. Then during their third year of marriage Bob changed jobs, so the two of them relocated. They still, however, make regular trips back home to see everyone. The beginning of each visit is devoted to small talk and bringing everyone up to date. Afterwards, the conversation wanes; dialogue seems stuck at this superficial level. Emily and her mother-in-law are grateful for the television that fills the long moments of silence; this "third party" gives them a welcome excuse to keep their conversation to a minimum.

Although the parties believe there is more to their relationship, no one is willing to take the risk to change the communication pattern. Thus, the parties continue to rely on superficial communication to survive the weekend. Table 7.1 presents a summary of defense mechanisms.

COPING WITH DEFENSIVENESS

As discussed in the preceding section, people communicate defensively in an attempt to protect themselves. Although their frustration is often with themselves, they defend themselves by directing their frustration, anger, or anxiety toward others.

When we feel uncomfortable, we may engage in superficial dialogue.

TABLE 7.1   Defense Mechanisms at a Glance

Avoidance	We retreat from a problem in a relationship.
Psychological withdrawal	We feel uncomfortable in a particular situation, yet feel forced to be physically present.
Distancing	We prevent others from getting close to us.
Reaction formation	We behave contrary to the way we really feel.
Sarcasm	We use a biting sense of humor to keep people at a distance and to maintain control in a situation.
Outdoing others	We feel the need to top the achievements of others.
Overly critical communication	We judge or criticize the behavior of others.
Formula communication	We engage in superficial dialogue as a means of self-protection.

As a result of our discussion about defense mechanisms, we should be able to recognize defensive communication. The next logical step is to learn how to communicate more effectively when we encounter defensive behavior. Realistically, there is no escaping defensive communication; therefore, it helps to know how to combat defensiveness when we encounter it. Our increased understanding of defensiveness will help us break through the walls others erect in order to shield themselves. Our reward for having accomplished this significant task is a level of communication that is more meaningful. Meaningful communication leads to more fulfilling relationships at home, work, and school. Ultimately, we can begin to understand and value the other person's point of view.

■ The Nature of Communication Climates

We bring a particular state of mind with us when we engage in the act of communicating. This emotional atmosphere is known as the **communication climate.** It includes such factors as our feelings toward the person or persons with whom we are interacting, our attitude about the subject under discussion, and how we feel about ourselves in the particular interaction. The climate, therefore, often determines the degree of comfort we experience while interacting with others.

Jack Gibb (1961) differentiates between supportive and defensive communication climates. A **supportive climate** is one that encourages a free and open interaction between individuals. We can be ourselves and appreciate the differences of others. For instance, a family gathering in which members pore over photo albums and talk nostalgically of bygone days represents a supportive climate. Inhibitions lessen as the individuals get caught up in their reminiscences. The family members focus on their shared experiences and feelings. A **defensive climate,** on the other hand, inhibits the interaction between individuals. We attempt to hide our thoughts, feelings, and ideas as a means of self-protection. In addition, we tend to focus on the "otherness" of the people with whom we are communicating. Consider the following situation:

> Morgan, who is 21 years old and single, loves her job as a customer service clerk at the local Kmart. The job is interesting because she gets to meet so many different people every day. She is working on a degree in retail marketing and would like to move into management at her store someday. While behind the customer service desk, Morgan usually greets each customer with a smile and pleasant, "Hello, how can I help you today?" But, during the holidays, it is difficult to be so polite because everyone is rushed and long lines are constant. Morgan must deal with all different types of merchandise returns during the holiday season. Many customers want a refund without offering a receipt. Store policy clearly states that a receipt is necessary for a cash refund. One rather busy afternoon, Morgan begins each interaction by asking, "Where is your receipt?" This question sets the tone for the conversation and instantly puts the customer on the defensive.

In this example, Morgan creates a defensive climate, which makes the customer feel abused and unappreciated and less likely to shop at Kmart again.

A supportive climate invites self-disclosure and an appreciation for the differences of others.

The Gibb study identifies six "pairings" of behaviors that contribute to a defensive/supportive climate. In other words, for each of the six behaviors Gibb associates with a defensive climate, there is a counteractive behavior that contributes to a supportive climate. The follow subsections will focus on the Gibb pairings: evaluation versus description, control versus problem orientation, strategy versus spontaneity, neutrality versus empathy, superiority versus equality, and certainty versus provisionalism.

■ Evaluation versus Description

Highly evaluative communication contributes to a defensive climate. **Evaluative behavior** is judgmental; it attacks the individual rather than that person's actions. In the following example, Holly and Jim have just moved in together after dating for six months. They met at work and have spent every free moment together since their meeting. Both are divorced. Holly has two married adult children, while Jim has no children. They decided to move in together to see if they are compatible and to try to avoid some of the mistakes they believe they made in their first marriages. During the first few weeks of sharing a home together, they find it difficult to communicate their frustrations. In a particular stressful moment, parties resort to evaluative communication:

> **Jim:** Why don't you ever pick your stuff up around here? You're so lazy! I'm always the one who cleans up this place. You never care about anyone but yourself.

Holly: I'm not lazy! You're the one with the problem. You're always criticizing! Everything has to be "just so" all the time. You know what? You're impossible to please!

Jim: I can't believe how nasty you are!

Holly: How about you?!

In this exchange, both Holly and Jim become defensive, which is reflected by their communication with each other. In order to ensure a more supportive climate, Jim needs to use a technique known as **descriptiveness,** the ability to focus on observable behavior. If Jim were to explain to Holly why he has a problem with their messy apartment, the interaction would probably go more smoothly, perhaps something like this:

Jim: Holly, it bothers me that this place is so messy. Since we're having company this weekend, I was wondering if you could do some cleaning. How long will it take you to finish what you are doing?

Holly: Well, I don't know. I'm really busy today, but I'll try to get everything straightened up by tomorrow evening.

Jim: I'd really appreciate that.

In this dialogue, Jim attempts to focus on the problem he has with his partner's sloppiness rather than attacking Holly personally. When we have difficulty with others, it usually deals with their behavior; therefore, it makes sense to have our feedback focus on those actions.

COMMUNICATION IN ACTION

Evaluative versus Descriptive Communication

Consider an interpersonal relationship that is important to you.

1. Identify an aspect of the other person's behavior that you find irritating.

2. Write down your observations. Try to avoid using evaluative language.

   Evaluative: Bob always interrupts me because he has to be the center of attention.

   Descriptive: Bob interrupted me three times last night when I was telling the story of my first night of classes at the university.

3. Share your observations with a classmate. Practice descriptive statements about the observable behavior of others with your partner.

4. What are the advantages of descriptive language?

5. How can you use descriptiveness to improve your relationship with the person identified at the beginning of this activity?

6. How can the use of descriptive language enhance your confidence as a communicator?

■ Control versus Problem Orientation

Sometimes we try to resolve a conflict with a one-sided solution. When this approach is taken, one party decides it is the other party who needs to change. **Control** is a means of making the other party conform to our way of thinking. Furthermore, it suggests that there is only one way to see a problem. Consider the following:

> Melanie was rebellious as a teenager. She repeatedly challenged the authority of her parents by piercing her tongue and getting several tattoos, which contributed to tense family communication. Her parents both worked full-time and had little time to spend with her. When dialogue did occur, shouting and screaming were typical. Melanie's parents felt that she was the one with the problem, that she was the one who needed to change. They encouraged her to seek therapy, yet they refused to participate in family counseling.

With a **problem orientation,** the parties involved realize that several people contribute to the problem and that adjustment of behavior is necessary on all fronts. The focus of the discussion rests with the assumption, "We have a problem. Let's try to resolve it." This is illustrated in the following case:

> Debbie is Melanie's age. Like Melanie, she went through a rebellious stage during her teens. There was considerable tension in her household, yet Debbie's family did not assume that the problem was entirely hers. Instead, the whole family participated in counseling sessions. Over a period of several months the problems between Debbie and her parents improved. This meant, however, that all the parties involved eventually altered their communication.

■ Strategy versus Spontaneity

Efforts to manipulate interactions between people indicate that some **strategy** is in motion. This frequently creates a defensive climate between parties. Sometimes when we have a conflict with another person, we try to preplan the dialogue, often with disastrous results. When we discuss our differences with the other party, our comments can lack spontaneity and sincerity. Consider the following situation:

> A conflict is brewing between Paula and Ruth. They have been friends for over 20 years. The two friends met in high school and were two of only a few African American students in a predominantly white school. They went to college together and remained in contact when Ruth was promoted at her job and had to move to another state. Ruth recently moved back to her hometown. At first, the friendship returned to its old intensity and openness. But lately, Paula has stopped calling and inviting Ruth to movies or shopping. Ruth, in return, has increased her invitations,

only to be turned down by Paula. Paula always offers an excuse. Ruth has been troubled over the tension that has developed between them, so she invites Paula out for lunch. Ruth is nervous about the meeting and stays up until 2:00 a.m. planning what she wants to say. When they meet, Paula surprises Ruth by bringing up some unexpected points. Ruth's preplanned comments are inappropriate for their current conversation. The outing is a failure for both women.

Spontaneity is the opposite of strategy. **Spontaneity** refers to an open discussion of feelings. You know the major points you wish to bring up in a discussion, but you do not have an exact script for the interaction that is about to take place. "I feel bad about the present strain in our relationship and I hope we can repair the damage" will go much farther than a preplanned script.

■ Neutrality versus Empathy

Neutrality implies indifference toward another individual. This apparent disinterest can be interpreted as a lack of caring and can therefore have a negative effect on the communication climate. For example:

> Allan and Barbara have been taking classes together since they met in their first college class four years ago. As study partners, they have helped one another with tests, math homework, and physics labs. They have both returned to college after many years with the full support of their spouses and families. As full-time workers and part-time students, Allan and Barbara have depended on each other for support and friendship. Allan has decided to continue his education and go to law school. He wants to share his news with Barbara. When he sees Barbara in the college cafeteria, he can't wait to tell her. Barbara, however, shows little interest, prompting Allan to wonder why he was excited about telling her.

Empathy, the ability to look at something from someone else's perspective, is the antithesis of neutrality. Empathy communicates an understanding of the other person's viewpoint. In essence, it means taking the focus off yourself so that someone else's position can readily be seen. Consider the following circumstances:

> Jan's two children have been home from school for the past two and a half weeks because of a teachers' strike. Jan is angered by the disruption the strike has caused her boys' education, their family's daily schedule, and so on. Roberta, one of Jan's closest friends, teaches in the school district. Roberta visits Jan one afternoon following another unproductive negotiating session. She is frustrated by the long ordeal, but she firmly believes the strike is justified. Despite her differing views, Jan allows Roberta to discuss her feelings and explain her reasons.

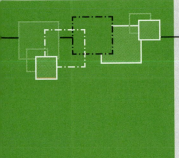

EMBRACING DIFFERENCE

Empathic Communication

In the two previous examples illustrating neutrality and empathy, Allan and Jan had different approaches to their interaction with their friends. Allan was hurt by Barbara's response. Jan, on the other hand, did not internalize Roberta's behavior. Jan was able to take the focus off herself and listen to Roberta with empathy.

1. Describe the effect the different approaches had on the friendships of Allan and Barbara and Jan and Roberta.

2. How did Jan's appreciation of difference help her as a communicator?

3. How can Jan's help you understand the importance of embracing difference?

Communication and TECHNOLOGY

Email Flaming and Defensiveness

More and more of us are using email to communicate with friends, family, and co-workers. Email is fast, inexpensive, instantaneous, and easy. We can even send photographs, reports, and other documents as attachments to our email. Email is a great way to send and receive information and stay in touch with friends or family who are far away. But, if used haphazardly, it can create defensiveness. Have you ever opened an email from a co-worker or friend and found an insulting or mean message that hurt your feelings or made you very angry? An email like this is called a flame. A flame is an example of defensive communication. Its goal is to hurt the other person's feelings, not to convey information. These messages are usually sent without real thought and as a reaction to the sender's immediate feelings. Flames do not solve problems or conflict and can only serve to intensify existing hurt feelings.

In order to avoid using flames and to use email to create a positive communication climate, follow these guidelines:

1. Carefully proofread every message you send. A misspelled word or typo could mean, for example, that the receiver misses an important meeting (the email says 1:00 and the meeting is actually at 2:00). The receiver is sure to be embarrassed and angry for missing the meeting and for receiving misinformation. One typo could cause defensiveness and conflict.

2. Allow time to pass before you send a message. Give yourself some time to reread and review your email before pressing the "send" icon. You may feel differently about the problem or conflict tomorrow. It is easy to write something to someone when you don't have to deliver the message face to face. Never write anything you would be unwilling to communicate in person.

3. Remember that email is not a private communication between you and the receiver. It is a permanent and sometimes public record of your message. If you don't want your message to be public, don't use email. Messages you send today could come back to haunt you tomorrow.

4. Ask yourself if email is the best way to deliver this message. Would it be better to use the

(continued)

Communication and TECHNOLOGY (continued)

telephone or discuss the problem face to face? Many of us use email to avoid conflict or to deliver messages that are unpleasant news. If you were the receiver, would you want to open your email and find this message?

5. Lastly, remember that the receiver will provide the emotion to the message. In other words, email is devoid of facial expressions, voice quality, and bodily movement—all things that help the receiver to interpret our message and provide some clues to the sender's meaning. Sarcasm, for example, is difficult to communicate via email. Whenever appropriate, use characters like :) and ;) to communicate a joke or happy/funny message (see Chapter 4).

The empathy displayed by Jan in this example creates a communication climate in which Roberta feels free to express her views because she knows they will be valued by Jan.

■ Superiority versus Equality

Superiority communicates an attitude that an individual is better, more important, or more valuable than someone else. Designed to intimidate others, superiority discourages people from expressing themselves freely and therefore can contribute to a defensive communication climate. Consider the following:

> Carol, a graduate teaching assistant, is lecturing to 50 first-year students in her Introduction to Philosophy course. This is the first time Carol has taught this course, and she is somewhat unsure of herself. A student raises his hand and asks Carol a question. Instead of answering the student's question, Carol cites her degrees in philosophy and describes her latest research project. This tactic is chosen intentionally to intimidate the students and to make them feel embarrassed to ask a question.

This response sets the tone for the remainder of the semester—a tense, defensive climate in which ill feelings dominate.

   Equality, treating others on a par with ourselves, represents a supportive climate. The dialogue between individuals tends to be much freer and more supportive

DILBERT: © Scott Adams/Dist. by United Feature Syndicate, Inc. Reprinted by permission.

because the status of the individuals does not interfere with the interaction. For example, if Carol had responded to the student's question by first acknowledging the importance of asking questions, the class as a whole would likely have proceeded more productively.

■ Certainty versus Provisionalism

We have all encountered individuals who believe that their way is the only way to proceed. Gibb refers to this type of person as one who has a high degree of **certainty,** one who believes that others cannot possibly contribute new knowledge to the situation. He or she does not see the value in differing approaches, viewpoints, or opinions. This individual frequently promotes defensiveness in others by inhibiting others from describing their ideas.

Provisionalism, on the other hand, is a willingness to explore new ideas. Individuals in this category realize that theirs is not the only way to look at a situation; they welcome input from others. For example:

> Karen and Angie are both receptionists for Dr. Johnson, D.D.S. Karen has worked for Dr. Johnson for three years. She is the senior member of the office. After eight weeks on the job, Angie suggests a different method for handling insurance claims to Karen. Rather than being threatened by Angie's suggestion, Karen recognizes the merit of the proposed change and decides to approach Dr. Johnson about implementing it. With Dr. Johnson's approval, Angie's idea saves the office several hours of work per week and the insurance claims are filed faster. Provisionalism, as illustrated in this example, creates a supportive communication climate that encourages an open exchange of ideas.

SKILL BUILDING

Writing Email

Review the story about Emma and Cara at the beginning of this chapter. After identifying the defense mechanisms used by each do the following:

1. Choose one of the characters.

2. With a partner or on your own, write two emails to the other character in the story. The first email should be a flame. In other words, write an email that creates further defensiveness and conflict. The second email should follow the guidelines listed in the Communication and Technology box on pages 139–140 to create a supportive communication climate.

3. Compare the emails. Which email was easier to write? Why? Which email will allow the parties to meet again and resolve their conflicts? Explain.

Serving Your COMMUNITY — Communication Climate

In an effort to understand the importance of a supportive climate, please engage in the following activity:

1. Please go back to the nursing home that you visited in the assignment in Chapter 6.

2. Spend another three hours assisting the residents.

3. Attempt to observe patterns of defensive behavior exhibited by the residents.

4. Schedule a meeting with the director.

5. When meeting with the director ask how he or she attempts to create a supportive climate in an effort to reduce defensiveness exhibited by the residents. Specifically ask the director to comment on the following:

   a. using descriptive language.

   b. resolving problems together.

   c. openly discussing feelings.

   d. appreciating the perspectives of those residing in the shelter.

   e. displaying a level of equality between himself or herself and the residents of the shelter.

   f. showing a willingness to explore new ideas.

6. How did this process help you appreciate the importance of creating a supportive climate?

STEPPING BACK FROM DEFENSIVE COMMUNICATION

If we find ourselves responding to someone else's defensive communication by behaving defensively in turn, it is time to step back and take stock of our actions or risk developing a habit of defensive communication. By analyzing the interaction, we can gain insight into the communication behavior of both parties and choose a more productive course of action than that provided by a defensive response. In the beginning of this chapter, Emma and Cara exhibited defensive communication behaviors. They are left feeling undervalued and unappreciated. If each had taken the time to reflect upon their working relationship and their communication, they might have been more willing to step back from their defensiveness and attempt to create a more positive communication climate. For example, Emma could have said to Cara, "I know you feel strongly about Christmas. I love the holiday, too. Can't we work together to find a way to celebrate it and include the other seasonal holidays as well?" This statement acknowledges Cara's feelings but also opens the door for a cooperative solution to their common problem and it invites Cara to communicate her ideas.

It is also time to step back if we find ourselves internalizing another person's defensiveness. This occurs when we perceive ourselves as the cause of someone else's defensiveness.

Finally, there are times when others are threatened by who we are, so they lash out at us. They may only see the differences between us, not the things we share. A number of emotions may account for this behavior: Anger, jealousy, and resentment are common reactions to such circumstances as our position at work, our perceived wealth, our attractiveness, or our popularity among our peers. If we realize that insecurities often motivate these individuals to communicate defensively, then it will be easier for us to detach ourselves from their defensiveness. By stepping back and analyzing their behavior, we reduce our chances of becoming defensive in return. this is the first step toward creating a supportive communication climate.

ETHICS in Communication
Creating a Positive Communication Climate

In the vignette at the beginning of the chapter, Cara and Emma engage in defensive communication. Their use of defense mechanisms leads not only to ineffective communication, but also to low productivity at Safe House. Emma's shouting and Cara's withdrawal from the interaction and her subsequent discussions with others behind Emma's back do not solve the problem they have. Tanya tries to mediate between the two, but is unsuccessful. Clearly, Emma and Cara are engaging in ineffective and unethical communication.

1. The Gibb study provides us with some clues to their communication problems. What type of communication is Emma using? What type of communication is Cara using?

2. What specific defense mechanisms are Emma and Cara using?

3. How can they improve their communication in order to create a positive communication climate?

4. Have you ever been in a situation like Emma or Cara? How did you communicate?

SUMMARY

Defensiveness is our response to a threatening situation, one that makes us feel anxious, uncomfortable, or fearful. Defensive communication acts as a shield that protects us from others, yet it creates barriers to effective communication.

We use a variety of defense mechanisms when we feel threatened by a situation or by another person. These include avoidance, psychological withdrawal, distancing, reaction formation, sarcasm, outdoing others, overly critical communication, and formula communication.

Since all of us use defensive communication and encounter its use by others, it is only natural that we should be interested in learning how to cope with defensiveness. Jack Gibb suggests that creating a supportive communication climate helps alleviate much of the tension and inhibitions that exist between people. In his work, he identifies six pairings of behaviors that contribute to either a defensive or supportive communication climate: evaluation versus description, control versus problem orientation, strategy versus spontaneity, neutrality versus empathy, superiority versus equality, and certainty versus provisionalism.

In addition to Gibb's techniques for establishing a supportive communication climate, another way to cope with defensiveness is to step back from the other person's defensive communication. In order to do this, we must first realize that it is the other person's insecurities that trigger the undesirable communication. Our ability to avoid internalizing the defensiveness of others allows us to analyze their communication and minimizes our chances of becoming defensive in return.

REVIEW QUESTIONS

1. Why do people behave defensively?
2. List eight defense mechanisms that emerge in social situations. Write a short example of each.
3. Why is reaction formation a difficult behavior to change?
4. Differentiate between avoidance and psychological withdrawal.
5. What are the benefits of alleviating a defensive climate?
6. Briefly explain six ways to create a supportive climate.
7. Create or describe a situation in which empathy is used to establish a supportive climate.
8. How does internalizing another person's defensiveness stifle effective communication?

KEY CONCEPTS

defensive communication
defense mechanisms
avoidance
psychological withdrawal
distancing
reaction formation
sarcasm
outdoing others
overly critical communication

formula communication
communication climate
supportive climate
defensive climate
evaluative behavior
descriptiveness
control
problem orientation
strategy

spontaneity
neutrality
empathy
superiority
equality
certainty
provisionalism

Interviewing

AFTER STUDYING THIS CHAPTER, YOU SHOULD

understand

- *open* and *closed*, *primary* and *secondary*, and *neutral* and *leading* questions.
- the function of each of the following interview parts: the opening, the body, and the closing.

be able to

- construct and conduct an informational interview.
- prepare a resume and cover letter for an employment interview.
- apply techniques to improve your communication in an employment interview.

CHAPTER 8

George is very excited. He is about to become the first member of his family to earn a college degree. It has taken him several years of night classes to graduate and now he is going to have his first job interview for a management position at a local engineering firm. He and his family have sacrificed their time together as well as the family savings for George to get his degree, but now it will all be worth it. This new job promises a large increase in pay and excellent benefits.

As he waits in the "holding" room with the other interviewees, George is confident that he and the recruiter will hit it off. George rehearses his opening comments about the score of the last local baseball game and how great the championship was for the city. He knows the interviewer will be impressed by his knowledge of sports—a very popular topic at the office. George knows he will fit in with the other "guys."

A young African American woman calls George's name and motions for him to follow her. When they reach the interviewing room, Gloria offers her hand for George to shake and invites him to sit down on one of the chairs in the room. George shakes her hand and asks, "When will the recruiter arrive? I am awfully anxious about this interview and hope it will begin soon."

George's jaw drops when Gloria hands him her business card that reads, "Gloria McFerson, Senior Recruiter." She says, "The recruiter is right here and I'd like to begin the interview right now. I know you must be nervous, but try not to be. I just want to spend a few minutes getting to know you and discussing your qualifications for the position."

■ ■ ■ ■ ■

In this chapter, we'll see how the concepts of perception, listening, self-concept, self-disclosure, and communication climate affect the interviewing process. In addition, we will learn about interview organization, questions, and types of interviews.

Like George, we all feel uneasy when we interview for a job. When we think about being interviewed, one word may come to mind: *fear*. What are some factors that contribute to our anxiety? First, there is the risk of participating in an interview. We are not certain about whether we will get the job, and if we do not, can we handle the rejection? Second, it is difficult to interact with someone we have just met, especially when we realize this person will be judging our responses. And third, many of us are unsure about how to conduct ourselves during an interview. This chapter attempts to alleviate some of our anxieties about interviewing by explaining what an interview is and how we can improve our part within the interaction.

An **interview** is a planned and purposeful interaction between two parties in which questions are asked and answers are given. The party who asks the questions is the **interviewer;** the responding party is the **interviewee.** The "interviewer" can be more than one person, such as a group of board members, department personnel, or panel members. When we think of interviews, the first kind that comes to mind is the employment interview. There are, however, several other types of interviews: physicians gather information from their patients; mortgage loan officers gather information from prospective homeowners; contractors ask customers about the special features to be included in their kitchen, bathroom, or sunroom; and reference librarians ask patrons about the kind of information they need to answer their questions. A wide variety of careers and jobs require you to understand the dynamics of an interview.

The interview builds on several of the concepts discussed earlier in this book. For instance, *listening* plays a crucial role in the interviewing process, since both participants must actively listen to each other's responses. Questions need to be worded with precision and clarity so that they communicate the intent of the sender, so *language* is important. *Nonverbal communication* is also crucial to the process. Participants need to observe both deliberate and accidental responses. Both parties need to be sensitive to their own interactions in order to respond appropriately to the other party's communication. A *supportive climate* set by the interviewer will allow for more *self-disclosure*. Most importantly, like all other communication interactions, a successful interview hinges on both participants understanding and appreciating the other's diverse approach to the situation. The interviewer and the interviewee come to the interview with their own past experiences, culture, and social roles.

INTERVIEW QUESTIONS

Interviews contain a wide range of questions. While interviewers must formulate appropriate questions, interviewees should try to anticipate the types of questions that will be asked. On a job interview, for example, we expect to be asked about former positions we have held or why we think we are qualified for the job. Anticipating such questions can help us feel more comfortable with the interviewing process and, in turn, increase our ability to respond to questions. Several kinds of questions emerge during an interview, including the following pairings: open and closed, primary and secondary, and neutral and leading.

OPEN AND CLOSED QUESTIONS

Open questions are nonrestrictive questions designed to give the respondent maximum latitude in formulating an answer. They provide an opportunity for interviewees to reveal more information about themselves: their feelings, philosophies, and biases. A question such as "What are your feelings about the war in Iraq?" allows us to voice our opinion about the issue. At the same time, open questions are often successful in establishing an atmosphere of give and take between the interviewer and interviewee.

Open questions can be problematic, however. Consider the fact that our response to an open question, both in terms of the subject matter covered and the amount of time used, is beyond the interviewer's control. In fact, much of the information we yield in response to an open question can be far removed from the interviewer's purpose. For example, if our response to the question about the war in Iraq digressed into a discussion of the torture of detained combatants, the interviewer would be getting more than he or she bargained for (in this case, the interviewer was simply looking for some indication of degree of public support for U.S. involvement in Iraq). Consider, too, that inexperienced interviewees or those with a low self-esteem might feel particularly anxious about responding to open questions because they are afraid to disclose personal information or they are afraid that their responses might be too off-base.

Closed questions are designed to elicit specific feedback from the respondent. They are especially useful in conducting surveys or polls in which the interviewer plans to statistically compare the responses. The interviewee's responses to closed questions should be brief.

The following series of closed questions could be used in a public opinion poll:

1. Do you support U.S. involvement in Iraq?
2. Should the United States have a permanent presence in Iraq?
3. When should the United States withdraw from Iraq?
4. Are the wars in Iraq and Afghanistan connected?

These questions, and several more like them, are necessary in order to gauge the public's attitude and knowledge of the war in Iraq. It might take dozens of closed questions to determine the attitudes expressed in response to just one open question. Closed questions, however, are not meant to probe or explore another person's feelings or values; rather, their intent is to simply gather facts or discern what is already suspected by the interviewer.

■ Primary and Secondary Questions

Primary questions are those questions that introduce a major area of discussion to be guided by the interviewer. Whenever the interviewer summarizes one area of discussion and then moves in a new direction, the initial question he or she asks is known as a primary question. For example, a sportscaster might kick off each new

Most polls include closed questions because the answers can easily be compared.

area of an interview by asking the following questions of a baseball manager whose team just clinched the American League Pennant: "What did you say to your players before the start of today's game?" "What was the turning point in this deciding game?" "Did you ever lose confidence in your team?" "Who do you plan to start in game one of the World Series?" The sportscaster is able to introduce several key issues, each with a separate primary question. Interviewers generally prepare primary questions ahead of time. By the same token, interviewees can usually anticipate that some of these questions will be asked during the interview.

Secondary questions are designed to gain additional information from the interviewee. The interviewer is asking that we clarify or expand our response to the primary question. General questions such as "What do you mean?" "I don't think I fully understand your point," or "Why do you say that?" can be used, or the secondary questions can be more specific. For instance, as a follow-up to the primary question, "Who do you plan to start in game one of the World Series?" the sportscaster might ask: "Will his arm have enough rest with only three days off?" "Are you worried about the number of walks he gave up during the two games he pitched in the Championship Series?" Certain nonverbal behaviors also can function as secondary questions. A raised eyebrow or a searching look might indicate that the interviewee needs to clarify or expand on his or her response to the last question.

Secondary questions also provide an opportunity for both parties to clear up any misunderstandings about statements made earlier in the interview because they allow us to check our perceptions. In addition, they allow the interviewee to give more detailed answers. Ultimately, this may affect how the interviewer interprets information, or reaches a decision, in the case of job interviews.

COMMUNICATION IN ACTION

Recognizing Types of Questions

After reading each question, determine whether it is (a) open or closed, (b) primary or secondary, or (c) neutral or leading.

1. What experience do you have with Microsoft Word?
2. When you say you have great people skills, what do you mean?
3. Why did you choose to major in political science?
4. You are looking for a challenging career, aren't you?
5. Don't you wish all days were as beautiful as today?
6. Which college course helped you to develop your writing skills?
7. What do you think about censorship?
8. Could you explain why you are applying for this position?
9. What questions do you have about the position?
10. Having a strong policy against sexual harassment is great for the company, isn't it?

How can determining the types of questions help you enhance your confidence as a communicator?

■ Neutral and Leading Questions

Neutral questions are those questions that reveal nothing of the interviewer's biases, preferences, or expectations. There is no "right" or "wrong" response to such questions as "Are accounting courses better at night or in the day?" "How do you like to spend your leisure time?" **Leading questions** are designed to move the interview in a specific direction. "Don't you agree that part-time students who work are more serious about their courses?" "Television coverage can make or break a politician's career, wouldn't you agree?" In the preceding questions, the interviewee is being led to a specific response. Leading questions can create problems, however. People can become extremely defensive when they feel forced to give responses that do not truly represent their views. This can increase the level of tension within the interview.

ORGANIZING THE INTERVIEW

How do we incorporate the different types of questions discussed in the preceding section into the interview itself? To answer this question, we need to explore the issue of organizing the interview. While the following discussion is presented from the perspective of the interviewer, it should be of equal value to the interviewee. An awareness of the interview's structure can help the interviewee anticipate the types of questions he or she will be asked.

In many ways, the structure of an interview follows the pattern of a speech, which we will discuss in Chapter 13. Consequently, there are three parts to the interview: the opening, the body, and the conclusion.

■ The Opening

The **opening** begins the interview. Its general function is to establish rapport between the two parties and to clarify the interview's purpose and scope. What the interviewer says during the opening generally sets the tone for the rest of the interview. His or her ability to create a positive communication climate (see Chapter 7) depends, in part, on how interpersonally skilled he or she is. One way to create a positive climate is to create common ground with the interviewee. Common ground means that the interviewer and the interviewee share an interest, value, and past experience. Because the interviewer and interviewee are coming to the situation from different perspectives and with different and diverse approaches, it is important for the interviewer to find something he or she shares in common with the interviewee.

The opening is an appropriate place to ask some general questions in order to relax the interviewee. These warm-up questions, often open in nature, give the interviewee an opportunity to express himself or herself in general terms: "Did you have any trouble finding the office?" "Have you been enjoying this unseasonably warm weather?" This process often reduces the tension for both interviewer and interviewee alike. The sequence should remain brief, however, lest the interviewee become nervous about supplying "correct" answers to these questions.

■ The Body

The next segment of the interview is the **body.** This is where the major part of the interview occurs. In developing the body, we must first determine the degree of flexibility we feel is appropriate for the interview. We might characterize the body in many ways. Charles Stewart and William Cash describe several methods to organize your questions. Three of the most important are highly scheduled, moderately scheduled, and nonscheduled (2008, pp. 86–89).

Highly Scheduled Body

A *highly scheduled body* includes all the questions that the interviewer plans to ask. Most of these questions are closed, leaving little opportunity for secondary questions to arise. Marketing surveys and public opinion polls follow a highly structured body. In employment interviews, the highly structured body generally works best for the inexperienced or untrained interviewer. The security of having a prepared list of questions in advance simplifies the process, especially for the novice. For instance, a newly promoted store manager may have little or no experience interviewing others for a position in sales. For her first interviewing experience, a prepared list of questions might be a wise choice. She can move from one question to the next, taking time to listen to the response given after each question. What a highly scheduled body does not invite, however, is a spontaneous exchange between interviewer and interviewee. This is generally achieved during a moderately or nonscheduled interview, where the interviewer is more experienced.

Moderately Scheduled Body

In a *moderately scheduled body*, the interviewer determines the primary questions ahead of time. These serve only as a foundation for the rest of the interview, however. The interviewer proceeds on the premise that the interviewee's responses will trigger secondary, related questions. In other words, the interview is open to give and take between the two parties. The moderately scheduled interview offers flexibility and a sense of naturalness. It is an excellent format for someone who has experience as an interviewer.

For example, the interviews conducted by Oprah Winfrey follow a moderately structured format regardless of the show's topic or the guests. Ms. Winfrey determines the topics she wants to cover prior to airtime. Once the initial questions are asked, however, she allows the interviewee's responses to dictate some of her follow-up questions. Of course, as a highly skilled interviewer, Ms. Winfrey is always able to bring the topic back into sharp focus if the conversation goes too far afield.

Nonscheduled Body

The *nonscheduled body* provides maximum flexibility for both the interviewer and interviewee. The interviewer works from an outline of topics, but no actual questions. According to Stewart and Cash, this type of interview works well when the topic is extremely broad, the interviewee is uneasy or reluctant to participate, or when the interviewer has little time to prepare a schedule of questions (2008, p. 86). For example:

> Linsey has been researching her informative speech topic of "crime on campus." As she walks to her car, she notices that the campus police have surrounded one of the buildings. She rushes over to the police officer in charge to find out what has happened. The officer says that she cannot speak with Linsey at that moment, but if she comes by the police station in 30 minutes, the officer can answer her questions. Linsey has little time to prepare a list of questions, so instead creates an outline of topic areas she hopes the police officer can elaborate on during the interview.

■ The Closing

In some respects, an interview's **closing** is similar to the opening. One of its purposes is to end on a positive note, reinforcing the positive climate created in the opening. To end an interview abruptly could destroy an otherwise positive climate. In "winding down" the interview, the interviewer might say, "I would be pleased to answer any questions you might have." This invitation provides the interviewee with an opportunity to ask a few final questions in order to clarify any uncertain factors: "Do the four store managers meet on a regular basis to discuss sales and advertising strategies?" "Do you encourage your managers to submit their suggestions for the company's advertising campaign?" After the interviewee's questions are addressed, the interviewer thanks him or her for participating in the session: "I'm glad you and I had this opportunity to talk. Thanks for coming in today."

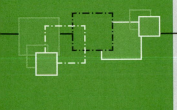

EMBRACING DIFFERENCE

Interviewing Styles

Jon Stewart, Oprah Winfrey, Barbara Walters, and Chris Matthews are all successful interviewers. Observe two of the above personalities and answer the following questions:

1. What types of interviews did you observe?
2. What was the primary goal of each interview?
3. How did the interviewers set the climate for the interview?
4. What types of body language did each interviewer use?
5. What types of questions did the interviewers ask?
6. How were the interviews concluded?
7. List the differences in the interviewers' approaches to the interview.
8. How can the differences used by the interviewers help you as a communicator?

ETHICS in Communication

The Employment Interview

In the scenario at the beginning of the chapter, we learn about George and his interview with Gloria McFerson. George is the first one in his family to graduate from college and now that he has earned his degree in engineering, George is excited to interview for a full-time position as a project designer. Of course, he is nervous before the interview and practices things he might say to connect with the recruiter. For example, George rehearses his comments about the latest sports scores.

When Gloria McFerson, a young African American women, enters the room, George mistakenly assumes she is a secretary or administrative assistant. Gloria is, of course, a recruiter and will be conducting the interview with George. Gloria ignores his preconceived notions of her and continues the interview in a professional manner. As you think about Gloria and George and their overall communication behavior, answer the following questions:

1. What assumptions does George make about engineers? What assumptions does he make about Gloria McFerson? Why do you think he makes these assumptions?

2. What could George have done before the interview to increase his chances of succeeding in this interview? How might you have changed his communicative behavior during the interview?

3. Explain why Gloria's communication is both ethical and effective.

4. Have you ever been in the same situation as George or Gloria? Describe your communication behavior.

TYPES OF INTERVIEWS

We have many opportunities to participate in interviews, including those related to job hiring, parent-teacher conferences, and questioning salespeople about particular consumer products, among others. There are many different types of interviews. These include the information-giving interview, such as a job orientation; the information-gathering interview, such as a survey or research interview; the selection or employment interview; the problem-solving interview; and the persuasive interview, such as that used in cars sales or fundraising (Stewart & Cash, 2008, p. 5). In addition, the counseling interview takes place between a therapist and a patient, and an exit interview is often required when we leave a job. Of the numerous interviews conducted daily, two are especially significant: the informational interview and the employment interview. The informational interview is presented from the interviewer's perspective; in it we discuss how to conduct this type of interview. In the section on the employment interview, the focus shifts from interviewer to interviewee. Preinterview preparations are explained, followed by a discussion of communication skills designed to improve our performance during an employment interview.

■ The Informational Interview

The purpose of an **informational interview** is to acquire facts about a specific topic. Perhaps our purpose is to gain an understanding of a company procedure or policy, to elicit an octogenarian's oral history, to determine the strategies used by the local high school football coach, or to learn about the successful techniques of a prominent business executive. Most importantly, you may use an informational interview to solicit support material for your speeches (see Chapter 12). In all these cases, we

Jon Stewart, host of the Daily Show, *is a skilled interviewer.*

must interview someone knowledgeable in a specific area. There are several steps to consider when conducting an informational interview. These include (1) developing the objective, (2) adequately researching the subject, and (3) carefully planning the interview questions.

Developing the Objective

A clearly defined interview objective serves several purposes; namely, (1) it communicates the intent of the interview, (2) it helps the interviewer develop appropriate questions, and (3) it establishes a time frame for the interview. By having a clear picture of the interview's intent, both parties better understand the purpose of the interaction and the importance of each of their roles. Having a good idea of where the interview is headed allows the interviewer to outline meaningful questions that remain focused on the stated purpose. Finally, a clearly established objective helps determine a reasonable time frame for the interview. This forces the interviewer to take into consideration the interviewee's time. For example:

Ineffective objective: To learn about your business.

Effective objective: To learn the procedure that your company uses for hiring accountants.

Ineffective objective: To learn about the newspaper business.

Effective objective: To learn about the different types of publishing software.

The first statements in the preceding list are vague, while the second statements clearly establish the parameters of each interview. The interviewer can then proceed to develop concrete questions, while the interviewee has a strong sense of the direction of the interview.

Researching the Topic

If the purpose of the interview is to gain information, it is advisable to research the topic ahead of time. Researching the topic helps the interviewer determine what he or she needs to find out during the interview, it prepares the interviewer to ask pertinent questions, and it enhances the interviewer's credibility with the interviewee. Furthermore, researching the topic avoids wasting interview time asking questions that could already have been answered by doing some groundwork. A basic understanding of the interview topic allows the interviewer to respond to the interviewee's comments by asking spontaneous follow-up questions. This task becomes difficult if the interviewer is generally unprepared for the interaction.

Planning the Interview Questions

Once the interview objective is determined, the interviewer is ready to develop interview questions. In part, the purpose of the interview dictates the types of questions used; an oral history, for example, tends toward open questions because its purpose is to learn about the individual's experiences. As discussed earlier in this chapter, open questions encourage the interviewee to reveal personal thoughts or attitudes concerning a particular topic. Open-ended primary questions should be formulated prior to the interview, as should some anticipated follow-up questions. Other secondary questions are interjected during the interview, since they grow out of the interviewee's responses. Whatever questions are used in the interview, they should conform to the structure (high, moderate, or none) deemed most suitable by the interviewer.

Example: Informational Interview

The purpose of this interview is to gather information about obtaining financial aid for college from the Director of Financial Aid Services. It might cover the following three points:

I. Objective: To discover the background and history of financial aid
    a. What is financial aid?
    b. When did financial aid begin?
    c. Why did financial aid become necessary?
    d. Who started financial aid?
    e. Where did financial aid originate?

II. Objective: To find out about the different types of financial aid
    a. What are the types of financial aid available?
    b. What are the requirements to receive financial aid?
    c. What are the eligibility requirements for each type of financial aid?
    d. Why should I apply for financial aid?
    e. How will financial aid benefit me and my family?

III. Objective: To find out how to get financial aid
    a. How do I start the financial aid application process?
    b. Whom do I speak to about getting financial aid?
    c. Where I should I apply?
    d. When should I begin seeking financial aid?

THE EMPLOYMENT INTERVIEW

For an employer, the purpose of an employment interview is to uncover information about potential employees and to use that information to hire a new employee; for an applicant, the purpose is to find out more information about a position and to persuade the employer to hire him or her. Such factors as experience, educational background, interpersonal skills, and appearance enter into the employer's decision-making process. In the past, some employers selected applicants on factors not related to job performance, such as gender, race, or religion; today, guidelines prohibit this practice. The Equal Employment Opportunity Commission (EEOC) has developed strict guidelines for interviewing and testing potential employees. Both employers and employees should be aware of these guidelines, in addition to state laws that govern hiring. In this section we will focus on two aspects of the employment interview: preinterview preparations and communication skills during the interview.

PREPARING FOR AN INTERVIEW

There are several ways for an applicant to prepare for an employment interview. Take the time to assess your employment potential, to compile a clearly structured resume, to write a solid cover letter, to research the company or organization, and to evaluate the interviewer's perspective in the interviewing process. Each of the steps described in this section has the potential to make you a better prepared, more confident employment candidate.

■ Self-Assessment

In assessing your employment potential, you want to evaluate your suitability for a particular career. To do this, you must appraise your capabilities and talents in order to determine how well you might fit a particular position. Self-assessment involves asking yourself such questions as (1) Why am I interested in this position? (2) How important is my work to me? (3) Do I have the necessary background for this job? (4) Could I grow into the position?

Many people look to their job to fulfill personal interests. For instance, a person who enjoyed doing research as a history major in college also might enjoy being a research assistant for an advertising firm. It is equally important to take stock of such personal qualities as motivation, intelligence, and sensitivity, because these directly affect your work behavior.

Do any of your personal accomplishments make you a viable candidate for a particular position? For instance, during your term as president of your son's school's Parent-Teacher Association, you probably demonstrated supervisory abilities that are applicable to a management position. Likewise, if you were responsible for financing your college education, you certainly demonstrated your ability to manage a budget.

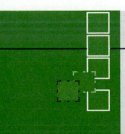

SKILL BUILDING

Preparing for Employment

As you prepare to write your resume and then to interview for jobs, take a few moments to write down your skills, work experience, accomplishments and honors, goals, and strengths and weaknesses.

1. Work experience: jobs, length of employment, skills used
2. Special skills: computer, languages, artistic (music, design)
3. Accomplishments and honors: work, school, community
4. Career goals
5. Strengths and weaknesses: oral and written communication, leadership, small-group work, motivation, dealing with stress, conflict resolution

Self-assessment forces you to realistically examine and evaluate your strengths and weaknesses. This internal review helps you to get a better sense of yourself and at the same time helps you to decide whether or not you are a good candidate for a particular job.

■ The Resume

A **resume** is a short account of one's qualifications for a particular position. The purpose of a resume is to present one's educational and experiential backgrounds, emphasizing his or her relation to the job under consideration. The resume requires thoughtful preparation and organization, because it is often a key factor in determining which applicants get interviews.

A carefully prepared resume should include the following information: (1) the applicant's name and current address, (2) current place of employment, (3) prior employment and related experience, (4) education/training, and (5) awards, honors, and professional recognition. In addition, the resume may include (1) activities and experiences that highlight leadership potential, (2) career goals, and (3) references. Figure 8.1 presents a sample resume.

■ The Cover Letter

The **cover letter** is a short letter that introduces you to a prospective employer. Its overall intent is to express your interest in the job and to create a positive first impression. To achieve this goal, the letter must be free of grammatical errors. Additionally, the cover letter should be tailored to the particular job vacancy. You want the organization or company to believe your letter is written expressly for them.

The first paragraph states your reasons for writing to the company. This is the place to indicate the specific position you are applying for and why you are applying for that position.

In the second and third paragraphs, explain your interest in the position and, more importantly, what you can do for the employer. Refer to specific professional or academic experiences, as well as job experiences, that contribute to your qualifications for the position. For instance, college courses in public relations and an internship at the county welfare department are details worth mentioning in a cover letter for a public relations position at the community hospital. This information gets the attention of those individuals who screen applications.

Next, refer to the enclosed or attached resume, which summarizes your training and experience. Also mention where the employer can check your credentials.

In the final paragraph, indicate your desire for a personal interview. You can suggest possible dates or simply indicate your flexibility. Remember, do what you can to encourage further communication. You may wish to call on a certain date to arrange an interview or to find out when a company representative plans to be in the area (such as on your college campus) so you can set up an interview then. Figure 8.2 presents an example of a cover letter.

In recent years, more and more companies are accepting applications (resumes and cover letters) via email. In addition, several websites allow you to post your resume for companies and recruiters to see and evaluate.

MARTIN GABRIEL SENDEJAS

6941 VAN BUREN AVE., WHARTON, OH 45863 • 419-321-0742 • CELL: 419-731-6931 • E-MAIL: mgsditto@hotmail.com

OBJECTIVE Electrical Engineering Technician

PROFESSIONAL PROFILE

- Enthusiastic, rising electrical engineering technology professional with relevant experience and expertise in use of high-tech equipment for analysis, documentation, and presentation; NC programming; computer hardware interface; and circuit design/PCB construction.
- Honest, reliable, punctual team player who exceeds expectations.
- Motivated achiever and problem-solver who will do what it takes to get the job done.
- Solid communicator who can explain technology in easy-to-understand terms; fluent in Spanish; studied nine years in a Spanish-speaking country.
- Computer-proficient in Windows, DOS, Linux/Unix, Microsoft Office (Word, PowerPoint, Excel), OrCAD, AutoCAD, Mathlab, Masm, D, C++, Visual Basic.

EDUCATION and TRAINING

- Bachelor of Science in Electrical Engineering Technology, Purdue University, Hammond, IN, May 2011; GPA: 3.43
  - Semester Honors for four consecutive semesters
  - Clare and Lucy Osterle Scholar
  - Harold C. Morgan Scholarship
- A+ Computer Service Technician, Computing Technology Industry Association

PROFESSIONAL EXPERIENCE

Sales Representative, Radio Shack, Lansing, IL, 08/2008–present
- Serve as electronics replacement and connectivity specialist.
- Assess customers in enhancing their in-home electronic devices.
- Increased sales by tailoring service to customers' needs and reducing amount of returned merchandise.

Maintenance Engineer, Holiday Inn, West Lafayette, IN, 08/2006–08/2008
- Juggled multiple responsibilities while maintaining hotel facility.
- Replaced and repaired electrical systems.
- Reorganized facility.
- Earned Worker of the Month Award, Sept. 2007.

Student, Purdue University, Hammond, IN, 08/2009–present
- Organized, planned, and built a Computer Numerical Control (CNC) machine that exceeded expectations and was considered one of the best projects of the semester.
- Conducted research to design, build, and test machine that drilled holes and could rout and engrave.

PROFESSIONAL AFFILIATIONS
- Member, IEEE

FIGURE 8.1 Sample Resume

6941 Van Buren Ave.
Wharton, OH 45863

January 15, 2010

Mr. Robert Gray, Staffing Specialist
Northern Electronics, Inc.
1605 Revere Street
Morton Grove, IL 60053

Dear Mr. Gray:

I am seeking a cooperative education or internship position in electrical engineering technology. Purdue University Calumet's Career Development Office informed me that Northern Electronics has several positions open for the Spring 2010 semester.

As you can see from my enclosed resume, I have extensive experience in electrical engineering technology from my studies at Purdue University Calumet and my work experience. I am fluent in Spanish and am computer-proficient in several software programs including AutoCAD, Masm, Windows, and Visual Basic. In my studies, I have earned a 3.43 grade point average while working part-time. I have received several scholarships and have earned semester honors for four consecutive semesters.

As an electronics replacement and connectivity specialist, I have experience with many different types of home and office electronics. I also have extensive experience with customer service. I am a member of IEEE.

I am available for employment beginning August 2010. I hope to complete an internship by June 2010 when I will earn my Bachelor of Science Degree in Electrical Engineering Technology. Please contact me at (419) 321-0742 or (419) 731-6931. My e-mail address is mgsditto@hotmail.com. I look forward to hearing from you soon.

Sincerely,

Martin G. Sendejas

enc.

FIGURE 8.2   Sample Cover Letter

■ Company Research

Finding out all you can about a particular company or organization will help you be better informed at the time of the interview. What kinds of things should you research? If the position is with a manufacturing company, learn about its products, the location of its plants, and the company's history, financial status, and growth potential. Websites like Vault.com and Wetfeet.com are designed especially for new college graduates and include company research, industry profiles, salary information, a day in the life, and much more. Other sources include websites such as Monster.com, Dice.com, and others that have already done the research for you. (See the Communication and Technology box on pages 162–163.)

Another sound practice is to conduct research in your field or discipline. Find out about such things as average starting salaries, trends, current and future problems, and what the work is like on a day-to-day basis.

■ The Interviewer

Ideally, a prospective employer comes to an interview prepared to ask pertinent questions of the applicant and to supply information about the company. In many instances, the interviewer alone determines whether or not the interviewee will be considered for the position. In a well-structured interview, the interviewer has a clear set of primary questions that constitute the body of the interview. Typical questions might include "What prompted you to apply for a job with our company?" "On your application you state that you have work-related experience. Would you please elaborate?" "What are your career goals?" "What qualities do you possess that would convince me to hire you over applicants with similar training for this position?" The interviewee's responses to these questions can be revealing; from them the employer assesses the applicant's general knowledge, ability to communicate, prior achievements, ambitions for the future, and suitability for the job. Table 8.1 lists some of the most popular questions interviewers ask in an employment interview.

TABLE 8.1   Possible Employment Interview Questions

1. Tell me about yourself.

2. Describe your work experience at _____.

3. Why did you decide on _____ field of study?

4. Why do you want to work in this industry?

5. How do you describe success?

6. What motivates you to do your best work?

7. What are your short-term goals?

8. What are your long-term goals?

9. What is your greatest strength?

10. Provide an example of how you used this strength to succeed.

11. What is your greatest weakness?

12. How has this weakness hindered your success?

13. How has your education at _____ prepared you for this position?

14. What about this position excites you the most?

15. Why did you apply to this company?

IMPROVING YOUR INTERVIEWING SKILLS

Anxiety and nervousness are common reactions to an impending employment interview. To a degree, relief is possible by immersing ourselves in the process, that is, by concentrating on the questions generated by the interviewer and by applying specific communication skills to our responses. These skills include effective listening, ethics, language, effective nonverbal communication, and asking questions. Although these topics are treated in previous chapters, their specific application to the employment interview is discussed in the following subsections.

■ Listening

Without question, listening is an important aspect of the interview. Effective listening requires that we do two things: (1) listen closely to detect the exact nature of the interview questions, and (2) listen to the interviewer's responses to our answers in order to gauge how well we are doing in the session, to learn more about what is important to the interviewer, and to be able to keep conversing intelligently. Be sure to use the listening skills we described in Chapter 3: paraphrasing, interpreting, and questioning. These skills will help you check your perceptions of the interviewer and the questions he or she is asking.

Communication and TECHNOLOGY
The Internet and the Job Hunt

The Internet is a wonderful tool for finding a job. Whether you are looking to change jobs or for your first job, the Internet can provide many kinds of information. For example, with a few clicks of the mouse, you can find information on resume writing (via regular mail or via email), company research, and job postings. Some websites offer forums and chatrooms for job seekers to network and share stories and advice. Here are a few helpful general sites:

1. Monster.com. This site offers information on every aspect of the job search. It can even match your qualifications with jobs posted by employers. It is useful for all types of careers and majors.

2. Collegegrad.com. This site is similar to Monster.com in that it offers general information on the job search. Collegegrad.com, however, is geared toward entry-level jobs. First-time job seekers will find specific information on how to prepare for the first job.

3. Careerbuilder.com. This site offers job listings nationally and internationally. Over one million jobs are listed and can be searched by location, industry, field, or specific job title.

There are also sites dedicated to specific fields or careers. Some of these include:

1. Healthcarejobsite.com is for nursing, medical professions, and pharmaceuticals.

2. Careerbank.com posts positions in accounting, banking, and other finance jobs.

3. Dice.com specializes in high-tech engineering and information technology positions.

Used with permission of Collegegrad.com

4. abcteachingjobs.com contains information on teacher certification by state and also job postings for elementary and secondary school teachers.

5. eLabRat.com posts jobs in science and chemistry and offers information about resume writing and interviewing for science-related jobs.

6. TalentZoo.com offers advice and job listings for job seekers in communication areas such as advertising, marketing, public relations, and media.

7. Hospitalityonline.com specializes in jobs with hotels, resorts, and restaurants.

8. Salesjobs.com is dedicated to sales professionals.

One of our chief concerns in an interview is to be able to provide intelligent answers to interview questions. In order to do so, we must first understand the question. Listening closely to the interviewer is essential; however, a second step is sometimes warranted—asking for clarification when we do not fully understand what the interviewer wants. For example, to make sure that we are on target, we might paraphrase an interviewer's question this way: "Am I interpreting your question correctly? You want me to explain what steps I would take to correct an employee's chronic tardiness?" When the interviewer confirms that we have understood the question correctly, we feel comfortable offering our response.

Following our answer, the interviewer may make some comments before moving on to the next question. Listening to this feedback is just as important as listening to the questions themselves, because it provides us with clues concerning our performance. For instance, if the interviewer clearly misunderstands our reply, we need to clarify our position in order to eliminate the misunderstanding. This problem can be rectified only if we are listening closely to the feedback being given.

Finally, by listening carefully to the interviewer's questions and feedback, we can avoid asking questions or making comments about something that has already been mentioned in the interview. When we are nervous, this happens more frequently. The key here is to shift the focus away from ourselves (that is, our preoccupation about how stressful this interview is) to the other party, to pay close attention to the interviewer's message.

■ Ethics

One of our objectives during an interview is to present an honest picture of ourselves. This requires that we represent our skills accurately and that we take responsibility for any difficulties that we may have had in previous jobs. Misrepresentation of skills or experiences threatens both the likelihood that we will be selected for the position and, if we are selected, the chances of maintaining our employment. Consider the following:

> Sean has just graduated with a degree in public relations. He secured several internships and feels well qualified to write press releases and create brochures and other print promotional materials. He tells a prospective employer at the local finance company that he has web page design experience in order to appear better qualified for the job; despite his misrepresentation of the facts, Sean lands the position. Two months later he is asked to create a new web page for the personnel department. It becomes immediately apparent to Sean's boss that Sean misrepresented his abilities during the job interview. Sean has jeopardized his employment with the firm.

During the interview, questions may be raised about our reasons for leaving a previous job. It is best to offer straightforward responses to such questions: "I saw no place to advance within the company's structure. After four years I grew tired of doing the same job day after day. I needed a change to feel self-motivated again." "I found myself increasingly frustrated by the unresolved problems and tension between my supervisor and myself. Because I saw no sign of improvement for the future, I decided to find another job." Avoid placing the blame on other parties; it suggests a weakness on your part, an inability to adequately work through difficulties with others.

■ Language

Answering interview questions with direct, precise language communicates both a knowledge of the subject and a confidence in our own abilities. Precise language, especially terminology related to a specific occupation or profession, demonstrates our familiarity with the field: "I've worked with children at two preschools during the past seven years. In my opinion, a preschool curriculum should stress the development of gross motor skills, socialization skills, and reading readiness skills." Furthermore, being able to provide direct, concrete explanations communicates our self-assurance: "Reading readiness includes teaching such concepts as letter recognition and sounds, numbers, left and right, and sequencing (first, second, third)." Conversely, vague or general responses indicate a lack of knowledge or expertise and an apparently weaker job candidate. The lesson here is to know the subject and to show the interviewer that we know the subject by expressing ourselves with appropriate language.

■ Nonverbal Communication

Nonverbal communication can indicate our level of confidence within the interviewing situation. When we are nervous, for example, we communicate our discomfort not only through our verbal responses, but also through our nonverbal behavior. Signs of discomfort include averting our eyes each time the interviewer looks directly at us, repeated shifting in our seat, wringing our hands, and forced smiles.

In an employment interview, we want our nonverbal communication to support our other efforts to appear confident in the interaction. In other words, our effort to listen carefully to the interviewer's questions and comments can be accompanied by our effort to maintain direct eye contact. If we look away when the interviewer speaks to us, we will seem nervous and uninvolved. Likewise, our verbal replies to interview questions can benefit from appropriate gestures and paralanguage. For example, when we talk enthusiastically about our career goals, we can add to that positive image by using hand gestures, by increasing the rate of our speech, and by raising the pitch of our voice. (Chapter 5 has an in-depth discussion of these and other nonverbal communication behaviors.)

■ Ask Questions

At the end of the interview, you will probably be asked if you have any questions for the recruiter. It is essential that you ask at least two questions to show you are prepared and interested in the position. These questions can illustrate that you have thoroughly researched the company and that you are motivated to know more about the interviewer and the position. Table 8.2 lists some possible questions you might ask during or at the close of an employment interview.

TABLE 8.2   Questions to Ask the Recruiter

1. What qualities do you want this employee to have?

2. How are employees evaluated and how often?

3. Why do you like working here?

4. What are the most positive aspects of working for _____?

5. What types of orientation or training do new employees receive?

6. Are there any opportunities for me to continue my education?

7. Based on my research. I noticed that this company did over $20 million in sales last year. How do you think the downturn in the economy will effect sales this year?

8. What are the opportunities for growth and advancement in this department?

9. How is the company responding to growing competition from _____?

10. Would you tell me what specific responsibilities I would have in this position?

Serving Your COMMUNITY   Interviewing Skills

In an effort to practice your interviewing skills and recognize different perspectives, do the following:

1. Volunteer for two hours at your local senior citizen community center as well as at your local high school. Before you leave each location, identify a resident of the senior citizen community center and a student from the high school. Please interview each person on the historic election of Barack Obama.

2. Develop a set of open and closed questions for each of the following categories:

   a. The impact of the election on the local community.

   b. The impact of the election on the country.

   c. The impact of the election on the world community.

3. How did this process help you appreciate difference and develop questions for different demographic groups?

SUMMARY

An interview is a planned interaction between two parties in which questions are asked by an interviewer and answers are provided by an interviewee. The interview consists of a variety of questions. Generally, each question can be classified as open or closed, primary or secondary, and neutral or leading. Open questions are designed to give the interviewee maximum latitude in formulating an answer, whereas the purpose of closed questions is to elicit specific feedback. Primary questions focus on the major concerns of the interviewer; secondary questions serve as a follow-up and are designed to gain additional information from the interviewee. Neutral questions reveal nothing of the interviewer's biases, preferences, or expectations; leading questions are designed to move the interview in a specific direction.

The basic structure of an interview is similar to that of a speech: Both have an opening, a body, and a closing. The opening begins the interview and sets the tone for the interaction. The body is the heart of the interview; it is where the questions are asked and the responses are given.

In the closing, the interviewer draws the session to an end, hopefully on a positive note.

Two types of interviews are especially significant: the informational interview and the employment interview. The purpose of an informational interview is to acquire facts about a specific subject. Generally, the most effective way to prepare for this type of interview is to develop an objective, research the topic, and plan the interview questions.

In an employment interview, the interviewer's goal is to uncover pertinent information about potential employees in order to select a qualified candidate; the interviewee's goal is to find out more about the position and to persuade the employer to hire him or her. The employer should be ready to supply information about the vacancy and the company offering the position. Before the interview, applicants should take the time to assess their employment potential, compile a well-structured resume, write a solid cover letter, research the company, and evaluate the interviewer's perspective on the process. There are specific ways to reduce anxiety and at the same time improve our communication in employment interviews. These skills include active listening, honesty, using direct language, using effective nonverbal communication, and asking questions.

REVIEW QUESTIONS

1. What is the difference between a primary and secondary question? Open and closed? Leading and neutral?
2. Explain the three ways to structure the body of an interview.
3. What steps are involved in preparing for an informational interview?
4. Why is it necessary to do a self-assessment?
5. What is the primary goal of a cover letter?
6. What specific communication skills can you use to improve your interviewing effectiveness?

KEY CONCEPTS

interview
interviewer
interviewee
open questions
closed questions

primary questions
secondary questions
neutral questions
leading questions
opening

body
closing
informational interview
resume
cover letter

CHAPTER 9

Communicating in Small Groups

AFTER STUDYING THIS CHAPTER, YOU SHOULD

understand

- definition of small-group communication.
- different types of groups.
- importance of norms, roles, cohesiveness, commitment, and arrangement to small-group communication.
- four phases a small group goes through to reach a decision.

be able to

- use the four decision-making methods.
- apply three communication techniques to improve your participation within a small group.

Most groups are formed to solve problems. At Sheldon Advertising, Brenda Sheldon has assembled a group of her employees to create a strategic plan for improving work performance for the coming year. The members of this special group have been selected by Brenda and reflect the different units within the company. The participants include the following:

Hannah, who represents the marketing unit, is an Irish American whose parents were born in Ireland, but she was born in the United States. Her ethnic background has greatly influenced the way she sees the world. She earned her college degree in communication and has worked at Sheldon Advertising for six years. Hannah is excited about being in this group. She has several ideas about how the marketing unit can expand and grow.

Mark, who represents the creative unit, is relatively new to the company. He is African American and earned his degree in art and design just two years ago. He feels somewhat uncomfortable being a part of this group. He hopes he can learn more about the advertising business by listening to his colleagues.

Raquel, who represents the accounting unit, has been at Sheldon Advertising for 12 years. She has a masters degree in accounting and heads the accounting unit. She would rather not be part of this group because she is uncomfortable working with others. She would rather work alone at her computer. Raquel damaged her hearing in an accident last year and has difficulty hearing when she is in small groups.

Darren, who represents the sales unit, loves to work in groups, and Brenda has asked him to lead the group in its initial discussions. He is usually the leader of any group he belongs to and believes he will be able to guide this group to create a brilliant strategic plan. His outgoing personality and overall confidence allow him to communicate with ease interpersonally and in groups.

At their first meeting, Darren asks the members to develop personal goals for next year. He then asks each member, one by one, to read aloud their goals. He actively listens to every participant and lets all members have an equal voice in the discussion, thus creating a positive communication climate. Hannah, Mark, and Raquel feel as if they are a vital and important part of the group because of Darren's communication.

■ ■ ■ ■ ■

Clearly, despite their different approaches to group communication and their perceptions of themselves and their co-workers, they are able to function very well as a group. This chapter discusses small-group communication and how our diverse approaches to it influence the overall effectiveness of the small-group process.

In the previous chapters, we discussed intrapersonal and interpersonal communication. Everything we have learned up to now is relevant to small-group discussion. Specifically, understanding the differences among people will help us function effectively in a group setting.

The complexities of small-group communication make it a fascinating area to study. Because so much of our time is spent in small groups, acquiring skills in this area will help increase our confidence and self-esteem. By participating in small groups, we have an opportunity to learn a great deal about ourselves, especially from the feedback other group members provide. At the same time, our participation increases both our understanding of how others communicate and our general knowledge of various issues and topics.

AN OVERVIEW OF SMALL-GROUP COMMUNICATION

Our lives are filled with group activities: business meetings, dinners with friends, bowling teams, study groups that review for midterms and finals, bridge games, community service, and planning committee meetings. Communicating in small groups requires special understanding and skill.

The dynamics of small-group communication are vastly different from those of either *dyadic* communication (two parties) or public communication (speaker and audience). Although small-group communication retains some of the spontaneity of interpersonal communication, it has the added pressure associated with interacting in public.

Small-group communication involves a small number of people who share a common goal or objective and interact face to face. Most small groups are composed of three to eight members, with five being the optimum number. Face-to-face communication means that people interact with each other on a personal level, either verbally or nonverbally; it is not enough to simply be designated a "member" of a group. A common goal or purpose binds the group together. Consider the shared purpose of individuals charged with raising money for the youth soccer league. This shared goal contributes to an overall feeling of belonging to the group. Finally, efforts to meet a goal or reach a decision demand that members work cooperatively. At various times during a group's interactions, individuals voice their suggestions or ideas; their comments or actions end up influencing the group as a whole.

In this chapter we shall discuss several aspects of small-group communication, ranging from types of small groups, to variables of the group process, to decision-making methods, to our verbal and nonverbal participation in small groups. The concepts covered in preceding chapter—perception, listening, verbal communication, nonverbal communication, understanding relationships, and building a positive communication climate—determine to a large degree how successfully we communicate in small groups. The relationship between these factors and small-group communication will become more apparent as you read this chapter.

TYPES OF SMALL GROUPS

Small-group communication occurs in a variety of situations, ranging from loosely structured social gatherings to highly structured public presentations. You may participate in groups in this class or other classes, at work, or socially. All groups are formed to meet a specific goal or objective. There are four types of groups: knowledge-gaining, personal growth, social, and problem-solving.

Knowledge-gaining groups come together to learn or experience new things. The members may even come together to gain or improve a skill. For example, a painting class, the Young Republicans, soccer teams, and book clubs are formed to help the members share knowledge and learn. **Personal growth groups** focus on the individual and his or her personal well-being. The members come together to support one another as each person struggles with personal challenges. Counseling or therapy groups could be considered personal growth groups. Yoga classes, Alcoholics Anonymous, and health support groups such as Y-Me (for breast cancer survivors) are examples of personal growth groups. The purpose of **social groups** is not to solve problems or accomplish specific tasks, but to interact with others on an informal basis and to maintain interpersonal relationships. Members may meet once a week to play softball, watch and discuss a film, or meet for a drink after work. Finally, **problem-solving groups**, also called **task-oriented groups**, come together to answer a question or provide a solution to a problem. Most groups formed at the workplace are considered problem-solving groups. Your group may have to manage a budget, hire a new employee, or create new rules for workplace behavior. We will discuss problem-solving groups in more detail in Chapter 10.

One important note: Groups can fit into one or more of these categories. For example:

> Bonita has always been an active person. She loved to play sports such as volleyball and soccer. Last year she had an automobile accident that left her unable to do many of the things she once loved to do. Her doctor suggested she enroll in a water aerobics class in order to exercise her muscles. During the first few classes, Bonita met two other women who were also in automobile accidents. The three women became close friends and now go out for coffee after each class.

In Bonita's case, her water aerobics class could be categorized as a knowledge-gaining group (coming together to learn new things), a personal growth group (each member dealing with personal struggles), and a social group (maintaining interpersonal relationships).

Personal growth groups, like this yoga class, focus on each person's well-being.

EMBRACING DIFFERENCE

Group Norms

Cindy works for AU Yukomo Electronics, an international technology company. The company had a retreat for executives in Las Vegas on building customer relations. She attended meetings with two different leaders the first day of the conference. Raúl, the leader of the first group, expected participants to speak up equally during the workshop. Ursula, the leader of the second group, employed a different approach to group behavior. She believed that participants should play multiple roles within a group, such as task and maintenance roles.

Cindy wanted to do her best at these meetings. The knowledge of Raúl's and Ursula's small-group communication strategies impacted the way she behaved in both meetings.

1. How does Cindy's awareness of different approaches to norms and roles in small groups enhance her skill as a communicator?

2. How can Cindy's experience help you when you are a member of a small group?

VARIABLES IN SMALL-GROUP COMMUNICATION

What factors contribute to the communication that takes place in a small group? This section explores a number of variables affecting group communication, namely, norms, roles, cohesiveness, commitment, and arrangement.

■ Norms

In part, the communication behavior of small groups centers around **norms,** rules that dictate how group members ought to behave. Whether these norms are implied or openly expressed, they often provide a basis for predicting the behavior of group members. Consider the following:

> During the first few class meetings, Chris noticed that his sociology instructor, Dr. Vasquez, ignored students who asked questions without raising their hands. As Chris actively listened to Dr. Vasquez's lecture on racism and the economy during the third week of class, he had several questions about the membership of labor unions and the unions' ability to speak for minority issues. Chris shouts out questions in his other classes, but he knows Dr. Vasquez will not answer his questions if he does not raise his hand.

Chris understands that a norm for his sociology class is to raise his hand in order to have a question answered by his instructor.

■ Roles

Roles are a set of expected behaviors each member of the group must follow. Think about the roles you may play in your life today. Are you a friend? Parent? Supervisor? If you are reading this book, you have probably taken on the role of a student. As a student, you are expected to study, attend class, participate in class discussion, and so on. Members of every group also play a role or roles. Specifically, there are three types of roles we can play. These are task, maintenance, and dysfunctional or negative roles.

We play **task roles** when we are concerned about meeting the group's goal or objective. We are focused primarily on getting the job done or the task completed. Beebe and Masterson summarized the types of roles we can play (2006, p. 82).

Initiator/contributor	Proposes new ideas or approaches to group problem solving; may suggest a different approach to procedure or organizing the problem-solving task.
Information seeker	Asks for clarification of suggestions; also asks for facts or other information that may help the group deal with the issues at hand.
Opinion seeker	Asks for clarification of the values and opinions expressed by other group members.
Information giver	Provides facts, examples, statistics, and other evidence that pertain to the problem the group is attempting to solve.
Opinion giver	Offers beliefs or opinions about the ideas under discussion.

Elaborator/clarifier	Provides examples based on his or her experience or the experience of others that help to show how an idea or suggestion would work if the group accepted a particular course of action.
Coordinator	Tries to clarify and note relationships among the ideas and suggestions that have been provided by others.
Orienter/summarizer	Attempts to summarize what has occurred and tries to keep the group focused on the task at hand.
Evaluator/critic	Makes an effort to judge the evidence and conclusions that the group suggests.
Energizer	Tries to spur the group to action and attempts to motivate and stimulate the group to greater productivity.
Procedural technician	Helps the group achieve its goal by performing tasks such as distributing papers, rearranging the seating, or running errands for the group.
Recorder	Writes down suggestions and ideas of others; makes a record of the group's progress.

Maintenance roles deal with the relationships within the group. When we play a maintenance role, we are concerned about other people's feelings, creating a positive communication climate, and solving or mediating conflicts (Beebe & Masterson, 2006, p. 82).

Encourager	Offers praise, understanding, and acceptance of others' ideas and suggestions.
Harmonizer	Mediates disagreements among group members.
Compromiser	Attempts to resolve conflicts by trying to find an acceptable solution to disagreements among group members.
Gatekeeper and expediter	Encourages less talkative group members to participate and tries to limit lengthy contributions of other group members.
Standard setter	Helps to set standards and goals for the group.
Group observer	Keeps records of the group's process and uses the information that is gathered to evaluate the group's procedures.
Follower	Basically goes along with the suggestions and ideas of other group members; serves as an audience in group 3discussions and decision making.

Individual roles can hinder the group's ability to meet its goal or objective. Individual roles interfere with the task and maintenance roles because the group member is more interested in him- or herself than in the overall welfare of the group.

Aggressor	Destroys or deflates the status of other group members; may try to take credit for someone else's contributions.
Blocker	Is generally negative, stubborn, and disagreeable without apparent reason.
Recognition seeker	Seeks the spotlight by boasting and reporting on his or her personal achievements.
Self-confessor	Uses the group as an audience to report personal feelings, insights, and observations.
Dominator	Makes an effort to assert authority by manipulating group members or attempting to take over the entire group; may use flattery or assertive behaviors to dominate the discussion.
Help seeker	Tries to evoke a sympathetic response from others; often expresses insecurity or feelings of low self-worth.
Special interest pleader	Works to serve an individual need; speaks for a special group or organization that best fits his or her own biases (Beebe & Masterson, 2006, p. 84).
Joker/clown	Makes little effort to participate in the task; uses inappropriate humor, sarcasm, or other distracting communication.

ETHICS in Communication

Understanding Group Roles

Within a small group, each member will play several roles at any given time. We may play a take, maintenance, or individual role throughout the group process. If we take a look at the beginning of the chapter, we can see that each member will have a significant impact on the group and the group's ability to create a strategic plan for improving work performance.

Hannah likes to work in groups and is eager to offer her ideas. Mark, unlike Hannah, is shy and a bit unsure of himself. He is energetic and eager to learn new things. Raquel is uncomfortable working in a group and would much rather work alone. She does not want to be in this group and states it clearly. Darren, the appointed leader of the group, loves working in groups and is

excited for the challenge of developing a plan. The success and failure of the group will rest on his ability to motivate and guide the group. As you think about these group members, answer the following questions:

1. What specific roles do you think Hannah, Mark, Raquel, and Darren will play in their small-group discussions? Why?

2. What special roles would each not play? Why?

3. What communication principles discussed in Chapters 1–8 should each character practice if they want the group to be successful?

4. Have you ever been in a small group? What roles did you play?

A breakdown in group cohesiveness can lead to conflict.

■ Cohesiveness

Cohesiveness is a demonstrated sense of purpose within a group. A cohesive group works together as a unit to solve problems, reach goals, or accomplish a specified task. Cohesiveness develops as individuals in the group become more committed to a project, as they get to know one another better, and as trust among them grows. For example, individuals serving together on a committee for the first time are likely to be reserved with one another. If, however, during their subsequent interactions they recognize the shared purpose among themselves, they will likely proceed with renewed enthusiasm. Decisions can be reached more easily this way. The importance of cohesiveness is evident in a group's accomplishments; generally speaking, the achievements are greater in a group that works cooperatively. Without cohesiveness, the task may take longer and more conflicts may occur during discussions.

■ Commitment

Commitment, the motivation of members to meet the goals of the group, also plays a significant role in the outcome of small-group interactions. Are the members genuinely committed to the stated goals of the group? Do they identify with the values expounded by the group? If the answer to these questions is yes, then the members are likely to be more productive and work as a cohesive unit. For example:

Seven elementary school teachers are charged with studying a plan to implement a computer curriculum in grades one through three. Five of the seven teachers (Jan, Maria, Cara, Eli, Doug) are enthusiastic about the idea; as a result, they devote considerable energy to writing their recommendations to the school administration. They engage in thoughtful discussion and actively listen to each other's ideas and suggestions. The remaining two members (Rose and Cecilia) have little interest in the project, which is apparent by their minimal participation during meetings. Rose and Cecilia do not hinder the others from completing the task, but they do not help either.

Commitment, then, can energize or renew a group's interest in achieving a goal.

There are some potential drawbacks to commitment. First, we are often blind to others' viewpoints because we are convinced that ours is the best (and only) way. Second, when we are committed to a project, there is a tendency to try to persuade others to see things as we do. At times the pressure we apply is overbearing.

■ Arrangement

Another variable that affects group participation is the communication **arrangement,** the physical placement of the individuals within the group. Is everyone sitting in rows, around a conference table, or on the floors and couches in someone's living room? Many groups meet virtually using the Internet. Meeting online through chat rooms, instant messaging, video, and email can greatly impact the effectiveness of the small group. Be sure that everyone in the group has access to the needed technology and understands the logistics of meeting via technology. See the Communication and Technology box on page 184 for more information.

Often the placement of individuals in the group determines the amount of interaction that takes place. For example, if a group is arranged in a row, direct eye contact is limited, especially for those who are seated at either end of the row. Dialogue is generally limited to those sitting next to one another. Interaction is increased when members are able to see each other better. When we have a better view of those we are talking to, it is easier for us to detect the feedback others send and alter our message, if necessary. Having group members seated in a half-wheel or circle facilitates direct eye contact and greater participation among everyone.

The variables in small-group communication are defined in Table 9.1.

TABLE 9.1	Variables in Small-Group Communication
Norms	Rules that dictate how group members ought to behave.
Roles	Set of expected behaviors each member of the group must follow.
Cohesiveness	Demonstrated sense of purpose within a group.
Commitment	Motivation of the members to meet the goals of the group.
Arrangement	Physical placement of the individuals within the group.

PARTICIPATING IN SMALL-GROUP DISCUSSIONS

Thousands of groups meet each day to discuss issues and make decisions. Asking a small group of individuals to solve a problem or come up with a strategic plan suggests a belief that collectively a better decision can be reached than by asking an individual to do the same thing. Of course, this is not true for all types of decisions. Some decisions are highly personal, such as the brand of toothpaste we choose or the kind of car seat we purchase for our child. However, participating in small-group decision making can be more effective if we understand that every group decision is reached as a result of going through specific phases.

■ Phases of a Discussion

Every small-group decision is a process that goes through several phases. In order to become better participants in the process, it is helpful to recognize that decision making is frequently a slow, frustrating exercise that requires considerable patience and tolerance. In the subsections that follow we shall explore four phases of the decision-making process of a small group: orientation, conflict, emergence, and reinforcement (for a detailed discussion, see Beebe & Masterson, 2006). Although groups may go through each of the phases, they may not do so in a linear fashion. In other words, groups often retreat to earlier stages before moving through all stages. Furthermore, a basic understanding of these phases provides a framework for the skills discussed in the final section of this chapter.

Orientation Phase

During the **orientation phase,** or the beginning of a group discussion, members are chiefly concerned about establishing a comfortable social climate. Dialogue is apt to be guarded and superficial as members pay particular attention to "getting along" with everyone. This is also a time for individuals to become acquainted with the subject about to be discussed. For example:

> The library administration appoints a five-person committee to decide how to spend an additional $100,000 on library materials during the remaining two months of the fiscal year. At the initial meeting the committee members discuss the circumstances surrounding the acquired funds and voice their pleasure at being involved in this assignment. Everyone is in agreement that they can work out an equitable way to spend the allotted money. One member says, "I feel as if we've hit the Powerball lottery! I can't wait to spend this money."

Conflict Phase

As ideas begin to surface regarding the decision making, it is natural for disagreement and tension to surface as well. This stage is known as the **conflict phase.** It would be unrealistic to expect a group to reach a decision without first experiencing conflict. The degree of conflict, however, varies from one group to the next and influences how much time is spent in this particular phase of the process. Our tolerance during this phase is particularly important (more on this in the final section of this chapter).

As individuals become passionate about their ideas and coalitions (subgroups) start to develop, the interaction becomes less inhibited. When individuals align themselves for or against a particular proposal, tension intensifies the differences of opinion.

> The library committee is now splintered into two coalitions, each having a vastly different idea about what kinds of materials and equipment to purchase. One group proposes that the majority of the money be used to purchase print materials: "The library should maintain its image as an institution that provides books on all subjects." The other group favors audiovisual materials: "We disagree. The patrons who use the library today want to check out compact discs, DVDs, and computer software."

How will they be able to resolve this problem?

Emergence Phase

As discussion continues, most groups grow anxious to reach a decision. This stage is called the **emergence phase.** In an effort to reach a consensus, there is a tendency among those members who expressed dissent during the conflict phase to now take a more ambiguous stand. These individuals attempt to disengage themselves from the passionate stands taken just a short time ago, but at the same time they avoid embracing the opposing position wholeheartedly. Ambiguity replaces passion as a modified form of dissent. As coalitions dissolve and dissent weakens, there is a gradual shift toward an apparent decision. Let us look once again at our library committee:

> A decision to purchase more audiovisual material is gaining favor. Those who voiced strong opposition during the conflict phase now make ambiguous comments about the same proposal. These comments reflect a shift in attitude from dissent to resigned acceptance: "The public would probably react enthusiastically to a larger collection of feature-film DVDs."

Reinforcement Phase

In the final phase of the decision-making process, consensus is achieved; this is called the **reinforcement phase.** Members typically reinforce their positive feelings concerning the decision and also show their support of one another. Dissent all but vanishes.

> The members of the library committee applaud their efforts and state that they acted on behalf of the public which they serve: "Our patrons will be thrilled with all the new materials we've agreed to purchase. Everyone on the committee did a terrific job."

TABLE 9.2   Phases of a Discussion

Orientation phase	A time for establishing a comfortable communication climate and becoming familiar with the topic.
Conflict phase	Disagreements surface; tension is a natural by-product.
Emergence phase	There is a gradual shift toward an apparent decision.
Reinforcement phase	Consensus is achieved; dissent all but vanishes.

The example of the library committee used throughout this discussion of orientation, conflict, emergence, and reinforcement phases is idealistic; few group discussions go so smoothly. Even the most heated, emotionally tense discussions, however, proceed through these phases. In the final section of this chapter we will learn skills to help us cope with the frustrations of small-group discussions and to help us successfully participate in the process.

Small-group discussion phases are summarized in Table 9.2.

DECISION–MAKING METHODS

As we have said, most groups find it difficult to reach a decision, especially one that every member agrees is the best decision. According to Brilhart, Galanes, and Adams (2001), the three most used methods are (1) decision by leader, (2) decision by majority vote, and (3) decision by consensus. Let's look at the different options your group has for reaching a final decision.

Decision by the leader of the group is quick and simple. This may be appropriate when time is of the essence or for routine decisions. There are several disadvantages, however. This method may cause resentment, lowered cohesiveness, half-hearted support for the decision, and an unwillingness to contribute to future group decisions (Brilhart, Galanes, & Adams, 2001, pp. 283–284).

Decision by majority vote is democracy in action. Every member of the group gets a chance to vote for a decision, and the decision with the most votes is chosen as the group's final decision. This method is quick because only a simple raising of hands or saying of "yea" or "nay" is required. The disadvantage is that there will be members of the group who will lose. They may feel their ideas were not given a fair hearing. This may cause cohesiveness and commitment to suffer and may hurt the overall productivity of the group.

Decision by consensus is the genuine agreement among members that an appropriate decision has been made; it is not the result of pressure applied by others in the group. If, for instance, members of a group, as a result of peer pressure, feel they must agree with a decision, then a true consensus has not been achieved. A consensus allows the group to reach closure on an issue or to complete the group's task. A group should be careful to avoid at least the following two things when engaged in the decision-making process: (1) making premature

OK, THE BOARD HAS FINALLY COME TO A CONSENSUS HERE...

TWO LARGE PEPPERONI'S ON THIN CRUST, WITH LIGHT CHEESE AND EXTRA SAUCE...

THE EFFICIENCY OF COMMITTEE MANAGEMENT

10-14

©1997 Wiley Miller/ dist. by Washington Post Writers Group
http://www.wileytoons.com
E-mail: wiley@wileytoons.com

decisions and (2) succumbing to pressures to conform. A premature decision often indicates a lack of analysis by the group. Many sides of an issue or decision need to be explored before a consensus is reached. Sometimes individuals feel pressured to comply with a stand taken by other members who are in positions of power (see Chapter 6). We have all experienced instances when we have felt it is wiser to agree with a supervisor, parent, teacher, or some other person in authority than to subject ourselves to their displeasure. Our agreement does not constitute a true consensus.

One other concern when trying to achieve consensus is groupthink. **Groupthink** is the illusion of consensus among the group members (Beebe & Materson, 2006; Cline, 1990). When there is too much consensus, groups may stop critically analyzing ideas, suggestions, and decisions. Members begin to believe that the group is "invincible" and that any decision made by the group will be a good one. We can avoid groupthink by critically analyzing all ideas and by using our responsive listening skills, such as paraphrasing, interpreting, and especially, questioning.

COMMUNICATION SKILLS WITHIN SMALL GROUPS

Small-group communication challenges our ability to communicate effectively with others. It requires that we make constant adjustments to the various personalities within the group, that we exert a special effort to make our message understood by others, and that we, in turn, strive to understand the views held by other individuals in the group. Furthermore, the potential for conflict and communication breakdowns is substantially higher in small groups than it is in one-to-one encounters. This is particularly true for task-oriented or problem-solving groups, where ideas are apt to clash. Fortunately, we can overcome these obstacles by applying specific skills in the areas of verbal and nonverbal participation and by maintaining a positive communication climate.

■ Verbal Participation

As a member of a small group, each of us has an obligation to let others know our ideas or positions regarding a specific topic. While the degree of participation varies with each member, it is important to remember that a lack of participation fails to serve the best interests of the group. Sometimes groups are dominated by one person who tries to monopolize the conversation. What can be done to

COMMUNICATION IN ACTION

Communication Skills within Small Groups

1. Begin by forming an even number of small groups (one group should be designated A and another B), each with five members. Have each group select one of the following topics to discuss:

   a. Should a city's public funds be used to purchase and display a Nativity scene?

   b. Should smoking be prohibited on campus?

   c. Should we allow government law enforcement agencies to lessen our free speech in order to step terrorism?

   d. Do television commercial that advocate the use of condoms for "safe sex" erode the morality of our nation?

2. Group A discusses its selected topic for 20 minutes. Members should concentrate on practicing the communication skills discussed in the previous section: verbal participation, nonverbal participation, and maintaining a positive communication climate. During this discussion, each member of group B observes one member of group A. (Note: These pairings should be decided prior to the discussion.)

3. At the end of 20 minutes, members of group B begin discussing their topic. Group A observes their communication skills.

4. At the conclusion of the second discussion, each set of partners from group A and group B meets to give each other feedback on their participation within the group. Use empathy and descriptive language when communicating with your partner.

5. How can practicing small-group communication skills in the above activity increase your confidence as a communicator?

remedy this situation? To steer the attention away from this person, one can ask someone else in the group a pointed question, such as "What course of action would you suggest?" or "How will the proposed schedule affect people who work in your department?"

Questions serve many purposes: (1) They maintain your involvement in the group discussion, (2) they can refocus the group's attention or provide direction for a discussion that has strayed from the main points, and (3) they can be used to draw other members of the group into the discussion, especially quiet members. Any group member can use the technique of asking questions to improve the quality of the interaction.

As this woman is doing here, by 2012 millions of us will be working in virtual teams or groups.

Nonverbal Participation

Another way to communicate our feelings is through nonverbal participation. Perhaps the most effective nonverbal behavior is that which communicates our agreement with or support of an idea. The simple act of nodding our head or smiling when someone makes a humorous comment offers encouragement to the person who is speaking. When we perceive another group member's nonverbal signals as negative (that is, a head shaking no, a glaring look, or eyes directed away from the person talking), there are specific actions we can take. One method is to ask the person why he or she disagrees with what is being said or proposed to the group. Another similar method is to confront the person about his or her negative nonverbal communication by saying something along these lines: "I noticed you shaking your head a moment ago. Are you having a difficult time understanding or accepting my proposal? I'll try to clarify my position if you want." The person's response to our comments and questions will indicate whether we have perceived this person accurately; then we can proceed accordingly.

Maintain a Positive Communication Climate

A positive communication climate, discussed at length in Chapter 7, encourages discussion among group members. During the orientation phase of a group discussion, the climate is likely to remain positive; however, this is not always the case during the conflict phase. As individuals begin to take sides on an issue or proposal, the climate can quickly change. Our efforts to reduce defensiveness can restore a positive climate and at the same time improve the overall interaction.

The group process is disrupted when one or two people dominate the discussion and others begin to withdraw from it. How do we combat this? When a group discussion deteriorates to the point where individuals resort to name calling or threaten to walk out, we can remind everyone involved to avoid personal attacks on others. Instead, the discussion should focus on the issue at hand. We also can remind group members to allow others to voice their opinions without being interrupted. This forces us to listen attentively. If we have any questions, we can ask them after the person stops speaking. Finally, our comments, including the feedback we give to others, should be descriptive (not judgmental) and reflect our empathy for the positions taken by these individuals. Group discussion will progress more smoothly when these steps for maintaining a positive climate are taken.

Communication and TECHNOLOGY
The Nature of Virtual Teams

The development of new technologies like wireless Internet allows us to do our work just about anywhere. As students, we can take our laptops, BlackBerries, or iPhones to our local coffee shop to do research for a term paper, listen to a class lecture, or answer email from small group members. According to the WorldatWork group (Rhodes, 2007), as many as 28.7 million people worked remotely at least one day per month in 2006. In addition, 70 percent of professionals have worked virtually with others and 46 percent do so at least once a week (O'Grady, 2003). Telecommuting is gaining acceptance in the workplace and workers want it. Nearly 40 percent of information technology workers, for example, would take a pay cut by 10 percent if they were able to work from home at least part of the time (Perez, 2008).

At school or at work, we rarely work alone. We collaborate through social network sites like Facebook, LinkedIn, and MySpace. We will be working in virtual groups.

A virtual team is "a group of people who work interdependently with a shared purpose across space, time, and organizational boundaries using technology" (Lipnack & Stamps, 2000, 18). Some teams may meet face to face, while others may never see the other members of their team. The virtual team's primary focus is completing a task or solving a problem. Team members use email, videoconferencing, message boards or chat rooms, Wikis, Googledocs, and fax to communicate with one another. Many workers telecommute from their own homes.

In contrast to traditional groups, which have a size of 3–8 members, "there is no right size for virtual teams. Size depends first on the task at hand and second on the unique constraints and opportunities of the situation" (Lipnack & Stamps, 2000). So, a virtual team could have ten members, all in different states, in different time zones, and never meet face to face.

In Chapter 10, we will explore the roles of leadership and trust in virtual teams.

Serving Your COMMUNITY

Communication in Small Groups

In an effort to recognize the communication behaviors within a small group, do the following:

1. Identify a community group that meets regularly.

2. Attend at least three meetings.

3. Observe the communication behavior of the group members paying attention to each of the following variables:

    a. norms.

    b. roles.

    c. cohesiveness.

    d. commitment.

    e. arrangement.

4. Schedule a meeting with an officer of the organization to discuss your observations.

5. Provide a summary of what you have observed. Comment on the following variables:

    a. verbal participation of group members.

    b. nonverbal participation of group members.

    c. climate within the group.

6. Provide an opportunity for the officers of the organization to give feedback on your observations.

7. Compare and contrast your perception of the group communication behavior and the perception of the officer(s).

8. How did this process help you recognize the different ways groups communicate?

SUMMARY

Small-group communication is communication involving three to eight individuals who share a common purpose, feel a sense of belonging, and usually meet face to face. Small-group discussion occurs in knowledge-gaining groups, personal growth groups, social groups, and problem-solving groups.

Several variables affect small-group communication, including norms, rules that dictate how group members ought to behave; roles, a set of expected behaviors; cohesiveness, the demonstrated sense of purpose within a group; commitment, the motivation of members to meet the goals of the group; and arrangement, the physical placement of the individuals within the group.

Effective small-group participation is based on two facts: (1) Every group decision is reached as a result of moving through specific phases, and (2) the use of special communication skills improves our communication. The four phases of the decision-making process include the orientation phase, where the climate is established and the members acquaint themselves with the topic; the conflict phase, in which disagreements surface; the emergence phase, in which the desire for the group to reach a decision takes hold; and the reinforcement phase, where members voice their support for the decision that has been reached and for one another. Groups use one of three decision-making methods: decision by a leader, decision by majority vote, and consensus. When trying to achieve consensus, groups should avoid groupthink, the illusion of a small-group consensus.

Finally, our effectiveness within groups depends on how skillfully we communicate in the following areas: verbal participation, nonverbal participation, and maintaining a positive communication climate.

REVIEW QUESTIONS

1. Define small-group communication.
2. How is small-group communication similar and different from the other forms of communication?
3. What are the four types of groups?
4. Briefly describe the following variables that affect small-group communication:
    a. norms
    b. roles
    c. cohesiveness
    d. commitment
    e. arrangement
5. What are the four phases of small-group decision making?
6. What are the strengths and weaknesses of each of the decision-making methods?
7. List and describe three communication skills that can improve our participation in small groups.

KEY CONCEPTS

small-group communication
knowledge-gaining groups
personal growth groups
social groups
problem-solving groups
task-oriented groups
norms

roles
task roles
maintenance roles
individual roles
cohesiveness
commitment
arrangement
orientation phase

conflict phase
emergence phase
reinforcement phase
decision by the leader
decision by majority vote
decision by consensus
groupthink

Solving Problems Using Small Groups

AFTER STUDYING THIS CHAPTER, YOU SHOULD

understand

- why and how to use small groups to solve problems.
- the five types of problem-solving formats.
- the small-group discussion questions of fact, questions of value, and questions of policy.
- the importance of an agenda.
- the definition of leadership.
- the three perspectives of leadership.

be able to

- list the steps involved in formulating a discussion question.
- create an agenda, establish criteria, generate possible solutions, and choose the best solution.
- compare and contrast democratic, autocratic, and laissez-faire styles of leadership.

We learned in Chapter 9 about the Sheldon Advertising problem-solving group and its goal to create a strategic plan for improving overall work performance throughout the company. Each member of the group represents a unit within the company. Hannah represents the marketing department, Mark is part of the creative team, Raquel is an accountant, and Darren represents outside sales. Darren has emerged as the leader of the group and is trying to develop and maintain a positive and supportive communication climate. But, as in every small group, conflict has occurred and the members are beginning to use defensive communication in and out of their meetings.

Before the last meeting, for example, Raquel had taken it upon herself to generate a list of possible solutions or ways to increase work performance. She presented the list to the group and asked the group to choose one, "so we can get this experience over with and go back to our real jobs." Darren thanked Raquel for taking the initiative to do the extra work outside the group but stressed that the group was several meetings away from finding a solution. "Why don't we hold on to your list and use it as a basis for our next discussion then? Are we all agreed?" The members nod in agreement. "OK then," said Darren, "what did our attempt at gathering research turn up? Who would like to share their information first?"

■ ■ ■ ■ ■

Working in groups can be very frustrating, but it can also be an efficient way to solve problems. This chapter discusses small-group communication and how our diverse approaches to working in groups influence the overall ability of the small group and its leader to complete tasks and solve problems.

SOLVING PROBLEMS AS A GROUP

As we discussed in Chapter 9, groups are used at work, school, and home. We rely on groups when there is a problem to be solved because small groups can be more effective than having a single person work on the problem. Specifically, small groups arrive at better solutions and have more resources, and a decision made by a group is more likely to be accepted by the whole group. Small groups arrive at better solutions because members "check on" one another. There is always someone to ask another question or offer a competing idea. Poor ideas are more readily pointed out and discarded. More resources are also available to small groups. As an individual, you are limited by your past experience, knowledge, and special talents. But, imagine the combined resources of five individuals. The differences each member brings to the group are truly an asset. Lastly, groups are more effective because decisions made by a group are more accepted by the whole. Of course, if members of the group are part of the decision-making process, they will "own" the final decision and want it to be successful. In addition, a decision reached by a group instead of an individual will take into account more views, ideas, and suggestions. These decisions are more acceptable to the group than decisions made by a person in authority. For example:

> Lisa Morrow, the current state senator, has decided to run for reelection. In order to win, she knows she must campaign vigorously on many different issues in several diverse areas of her district. As she puts together her reelection team, Senator Morrow asks Joe Koch to be her advisor on regional transportation because of his experience in mass transit. She also asks Dee Williams to serve as her advisor on farm and agricultural issues. Dee has been a farmer for 20 years as well as a lobbyist for the local farmers' association. Lastly, Senator Morrow enlists the help of Sydney Wells, a political communication specialist. Each of the members of her reelection team brings his or her special talents, knowledge, and expertise.

We begin this chapter with a discussion of problem-solving formats and then discuss the process of solving problems and the role that leadership plays in the overall process.

TYPES OF PROBLEM-SOLVING FORMATS

All groups use a format or structure when they meet to solve problems and complete tasks. The format chosen by the group is a reflection of the kind of problem the members are facing. Some formats require privacy to ensure frank discussion, while other groups operate in public and may even engage the audience in the process of solving the problem.

A **committee** is a small group of people assigned a task by a larger group. Although the group has a specific function, "business" tends to be conducted rather informally. For example, a campus club committee charged with planning programs for the year is likely to conduct its business in a member's home, with the discussion taking place while refreshments are served. A faculty textbook-selection committee meeting is slightly more structured—group members take minutes and cast votes over competing texts.

A number of small-group discussions take place publicly. These group presentations range from the less structured forum, to the panel discussion, to the highly structured symposium. Generally speaking, in a **forum**, a group presents its ideas to an audience, which is then invited to join the discussion. A town meeting is typical of a forum. A second type of public small-group discussion occurs when a **panel** of individuals attempts to solve problems or inform an audience about a topic. In many cases, a chairperson is selected to act as a moderator. (Although the audience may ask panel members questions, the role of the audience is diminished.) The more structured **symposium** includes a small group of speakers who share a topic, but who discuss it individually, often focusing on a specific aspect of the topic. A symposium on the September 11, 2001, terrorist attack on the World Trade Center and the Pentagon, for example, might include separate presentations on the hijacking, the role of New York City firefighters and police, and the victims. The presenters listen, along with the audience, to the comments of their fellow participants. Interaction among the speakers and between the audience and speakers is minimal.

Focus groups are used to discover what people are thinking and feeling and are primarily used by advertisers and marketers. Advertisers, for example, want to know what you think about the new sandwich at McDonald's or the new clothing line at the Aeropostale in order to advertise these products more effectively. Members of a focus group offer information but do not make decisions. Their opinions and thoughts are used as supporting material when others make the final decisions. A facilitator or leader encourages and guides the group through a series of questions, probing the members for specific feedback on the product or idea.

THE PROCESS OF PROBLEM SOLVING

As we have said, frequently the task of a small group is to discuss a question or resolve a problem. As participants, we feel more comfortable if we adequately prepare for the discussion in advance. Just as we feel ready to take an exam when we have read the assigned texts and studied our class notes, the same applies to our participation in a group discussion. Necessary preparation includes assessing the

A panel of speakers presents ideas to an audience.

question, gathering material, developing an agenda, establishing criteria for the solution, and generating solutions before choosing the best solution. The first step is assessing the question.

■ Assessing the Question

One of the preliminary steps of small-group discussions is to assess the question before the group. Knowing this will help you decide how to proceed. To help focus the discussion, one useful exercise it to first determine whether the question is one of fact, value, or policy. A second step involves formulating the question. Both of these steps help shape the discussion that follows later.

Types of Questions

When dealing with a **question of fact,** the group argues whether a statement is true or false. Its purpose is to explore a "fact" and draw some conclusions based on its accuracy. A group of jurors, for example, must weigh the statements of various witnesses in order to judge whether these statements are true or false.

A second type of question centers around **value.** The group in such a situation must determine the morality of an issue, that is, whether something is good or bad, right or wrong. For instance, our jury must decide whether a defendant's actions are unlawful and, therefore, punishable by law, or whether the actions do not violate present laws.

Finally, with a **question of policy,** the group must decide if any specific action is in order. Such a decision often rests on taking another look at questions of fact and value that help shape policy. For example, if our jury decides in favor of the defendant (based on weighing earlier questions of fact and value), it might have to tackle the sticky issue of how much to award the defendant in damages—should the defendant be entitled to damages, and if so, how much?

Formulating the Question

Once the group determines whether the question is one of fact, value, or policy, the next stage is to formulate the question. Is the question stated clearly? Is the question neutral? Does it promote discussion? These three factors should be considered when constructing the question.

Is the question clear? "Do you feel that music videos are eroding traditional values?" Each member of the group may have a different interpretation of "traditional values" in the preceding question. To ensure that each member understands the topic, it is best to use concrete language, as discussed in Chapter 4. Additionally, it is useful to construct a question that contains only one idea; the more complicated the question, the greater is the confusion among group members.

Now consider this question: "Do the sexual themes portrayed in rock videos harm adolescents by influencing their attitudes toward sexual relationships?" In this second question the language is concrete, providing the group with a greater sense of direction than the first question allowed.

Is the question neutral? In constructing the question, care should be taken to avoid alienating group members. "Should the racist practice of the school board be

COMMUNICATION IN ACTION

Assessing Discussion Questions

Identify the following as questions of fact, value, or policy:

1. Does lowering your blood cholesterol level reduce your risk of developing heart disease?
2. How can the laws be changed to reduce the number of gun-related deaths?
3. Is it important to have an ideologically balanced Supreme Court?
4. Should parents receive a tax credit if their children attend private schools?
5. Many psychologists agree that viewing violence on television can lead to acts of violence by individuals. Is their stand on this issue useful?
6. Should cloning be allowed for infertile couples?
7. How can understanding the differences between questions of fact, value, or policy increase your confidence as a communicator?

stopped?" This question would undoubtedly provoke some individuals and might lead to an unproductive conflict within the group. A question can be **neutral**, that is, one that does not "take sides," yet still promote natural conflict and discussion among group members. For example, "What steps should the school board take to celebrate diversity in the schools?" Because the second question neither condones nor attacks the present policies of the school board, it is unlikely to alienate group members before the discussion starts. Its neutrality can lead to a more fruitful discussion.

Does the question promote discussion? The question should be one that generates a meaningful, engaging discussion. Controversy frequently stimulates members to participate in a discussion. A question that is controversial, then, should successfully accomplish this task. "Are the welfare agencies and juvenile courts justified in returning abused children to their homes?" This question does not suggest that there is a simple answer. The issue is obviously a complex one and can certainly lead to a lengthy debate. Table 10.1 provides a checklist for formulating the question.

TABLE 10.1   Formulating the Question

Is the question clear?	Use concrete language. Construct a question that contains one idea.
Is the question neutral?	The question should avoid "taking sides."
Does the question promote discussion?	Controversy may stimulate discussion.

Primary and secondary sources help groups make decisions.

Gathering Material

Once the discussion question is decided, the next step is to gather research material. This process is discussed at length in Chapter 12; however, a brief review is included here as well. To support our position or contentions, we need to gather reliable information that is culled from either **primary sources,** documents such as letters, manuscripts, and taped interviews, or **secondary sources,** interpretations of primary material. For example, to prepare for a discussion on former President Bush's reaction to the terrorist attacks, we would want to examine his personal copy of his address to the nation. This primary source, however, is unavailable to the general public. What is available in its place is a wide range of secondary sources: newspaper accounts, reports by television journalists, and analyses in magazines and journals. Of course, sources that include a transcript of the president's message, such as the *New York Times* or *Vital Speeches of the Day*, are considered to be more accurate than interpretations of his message that appear in other periodicals. Furthermore, assessments of the meaning and impact of Bush's message are offered by many, but those of noted authorities are better secondary sources than those of lesser known individuals. And remember, whenever you use another person's information, be sure to give the source credit (see Chapter 12 for more on this).

The Agenda

Our preparation for a discussion should include an **agenda,** an outline of the points to be discussed. One member of the group may be asked to prepare the agenda (this individual may assume a position of leadership within the group). Although the group is likely to shift back and forth as the members discuss the topic, an agenda will help them stay focused. The agenda should allow for adequate time both to discuss the problem and to explore several solutions.

It is important to let all group members have an opportunity to share their ideas. This process guarantees that several different approaches to the problem will be explored and adequately discussed before moving on to a solution. Even after a tentative solution is reached, the group is likely to debate the positive and negative aspects. The agenda should take this fact into account.

Establishing Criteria for the Solution

Before finding a solution, the group must first decide on the criteria for a good solution. **Criteria** are the minimum requirements a solution must have to be acceptable. For example, if a group of student leaders from several student organizations is

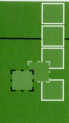

SKILL BUILDING

Preparing for a Discussion

1. Your group needs to find a solution to the campus parking problem. Formulate a discussion question.
2. What kinds of resources would you use to gather information about the subject?
3. Develop an agenda for the discussion. Take into account the various arguments, both pro and con, surrounding this subject. Consider how much time to allow for each point discussed.
4. Share your agenda with a small group to elicit feedback.
5. Use this feedback to improve your agenda.

planning a homecoming celebration, the group members would need to know what specific events need to be scheduled and when. Specifically, the solution—or in this case, the schedule of events—must include a parade and a dance, and these events must be scheduled in conjunction with the football game on Saturday morning. The more specific the criteria, the easier it will be for the group to make its final decision.

■ Developing Possible Solutions

Now that the group has established its criteria, it is time to develop possible solutions. This is the time for members to be creative and to generate as many possible solutions as they can. It is not the time to be evaluative or critical. The group hopefully has established a positive and supportive climate (see Chapter 7) and will allow members to voice even the wildest of ideas and possible solutions. If the group is stalled, it may use brainstorming. **Brainstorming** encourages creativity and the free flow of ideas. Members throw out ideas while other members write them down. This generates a long list of possible solutions. For brainstorming to be effective, the members should refrain from evaluating ideas or offering negative feedback. In addition, members should "piggyback" on one another's ideas, thus combining two or three people's ideas to generate a new solution (Beebe & Masterson, 2006, p. 144).

■ Choosing the Best Solution

Through brainstorming, research, and discussion, the group has developed a list of possible solutions. The group must know how to choose the best solution to solve the problem. The first step is to evaluate each idea according to the criteria set. Any idea that does not meet the minimum criteria must be discarded. Second, the members must decide which ideas best meet the criteria. As we discussed in Chapter 9, consensus is the best way to come to a decision, and the group members should strive for a true consensus among all the members.

LEADERSHIP

Regardless of a group's purpose, whether it is planning a class reunion or deciding which computer to purchase for the office, the group's success depends, in part, on its leadership. **Leadership** is the ability to exert influence on a group by providing a sense of direction or vision. This influence can come from an individual designated as the leader or can be shared by several members of the group. Leaders can also empower the members of the group. When members are empowered, they have the power to make decisions, be creative, and explore their own potential (see Chapter 6). An effective leader can create opportunities for the members and thus empower them. Obviously, group leaders possess one or more types of power (expert, legitimate, referent, coercive, and reward, as discussed in Chapter 6), and their power can affect the overall group's decision-making process.

In this section we shall discuss a variety of leadership perspectives, ranging from the trait perspective with its "born leaders," to the situational perspective with its democratic, autocratic, and laissez-faire styles, to the functional perspective with its shared leadership by means of task-related and process-related behaviors. Knowing about these perspectives can help us to recognize the leadership roles played by others and assist us in developing our own leadership capabilities.

■ Trait Perspective

The **trait perspective** of leadership suggests that certain individuals are born leaders because they possess such qualities as a forceful personality, marked intelligence, and dynamic communication skills. While we can think of individuals who have these characteristics, they are not necessarily effective leaders when placed in small groups. Why? This perspective has some serious flaws. The chief flaw with the trait perspective is that its outlook is too narrow: It does not take into account the other individuals in the group. The leadership qualities just described do not guarantee that an individual will be a successful leader. So what if Angela is aggressive, intelligent, and a skillful communicator? If she has no interest in a group's intended purpose or function, she may prove to be an ineffective leader.

■ Situational Perspective

In most groups the type of leadership required depends on two chief ingredients: (1) the reason for the group's existence (that is, to set a preliminary budget or to plan a surprise birthday party) and (2) the composition of the group, including how these individuals interact. In other words, each group creates a new situation, and this situation dictates which style of leadership is most appropriate. This is called the **situational perspective.** We frequently label a leader's style as democratic, autocratic, or laissez-faire. Let us take a look at what each of these means.

A **democratic leader** demonstrates his or her confidence in the group by involving group members in decision-making matters. Rather than dominate the

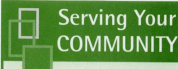

Serving Your COMMUNITY — Leadership in Small Groups

In an effort to help you understand the different styles of leadership, do the following:

1. Please volunteer for three hours at two of the following organizations within your community:
   a. the local hospice
   b. Girl Scouts or Boy Scouts of America
   c. the Salvation Army
   d. Boys and Girls Club of America
   e. an organization deemed appropriate by your instructor.

2. Observe the leadership communication behaviors of the people working.

3. After spending at least three hours at two of the above local organizations (a total of six hours), schedule a meeting with the supervisor or manager of the organizations.

4. Share your observations about leadership with the supervisor or manager. Ask each individual manager to comment on the strengths and weaknesses of the following leadership styles:
   a. the democratic style
   b. the autocratic style
   c. the laissez-faire style

5. Compare and contrast the responses from the two managers. Which type of leadership style is the more effective? Explain.

6. How did this process help you understand the different styles of leadership?

group, the democratic leader allows the group to decide who will tackle specific tasks or jobs. Such involvement generally increases both the group's cohesiveness and the overall satisfaction with the group process. We take pleasure in knowing that we have contributed to the group's efforts, that we have been personally involved.

The **autocratic leader** is a more domineering presence. This individual usually decides what direction the group will take; he or she assigns tasks to members, dictates the nature of all activities, and makes policy statements. The separation between "leader" and "group member" inhibits input from the group; the lack of involvement often leads to dissatisfaction on the part of group members. Because the process is more expedient under an autocratic leader, group members are frequently more productive. However, the satisfaction of participating in the decision-making process is absent.

A **laissez-faire leader** gives minimal direction or instruction to group members; rather, members have complete freedom to make decisions. The laissez-faire leader offers advice only when directly asked by the group or one of its members. Practically speaking, this style of leadership is the least effective of the three. The group often fails to make progress because it is unsure about where it is headed.

From the descriptions just given, we might easily conclude that the democratic style of leadership is the best approach. While this is true in many cases, there are instances when either an autocratic leader or a laissez-faire leader is wanted. Consider, for example, two groups who are given the same assignment in their public administration class: to write a job description for a town manager serving a population of 18,000. Group A has three members with no work experience and a fourth member who served for five years as a clerk in a mayor's office. Because of her experience, Julia "takes charge" of the group, especially after 15 minutes of floundering and indecision by the other members. Her role as an autocratic leader succeeds in mobilizing the group.

The four members of group B, however, all have work experience. Suggestions for the town manager's job description seem to come easily, and there is agreement among the group members about the necessary qualifications. For this group, a laissez-faire style of leadership is appropriate. There is no need to have a controlling presence when the individual members already function as a cohesive group.

Leaders, such as Bobby Jindal, Governor of Louisiana, must possess effective communication skills.

■ Functional Perspective

A **functional perspective** of leadership focuses on the kinds of leadership behaviors that any member of the group can exhibit that collectively result in the group's making progress. This perspective differs from the other leadership perspectives discussed so far because it does not promote the role of a single leader. Two primary types of behavior associated with functional leadership are task-related leadership behavior and process-related leadership behavior.

Task-related leadership behaviors include those actions designed to keep the group focused on the problem or question. Groups frequently get sidetracked from their intended function; to rescue them there are such task-related behaviors as initiating ideas, elaborating on the ideas of others, raising questions, and summarizing thoughts.

An individual who offers new or fresh ideas helps the group move closer to solving a problem. This is especially true if the group seems stuck on a particular point. When an idea generates enthusiasm, someone can take that idea a step further by elaborating on the subject. For example:

> Monica's idea is to make the theme of her class' forty-fifth high school reunion, "I Want to Hold Your Hand," a popular song by the Beatles in 1966. The planning committee likes her idea, and Jim responds by suggesting that this theme be carried out in the invitations and music. He thinks the invitations should request that all guests dress as they did during their senior year and that the band play songs popular during the early 1960s.

Another behavior that moves the group forward is asking questions. Even a simple question such as, "Where do we go from here?" refocuses the group's attention to the

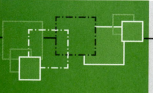

EMBRACING DIFFERENCE

Leadership Styles

Marisha is the newly elected president of student government. She has three committee chairs that report to her and are effective communicators with very different styles of leadership. Sam gives very little direction to his staff. He allows his committee to work through their critical decisions as a group. Bob, on the other hand, gives very clear direction to his staff, especially on financial matters. Omar gives his staff the opportunity to vote on every issue that emerges within the committee. Marisha realizes that leadership is situational and supports all of their different approaches to leadership.

1. Identify the different approaches to leadership exhibited by Sam, Bob, and Omar.
2. How does Marisha's appreciation of difference enhance her skill as a communicator?
3. How can the lesson learned from Marisha's behavior help you understand the importance of embracing difference?

Communication and TECHNOLOGY
Leadership in Virtual Teams

As we learned in Chapter 9, most workers spend much of their time in groups or teams. Very few workers spend their entire day working alone. Virtual teams, groups that work independently using technology, are fast becoming an essential part of business life. We become part of teams that live and work in different areas of the world and thus different time zones and in different cultures. Many times virtual teams fail to meet their goals or objectives. Ineffective leadership contributes to the failure of most virtual teams.

A new kind of leader is needed in a virtual team. Like other groups, an authoritarian leader may hinder the communication within the group, but in virtual teams, it is even more important that the leader allow members to communicate freely. According to the Stanford Graduate School of Business, "Relatively routine tasks, such as scheduling a meeting, become complex and fraught with interpersonal friction when one person's work day begins as another is sitting down to dinner or sound asleep. A simple email exchange frazzles nerves because of cultural misunderstandings, and information needed in one place sits on a desk in another because there's no routine mechanism to share knowledge" (Snyder, 2003).

In addition, the nature of the virtual team also requires a new leadership style. According to Charlene Solomon, "The complexities and subtleties of dealing with widely different personalities, cultures, and languages make communication far more difficult among virtual team members. There new challenges require diverse management skills, such as the ability to determine the best technology to facilitate communication, and the ability to engender trust and productivity among team members even when there is no direct supervision" (2001). Given the complexity of leading a virtual group, it is no surprise that an entire website is devoted to enhancing effective virtual team leadership, Leadingvirtually.com. It provides resources, blogs, articles, and discussion boards for virtual leaders. They offer the following:

1. Share the leadership tasks. Use a democratic style of leadership.

2. Facilitate a positive communication climate by building trust early. Use Icebreaker activities to help members get to know one another.

3. Encourage cooperation among the team members.

4. Encourage frequent contact among team members. Have members meet face to face, if possible.

5. Have a clear understanding of the technology necessary for the team to complete its task (virtual meeting platforms like WebEX or Go to Meeting, email, chat rooms, video conferencing, etc.).

6. Create a shared (cyber) space for team members to talk about things other than work.

task at hand. Finally, summarizing a discussion accomplishes two things: (1) It clarifies the various points by restating them, and (2) it brings into sharp focus what has already transpired and, by doing so, points out what remains to be done. This gives the group an opportunity to hear the ideas or arguments again and to ask for clarification if necessary.

The task-related behaviors just described go hand in hand with **process-related leadership behaviors**—those behaviors concerned with maintaining a positive climate within the group. These include such things as relieving tension, gatekeeping, and offering encouragement to other group members.

When the interaction within a group becomes tense, it is a relief to have some-one say, "Let's take a break for a few minutes," or to interject a little humor to ease the tension. An equally important function is carried out by a **gatekeeper,** one who attempts to regulate the flow of communication within the group. This role requires that the individual draw quiet members into the discussion (perhaps by asking a direct question) and, at times, take the center stage away from a group member who is dominating the discussion. The person who acts as a gatekeeper believes that each member has something to contribute to the group. Praising an individual's ideas, for example, can lead to increased self-esteem and satisfaction as a group member. When members feel better about themselves, the overall quality of the group process is enhanced.

EFFECTIVE LEADERSHIP COMMUNICATION

The success or failure of the group may rest on the leader's shoulders. To help ensure a positive outcome, leaders can take several steps. First, create and maintain a positive communication climate. Try to minimize defensive communication by including every member in the discussion and decision-making process. Second, recognize that each member brings diverse strengths and weaknesses to the group. One member may be an excellent researcher, but shy and hesitant during discussions. Effective leaders encourage members to use their strengths to help the group complete the task. Third, tolerate and use conflicts as a means to further the group's progress. Conflicts can "clear the air" and reveal problems within the group that must be addressed. Finally, attempt to keep the group on task. Without an effective leader, groups can flounder and drift for a long time and never meet the goal or objective.

ETHICS in Communication
Effective Leadership

At Sheldon Advertising, Darren has been appointed the leader of a problem-solving group made up of employees from different units. The group's task is to develop a strategic plan to increase the work performance of all employees. Although Darren was appointed the leader, he has also become the emergent leader. All the members of the group (Hannah, Mark, and Raquel) look to Darren for direction and advice. He knows that the group's success rests on his shoulders.

Darren uses his communication to effectively guide the group through all the phases of the small-group process. Think about Darren and his group while addressing the following:

1. What specific communication skills is Darren using?

2. Describe what kind of leader Darren is in this small group.

3. How can Darren ensure his group will be successful?

4. Have you ever been the leader of a small group? What specific communication skills did you use to help your group successfully finish its task?

SUMMARY

Small groups are effective in solving problems because they arrive at better solutions and have more resources, and because the decision is more likely to be accepted by the larger whole. Small-group formats include committees, forums, panels, and symposiums. Focus groups help advertisers discover our views on ideas, products, and issues.

Several steps help the group solve a problem: (1) assessing the question, which includes determining whether the question is one of fact, value, or policy, and formulating the question, which means deciding whether the question is clear, whether it is neutral, and whether it promotes discussion; (2) gathering material, either from primary or secondary sources; (3) having an agenda or outline of the points to be discussed; (4) creating criteria for the solution; (5) generating possible solutions; and finally, (6) choosing the best solution.

Leadership is the ability to exert influence on a group by providing a sense of direction or vision. It is defined by a variety of perspectives, ranging from the trait perspective, with its notion that certain individuals are born leaders, to the situational perspective, in which the group situation dictates the most appropriate leadership style (democratic, autocratic, or laissez-faire), to the functional perspective, which focuses on the kinds of leadership behaviors any group member can exhibit that result in the group's making progress. Effective leaders try to create and maintain a positive communication climate, acknowledge the diverse strengths and weaknesses of each group member, use conflicts in a positive way to further the group's objective, and keep the group members on task.

REVIEW QUESTIONS

1. Why are small groups an effective way to solve problems?
2. Differentiate between a question of fact, a question of value, and a question of policy. Give examples of each.
3. List three factors a group should consider when formulating its discussion question.
4. Why is an agenda necessary for small-group discussion?
5. How can a group develop possible solutions?
6. Define leadership.
7. Compare and contrast the situational and functional perspectives of leadership.
8. What are the communication strategies of an effective leader?

KEY CONCEPTS

committee
forum
panel
symposium
focus groups
question of fact
question of value
question of policy
neutral questions

primary sources
secondary sources
agenda
criteria
brainstorming
leadership
trait perspective
situational perspective
democratic leader

autocratic leader
laissez-faire leader
functional perspective
task-related leadership
    behaviors
process-related leadership
behaviors
gatekeeper

CHAPTER 11

Selecting a Speech Topic and Adapting to the Audience

AFTER STUDYING THIS CHAPTER, YOU SHOULD

understand

- ■ the four ways to use yourself as a source for topics.
- ■ the three aspects of the situation you need to analyze before choosing a topic.
- ■ three demographic factors of an audience.
- ■ six other audience characteristics.

be able to

- ■ develop three types of surveys to gather information from an audience.
- ■ adapt a topic to fit audience needs.
- ■ brainstorm a topic individually or in a group.
- ■ develop a specific-purpose statement.
- ■ develop a thesis statement.

Rolanda is trying to choose a topic for her first speech. The goal of the speech is to inform her audience about a topic that is important and interesting and must be three to five minutes in length. Rolanda has always been active in her community. She has volunteered at the local homeless shelter, served as a mentor in the Big Brothers Big Sisters program, and tutored at-risk students at her neighborhood elementary school. As a student, Rolanda is majoring in sociology and hopes to be a social worker. Her instructor emphasized that students should choose a topic they are passionate about and have some past experience.

As a way to find out what her classmates (audience members) know about the local agencies and programs that help people in need and to find out what they are interested in learning about, Rolanda distributes a survey. Although the results are varied, everyone in the class seems interested in mentoring. Several students indicated that they had mentors as children and others would like to become involved in mentoring. Rolanda decides that mentoring is too broad a topic to cover in the limited time she has, so she decides to focus on the Big Brothers Big Sisters program and her experiences as a mentor. To further narrow her topic, however, she will have to do some research.

■ ■ ■ ■ ■

In this chapter, we will look at the process we go through to choose a topic when we engage in public communication. Specifically, we will discuss the need to analyze yourself, the situation, and the audience. Understanding the unique interests, knowledge, and enthusiasm you possess, and understanding the diversity of your audience can help you to develop an interesting and thorough public presentation.

SELECTING A TOPIC

Throughout our lives we are asked to deliver speeches, whether it is a presentation at work, a toast at our friend's wedding, a campaign speech, a victory or concession speech following an election, an after-dinner speech, a eulogy for a departed friend, or an assignment for a communication class. Like Rolanda, a question speakers often ask is, "What can I talk about that will interest my audience?" Frequently, the very nature of the occasion dictates the topic we select. For example, your supervisor may ask you to discuss the strengths and weaknesses of the new software program your department just adopted. Some speaking situations (for instance, the communication classroom) require more imagination on our part. For such occasions, we can look to ourselves, the situation, and our audience, or try brainstorming to develop an interesting topic.

YOURSELF

Sometimes the best place to look for a speech topic is yourself. It is logical to assume that you will deliver a more interesting and effective speech if you are comfortable with the topic. Through self-reflection, you can draw from your own concerns, experiences, knowledge, and curiosity to select a topic. You are a unique person with much to share with your audience.

■ Concerns

One of the most important factors that can assist you in selecting a topic is to choose something that is important to you. By doing so, you communicate sincerity to your audience, which, in turn, enhances the quality of your delivery by communicating your enthusiasm. In addition, when you pick a topic that you care about, it is easier for you to concentrate on it during the delivery. You both look and feel more confident before your audience. This positive feeling may inspire you to want to share your concerns with the audience. Consider the following:

> Jovan has always helped to take care of his brother, Milo. Milo has a spinal cord injury and Jovan's family must help him with his daily needs. For Jovan's informative speech, he wants to discuss stem cell research and the promises it holds for people like his brother.

It is easy to communicate your enthusiasm when you choose a topic you feel strongly about.

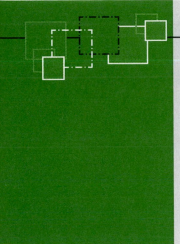

EMBRACING DIFFERENCE

Understanding Yourself

Now it's your turn. Answer the following questions as a means to find an appropriate topic for your first speech.

1. What issues, beliefs, or concerns evoke a passionate response from me?
2. What unique areas tap into my background as an "expert"?
3. List three topics that pique my curiosity.
4. How does your appreciation of your uniqueness help you to select an appropriate speech topic?
5. How does the experience of choosing a speech topic help you to understand the importance of embracing difference?

■ Experience

Your own experiences also can help you select a speech topic. Since you are a unique person, you have something special to bring to your audience. Drawing from your own experiences can provide a rich source of topics for you. Furthermore, when speaking from your own experiences, it is easier to visualize what you are talking about, which makes the entire public-speaking experience easier. The following example illustrates this:

> Jeanine contracted cerebral palsy at the age of one. During her childhood she underwent several operations to alter the fixed stiffness in some of her limbs, and as a result, she is now leading a rather normal life. She wanted her audience to realize how important it is to not stereotype people with disabilities. When discussing cerebral palsy, Jeanine described her own experiences and emphasized how she was able to overcome many of the disease's crippling effects. As she spoke, she could help the audience visualize the different stages of recovery she went through with the disease, and as a result, her speech was very convincing.

While Jeanine's topic is a dramatic one, other personal experiences can be the basis for equally compelling speeches. Consider, for example, renting your first apartment, the thrill of hang gliding, or the birth of your first child or grandchild.

■ Knowledge

Your knowledge about a given topic serves as a reservoir of information you can share with your audience. You know intuitively which points are important to include in your speech and which to omit. This is a distinct advantage over having

Your past experiences can often be used as a speech topic.

to research a totally unfamiliar topic and then having to sift through the information to decide what to include or leave out. Consider this example:

> Jeff is employed by the A. E. Public Relations Corporation and has a bachelor's degree in public relations. His company is committed to public service, so his supervisors graciously donated Jeff's time to the local women's shelter, the Haven House. The director of the Haven House asked Jeff to prepare a 40-minute presentation to the staff on techniques of fund raising, including creating a new brochure. Since Jeff's specialty is graphic arts, he decides to prepare several different types and designs of brochures so that the staff can have a foundation to work from. His presentation, then, will focus on how the staff can use his designs to help attract more contributors and increase the awareness of the shelter's mission in their new brochures.

Jeff's knowledge of graphic arts allowed him to capably present a speech on the related topic of brochures. Picking a topic that you are familiar with also will help increase your confidence before a group, because you will be comfortable with the fact that you have a certain level of expertise concerning your topic.

■ Curiosity

The process of learning is lifelong. An idea, an event, or a well-known personality may have piqued your curiosity at some point, and now you want to learn more about it in order to share your knowledge with others. Your enthusiasm for the subject will likely contribute to a dynamic presentation. For example:

Mariaha has always been a history buff. Her grandparents have told her stories about the day President John F. Kennedy was assassinated. She knows that some people believe that Lee Harvey Oswald did not act alone and that many others may have been involved. In her research, she discovered information about the "dancing bullet" theory and wanted to share this with her class. Her curiosity proved to be the foundation of an exciting presentation.

THE SITUATION

The second step in choosing an appropriate topic is to analyze the **situation** in which you will be speaking. Specifically, you want to consider the size of your audience, the time limit, and the size and shape of the room.

The size of the audience or the number of people in the audience is very important. Some obvious adjustments need to be made in developing your presentation based on the audience's size. For example, with a larger audience, you may find it necessary to be more formal in your presentation, right down to the way you deliver the speech. With a large audience you are less likely to interact directly with members of the audience. In addition, it is more difficult to respond to feedback because it is so difficult to establish direct eye contact with members of the audience. Conversely, you will probably find that with a smaller audience you can present a speech with abstract ideas, because it is easier for you to detect any nonverbal feedback the audience generates and act on it. Consider the following:

> Professor Gerard's lecture was on the subject of how the media create pseudo-events. As he was explaining the concept of a pseudo-event, he noticed a look of confusion on Andrea's face. Because of the relatively small size of the group, he was able to detect her nonverbal cue and respond to it. To further illustrate his point, he used the story of Terri Schiavo, a woman who eventually died when her feeding tube was removed at the request of her husband. Dr. Gerald pointed out that many people believe that the media inflamed the feelings of the Right to Life movement by focusing all its attention, 24 hours a day, on this one woman's case.

Another fact to consider concerning the situation is time limit. For your speaking assignment in this class, you will have a relatively short amount of time. Outside the classroom, however, you may have to speak for 30 minutes or longer. The time limit will greatly impact the amount of information you can effectively convey. You may want to pick a very specific topic and cover it in-depth. Another option may be to choose a broader topic and cover only the major ideas. Either way, you must consider the length of time you have to present your material. For example, Debbie, a single mother of three children, was asked by her daughter's fourth grade teacher to teach the students how to make a kite. She was given one hour to talk about kites and to have the children actually build and fly a kite. Debbie decided that it would be more effective to spend her time demonstrating how to construct a kite instead of discussing the different types of kites or the physics behind how a kite flies. She brought materials for each child to build his or her own kite. Debbie's talk will be more successful because she took into account the amount of time she was given for her presentation.

The third consideration concerning the situation is the size and shape of the room. Specifically, you will want to know how the seats are arranged, what the lighting is like, and how much space there will be for you to move around the room. Knowing the size and shape of the room will help you to choose appropriate visual or audio aids and will also help you to adjust your delivery style so that everyone in the room can see and hear you. Xavier was selected by his local electricians' union to discuss his experiences as a contract negotiator. All the members were invited to attend the presentation, so the event would have to take place in the very large union hall. The hall holds five hundred people, and has very poor lighting but is equipped with a sound system and a computer system capable of projecting images so all can see. Xavier decides to adjust his topic and focus on the actual contract because he can use the projection system to show how the specific negotiations progressed using several charts and graphs.

It is important to consider the size of the audience, the time limit, and the size and shape of the room when choosing your topic. Each of these elements can have a great impact on what your topic is and how you present your material.

THE AUDIENCE

Audience analysis goes hand in hand with selecting and developing the speech topic. For instance, preparing for a speech on "safe sex" depends, in part, on the audience. Consider the different approach you would take when talking to 150 ninth grade students from the approach you would take when talking to 15 administrators of social service agencies. Many factors such as audience attitudes, needs, age, sex, and knowledge must be taken into account.

Before developing any speech, consider the audience; your efforts to develop an effective speech will be wasted if you fail to consider whom you are talking to. For example, your speech is headed for failure if your audience has no interest in your topic, if the information you are providing is beyond the audience's level of comprehension, or if your message runs counter to beliefs firmly held by the audience.

What criteria do you use to assess your audience? This section will explore the areas of demographics, characteristics of an audience, appropriate methods for gathering audience information, and adapting to the audience.

DEMOGRAPHIC FACTORS

Segments of the population are routinely analyzed according to **demographics**, that is, easily identifiable characteristics such as age, sex, and ethnic/cultural/religious background. Demographic analysis of an audience should be considered for

COMMUNICATION IN ACTION

Finding an Appropriate Speech Topic

To help in the process of finding a topic for your first speech, do some self-analysis.

1. What do you do in your free time?
2. What are you favorite subjects in school?
3. Is there a cause, issue, or concern you feel passionately about? If so, describe it.
4. What unique experiences have you had?
5. What do you consider yourself knowledgeable about?

How can you use the answers to these questions to find a topic for your speech? Make a list of four possible topics.

the purpose of preparing a public speech because it can assist you in tailoring the topic to a specific audience.

■ Age

The composite age of the audience often plays a role in the selection of a speech topic, because some topics are better suited to one age group than another. These topics are based on the unique frame of reference of a particular audience. Topics based on the Vietnam War, for example, will have a different impact on those Americans who "lived the war" via the front line or who worked for the war effort "stateside" than on those Americans too young to have anything but secondhand experience.

The age of the audience also can affect how you develop the topic. It may even be a primary factor in determining how you will discuss a topic that you consider highly sensitive. In such cases, your choice of words might change with the audience's age in an effort to not alienate them. The age of the audience suggests a general frame of reference that may or may not be in tune with the topic. Consider the following:

> Antonio has recently been elected a member of the local public school board. In recent months, the board has been discussing the issue of sex education in the classroom. Antonio is the only board member under the age of 40. Many of the other board members were teenagers during the rebellious 1960s and early 1970s and experienced the "free love" movement. Since Antonio is speaking in favor of abstinence education in the classroom, he is cautious as he puts his words together. He knows his audience is sensitive to the issue, so he avoids language that might inflame their feelings.

As you become more sensitive to the age of your audience, you should find yourself feeling better able to communicate with them.

■ Sex

As our society changes, so do the attitudes we hold concerning sex roles. Consequently, there are very few topics that are regarded as strictly "male" or "female." More men are spending time participating in child-rearing responsibilities, while more women are spending a significant amount of time expanding their careers. It would be dangerous, then, to cling to outdated stereotypes that categorize people's interests according to sex roles. In fact, men and women often have similar responses to a topic.

We cannot, however, avoid the fact that many people are raised in an environment filled with sexual stereotypes, and it would be impossible for those individuals not to be influenced by those stereotypes. An all-female audience, for example, may have a high level of knowledge concerning child care; likewise, an all-male audience may be familiar with the standings of the hometown football team. Still, it is important to remember that not all members of a gender group will possess knowledge about a particular subject.

■ Ethnic, Cultural, and Religious Background

The United States has been aptly labeled as a beautiful patchwork quilt of racial, ethnic, and cultural groups, as well as of diverse religions. Although we are bound together in our society, we also retain all the unique qualities of our heritage. This is as true today as it was during the great wave of immigration during the 1800s and early 1900s. It is important to keep these differences in mind when you prepare your speech so as to not alienate a particular segment of the audience. On the other hand, discovering that the audience's background is similar to your own, or that because of its cultural or ethnic background it is sympathetic to your topic, makes it easier for you to prepare your speech.

AUDIENCE CHARACTERISTICS

In addition to the demographic factors just discussed, it is possible to assess an audience based on such criteria as knowledge, attitude, needs, societal roles, occupation, and economic status. Knowledge of these characteristics can help you adapt or adjust the speech to fit the audience. This applies to both the structure of the speech and the style of delivery you choose.

■ Knowledge

The amount of information the audience possesses about your topic may give you some insight concerning the way you want to approach the speech. If your audience is unfamiliar with your topic, you may need to take an elementary approach; on the other hand, if your audience is familiar with the topic, you can take a more detailed approach. For example, if you select the subject of identical twins as your topic, for a group of expectant parents whose knowledge of the subject is limited, a successful speech would likely focus on raising twins, with perhaps a brief biological explanation of how twins are created. If, however, your speech is directed at a group of biology majors, the genetic factor would likely be the focal point of your talk. With this group, the level of detailed information would be much greater.

■ Attitude

Generally speaking, at the outset of a speech, the audience has formulated an attitude toward both the topic and the speaker. Knowledge of the audience's attitude toward the topic can help you adapt what you say to the group. Consider this example:

> Elizabeth Jones, the assistant superintendent, plans to speak to a group of disgruntled parents about the school board's recommendation to close Taft Elementary School at the end of the year. Realizing that her audience strongly opposes this action because their children would have to ride a bus to school instead of walking, she begins by stating that the board gave serious attention to this issue and regretted having to make this difficult decision. Her opening remarks are meant to reduce some of the audience's hostility, so she can proceed to explain the reasons for the board's decision.

In the situation described above, it is reasonable to presume that the sentiment toward Elizabeth was probably negative prior to her speech. Her remarks were intended to diffuse some of the natural resentment both toward an unpopular board decision and toward herself as president of the school board. Had Elizabeth not taken the audience's resentment into account, her speech would not have been as sensitively prepared.

■ Needs

According to Abraham Maslow, people have the same basic needs, which are best understood when explained in terms of a hierarchy. These needs are classified as physiological, safety, belonging, esteem, and self-actualization (1970, pp. 35–58).

As a speaker who is familiar with **Maslow's hierarchy of needs**, you can develop your topic according to the appropriate audience need. What does this mean? First, it means examining the topic you have selected (this time from the audience's perspective) and asking yourself, "What is the connection between my topic and people's needs as identified by Maslow?" What, for example, is the relationship between the threat of nuclear disaster (your topic) and Maslow's hierarchy of needs? Answer: This topic appeals to the audience's need for safety. Second, once you have established the link between your topic and the audience, you can begin the process of adapting your speech to appeal to these needs. Need identification is simply one more way of analyzing the audience.

Physiological needs are the lowest level needs on Maslow's hierarchy; food, water, and air are examples. A speech on the refugees of genocide in Darfur relates to physiological needs on Maslow's hierarchy because it appeals to the physiological needs of the members of the audience and therefore most likely evokes their sympathy and interest. You might, for example, develop a speech that informs your classmates about international programs trying to alleviate the hunger and starvation of the Darfur refugees.

Safety needs, the second level on Maslow's hierarchy, refer to our desire to feel secure. They function on two levels: (1) physical security and (2) personal security in social situations. The example given earlier about the threat of nuclear disaster deals with physical security. A speech that focuses on the difficulties of social interactions also may relate to an audience's need for safety. For example, a possible speech topic could inform the audience about three techniques to increase their confidence during their first day at a new job.

The **need to belong** refers to the desire to be part of a group. The group, of course, may vary in composition. Some individuals join Los Latinos (a Hispanic organization) because of their desire to be part of a group that is popular on a college campus and want to be with people who share a common culture. Other individuals participate regularly in religious organizations because they enjoy being with people who hold convictions similar to their own. If your audience happens to be 25 students taking a course entitled "Introduction to News Writing and Editing," you may want to persuade the members of this class that joining the student newspaper staff can help them feel more involved in campus activities.

Esteem needs, the desire for influence or status within the social structure, are next on Maslow's hierarchy. Figure 11.1 illustrates Maslow's hierarchy of

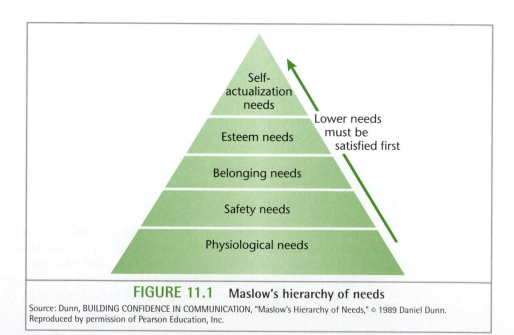

FIGURE 11.1   Maslow's hierarchy of needs

Source: Dunn, BUILDING CONFIDENCE IN COMMUNICATION, "Maslow's Hierarchy of Needs," © 1989 Daniel Dunn. Reproduced by permission of Pearson Education, Inc.

needs. Everyone wants to feel important and needed in their lives. Consider the following situation:

> Tyler Laufer is raising two sons on his own. For support, he joined Parents Without Partners and is now the executive director. Tyler has been asked to speak to the members of a new chapter. He plans to speak about the importance of the organization, but he refines his topic to persuade the members that they can shape the future of their chapter by serving as officers during the coming year.

Self-actualization is perceiving that you have reached the highest level of your potential. Maslow emphasizes the importance of reaching your full potential as you grow toward self-actualization. On the day before the co-ed volleyball league championship, you attempt to persuade your teammates that you can win the match because you have practiced hard and are well prepared. Your pep talk helps to build the team's self-confidence and inspires them to play their best.

■ Societal Roles

We wear several "hats" during the day. Right now, as you read this textbook, you are playing the role of college student. At home, you may also be a mother or father, brother or sister, aunt or uncle, spouse or partner, grandmother or grandfather. At work, you may be a cashier, server, supervisor, manager, or intern. A **role** is a group of expected behaviors placed on us by our society or culture (see Chapter 9). The roles that we play each day shape our experiences and knowledge about many topics. For example, a grandmother may know many home remedies for a common bee sting, or a woman who has been a supervisor for 20 years knows much about employee training. It is important to understand and appreciate all the roles your audience plays in their lives outside of the university. This will help you choose an appropriate topic and be able to adapt it to the audience.

■ Occupation

Unlike the college classroom, which includes students with a variety of majors, roles, and backgrounds, many public-speaking situations have an audience with a similar occupation. For example, you may be asked as the supervisor of technical support to inform the nursing staff on how to use the new computer software to track patient care, or as the head server, you may be required to persuade the kitchen staff to be more precise in communicating to the servers about daily specials. In each of these examples, the audience shares a body of knowledge or interest because they have the same occupation. This kind of audience will understand technical language or jargon, and this can help you relate your topic to them more easily.

■ Economic Status

Economic status or income level is another characteristic you will want to know about your audience. Mick wanted to persuade his audience to spend their spring break in a tropical location such as Cancun or the Virgin Islands. After doing

An audience's occupation may influence your topic selection.

some audience analysis, Mick realized that almost all of his fellow students work full-time so that they can afford their college tuition. It is unlikely that Mick's audience would be able to afford such an elaborate vacation. Instead, Mick chooses to persuade his fellow students to visit one of the local art museums during the spring break. Knowing the economic status of your audience can be important in finding an appropriate topic and a means of adapting the topic to it.

■ Gathering Information

How do you determine the demographics and characteristics of your audience described in the above section? Basically, there are three methods for gathering information: observation, interviews, and surveys (see Chapter 12 for a more detailed discussion). Whether you have an opportunity to observe your audience ahead of time, whether you manage to interview some of the members individually, or whether you prepare a survey for each member to complete, you will undoubtedly draw some inferences based on your observations and the responses you receive from members of the audience. In turn, these will be used to develop and adapt your speech to the audience.

Observation

Observation helps us learn about the audience. It is not difficult to determine such demographic factors as sex, age, and race. You also can note how a group reacts to what others say; in particular, how they react to other speakers. For example, if you are scheduled to conduct a workshop on bathroom plumbing repair at the local hardware store, you may want to attend a couple of workshops prior to your speech. This gives you a chance to observe how the class reacts to the different speakers' styles, content, and so on. Use this information as you work on developing your speech. Are there any special appeals you can make because of the group's composition, attitudes, and needs? In a communication class you have a perfect opportunity to practice this method.

Interviews

A more time-consuming method of gathering information is the **interview.** In an interview, your purpose is to gain background information about the audience by asking another party specific questions. This approach is especially useful in situations in which you have been asked to speak to an audience about whom you know nothing. To avoid speaking to the group "blindly," you would want to ask one of the members (probably the person who invited you to speak) about the audience's interests, age, knowledge about the topic, and so on. His or her response to your questions will help you prepare a more appropriate speech. Further information on constructing interview questions and conducting an information interview can be found in Chapter 8.

Communication and TECHNOLOGY
Using Online Surveys for Audience Analysis

Using a questionnaire or survey can help you learn about your audience. Surveys can discover information about your audience's demographics, occupation, societal roles, and most importantly, their knowledge and attitudes about your topic. With the results, you can more easily adapt your topic to the audience. One of the problem with surveys, however, is that they can be time consuming to fill out and in most classrooms, there is just not enough time for all the speakers to distribute a survey.

One possible solution is the use of Internet survey websites. SurveyMonkey, Zoomerang, and Question Pro all offer survey distribution at little or no cost. These websites help you create a variety of questions: open-ended, closed, and scaled. The programs are easy to use and each takes the user through a step by step process to create and distribute the survey. The survey can contain 10 to 20 questions depending upon the website and the results are immediate. All of these websites provide you with a detailed analysis of the results as well as pie or bar graphs illustrating a summary of your audience's answers.

If your class has a course website, each speaker can post a link to his or her survey. If not, the speaker can send an email to each audience member with the link to the survey embedded in the message.

Using online surveys is a fast and efficient way for any speaker to do a thorough audience analysis.

Surveys

Surveys can pose a variety of general questions, such as number of years of education, marital status, age, and income bracket, and they can ask questions that relate to a specific topic, such as "Are you an organ donor?" "Do you believe that the United States should make flag burning illegal?" or "What is the best restaurant in town?" Such specific questions can help you to analyze an audience's knowledge, attitudes, and needs concerning your selected topic. You can choose from three types of surveys: closed, open, and graduated scale.

In a **closed surveys,** the respondent must select an answer from two or more choices:

Did you vote in the last presidential election?
Yes _____ No _____ Don't remember _____

While a survey composed of questions such as the preceding does not provide much detail, it does offer additional information in a limited way. Because responses are clear-cut, you can generally detect whether or not there is a consensus of opinion among the members of the audience. If there is, you will have a better idea of how to develop your presentation.

An **open survey** gives respondents the opportunity to fully express their feelings:

Why don't the majority of Americans vote?

Responses to such questions, which tend to be more detailed, often provide insight about people's reasons for feeling strongly about a topic. Despite the sense of "knowing" the audience better, there is the drawback of having to sift through a great deal of extraneous information in an open survey.

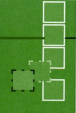

SKILL BUILDING

Understanding Audience Analysis

Analyzing your audience can help you select an appropriate topic for your speech and will also help you adapt the topic to the audience. Answer the following questions about your audience:

1. What are the ages of your audience members?
2. How many men and women will be in attendance?
3. What are the ethnic/cultural/religious backgrounds of the audience?
4. Describe the general characteristics of the audience, such as knowledge, attitudes, needs, societal roles, occupations, and income levels.

How can you use the answers to these questions to help you choose a topic? After choosing a topic, how can these answers assist you in adapting the topic to this particular audience?

The **graduated scale,** also known as the **Likert scale,** gives individuals the opportunity to rank their feelings on a continuum:

For the following statement, circle the number that most accurately represents your feelings:
   The majority of the American public does not vote because elections are held on a workday instead of the weekend.

1	2	3	4	5
Strongly agree	Agree	Undecided	Disagree	Strongly disagree

The responses can indicate the intensity of audience feelings toward a particular topic. This information is valuable to a speaker.

Observations, interviews, and surveys are tools to assist you in choosing an appropriate topic. Rolanda, at the beginning of the chapter, began with the topic of local agencies and programs to help people in need. After distributing a survey to her audience, she was able to determine that mentoring children was a topic that interested almost everyone. Thus, a thorough audience analysis made topic selection easier for Rolanda.

BRAINSTORMING

If, after you have considered yourself, the situation, and the audience, you find that you still have a difficult time deciding on a suitable topic, try brainstorming. Brainstorming, a spontaneous method for generating ideas, also can help you to select a speech topic. This process involves listing as many ideas as you can within a given amount of time, either by yourself or with a group. Alex Osborn, noted authority on the subject, maintained that in brainstorming two basic principles must always be followed: (1) Defer judgment on all ideas and (2) strive for quantity (1979, p. 141).

Perhaps the best way to individually brainstorm is to write down as many topics as you can within five to ten minutes (five minutes if you think fast). Do not discard or reject any ideas that come to mind; that can be done later on. What is important here is to get as many ideas on paper as you can. As you do this activity, you may find that one idea triggers another; this free association often produces several good topics. What happens, for example, when you begin with the word *food?* Manuel ended up with the following list:

food
hamburgers
hot dogs
baseball
World Series
New York Yankees
baseball stadiums

Manuel's first thought upon hearing the word *food* was *hamburgers. Hot dogs* came next because he always associates one with the other. *Hot dogs* reminded him of baseball; Manuel loves to eat hot dogs at *baseball* games. From *baseball* he jumped to the *World Series*. He hoped his favorite team, the *New York Yankees* would be in the World Series this year at their new *stadium*. From this list he decided on a speech topic: the newly constructed home for the New York Yankees, Yankee Stadium. Now you try it! Using the same starting point, see where food takes you. Give yourself three or four minutes.

Group brainstorming, an extension of individual brainstorming, maintains the two principles just discussed, that is, defer judgment and strive for quantity. There are advantages, however, to having a small group toss out ideas: (1) The number of possible topics increases dramatically, (2) one member's suggestion often triggers a chain reaction among the rest of the group, (3) a healthy competition often develops between members (each member tries a little harder to express an idea that captures everyone's attention), and (4) good ideas receive reinforcement from others.

ADAPTING TO THE AUDIENCE

Once you have chosen a topic based on your analysis of self, situation, and audience or through brainstorming, you are now ready to adapt your topic. Specifically, analyzing an audience takes considerable time and effort; however, this generally translates into a better understanding of your audience. How do you use the information you have gathered (through observation, interviews, and surveys) about an audience's demographics and such related characteristics as knowledge, attitudes, needs, societal roles, occupation, and economic status? Simply stated, you must use these data to adapt your topic to your audience. Adapting your topic means that you create a relationship between you, the topic, and the audience. Specifically, there are four strategies you can use to adapt to the audience:

1. *Make a personal connection to the audience.* In other words, show the audience how you relate to the topic or why you are concerned or interested in the topic. The audience wants to know why the topic is important and worthy of their attention. You may indicate why you chose the topic, or explain your past experiences with the topic. Audiences are more apt to listen to a speaker who is like them in some way. Demonstrating your relationship to the topic will also create a connection between you and the audience.

2. *Be sure to define all your terms.* From your thorough analysis, you have a pretty good idea what the audience may or may not already know about the topic. One way to adapt to the audience is to clearly and precisely communicate your ideas. This means that as you develop your speech, be sure to explain and define all the terms or concepts about which the audience may have little knowledge.

3. *Address the audience's needs, concerns, and interests.* Indicate to the audience that your topic is relevant to their experiences, desires, or curiosity. Audiences will listen to speeches that have a direct connection to their lives. Make your topic relevant to them and they will want to listen.

4. *Use vivid example or stories to make your topic come alive.* Since childhood, we all love to listen to stories. Your audience will more easily relate to your topic if

you get them involved in a story about you or a compelling character. As you begin to develop your speech, keep in mind all the things you have learned about your audience and use them to find or create a story that the audience can relate to.

For example, perhaps you realize that your audience, 80 percent female between the ages of 20 and 45, has a very positive attitude about preschool education. Obviously, a speech that advocates additional state funds for preschool education should be well received. Your next step, then, is to develop your topic with this in mind. You decide that you can tell your own story (of finding an affordable preschool for your three-year-old daughter Sydney) as a means of creating a relationship between you, the topic, and the audience. Furthermore, you realize you will need to find source material that shows how quality preschool education positively affects not only the child, but also the whole community (of which your audience is a member).

You will be a better public speaker if you can take what you have learned about your audience and temporarily become one of its members as you begin to develop your speech. Your efforts to empathize with your audience, a skill so essential to successful interpersonal communication, will lead you to a successful public presentation. The next two chapters will take you through the process of preparing your speech; gathering information about your topic is treated in Chapter 12, while organizing your speech is the subject of Chapter 13.

THE SPEECH PURPOSE

After choosing a topic and determining the best way to adapt it to your audience, you must establish the purpose of your presentation. If your stated purpose is in line with the expectations of the audience, you will likely feel more comfortable about presenting your ideas. The development of your speech purpose usually follows three steps: (1) determining the general purpose, (2) determining the specific purpose, and (3) creating a thesis statement.

ETHICS in Communication
Adapting to the Audience

Rolanda, at the beginning of the chapter, struggles to find an appropriate topic for her first speech. After a long process, Rolanda is able to find and develop an appropriate topic that will be ethical and effective. How was Rolanda able to accomplish this? Answer the following questions:

1. How did Rolanda assess her audience? What role do demographics play in her decision?

2. Why are Rolanda's own interests so important in her final topic decision?

3. As you think about your own first speech, how will you address your needs and the needs of your audience?

■ General Purpose

Establishing the **general purpose** of your presentation means deciding whether your overriding goal is to inform, to persuade, or to entertain. In most instances, your purpose is to inform or to persuade, although these frequently overlap. When your purpose is to inform, your chief concern rests with presenting information as clearly and accurately as possible. For example, as Human Resources director, you set a time and date to explain each of the three medical plans now available to company employees. As you try to increase the audience's understanding of your topic and to broaden their knowledge, clear, descriptive language is essential.

When your purpose is to persuade, you want to go beyond simply presenting information. With this type of speech, your primary goal is to induce change in the audience; that is, you want to move them to action. Your goal as a speaker is to get the audience to empathize with your position, to feel the concern that you feel. If you are successful, the audience will be motivated to change. You are scheduled to speak to 10 employees about XYZ health maintenance organization, one of three health plans to be voted on by the group. As a representative of this health insurance company, your aim is to convince (persuade) the group that XYZ is the best plan on the market. While you are concerned about presenting the information clearly, your speech goes one step further—it asks the audience to respond in some way.

When your purpose is to entertain, you strive to make others happy. This is usually accomplished by interjecting humor into your speech. Jon Stewart and David Letterman make entertaining presentations on their nightly television shows. Although their monologues sometimes fail to draw laughter, their overriding purpose is to entertain.

■ Specific Purpose

In order to make your speech more manageable, both for you to develop and for your audience to understand, you must determine its specific purpose. Stated in a single sentence, your **specific purpose** takes into account the following factors: (1) what you hope to accomplish, (2) which aspect of the topic you will cover, by narrowing your topic, and (3) your intended audience. This process moves you from your general purpose (to inform, to persuade, or to entertain) to a more focused speech topic. Consider the following:

> Amy, a first-year speech student, must give a four-minute informative speech. She was advised to describe something to her audience and to base her speech on a personal experience. Amy knew she would be more convincing if she discussed a topic she cared about. She wrestled with several topics before finally deciding on the topic of parenting. Amy just had her first child three months ago and is very concerned about raising a self-confident and happy daughter. Because parenting is a broad topic, she knew she would have to narrow its focus. After some additional thought, she decided to focus on disciplining children.

When Amy began developing her speech, she started with the general purpose "to inform." Now she has to determine which aspect of parenting she wants to talk about. Her first attempt to narrow her topic produced the following results:

Specific purpose 1—to talk about parenting. Would an audience have a strong sense of the speech purpose after hearing this statement? Probably not. Amy still needs to decide exactly what she wishes to tell her audience. She tries it again, this time with better results.

Specific purpose 2—to inform the audience about the importance of parental discipline. Amy is now offering more information, but she still is not telling us anything specific. Amy needs to be more specific. For example, she may want to determine the different ways to discipline a preschool child. By doing so, she will have a better idea of what to share with her audience. Upon further reflection, Amy comes up with the following.

Specific purpose 3—to inform the audience about three ways to effectively discipline a preschool child. This shows some improvement, but Amy still has not identified the group to whom she wishes to deliver the speech. This seemingly minor point is important, because it helps her to keep her audience in mind as she delivers her speech. Here is Amy's final effort.

Specific purpose 4—to inform my class about the three ways to effectively discipline a preschool child. Do you see what Amy has accomplished? She has moved from a very general treatment to a more specific treatment of the topic. As a result, Amy should have an easier job constructing an effective speech because she has created specific guidelines for herself.

What process can you use to develop your specific-purpose statement? Let us analyze the preceding example. Amy's Final statement, "To inform my class about the three ways to effectively discipline a preschool child," clearly states her specific purpose. Note that it is written in the form of a statement, not a question, that it contains only one idea, and that the language is concrete. Also note that Amy needed to revise her statement several times before constructing an effective one. You must refine your statement until it includes all the components just mentioned.

THESIS STATEMENT

Once you have constructed an effective specific-purpose statement, the next logical step is to develop your thesis statement. A **thesis statement** includes the major ideas of your speech; at the same time, it refines your specific purpose.

Whereas the specific-purpose statement lays the groundwork for constructing your speech, the thesis statement reflects the outcome of your research (see Chapter 12). In fact, your research may cause you to construct a thesis statement that is different from the one you initially envisioned. For example, prior to conducting any research on your topic, "leading causes of death for women," you develop the following specific-purpose statement and thesis statement:

Specific purpose—to inform my classmates about the two leading causes of women's death.

Thesis statement—The two leading causes of women's deaths in the United States are automobile accidents and cancer.

Your research, however, turns up different evidence; you must now change your thesis statement to reflect your findings:

Amended thesis statement—The two leading causes of women's deaths in the United States are heart disease and cancer (Center for Disease Control, 2007).

In constructing your thesis statement, there are a few guidelines to follow: (1) Put your thesis statement in a complete sentence, (2) avoid general or vague language, and (3) preview the main ideas. By taking these factors into account, your thesis statement will provide a good basis for developing the major ideas in your speech.

The previous section included this example of a specific-purpose statement: "To inform my class about the three ways to effectively discipline a preschool child." Fine-tuning resulted in the following thesis statement: "Three ways to discipline a preschool child are time-outs, scolding, and praise." While this thesis statement refines Amy's specific-purpose statement, it also reflects what she wants her audience to remember after her presentation.

Serving Your COMMUNITY   Demographics and Audience Adaptation

Demographics can play a major role in topic selection and in adapting the topic to the audience. To illustrate this point, assume you want to focus an informative speech on the events of 9/11, then:

1. Contact your local senior residential community and volunteer to assist the residents.
2. Spend at least three hours volunteering with the residents.
3. During your time with them, interview at least three people about their memories of 9/11 and the impact the events had on their lives.
4. Interview at least three of your classmates about the same topic.
5. Compare and contrast the points of view of each group.
6. How would you integrate the diverse points of view into your presentation for:
   a. residents at the retirement center?
   b. classmates?
7. How did this process help you appreciate differences in audience demographics?

SUMMARY

Selecting a topic is the first order of business in preparing a public speech. A key variable in the selection process is you—your concerns, experiences, knowledge, and curiosity often provide excellent speech topics. Another key element is the situation. Knowing about the size of your audience, the time limit, and the shape and size of the room will help you determine an appropriate topic.

You can increase your understanding of the audience by assessing such things as audience demographics, including age, sex, and ethnic/cultural/religious background, and the additional characteristics of knowledge, attitudes, needs, societal roles, occupation, and economic status. What you learn from your assessment can help you choose a topic and adapt it to fit your particular audience. How do you gather these data? Basically, there are three methods: observation, interviews, and surveys. Surveys can include closed questions, open questions, or those on a graduated scale (or combinations of all three). If after careful examination of yourself, the situation, and the audience you still do not have a topic, consider brainstorming. Brainstorming, either by yourself or with your peers, is an alternative method for exploring additional topics.

Your observations, interviews, and surveys provide a great deal of information about your audience which you must now use to adapt the topic selected at the beginning of this process to the audience you have come to better understand as a result of the assessment process.

Once you have selected your topic, you must determine the purpose of your presentation. The development of your speech purpose usually follows three steps: (1) determining the general purpose (to inform, persuade, or entertain), (2) determining the specific purpose, and (3) creating a thesis statement. The move from general purpose to specific purpose helps you focus your topic by taking into account such factors as (1) what you hope to accomplish, (2) which aspect of the topic you will cover, and (3) your intended audience. With some fine-tuning you develop your thesis statement, which includes the major points of your speech.

REVIEW QUESTIONS

1. What factors in your background can assist you in choosing a topic?
2. How can the elements of a situation affect your topic selection and how you develop the topic?
3. Why is knowing the demographics and other characteristics of your audience so important in choosing and developing a speech topic?
4. How can you incorporate an audience's need for esteem in a speech on corporate advancement?
5. Describe three types of questions you might ask your audience before choosing your topic.
6. How can you adapt your speech topic to a specific audience?
7. What factors should be included in your specific-purpose statement?
8. What factors should be included in your thesis statement?

KEY CONCEPTS

situation	self-actualization	graduated scale
demographics	role	Likert scale
Maslow's hierarchy of needs	observation	general purpose
physiological needs	interview	specific purpose
safety needs	survey	thesis statement
need to belong	closed survey	
esteem needs	open survey	

Researching and Using Supporting Material for Your Speech

AFTER STUDYING THIS CHAPTER, YOU SHOULD

understand

- six potential sources of information for your speech.
- seven forms of supporting material that may be used in your speech.
- six different types of presentational aids.

be able to

- locate reference and periodical sources at the library or on the Internet to use in your speech.
- properly document sources used in your speech.
- avoid three special problems associated with the use of presentational aids.

Rolanda is on her way to the campus library to do the research necessary to develop her speech. She knows that her topic, mentoring children, is interesting to the audience because of her thorough audience analysis, which included a survey. The topic is also very interesting to her because of her experience serving as a mentor with the Big Brothers Big Sisters program in her city. Her task now is to find as much information on mentoring children as possible.

After several hours in the library and on the Internet, Rolanda finds

- three recent newspaper articles describing the work of the Big Brothers Big Sisters program in her city.
- four books: an autobiography of an adult who was mentored as a child; two textbooks for a sociology course on children at risk; and one focusing on how to be a mentor.
- a lengthy newsmagazine article about children at risk and their need for mentoring.
- six scholarly journal articles written by educators, sociologists, and child psychologists.
- a speech by former Supreme Court Justice Sandra Day O'Connor that discusses mentoring.
- several websites, like mentoring.org, that discuss mentoring and opportunities for mentoring children in her community.
- the national website for Big Brothers Big Sisters (bbbs.org). Rolanda sent their director an email requesting information about the organization.

■ ■ ■ ■ ■

Obviously, Rolanda has found plenty of information for her speech. She must now read through it and determine the best way to organize it so she can clearly communicate it to her audience. In this chapter, we discuss how to find material, both in and out of the library, to support your topic. A diversity of source material will add to the fullness of your speech and strengthen your overall arguments. The more diverse your source material, the greater chance you have of connecting with the multiple frames of reference of the audience. It will also help you feel more confidant about presenting the speech because you will know your research is credible and interesting.

Regardless of your topic, integrating evidence into your presentation helps you to construct and develop your ideas more logically. In your presentation, you will be making a claim (the thesis statement described in Chapter 11). Your claim must be supported with various forms of evidence. Furthermore, the added documentation helps you to inform your audience more accurately and thoroughly and increases the credibility of your arguments. Rolanda has already done a great job of collecting and organizing her supporting material. In this chapter we shall take a look at the types of information available to you, where to look for these sources, how to cite them in a speech, and the kinds of supporting material you can use as a speaker.

SOURCES OF INFORMATION

When contemplating supporting material for a speech, it is important to know the kinds of materials available and where they can be found. In this section we shall discuss such important sources as personal experiences, interviews, and, in the subsequent two sections, information that can be found in the library and on the Internet.

■ Personal Experiences

Speeches that relay personal experiences add a special dimension to public presentations. Whether the speech topic is a personal experience—hiking through Yellowstone National Park, your first day on a new job, delivering a child at home, doing yoga—or whether personal experiences are included to augment an aspect of the topic (that is, interjecting a brief story about your effort to stop smoking as a way to reduce hypertension), the overall effect is one of adding "life" to the talk. No one knows better than you the significance of a particular experience, and the public speech provides you with an opportunity to successfully communicate these personal feelings.

The speech that focuses on personal experiences is ideal for the novice speaker. Being intimately acquainted with the subject, the individual can avoid some of the anxiety associated with public speaking; in its place is the feeling of confidence that comes from knowing the subject. In addition, using your diverse experiences encourages the audience to appreciate you as a speaker and helps increase your credibility.

■ Interviews

While searching for sources of information for your speech, remember that the experiences and knowledge of other people can enhance almost any topic. These people may range from professionals to researchers to practitioners. Look for someone who has something special to bring to your topic—an individual who possesses some unique knowledge that can be used to enhance the quality of your presentation (see Chapter 8 for a detailed discussion about interviewing).

FINDING SOURCES: THE LIBRARY

In addition to using yourself and interviewing others, the academic or public library is usually the next best place to search for supporting materials. Several areas of the library can help you research your topic in order to prepare a more thorough speech. These include the classification system used by the library, the online catalog, indexes and databases, and the Internet.

■ Classification Systems

The first step in doing research in the library is finding out how your topic has been classified by the library. All source material is cataloged and shelved by subject area, so that like materials are located in the same place. There are two classification systems, Dewey Decimal and Library of Congress (LC). In general, public libraries use Dewey and academic libraries use LC, but that's not always the case. Both use standard keywords (called *subject headings*) to classify and organize materials. These are useful to know when searching for books and journals relevant to your topic; ask a librarian for help in determining the best words to use. For example:

> Megan grew up in a family that loves cars. Her parents even turned their garage into a body shop so they could restore old Mustangs. Megan shares her parents' love for old cars. She would like to do her informative speech on the history of the Corvette. She begins her research by using the word *cars* to find books held in the library. The search results in "no holdings found." The librarian will tell her that her topic is found under *automobile*, not *cars*. Her search will now be much more successful now that she knows the right subject heading word to use.

■ Online Catalog: Library Holdings

In the past, library catalogs consisted of big banks of drawers that held rows and rows of 3" × 5" index cards organized by author, title, and subject heading. Today, all of this information can be accessed from any computer, located anywhere, that has Internet access. You can search your library's online catalog by an author, title, subject, or keyword to find out what books, periodicals, newspapers, encyclopedias, biographical sources, government publications, and other media are available. In some cases, the online catalog will include links which will take you directly to electronic versions of these materials.

◼ Books

Because of the amount of space books provide, treatment of a topic is frequently more in-depth than that found in newspaper, magazine, or journal articles. Rarely, however, does a speaker have time to read an entire book to get information about a topic; more commonly, a section or chapter of a book is used for that purpose.

Specialists in a field often write books. Because books take longer to publish, however, the information they contain may be more dated than what can be found in either periodicals or newspapers. When timeliness is not an important factor, books often make excellent sources of information.

◼ Newspapers

An excellent source of supporting material for current topics is the **newspaper.** Articles tend to be brief, but focused. Daily newspapers routinely include detailed accounts of events and reactions to those events, as well as factual and statistical information. For example, in the January 21, 2009, issue of the *New York Times*, there are dozens of articles about Barack Obama's inauguration. The topics include the size of the crowds in attendance, the Inauguration ceremony, Obama's speech, and the inaugural balls.

Because most major news stories require a second source to verify the position taken in the article, there is a great deal of pressure to describe the situation accurately. Even so, newspapers often have a bias, a fact that public speakers should understand.

◼ Periodicals

Periodicals, written sources published at regular intervals (that is, weekly, monthly, quarterly, or semiannually), provide a wealth of factual and interpretive information on hundreds of topics. Speakers can rely on these sources to add substance to their presentations.

Magazines have a longer interval between issues than daily newspapers, which allows the writers to devote more time to researching the topic and to put into perspective the circumstances surrounding a particular event. Generally, magazine articles are more in-depth than newspaper articles because of the additional time provided for research and because of the greater amount of space allotted to these stories.

As you consult magazines for information, keep in mind that many magazines (like newspapers) have a particular bias. For instance, to get varying perspectives on the subject of mothers who work outside the home, you might read articles in *Family Circle*, a traditional women's magazine; *Newsweek*, where the approach is likely to be neutral and matter-of-fact; and *Ms.*, which provides a feminist perspective. Using all these types of magazines allows a more thorough examination of your subject.

Journals contain research findings carried out in a particular field, such as medicine, social welfare, electrical engineering, or communication. They are also valuable resources for supporting material to enhance your speech. You might look at journal articles for several reasons: to get data and statistics provided by research studies, to get commentary on a subject by specialists, or to get more in-depth coverage of a topic. To continue the example from above, you might want to look in *Signs*, a journal of women's studies or *Management Communication Quarterly*, a journal of business management. Each of these journals will provide you with more specialized information concerning working mothers.

■ Encyclopedias

Nearly everyone has had an occasion to look up information in a general encyclopedia, such as *World Book* or *Encyclopaedia Britannica*. However, most libraries also own specialized encyclopedias published for numerous disciplines. Titles often found in the reference collection include *International Encyclopedia of the Social Sciences*, *McGraw-Hill Encyclopedia of Science and Technology*, *Encyclopedia of Women's History in America*, and *Encyclopedia and Dictionary of Medicine and Nursing*. These sources include signed articles written by scholars in the field and are often accompanied by bibliographies or references to related works.

■ Biographical Sources

If your topic focuses on the accomplishments or fame achieved by a well-known individual, there are many biographical reference sources that await you. For example, *Biography Index*, published since 1949, contains citations to both periodical articles and books written about well-known people. *Current Biography* is a monthly publication with an annual accumulation called *Current Biography Yearbook*. This source includes biographical sketches of many living persons. The articles usually conclude with a brief list of additional references. Finally, there are several *Who's Who* biographical dictionaries that contain background information on thousands of individuals. Those considered standard reference sources include *Who's Who*, *Who's Who in America*, *Who's Who of American Women*, and *Who's Who in American Politics*.

■ Government Publications

Perhaps your speech topic necessitates that you have current statistics to report to your audience. For example, are more men or women involved in fatal automobile accidents? How many Americans died of AIDS in 2009? *Statistical Abstract of the United States* would be an excellent place to check for these figures. A few worth mentioning include *Stat-USA*, available online from the U.S. Department of Commerce at http://www.stat-usa.gov/; the Federal Bureau of Investigation's *Uniform Crime Reports*, online at http://www.fbi.gov/ucr/ucr.htm; the U.S. Department of Justice's website at http://www.usdoj.gov/; and the *Congressional Record* (http://www.gpoaccess.gov/crecord/). This last source is particularly useful when researching how an issue was debated on the floor of the House of Representatives or the Senate.

To track down the thousands of government documents made available each year, check the *Catalog of U.S. Government Publications* at http://catalog.gpo.gov/. There you can search for documents by author, title, subject, and keyword.

■ Other Media

Audiovisual sources, including radio and television broadcasts, films, sound recordings, and videos, have both advantages and disadvantages for the public speech. First, we shall consider radio and television broadcasts. As information sources, the chief advantage of radio and television news broadcasts is their immediacy. When news stories receive considerable attention via television, radio, and Internet (which is especially true for such crises as the events of 9/11/01; natural disasters such as floods, earthquakes, and volcanoes; and important political events such as the 2008 presidential election and inauguration in 2009), vast audiences are reached. Therefore, when you incorporate information from the broadcast in your speech, several members of your audience will likely instantly recognize what you are saying. You and your audience share a common ground, which increases the audience's understanding of your message. Another advantage of these sources is their dramatic nature. For example, coverage of the same issue in such print media as newspapers and magazines cannot compete with the drama of a live broadcast.

Films and audio recordings are good sources for reflecting the moods and attitudes of a particular time. Consider, for example, the way popular/rock music, motion pictures, and television comedies and dramas all reflect what our society is like during a specific period. A song, a film clip, or a clip from a television program can portray a "slice of life" to your audience.

Finally, videos, especially commercially produced educational videos, also can provide useful background information, particularly for an informative speech in which your purpose is to educate your audience. Excerpts included in your presentation can effectively complement your verbal explanations. YouTube.com is also a valuable resource for video clips.

This brings us to the disadvantages or drawbacks of using audiovisual sources. Incorporating material you gather from the types of media just discussed poses two problems: (1) having adequate time in your speech to "set up" or introduce the material, and (2) operating the necessary machinery (computer, CD, MP3 player, or DVD player). You must consider these special conditions when contemplating the use of audiovisual materials in your presentation.

■ Indexes and Databases

Doing research doesn't mean having to check each journal, magazine, or newspaper that may have information relevant to your topic individually. Virtually every library offers a variety of periodical indexes which lets you search for a topic in hundreds of publications at once. The H. W. Wilson Company publishes *Readers' Guide to Periodical Literature*, which indexes nearly 400 popular periodicals in an alphabetical topical arrangement. It also publishes specialized periodical indexes such as *Education Index* (covering almost 700 education journals), *Business Periodicals Index* (over 800 journals), *Social Sciences Index* (600 journals), and *Humanities Index* (550 publications).

Large libraries also have newspaper indexes on hand, most notably the *New York Times Index*, *Wall Street Journal Index*, *Washington Post Index*, or the *National Newspaper Index*. All of the indexes mentioned are available online.

Computers have made doing thorough research even simpler. Many libraries offer electronic access to all of the H. W. Wilson indexes through *WilsonWeb*, where you are able to search for a topic across all of their indexes at the same time. More and more articles are becoming available in electronic format, and when your search results include these, *WilsonWeb* provides a link to the full-text. In these cases, the entire article appears on your computer screen where you can read and/or print it. Your library may also offer online access to other, more specialized, electronic databases where you can search for articles about communication (ComAbstracts), sports (SPORTDiscus), psychology (PsycARTICLES and PsycINFO), and legal/corporate/compliance issues (Lexis-Nexis). Electronic journal archives, such as JSTOR and Project MUSE, provide online access to hundreds of journals in a variety of disciplines.

Your library also offers large databases of information online. E*Subscribe offers access to more than 1.2 million research reports, journal articles, and other education-related materials from ERIC, the Education Resources Information Center sponsored by the U.S. Department of Education. Medline Plus, from the U.S. National Library of Medicine and the National Institutes of Health, offers extensive information from the National Library of Medicine. PAIS International contains references to more than 553,300 journal articles, books, government documents, statistical directories, grey literature, research reports, conference reports, and publications of international agencies from over 120 countries throughout the world. MLA International Bibliography, from the Modern Language Association, has over a million records dealing with literature, language, linguistics, and folklore. AGRICOLA is the definitive database for information about agriculture and related issues, providing abstracts and indexing for hundreds of resources about agriculture, agronomy, animal science, biology, chemistry, ecology, forestry, nutrition, pollution, and zoology. You can use all of these databases, and many more, to obtain abstracts of articles and bibliographic information; in many cases full-text articles are also available. A reference librarian can help you determine which database(s) will be most appropriate for your topic.

COMMUNICATION IN ACTION

Finding and Evaluating Periodicals

Using several of the indexes listed above, find at least three articles about the following topics:

1. women's professional sports.
2. the Challenger shuttle accident.
3. laser eye surgery.

Which of these articles would be appropriate for use in an informative speech? How can integrating periodicals into your presentation strengthen your confidence as a communicator?

USING THE INTERNET: WORLD WIDE WEB

Most colleges and universities are connected to the information superhighway or the Internet. The Internet is a network of computers from around the United States and the world. From your computer, you can access information from millions of websites. To begin your search, you must first choose a search engine. A search engine will provide you with a list of possible websites that may be helpful. Use several different search engines because each uses different criteria in selecting and organizing relevant websites. Yahoo!, Ask.com, and Google are just a few available. For example, with the Yahoo! search engine, you use the keywords *vegetarian* and *cooking*. Yahoo! will provide you with over 58 million "hits." You then must choose a subcategory and begin sorting through the list to find credible sources. In this example, you can choose sites concerning recipes, cookbooks, restaurants, festivals, and medical information.

It is important to understand that just because information is on the Internet does not mean it is credible or true. When accessing information from the Web, you need to ask four specific questions. First, who is the source of the information? Is the source biased? Does he or she have a vested interest in the information? Is the source an expert? Second, how old is the information? When was the last time the site was updated? Third, is the information verifiable elsewhere? In other words, can you cross-check the information from other sources? Finally, is an email or other contact information provided? You may need to clarify or verify information on the site. Websites that do not provide other contact information should be regarded very carefully. Table 12.1 lists four important questions to ask about the credibility of any website.

■ Using Email

If you are using your college or university's online resources, you probably have an email address. Your email account allows you to send and receive messages from anyone online. Email is a valuable tool when doing research for your speech. Specifically, you can request information from experts in the field or others who have experience with your topic. In the beginning of this chapter, Rolanda sent an email to the director of Big Brothers Big Sisters. When sending emails, be sure to identify yourself, what specific information you are seeking, and why you want the information.

TABLE 12.1   Four Questions to Ask about Websites

1. Who is the source?

2. How old is the information?

3. Is the information verifiable elsewhere?

4. Is an email or other contact information provided?

Google is one of many search engines that you can use to find source material on the Web.

CITING SOURCES

An important part of constructing your speech is to indicate your sources of information. This process should enhance your credibility, especially if you are planning to present a controversial argument. More important, it is unethical to omit mentioning whose ideas you are borrowing for your speech. When you use the ideas of another and do not indicate where those ideas come from, you are plagiarizing.

In written material, you must provide a citation for any source material. Its purpose is to indicate where someone else could find the data you used. A citation should indicate whose idea is being used and the source from which it was obtained. In order to give proper credit to others, you should include a citation after every direct quote, as well as for those times when you paraphrase someone else's ideas. Several stylebooks describe the proper format for citations. Your instructor may require that you use a specific style manual for citing sources in your speech outline (see Chapter 13).

It is necessary to give credit orally to a source you have used. This is known simply as the **oral citation.** For example:

In her informative speech on the "Science of *Star Trek*," Tavaughna cited a recent article on the possibility of creating phasers, a weapon used in the *Star Trek* series. She said, "Dr. Lawrence Krauss, author of *The Physics of Star Trek*, said in a May 2009 *Scientific American* article, 'Phasers are

SKILL BUILDING

Using the Library

Now that you have decided on a topic for your first speech, it is time to do some research. Go to your library and check the following reference sources for possible supporting material:

1. Your library's online catalog for books.
2. *Readers' Guide to Periodical Literature* (bound volumes) or *WilsonWeb* (online).
3. *New York Times* or other newspaper index.
4. Online database(s) appropriate for your subject, such as E*Subscribe, MedlinePlus, MLA, or others.
5. Internet for any websites.

List the possible source material you found. Which of these is the most useful? Why? Which of these is not useful? Why?

like lasers, really—they are directed-energy weapons. But the problem with a real phaser is that it would be pretty hard to generate the energy to heat something or someone up to a billion degrees to vaporize them. You would get some recoil, too" (Hadhazy, 2009). This statement lets Tavaughna's audience know that the idea originated with someone else.

As you gather information for your speech, you may wish to prepare a bibliography of all your sources. The bibliography should include all the sources you use, even if they are not directly cited in the text of the speech. The style manuals used for citations also should be used for these bibliographic citations. Whenever questions arise about the information you have presented in your speech, you can refer to your bibliography to direct the questioner to particular magazines, books, films, and online sources. A thorough bibliography, appended to your speech outline, usually indicates a well-researched speech.

Communication and TECHNOLOGY

Limiting Your Web Frustration

Ten billion searches for information are conducted each day, according to ComScore (2008). Specifically, 69 percent of the Internet users each day use a search engine (Fox, 2008). The Internet provides us with access to limitless information and we don't even have to leave our homes. With a few clicks of the mouse, we can find information, for example, about environmental topics like the diminishing rain forest and global warming, or the latest scores for our favorite sports teams, and we can even find the full text of the President's last national address. But, the Internet can be frustrating to navigate and even dangerous to our speech purpose or goal. In order to limit your frustration and to successfully find the information you need to support your main ideas in your speech, consider the following:

1. Search Engines Limit the Information You Can Find.

Google is the most popular search engine as almost 59 percent of all searches use it. Yahoo! is the second favorite with over 22 percent (ComScore, 2008). Yahoo!, students' favorite search engine, indexes only about 7 percent of the information available on the Web (Goss, 2000). That means, for example, when you search for information on the history of affirmative action in the United States, Yahoo! will leave out 93 percent of the information available. Always use more than one search engine. Others include

www.msn.com

www.aol.com

Any of these search engines can help you access information on your topic.

2. Define Your Topic Carefully.

There are several things to consider before doing a search. First, try several different terms for your topic in order to find relevant information. For example, to find information about the history of the Internet, you might use these key words: *Internet, World Wide Web,* and *information superhighway.* Second, if your topic is too broad, you may find yourself overwhelmed with "hits" or websites that apply to your topic. Doing a search on "baseball" for example, will provide you with over 1,000,000 sites. You could not possibly check all of these sites. Narrow your topic to the World Series of 2009 or the invention of baseball. These topics are more manageable. Third, some topics are difficult to search for on the Internet because of the nature of the words used to do the search. Specifically, searches on topics like breast cancer, self-breast examinations, and sexual harassment will turn up pornographic sites.

3. Use the Links Provided.

Many websites will lead you to other sites that are similar in content via a hyperlink. Use these links to find sites your search engine may not know about. Be careful, however, to keep track of your path. Jeffery Schantz states, "They [students] forget a hyperlink can, and often does, take them to an entirely new source. That's a problem when they try to document sources. They may inaccurately attribute sources and may have trouble retracing the steps that led them to a specific source" (1999, p. 4).

4. Check the Credibility of the Source.

Users of the Web often believe that if something is online, it must be true (Goss, 2000). Anyone can develop, design, and maintain a website and just about any information can be included on that website. It is your ethical responsibility to provide your audience accurate and reliable information. Earlier in this chapter, we discussed the questions you should ask about any information you find on the Internet. In addition, according to Goett and Foote, remember "Web pages are created for advertising, sales, advocacy, education, reference, and entertainment. Students need to recognize that these goals may bias the presentation of factual information. Recognizing such bias does not mean that a source be discarded, since we sometimes wish to examine all sides of controversial issues, but it does caution about accepting facts and figures gathered from Web pages at face value" (2000, p. 92).

5. Avoid Plaigarism.

Plagiarism is using someone else's words or ideas without crediting that person at the time of use. Anytime you take information from a website, you must credit the source by providing a citation. Even if you paraphrase or summarize information, a citation must be provided. Because information can be downloaded right from the Web to your computer, don't be tempted to "cut and paste." Don't take ideas that belong to someone else and pass them off to the audience as yours.

Using the Internet to find supporting material can be easy and fun if you follow these guidelines.

FORMS OF SUPPORT FOR YOUR SPEECH

In an effort to present your ideas clearly and convincingly, it is important to include evidence to support those ideas. The purpose of using supporting material is to supplement your major ideas, and this, in turn, adds credibility to your position. A diversity of source material will make your argument stronger. An added benefit is increased self-confidence, because you know that the argument you are presenting is thorough and well documented. It will also help you to relate your ideas to the unique and varied frames of reference of your audience. Several different types of supporting material are discussed in the following subsections.

■ Examples

One of the strongest types of support is the use of examples. **Examples** are statements that attempt to illuminate the facts. They can be very effective in your effort to involve the audience in your presentation. Moreover, they help to clarify your presentation by reinforcing the points in your arguments. This assists the audience in following the progression of your ideas. A properly used example is one that is relevant and relates to the major ideas of your presentation. Let's take a look at three types of examples.

Factual Example

A **factual example** is something that you have observed. It grows out of your own experience, and as with any good example, it helps to reinforce a point. When the example is believable, it keeps the audience involved in your presentation and can lead to greater interest on their part. Consider the following:

> Dave is a psychology major and his topic for his first speech, "emotional pain," needed the focus of a specific example to illustrate one type of emotional pain. He recalled attending the funeral of a friend's teenage daughter who was killed in an automobile accident and the pain he witnessed there. The language Dave used to describe the situation— people sobbing uncontrollably, the parents needing to be supported by other family members, and so on—captured the emotional pain this family was experiencing and earned the attention of the audience as well.

Hypothetical Example

A **hypothetical example** is one that invites the audience to imagine a situation created expressly for the speech they are listening to. It is an effective way to capture the audience's interest, because it involves them directly in the process. Consider the following:

> Denise, a member of the Highland election board, was addressing a local women's group. Her purpose was to inform the audience of the procedure for registering voters. She believed her speech was crucial to increasing voter turnout in the upcoming off-year election. To emphasize her point,

she created a hypothetical situation—she asked the audience to imagine that they were living in some areas of Afghanistan. She spoke of Rebecca, a young woman who is not allowed to leave her home without a male escort or to attend school. Of course, like all other women in Afghanistan, she cannot vote. While not an actual case, Denise's example dramatically expressed her feelings that our freedom should not be taken lightly. She then moved back to her original theme: We need to be aware of the registration process and exercise our right to vote.

This example works because it kept the audience involved in the presentation and served to reinforce the central purpose of the speech.

Examples, then, can play an important role in your presentation because they can help clarify and reinforce your ideas. In addition, they add a personal touch to your presentation by providing a safe way to relay your personal feelings to your audience.

ANECDOTES AND STORIES

Anecdotes, brief narratives, and stories help to personalize your ideas. They can help you make abstract ideas come alive for your audience. In other words, anecdotes and stories put a human face on an issue.

For example, in her speech at the Democratic National Convention in 2008, Michelle Obama said:

> I come here as a daughter—raised on the South Side of Chicago by a father who was a blue-collar city worker and a mother who stayed at home with my brother and me. My mother's love has always been a sustaining force for our family, and one of my greatest joys is seeing her integrity, her compassion, and her intelligence reflected in my own daughters. My dad was our rock. Although he was diagnosed with multiple sclerosis in his early thirties, he was our provider, our champion, our hero. As he got sicker, it got harder for him to walk, it took him longer to get dressed in the morning. But if he was in pain, he never let on. He never stopped smiling and laughing—even while struggling to button his shirt, even while using two canes to get himself across the room to give my mom a kiss. He just woke up a little earlier and worked a little harder. He and my mom poured everything they had into me and Craig. It was the greatest gift a child can receive: never doubting for a single minute that you're loved, and cherished, and have a place in this world. And thanks to their faith and hard work, we both were able to go on to college. So I know firsthand from their lives—and mine—that the American dream endures (2008).

Michelle Obama tells the story of her childhood and of her parents to put a human face on illness, education, and hope. Like examples, stories and anecdotes should reinforce or clarify your overall argument.

■ Statistics

Why use **statistics** in a public speech? The reasons are clear. First, people have an easier time conceptualizing ideas that are presented in numerical terms; somehow things seem real when you quantify them. Take the issue of poverty: you see the epidemic in a more serious light when you are told that 12.5 percent of the population lives in poverty (U.S. Census Bureau, 2008b). Second, statistics add credibility to your arguments because they document the points you are advancing. For example, a speech that attempts to persuade the audience to have a colonoscopy in order to prevent colon cancer is made more effective if it includes statistics to back up these claims. Possible statistics to support the claim could be (1) colon cancer is the third most common diagnosed cancer; (2) 141,000 Americans each year are diagnosed with this form of cancer; and (3) 60 percent of deaths could have been prevented with early detection through a colonoscopy (Centers for Disease Control, 2009).

Despite the support statistics offer, caution should be exercised regarding their use. The discussion that follows focuses on understanding statistics and using statistics.

Michelle Obama at the Democratic National Convention uses a story about her family to put a human face on several issues.

Understanding Statistics

In order to assess the value and limitations of statistics, a basic understanding of the methods used to compile statistics is desirable. Statistics are calculated in one of three ways: according to the median, according to the mean, or according to the mode.

The **median** is the middle point of a set of numbers, which means that half the numbers are above the midpoint and half the numbers are below the midpoint. In this set of numbers—6, 8, 9, 32, 37—9 is the median, because half the numbers are above 9 and half are below 9.

The **mean** is sometimes referred to as the "average." To calculate the mean, add all the values and divide the total sum by the number of numerals in the set. If one number is significantly higher or lower than the rest of the numbers, it can greatly affect the outcome of the mean. For instance, in the following set of numbers—3, 6, 9, 12, 15, 64—the number 64 would greatly raise the average of the combined scores.

The **mode** is the number that occurs most frequently in a set of numbers. In this set of numbers—1, 4, 7, 9, 9, 15—9 represents the mode because it occurs more frequently than any other number. Consider the difference in the median, mean, and mode for this set of numbers: 1, 12, 13, 37, 75, 75, 130.

Median: # 37
Mean: # 49
Mode: # 75

Using Statistics

As a speaker, it is important to be sensitive to the way you use numbers when developing your arguments. In fact, before deciding to use statistics in your talk, you should consider the following: (1) Is the statistical sample representative? (2) Do the statistics mislead your audience? (3) Are the statistics confusing to your audience?

It is your responsibility to make sure the statistics you use are based on a representative sample. Is the sample large enough? For example, in her speech about parking conditions at the university, Juanita reports that "nine out of ten students feel that there is a campus parking problem." While it appears that 90 percent of the students concur with Juanita's belief that there is a parking problem, there is something wrong with the data she used. Her sample of only 10 students is not large enough to draw any conclusions.

A second problem arises from the data. Are these 10 students representative of the total student body? After some questioning, Juanita reveals that the 10 students she interviewed were all late for their eleven o'clock classes, the busiest time of day on campus. Many were angry because they could not find a parking spot. In addition, the day she conducted her survey the university was hosting a statewide journalism symposium, which meant that there were more visitors on campus than normal. Both of these circumstances would render Juanita's findings invalid.

Another point to consider is whether or not the statistics might mislead your audience. Statistics can vary dramatically, depending on the particular numerical representation used, namely, median, mean, or mode. All three are ways of explaining numbers, yet each represents a different measure for the same data. Consider the following:

At a national conference of real estate agents, speakers cited various statistics to advance their own positions. For example, Angela, an agency owner, claimed that "with the average [mean] selling price of a home at $185,000, real estate commissions were providing a good income for brokers." Luke, a part-time sales representative and full-time college student, however, used $100,000 [the mode] as an argument for raising the commission percentage. With the median at $125,000, both groups chose to use related statistics to support their stand on the issue of real estate commissions.

SKILL BUILDING

Working with Statistics

1. The following is a set of test scores from an industrial psychology class:
   94 92 83 83 75 74 71 70 69 64 51 42
2. Please calculate the mean, mode, and median.
3. What is the potential problem with using this information?

This case illustrates that statistics are often selected because they support a position; it is this very selectivity that can mislead an audience.

While statistics can help you quantify a point you are trying to make, and thereby enhance your argument, you should be careful not to clutter your speech with too many statistics that may confuse or overwhelm the audience.

■ Authoritative Opinion

Authoritative opinion, the words or ideas of individuals knowledgeable about a topic, can add credibility to your presentation. Use of authoritative opinion also indicates that you are not alone in your thinking. When using an authoritative opinion, you should (1) verify that the testimony comes from a qualified source, (2) verify that the source is unbiased, and (3) accurately quote or paraphrase your source.

Two types of testimony include the comments of recognized authorities and the comments of persons uniquely qualified on a given subject. Comments made by the president of the American Bar Association concerning the legal qualifications of a Supreme Court nominee would be regarded as expert testimony by a recognized authority. On the other hand, if you are giving a speech on how to do your own picture framing, you might decide to include Ms. Sutter's suggestions for matting art prints and needlework because of her 15 years of experience in the custom framing business. Ms. Sutter is not a "recognized" authority, yet she is uniquely qualified on the subject of picture framing.

■ Comparisons

One way to make your arguments stronger is to compare to similar or different ideas, facts, or concepts. Analogies and similes can help you to clarify your message.

Analogy

An **analogy** compares the similar features in two seemingly different objects or situations. For example, "what racquetball does for Barb, needlepoint does for Chris." Two totally different activities reduce stress for these two women. If your speech topic is "ways to reduce stress," this analogy breaks down the topic into subpoints that are more easily understood, in part because the comparison drawn between the two activities is valid.

When you use an analogy, develop it completely so that the audience can follow the logic of your thinking, as in this example:

Barbara, president of her local chapter of PETA (People for the Ethical Treatment of Animals) was asked to speak to a group of high school students about the lack of humanity in hunting and trapping animals. She spoke of the different methods of slaughtering to demonstrate her point. In order for the audience to visualize what she was saying about the suffering of trapped animals, she compared it to the brutal treatment of prisoners of war incarcerated in Third World countries. She asked the students to imagine the torture experienced by some of our prisoners of

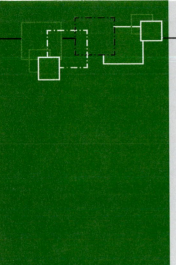

EMBRACING DIFFERENCE

Supporting Material

Hesla is intrigued by all stories in the media about alternative energy sources like solar and wind power. She plans to use the subject for her next speech assignment and knows she must narrow the topic and eventually develop a clear thesis statement. She also realizes that she must include a wide variety of supporting material to reach a diverse audience. As she begins to shape her presentation, she decides to include at least five different forms of supporting material in her speech.

1. What are some possible sources Hesla could use in her speech? Where might she find them?
2. How has Hesla's appreciation of difference helped her build her speech?
3. How can you use Hesla's experience to help you understand the importance of embracing difference?

war and then compared it to the brutal slaughter of innocent animals for recreational purposes. This analogy was compelling and drew the audience into the presentation.

Similes

Similes, like analogies, compare two things. But, unlike analogies, similes compare similar objects or situations using the words *like* or *as*. For example, you may argue that "giving a speech is as easy as riding a bike" or "learning CPR is like buying an insurance policy." The use of a simile not only helps you to clarify your message but also makes your message more vivid and creative.

■ Definition

When your speech includes jargon (terminology of a specialized group or activity) or technical terms that the average audience has difficulty understanding, you should define those terms using language that is more appropriate. For example, if the members of your audience have no experience with computers, you would need to provide definitions for such terms as *flash drive, Windows icons, and status bar*. Where do you turn for these definitions? Because specialized terms are often not defined in *Webster's*, you may need to consult one of the dozens of dictionaries that exist for specific disciplines (for example, art, construction, psychology, data processing, and biology).

PRESENTATIONAL AIDS

One of the most effective ways to clarify a concept or point is to include presentational aids in your presentation. **Presentational aids** are visual or audio support for your verbal message. A speech on arteriosclerosis (hardening of the arteries), for example, would be enhanced by an illustration showing what a clogged artery looks like. Your message is more likely to be understood if you include such visual aids as graphs, drawings, slides and movies, photographs, your body, or computer-generated presentational aids.

■ Graphs

Graphs are helpful when you wish to present statistics. Used appropriately, they can add clarity to your presentation and increase your audience's level of comprehension. There are three different types of graphs: (1) line graphs, (2) pie graphs, and (3) bar graphs.

The **line graph** is especially useful in demonstrating change over a period of time. For example, you want to communicate to your audience that the Hispanic population in the United States has increased in the past few years. After checking the U.S. Census Bureau, you find that 293,192,000 Hispanics were living in the United States in 2005; 295,896,000 in 2006; 301,621,000 in 2007 (2008c). A line graph can help show your audience the increase in Hispanic population (see Figure 12.1).

The **pie graph** (a pie shape divided into wedges) is helpful in demonstrating to an audience the way something whole is divided into parts or the way one part of a whole relates proportionately to the other parts. For instance, a pie graph of a municipal budget would show the relationship between public works spending and funds appropriated for education. The audience gains a visual sense of the way their

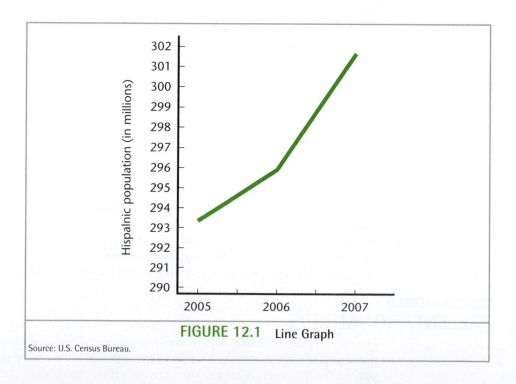

FIGURE 12.1 Line Graph

Source: U.S. Census Bureau.

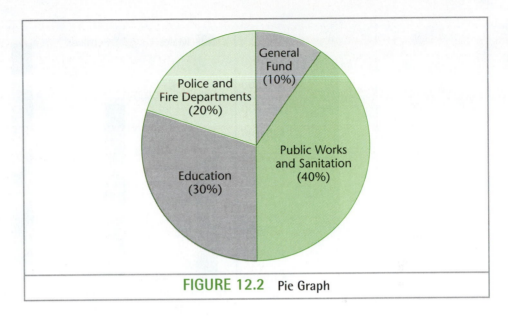

FIGURE 12.2   Pie Graph

tax dollars are spent. The pie graph in Figure 12.2 shows how a whole is divided into parts; here, a town budget.

A third type of graph is known as a **bar graph.** A bar graph is primarily used to show the way different items compare and relate to one another. For example, you want to persuade your audience to finish their college degrees because they could increase their yearly income. You create a bar graph (see Figure 12.3) that shows (1) men with a high school diploma earn on average $35,248 and women earn only 22,208; (2) men who earn an associate's degree earn on average $46,201 and women earn only $30,912; and (3) men with a bachelor's degree earn $67,980 and women earn only $40,684 (U.S. Census Bureau, 2008a).

■ Drawings

A drawing that is easy to produce can help the audience to better understand your topic. Your drawing need not be complicated, nor do you have to be an artist to use one. Consider the following:

> Evelyn, a volunteer at the Caring Place, a shelter for battered women and their children, wanted to inform her audience of single mothers about how easy it is to change the oil in their cars with little effort and at a great monetary savings. She obviously cannot bring a car into the center to demonstrate the process. Instead, she drew two diagrams, each illustrating the process of removing and replacing the oil and oil filter. These drawings helped complement Evelyn's oral presentation by simplifying the message, which increased the audience's understanding of this aspect of a car tune-up.

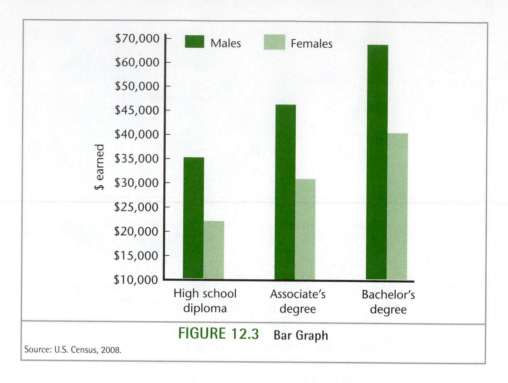

FIGURE 12.3   **Bar Graph**

Source: U.S. Census, 2008.

■ Movies and Video

Movies and video can be especially useful when you wish to stir the emotions of your audience. At times, a speaker might find it advantageous to show a movie clip to illustrate a point, as demonstrated by the following:

> Dagmar, a widow with three small children, belongs to a self-awareness group from her church. Currently, members of the group are discussing the importance of family communication. Each member is reading Judith Guest's novel *Ordinary People*. In addition, Dagmar has been asked to speak before the group on some aspect of family dynamics. She decides to talk about the importance of female family members expressing their feelings. She recalls how stirring and powerful the movie *Ordinary People* was and decides to show a scene between the mother and son. It brings several members of her audience to tears.

Movies and videos present a special kind of difficulty, however, because of the mechanics involved in operating the necessary equipment. If you choose to include slides or a movie, make sure you understand how to operate the DVD player, VCR, or other equipment. Take some extra time to practice before your actual presentation.

Your body can make a very effective presentational aid.

■ Photographs

Well-chosen photographs can capture an emotion, an attitude, or a special image. Furthermore, photographs that are directly related to your topic can have a powerful impact on your audience. Imagine, for example, the impact of a set of before-and-after pictures, the first depicting a child on the verge of starvation, the second showing the same child three months after having received food and medical attention. One drawback to photographs, however, is their size. Be sure that your photographs are large enough for everyone in the audience to see. For example, 4 × 6 photograph of the Grand Canyon will not be large enough to communicate its beauty, complexity, and size. It may be better to use PowerPoint or other software to show the photographs.

■ Your Body

You may wish to demonstrate or explain an important point in your speech by using your body. The movement of your body also can have an additional benefit—it helps reduce excess tension. Consider the following:

Michael has been studying dance since he was 12. He has been asked by the campus committee on cultural awareness to discuss the relationship between dance and culture. Specifically, he wants to demonstrate how the

Serving Your COMMUNITY — Effective Presentational Aids

Presentational aids are an important aspect of any presentation. To be effective, they must relate to the audience. Review your notes from the Serving Your Community box in Chapter 11. Then:

1. Create three presentational aids to support the topic of 9/11. Would your aids be the same for each audience (seniors and classmates)? Why or why not?

2. If you needed to create different aids for each audience, how would they be different?

3. When creating the presentational aids consider the following:
    a. Be sure the presentational aids support the main topic.
    b. Be sure the entire audience is able to see the aid.
    c. Consider the size and shape of the room as you develop the presentational aid.

4. How did this process help you appreciate difference as it applies to the creation and use of presentational aids?

twist, disco dancing, and break dancing grew out of the cultures of particular time periods. In order to make sure that the audience is familiar with these dances, Michael briefly demonstrates each one. Michael's "performance" adds a special quality to the presentation and assists him in advancing his theme.

■ Computer-Generated Presentational Aids

Computers can make it easier for you to prepare and use presentational aids. Charts, graphs, maps, diagrams, pictures, and many other aids can be produced using computer software. These aids are professional in appearance and enhance your overall presentation. PowerPoint or other presentation software may be available on your campus. Check with your computer lab instructor for help. One drawback to using presentation software is that it is easy to get carried away and prepare too many aids. Remember, presentational aids should not substitute for your arguments, but enhance the audience's understanding of them. (See the Communication and Technology box on page 291 for more information using PowerPoint.)

USING PRESENTATIONAL AIDS

It is important that your visual aids enhance your presentation, but that they do not become the center of your presentation. On the contrary, they should support the points you wish to make. If, for example, your audience becomes preoccupied with

ETHICS in Communication

Using Supporting Material

In the beginning of the chapter, we read about Rolanda and her search for supporting materials. She chose to inform her classmates about mentoring. Now that she has collected relevant information from a variety of sources, Rolanda must use this material to organize and support her ideas. How can she do this in an effective and ethical way?

1. Why is it important for Rolanda to document her source material? When should she use an oral citation during her presentation?

2. Why does Rolanda need to rely on a diversity of source materials?

3. How can using biased sources or manipulating data and statistics harm Rolanda's presentation?

4. As you think about your own speech, how will you ensure that you use supporting materials effectively and ethically?

---

a presentational aid (for example, a graphic picture or a breathtaking photograph), your message may get lost.

Too often speakers pay so much attention to a presentational aid that they forget to talk to the audience. It is crucial that you not speak directly to your presentational aid; instead, glance at it and then establish direct eye contact with the audience. By focusing exclusively on the presentational aid, you risk losing contact with the audience.

For your presentational aid to complement and enhance your presentation, all members of your audience need to be able to see it. Avoid making the audience squint or strain their eyes in an effort to see your aid. Also, when selecting your presentational aid, keep the size of the room in mind. What is the length of the room? How are the seats arranged? Ask yourself these questions to help you determine the appropriate size for your visual aids. If you have difficulty seeing the presentational aid when standing in the back of the room, chances are the audience will, too. Here are three additional pointers for use of poster board: (1) Use extra-wide markers in preparing graphs or drawings; (2) use dark colors, which show up better from a distance; and (3) make the characters large enough to see from a distance.

SUMMARY

An arsenal of supporting materials will help to make your speech clearer, more credible, and more accurate. In this chapter we identified several sources of information for your speech, including personal experiences, interviews, books, newspapers, periodicals, other media such as radio and television broadcasts, and the Internet.

In order to use these various sources, you must know how to find them in the library or online. The reference collection includes such helpful sources as encyclopedias, biographical materials, and government documents. Magazine, journal, and newspaper articles are accessible with the use of indexes such as *Readers' Guide to*

Periodical Literature, *Magazine Index*, and the *New York Times Index*, or databases such as ERIC, MLA, or PAIS. You can also use a search engine from your computer to find websites that contain useful information. Lastly, you may want to send an email requesting information from an expert or someone with personal experience with your topic.

After locating supportive material and deciding what to incorporate in your speech, you begin the process of developing the ideas in your speech. You are responsible for giving credit to others for any ideas of theirs that you use. This is done through oral footnotes during the delivery and in your bibliography.

Your efforts to find supporting materials for a speech generally produce a number of possibilities.

Depending on your topic, you will want to include one or more of these types of supporting material: examples, both factual and hypothetical; anecdotes and stories, and statistics; authoritative opinions; comparisons like analogies and similes; definitions; and visual aids, including graphs, drawings, movies and videos, photographs, your body, and computer-generated aids. Knowing how to incorporate appropriate forms of support increases your confidence during your speech. Furthermore, using a diversity of support material such as examples, statistics, stories, and other materials assists you in developing your ideas more completely, which is the purpose of using supporting materials.

REVIEW QUESTIONS

1. List six sources of information that provide supporting material for your speech.
2. What three steps are important to remember when interviewing someone?
3. List three resources you can find on your library's online catalog.
4. Explain how you can use the Internet to gather support material.
5. What four questions should you ask about information found on a website?
6. Why is it important to cite your sources?
7. Explain the benefit of using examples in a speech.
8. Explain the difference between median, mean, and mode.
9. What guidelines should you keep in mind when you plan to use statistics in your presentation?
10. Under what circumstances would you incorporate these presentational aids in your speech:
    a. line graph
    b. pie graph
    c. bar graph

KEY CONCEPTS

newspapers
periodicals
magazines
journals
oral citation
examples
factual example

hypothetical example
anecdotes
statistics
median
mean
mode
authoritative opinion

analogy
similes
presentational aids
line graph
pie graph
bar graph

CHAPTER 13

Organizing Your Speech

AFTER STUDYING THIS CHAPTER, YOU SHOULD

understand

- the three major parts of a speech.
- the five patterns that are useful for organizing the body of your speech.

be able to

- develop the body of your speech.
- construct the introduction of your speech.
- construct the conclusion of your speech.
- compose transitions, including transitional previews and summaries, for your speech.
- compose a full-sentence outline for your speech.
- develop a key-phrase outline for your speech.

Adam is majoring in hotel management and tourism. He works part-time at a local restaurant as a prep cook and hopes to one day manage a hotel in a tropical place. Adam's father is an airline pilot, so his family travels during every summer and school break. His favorite place to visit is Hawaii. For his informative speech, Adam's instructor has encouraged the students to share their personal experiences and passions. Adam decides to discuss his love for Hawaii, but first he must do extensive research.

He looks at several travel websites, reads articles in travel and food magazines, and interviews two people who live in Hawaii. Adam must decide how to organize his ideas. He knows that as the speaker, it is his responsibility to make his presentation easy to listen to and understand.

First, he tries to organize his ideas around planning a trip to Hawaii. Adam decides this would not relate to the audience because he knows that many members of his audience cannot afford to go to Hawaii (Adam wouldn't be able to go either if his father wasn't a pilot) and there is just too much information for a five-minute speech. Next, Adam decides to focus on one island in Hawaii, Oahu, and to tell his classmates about his favorite island. He narrows down this topic further and decides on three main points: the history of the island, the food at a luau, and the most popular tourist sites. This organization seems to work best for Adam, his audience, and the speaking situation.

■ ■ ■ ■ ■

As Adam discovered, there are multiple ways to organize ideas. Depending on your topic, the speaking situation, your audience, and yourself, you must decide which approach will help you to effectively communicate your information to your diverse audience. You can then be confident that the audience will listen to and understand your speech.

In this chapter, we will discuss the format of a speech. Specifically, a speech has an introduction, body, and conclusion. Chapter 11 concentrated on selecting a speech topic, determining the purpose of your speech, and analyzing the audience. Chapter 12 focused on gathering supporting materials for your topic. This chapter builds on the discussions of the previous two chapters.

As a speaker, you want your audience to find your speech not only informative and interesting, but also easy to follow. You are responsible for ensuring that members of the audience understand your speech. Remember from Chapter 3 that listening is very difficult, and as the speaker you need to make it as easy as possible for the audience to listen to your presentation. To do this, your presentation must be well organized. A well-organized speech will take your audience from a position of unfamiliarity with your treatment of a topic to a position of enlightenment.

Traditionally, a speech has three major parts: a beginning, a middle, and an end. These parts are known, respectively, as the introduction, the body, and the conclusion of a speech. Transitions between the major parts of the speech further clarify your presentation.

THE BODY

The body is the main part of your speech; as such, you begin your work here. Those ideas expressed in your thesis statement are fully developed in the body. For example, a speech on situation comedies might include the development of factors that contribute to a successful show: good scripts, appealing characters, and a degree of social commentary. Furthermore, it is in the body of your speech that you incorporate the supporting material gathered from personal experiences, interviews, sources of information found at the library, and the Internet. The ideas you wish to express in your speech can be shaped into logical, observable patterns. In fact, logically developed ideas contribute to a speaker's confidence and at the same time make it easier for the audience to follow the presentation. Two helpful steps in preparing the body include organizing your ideas and outlining.

■ Organizing Your Ideas

An element that helps create a logical flow of ideas is **sequence,** or order. Ideas that are organized in a definite pattern or progression help your audience follow the development of your talk. Generally speaking, certain topics are better suited for a particular organizational pattern, although there are no ironclad rules for selecting one over another. Ultimately, you must decide which pattern seems most appropriate for the development of your topic and the diversity or frame of references of the audience. Five organizational patterns may be used: causal order, problem/solution, spatial order, time order, and topic order.

Causal Order

Causal order establishes the fact that certain events are linked to other events that have precipitated them. When using a cause-and-effect format, first define the cause and then follow up by discussing effects. For example:

> Rashelle is a nursing student and works as a nurse's aide at State Hospital. She has been asked by her son's teacher to discuss the importance of hand washing to prevent getting colds and flu because many of the students have missed school due to illness. Her son and his classmates are in the fourth grade, so Rashelle knows she must organize her main ideas so that her presentation will make sense to them. She decides to organize her main ideas in a causal order. First, she will discuss how people don't wash their hands as often as they should after sneezing, blowing their noses, and using the bathroom. Second, she will discuss how cold and flu germs are transmitted to others and the resulting effects of fever, sore throat, nausea, and headache.

Problem/Solution

The **problem/solution** approach to organizing a speech involves identifying a conflict and then offering a potential course of action that will correct the problem. In most instances, the first part of the speech is reserved for discussing the problem; in the second part of the speech the speaker offers a solution to that problem. In most cases, the speaker is attempting to persuade the audience to follow the solution offered in the speech. This organizational pattern would be appropriate for the following topic: "Thousands of Americans suffer from hypertension [problem], but there are proven ways to reduce this condition, namely, controlling your diet, exercise, and medication [solution]."

Spatial Order

Spatial order refers to organizing the parts of a topic according to the relationship of their positions. This relationship can be geographic (the different wine-producing regions of France), rank ordered (the degrees of proficiency in karate), or directional (the exterior, then interior features of a house, car, boat). In the case of karate, the body of your speech might be organized around describing the specific techniques required for each rank from beginners (white belt) to experts (black belt).

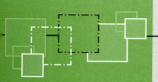

EMBRACING DIFFERENCE

Organizing Ideas

Before we can deliver our ideas to the audience, we must organize them. An effective organizational pattern will allow you to feel comfortable with the material and also clearly communicate the information to a diverse audience. Of the organizational patterns discussed in this chapter, which would work best for the following topics and their main ideas:

- Cities and towns are using fewer tax dollars for infrastructure like roads, bridges, and schools. If this trend continues, cities and towns will ultimately decay.
- The following steps are helpful when purchasing a new car: (1) research the different models; (2) select the model that is best for you; (3) visit several dealerships that sell the car; and (4) purchase the car at the dealership that gives you the best price.
- Chicago is a great sports team city because it is home to the Bulls, professional basketball; White Sox and Cubs, professional baseball; Blackhawks, professional hockey; and Bears, professional football.

1. Explain why you choose each organization pattern.
2. How does learning about the different approaches to organizing ideas help you understand the importance of embracing difference?

Time Order

Time order arranges ideas in a chronological framework. This pattern of organization is best suited to topics that present a step-by-step explanation (how to wallpaper a kitchen, how to cook a turkey) or a historical development. For example, Shelly is doing her speech on the history of the women's movement. Her three main ideas will correspond to the three "waves" of feminism. Within each main point, Shelly will discuss how women tried (and most times succeeded) in changing their lives for the better.

Topic Order

Topic order involves breaking down your main topic into smaller points that are pertinent to the main idea. For example, if the purpose of your speech is to define what a teacher is, you might discuss each of the following subtopics: (1) A teacher is someone who educates others, (2) a teacher is a role model, and (3) a teacher is someone who instills a love of learning. The order of the discussion may be unimportant, or you may view one subtopic as more important and want to address it first. That is something you must determine.

■ Outlining the Body

Why should you outline the body of your speech next? Is not selection of an organizational pattern enough to develop your speech? The answer is no. Your decision to adhere to a particular organizational structure is based on the way you view your total topic, including both its general and specific purposes. Outlining the body of your speech helps you to develop fully the points made in your thesis statement. Outlining is simply another step in the process of preparing a speech. To summarize what has happened so far, consider the following:

> *General purpose*: to inform
>
> *Specific purpose*: to inform my classroom audience about Hawaiian culture
>
> *Thesis statement*: To understand Hawaiian culture, we will discuss a brief history of Oahu, luau cuisine, and Oahu's tourist attractions.
>
> *Organizational structure*: topic order

The next step is the outline:

  I. Brief history of Oahu

 II. Luau cuisine

III. Oahu's tourist attractions

In other words, the task that awaits you is to construct an outline that develops the three ideas mentioned in your thesis sentence.

The main purpose of outlining is to help both the speaker and the audience follow the development of ideas in the speech. When constructing an outline for the body of your speech, it is sometimes helpful to use full sentences. Specific outlining rules follow, and each is related to the body of the speech.

Communication and TECHNOLOGY
Computer Software and Organization

Outlining and organizing your ideas for presentation can be frustrating. It is sometimes difficult to see how all the ideas fit together. You could put your ideas on note cards, spread them out on the floor, and begin organizing them until you have a complete outline. Today, however, computer software can help in this process.

Inspiration (http://www.inspiration.com), a computer software program, can help us organize, diagram, map, and outline ideas. Students can type in their ideas and then see how the ideas look using the "Diagram View" button. Then, using the "Outline" button, your ideas will appear in a hierarchical outline. Topics and ideas can be dragged into different places within the outline. The final outline can be converted into handouts, speaker's notes, and even presentational aids.

If you don't have access to Inspiration, Microsoft Word can also help with organizing and outlining your ideas. Depending on your version of the program, using the drop-down menu from "View," you can click on "Outline" or "Document Map." Each of these features will show you how your ideas (as typed into the document) are organized. The "Outline" function, however, will not include Roman numerals, letters, and the like. You will have to add them to the outline.

Organizing and outlining software is an excellent tool for creating your presentation. Be aware: The software works well only when it has good ideas to organize and outline. Make sure your research is thorough and well documented.

An Outline Consists of Coordinate and Subordinate Points

Coordinate points are the major ideas in a speech that grow out of the thesis statement. It is essential for the speaker to clearly identify the major points, because this helps clarify the direction of the talk for the audience.

Subordinate points are minor points that grow out of the major ideas. It is equally important to realize that your subordinate points should at all times support your major ideas. When analyzing and developing your presentation, be sure that a clear connection exists between your major and minor points. Furthermore, make sure you include at least two subordinate points for each coordinate point.

In the following example, the coordinate points (Roman numerals) represent the major ideas of the talk, while the subordinate points (letters) are minor points whose function is to support the major ideas.

I. A Brief History of Oahu, Hawaii
   A. "Oahu is the 3rd largest island in the chain of 8 major Hawaiian Islands, but it is home to 75% of the state's total population" (*Oahu Travel & Vacation Guide*, 2006–2008, par. 4).
   B. In the 1700s, King Kamehameha I united the islands of Hawaii. However, it was not until the 1800s when King Kamehameha III "established his royal court in Honolulu" that Oahu became "the seat of power in Hawaii" (*Hawaii Visitors & Convention Bureau*, 2007). To date, Honolulu "is the

eleventh largest city in the world" (*Oahu Travel & Vacation Guide*, 2006–2008).

C. According to *Oahu Travel & Vacation Guide* (2007), the average temperature is between 68 and 85 degrees year round. People enjoy the warm ocean waters, which have an average of 76 to 78 degrees year round. (*Oahu Travel & Vacation Guide*, 2006–2008). I can tell you from personal experience that Oahu is the most beautiful place I have ever had the opportunity to visit.

II. The best place to go for an authentic Hawaiian meal is, of course, a luau.

A. The one thing you are sure to find at a luau is Kalua pig. The word *kalua* indicates the *imu* (underground oven) in which the pig is cooked ("Luau Foods . . . ," 2008; Smith, 2008). First, the entire pig is seasoned with salt while the imu is prepared with "vegetation" and "hot rocks." Then, the pig is roasted inside the imu for five or more hours to give it a rich, smoky flavor (Smith, 2008).

B. Another food commonly served at Hawaiian luaus is poi. Poi is a thick, purple-colored paste made of pounded taro ("Luau Foods . . . ," 2008). Taro can only be cultivated by men and is named after the god Kane, provider of water and sun. There is to be no arguing or anger when poi is served; Polynesians brought poi to Hawaii back in 450 A.D. and is considered "sacred" and significant in Hawaiian culture (Yuen Hernandez, 2008).

C. Finally, it is nearly impossible to go anywhere on the island of Oahu without being served pineapple. From personal experience, I can tell you that pineapples aren't just served in tropical beverages. Pineapple can be served with any meal of the day, and it tastes just like candy! Perhaps you didn't know that the Delmonte and Dole Plantations are located on the island of Oahu ("Luau Foods . . . ," 2008). I took several photographs while driving past both plantations. Did you know that only one pineapple grows on one pineapple bush, and it can take up to two years to grow a single pineapple? According to resident Jaimi Dennis (2008), you can trick the pineapple into growing faster by covering the plant with a plastic bag and slipping an apple inside the tent. Gases emitted from the decomposition of the apple spur the growth of the pineapple.

III. Some of the tourist attractions on Oahu include Pearl Harbor, Diamond Head Mountain, and the North Shore.

A. One of the most popular places to visit on Oahu is Pearl Harbor. Pearl Harbor, the only U.S. naval base that is a national monument, was bombed by the Japanese in 1941. It was the catalyst for the United States' involvement in WWII. The event killed and wounded approximately 2,390 men (*Hawaii Visitors & Convention Bureau*, 2007).

1. The *U.S.S. Missouri* is the place where the United States and Japan signed their peace treaty (*Oahu Travel & Vacation Guide*, 2006–2008). General MacArthur "accepted the unconditional surrender" of Japan on the decks of this famous battleship (*Hawaii Visitors & Convention Bureau*, 2007, par. 6).

2. The *U.S.S. Arizona* was sunk by the Japanese at eight o'clock in the morning on December 7, 1941 (*Hawaii Visitors & Convention Bureau*,

2007). There are approximately 300 bodies still trapped inside the ship, which is why they built the memorial (*Oahu Travel & Vacation Guide*, 2006–2008). Visitors can take a boat shuttle to the memorial to visit a shrine engraved with the names of all the men who lost their lives as a result of the bombing (*Hawaii Visitors & Convention Bureau*, 2007).

   B. Diamond Head is another popular place to visit. One of the world's biggest craters, Diamond Mountain is situated on the South Shore on the east side of Waikiki. It received its name in the 1820s after British sailors "noticed small sparkling calcite crystals in the beach sand nearby the crater" (*Oahu Travel & Vacation Guide*, 2006–2008). It used to be an active volcano, but it hasn't erupted in over 150,000 years (*Oahu Travel & Vacation Guide*, 2006–2008).

      1. Visitors can hike 760 ft. to the top of the mountain (*Oahu Travel & Vacation Guide*, 2006–2008). Six years ago, my father and I climbed 99 stairs to the top of Diamond Head. The view is spectacular!

   C. In a personal interview with Hawaiian resident Jaimi Dennis (2008), I was informed that the North Shore is the most famous beach of all the Hawaiian islands.

      1. People visit this part of Oahu for laying out on the beach and boogie boarding, and many people sneak up there to visit the *Lost* set. But the North Shore is most famous for the Eddie Aikau Surfing Competition.

      2. Eddie Aikau Competition was inspired by surfer Eddie Aikau, who was famous for tackling 40′–50′ waves. No matter how high the waves were, "Eddie would go" (Burlingame, 1998, par. 15). This saying can be seen on t-shirts and bumper stickers all over the islands. Aikau was one of the crew members on a voyage from Hawaii to the Marquesan Islands (Burlingame, 1998). The canoe, Hokule'a, began flooding with water. Eddie went to get help and was never seen again (Burlingame, 1998). "The search for Aikau became the largest air-sea rescue effort in modern Hawaiian history" (Burlingame, 1998, par. 27). The Quiksilver In Memory of Eddie Aikau Big Wave International surf meet occurs only when the biggest waves descend howling upon Waimea Bay (Burlingame, 1998).

Each Idea in an Outline Is Discrete

Discreteness is the quality of being separate. Your ideas are said to be discrete if they have the ability to stand on their own. For your outline, this means making sure that only one idea is contained in each sentence. The two subordinate points in the following outlines are discrete, separate ideas. Each one achieves its goal of supporting the coordinate point. Look at the above outline. Each of the three main ideas is discrete and different from the other ideas.

Limit the Number of Major Ideas

It is wise to limit the number of major points you choose to include in a classroom speech. Your speech will be too lengthy or cumbersome if you include more than five major points; with too many main ideas, you run the risk of treating your topic superficially.

Serving Your COMMUNITY **Organizing Ideas**

It is important to organize your ideas so that the audience can understand your main ideas and can easily listen to your presentation. With a partner, do the following:

1. Volunteer for at least three hours with one of the following organizations:
   a. Habitat for Humanity
   b. Meals on Wheels
   c. A local hospital
2. Gather information about the importance of volunteerism from all the different people you communicate with throughout the three hours: supervisors/directors, other volunteers, employees, and those you are helping.
3. Organize your ideas into a one-minute presentation on the importance of volunteerism by using a full-sentence outline. Then, develop a key-phrase outline that could be used to present the speech to an audience.
4. Which organizational pattern discussed in this chapter works best? Why were the other patterns ineffective?
5. How did this process help you appreciate difference?

THE INTRODUCTION

The introduction is the place where you strive to create a "need to know" for the audience. What motivates an audience to listen to the development of your ideas during the body of your speech? Hopefully, your introduction gains their attention. An effectively constructed introduction can elicit support from your audience and ensure their attention. As a speaker, it is both exciting and encouraging to see an audience show signs of interest and involvement in the first minute of your presentation. The objectives of your introduction are threefold: (1) to capture the audience's attention, (2) to establish your credibility, and (3) to communicate the nature of your topic to the audience.

■ Drawing the Audience's Attention

Drawing the attention of your audience in the introduction is crucial if you expect to maintain their interest during the body of your speech. There are a number of ways to achieve this goal, including the following: a narrative, a startling statement, a rhetorical question, or a quotation.

Determining a suitable format for your introduction requires that you analyze both your topic and what you consider to be the needs of your audience. In

SKILL BUILDING

Developing a Speech Body

1. Choose one of the following topics:
   a. Making your favorite dinner
   b. Your ideal vacation
   c. Parking on your campus
   d. Last year's Super Bowl or other sports' championship
2. Create a speech body that contains three coordinate points and two subordinate points under each coordinate point.
3. Use full sentences in completing this task.

Chapter 11 we addressed the subject of topic selection and adapting to the needs of the audience. At this time you may find it helpful to review that discussion. Remember, that your audience will approach their interaction with you and your topic from diverse points of view. The more you know about their frames of reference, the easier it will be for you to create the "need to know" for them. Each of the following introductions could be used with the speech outline we prepared earlier in this chapter on mentoring children.

Narrative

An effective way to introduce a speech is to use a **narrative,** or story. It can enable the speaker to create a feeling of understanding with the audience. Because narratives are often based on personal experiences that the audience can easily identify with, they can capture the audience's interest right away. A narrative can be either factual or hypothetical as long as it relates to the central theme of the talk. Consider the following:

> Nearly forty years ago, a young surfer became famous for tackling 40- to 50-foot ocean waves. No matter how high or dangerous the waves were, he would fearlessly set out ride the tide. As a crew member on a voyage from Hawaii to the Marquesan Islands, the traveling vessel began filling with water. In an attempt to save the traveling passengers, the young surfer paddled away on his surf board to seek rescue. This man, Eddie Aikau, was never seen alive again. "The search for Aikau became the largest air-sea rescue effort in modern Hawaiian history" (Burlingame, 1998, par. 27). Today, The Quiksilver In Memory of Eddie Aikau Big Wave International surf meet occurs only when the biggest waves descend howling upon Waimea Bay (Burlingame, 1998).

Begin each presentation by gaining the attention of the audience.

This story puts an actual face on Eddie Aikau, which helps the audience visualize the tremendous impact of his sacrifice.

Startling Statement

A **startling statement,** one that shocks, arouses, or surprises an audience, will certainly capture their attention. Remember, however, that this statement must relate to the topic. If not, you may gain the audience's attention, but for the wrong reasons, making it difficult to bring the audience back to the topic later on. This is particularly true if you incorporate something gimmicky or humorous and then attempt to speak on a serious topic. The startling statement can be very effective if it is used properly. Consider this opening statement: "Did you know that Honolulu, Hawaii is the second cleanest place in the world (Honolulu: World's Second Largest, 2007)? According to the *Oahu Travel Guide* (2006–2008), Hawaii is one of the most remote places in the world, located in the South Pacific equidistant from Japan and California. This remote paradise has some of the cleanest air in the world and consistently warm weather, and Hawaiian residents have a higher life expectancy than anywhere else in the nation ('Health Status,' 2008). According to *Hawaiian Health Trends*, 'In 2000, the most recent year for which state estimates are available, people born in Hawai'i had a life expectancy of 80 years, three years longer than the U.S. average' ('Health Status,' 1994–2008)." The speaker's attempt to startle the audience was done for the express purpose of gaining interest in the topic.

Rhetorical Question

Try asking a rhetorical question to introduce your speech. A **rhetorical question** is one that is posed to the audience and later developed or answered in the talk. The speaker does not expect the audience to answer a rhetorical question; its purpose is to motivate the audience to think about the topic. If the speaker is successful, the audience will want to hear more. Consider the following:

Have you ever wondered what it would be like to travel to a tropical paradise? Take a moment to imagine yourself in a place free of stress and surrounded by breathtaking beauty . . . do you envision a secluded beach with white, sandy beaches and palm trees? Do you hear ocean waves crashing as interchanging shades of turquoise, cerulean, and royal blue water foam around your ankles? Imagine the most enchanting place in the world, and it won't even come close to experiencing the magnificence of Oahu, Hawaii.

In this example, the speaker asks the audience to think about their own desires to visit a tropical place. This is accomplished by including a question that the audience can easily relate to and understand.

Quotation

Using a **quotation** to introduce a speech involves taking someone else's exact words to support the ideas covered in your speech. Quotations are often dramatic in nature and can therefore elicit the audience's interest. After stating the quote, follow up by drawing a connection between the quote and the topic for the audience. Occasionally you may be forced to take excerpts from a lengthy quotation. When this occurs, be sure you are capturing the essence of the quote. Here is an example of a quote that could be used for our speech on Hawaii:

In 1921, author William Somerset Maugham said of Hawaii, "It is the meeting place of East and West. The very new rubs shoulders with the immeasurably old. . . . All these strange people live close to each other, with different languages and different thoughts; they believe in different gods and they have different values; two passions alone they share: love

Startling statistics about Hawaii can help gain the audiences' attention.

and hunger. And somehow as you watch them you have an impression of extraordinary vitality. Though the air is so soft and the sky so blue, you have, I know not why, a feeling of something hotly passionate that beats like a throbbing pulse through the crowds" (Daily Celebrations, 1999–2008).

In this example, the speaker uses a quote as a springboard for the speech, and it is successful because it is directly related to the topic. Note the brevity of the quote; with a lengthy quote you risk losing the audience's attention. Also, it is more difficult to deliver a quote because you are stating someone else's words and the speech patterns are likely to be unnatural to you. Because of these factors, a quote that is short and to the point will work better for most circumstances.

■ Establishing Your Credibility

After capturing your audience's attention, you must still address two remaining goals before moving to the body of your speech: (1) establishing your credibility and concern and (2) communicating the nature of your topic. Establishing your credibility as a speaker for a particular topic involves conveying your knowledge about the topic (for example, mentioning personal experiences or recently conducted research), as well as your concern. For our speech on Oahu, it would be important to tell the audience about any experience you have had in Oahu. You could relay a narrative about your own experiences, for example. This would communicate to the audience that you have hands-on experience, as well as knowledge found during your research. Specifically, Adam has decided to do his informative speech on Oahu, Hawaii. As part of his introduction and attempt to establish his credibility, he states, "For the past six years, I have traveled to Hawaii and learned a great deal about Hawaiian culture through personal experience, interviews, and extensive research."

When constructing your introduction, you want to communicate that your topic is important and that you are committed to sharing it. Ask yourself a few questions, such as "How does this topic relate to my needs?" and "Why do I want to share my views with this audience?" The answers to these questions will help you communicate your involvement in the topic.

■ Providing Information about Your Topic

In the last phase of your introduction, indicate what the body of your speech will include, stopping short of actually developing your ideas. Save that discussion for the body. What you should reveal to your audience is the purpose of your speech. For example, you would want to preview your main ideas of your speech on Oahu: the history, the cuisine, and tourist attractions. Your actual discussion of these subjects would follow in the body.

COMMUNICATION IN ACTION

Gaining the Attention of the Audience

1. Earlier in this chapter you developed a speech body. Using the same topic, write four different types of introductions:
   a. Narrative
   b. Startling statement
   c. Rhetorical question
   d. Quotation
2. As you write these introductions, ask yourself how you can capture the audience's attention.
3. How could you demonstrate your credibility as a speaker on this subject?
4. Share your introductions by forming small groups.
5. Elicit the feedback of your peers on how involved they become in your talk.
6. How does gaining the attention of the audience strengthen your confidence as a communicator?

THE CONCLUSION

The functions of the **conclusion** are (1) to draw your speech to an end, (2) to reiterate the central theme of your presentation (especially in an informative speech), and (3) to indicate to the members of your audience what you would like them to do (especially in a persuasive speech).

As you begin your conclusion, give your audience a cue so that they can refocus their attention. Phrases such as "in conclusion" or "in closing" generally work. Now use your remaining time to reinforce your speech's purpose or to ask something of your audience—either that they change the way they look at an issue or that they take some action. There are different techniques to achieve this goal, including the summation, the challenge, and the call for action.

■ The Summation

One way you can conclude your talk is with the **summation,** which reinforces the main points in your speech. For example, the following statement could be a meaningful close for our speech on Hawaii:

> In conclusion, today I have informed you about Hawaiian culture; more specifically, the beautiful island of Oahu, luau cuisine, and various tourist attractions.

■ The Challenge

Another way to end your speech is by **challenging the audience.** This occurs when the speaker calls on the audience to think further about the topic.

After speaking about his experiences in Hawaii, Adam concludes with the following:

> We all dream about going on vacation to somewhere tropical. I challenge you to take the step to make your dream a reality. Think about how you might plan a trip to Hawaii in the future.

■ The Call for Action

There are times when you want to persuade your audience to act. This is known as a **call for action.** Such a call necessitates going a step further than presenting information. Although the conclusion still grows out of the presentation's central purpose, you make an effort to inspire, motivate, or move the members of your audience to take a stand, change their behavior, or act on their beliefs.

TRANSITIONS

A **transition** provides a link between the main parts of your speech. There are three specific types of transitions: the transitional preview, the transitional summary, and the signpost. It helps to have a **transitional preview** after the introduction (to give your audience an idea of what is to come), to have transitions between the coordinate points in the body of your speech ("Now that I've explained the food at a luau, I'll move to the tourist attractions of Oahu."), and to have a **transitional summary** before the conclusion (to recap all the coordinate points). Transitions show the relationships between the ideas in your speech, while transitional previews and summaries allow the audience to hear the main ideas several times. Because the audience can miss a point during your presentation, previews and summaries provide an additional chance for them to follow and understand your speech. **Signposts** help the audience know where you are in the speech. Phrases such as "My first main point" or "In closing" help the audience follow along as you proceed through your presentation.

PREPARING THE SPEECH OUTLINE

For help in preparing and delivering your speech, use a speech outline. There are two types of speech outlines: the full-sentence outline helps you construct or develop your topic (see the earlier section on "Outlining the Body" for more discussion); the key-phrase outline helps prepare you for your presentation to the audience.

■ Full-Sentence Outline

The first step in constructing your speech is to prepare a **full-sentence outline**—one that uses full sentences to list the major and minor points, as well as the different forms of support in your talk. This process helps you to clearly delineate the different parts of your speech. An added benefit of this exercise is that you will feel more confident that you are presenting a well thought-out speech. As you develop your full-sentence speech outline, keep these techniques in mind: (1) Label the different parts of the speech, (2) use a consistent symbol system, and (3) attach a bibliography.

Your outline will be more effective if you take the time to label the different parts of your speech (introduction, transitional preview, body, transitional summary, conclusion). Make these labels in boldface print so that the different parts stand out. You can write these headings in the center of the page or place them off to the side.

As you construct your speech outline, it also is helpful to use a symbol system that follows standard outlining procedures. Those ideas of greater importance are placed farther to the left in the outline than ideas of lesser importance. The symbol system used in the following example shows the relationship between ideas. Major points are indicated by Roman numerals, subordinate points are designated by capital letters, followed by Arabic numerals for sub-subpoints.

When you develop a talk for a classroom presentation, you may be required to show the instructor the sources you used in gathering your information. These sources, including books, magazines, journals, newspapers, interviews, and Internet sites, should be listed in a bibliography that is attached to your full-sentence outline. Several style manuals exist that describe acceptable bibliography formats. Check with your instructor to see if there is a preferred one for your class. (See Chapter 12 for a more detailed treatment of this topic.)

We are ready to put together our speech on Hawaii. First, we will write a full-sentence outline.

■ Introduction

I. Did you know that Honolulu, Hawaii is the second cleanest place in the world (Honolulu: World's Second Largest, 2007)? According to the *Oahu Travel Guide* (2006–2008), Hawaii is one of the most remote places in the world, located in the South Pacific equidistant from Japan and California. This remote paradise has some of the cleanest air in the world and consistently warm weather, and Hawaiian residents have a higher life expectancy than anywhere else in the nation ("Health Status," 1994–2008). According to "Health Status" (1994–2008), "In 2000, the most recent year for which state estimates are available, people born in Hawai'i had a life expectancy of 80 years, three years longer than the U.S. average."

II. For the past six years, I have traveled to Hawaii and learned a great deal about Hawaiian culture through personal experience, interviews, and extensive research.

III. Hawaii is our nation's fiftieth state, but most Americans do not know anything about Hawaii's rich culture and how vastly it differs from the rest of American culture.

IV. Today, I am going to inform you about Hawaiian culture; specifically, how the islands were united, luau cuisine, and Oahu's tourist attractions.

Signpost

I. First, I am going to give you some background information on the beautiful island of Oahu.

■ Body

I. A brief history of Oahu, Hawaii
   A. "Oahu is the 3rd largest island in the chain of 8 major Hawaiian Islands, but it is home to 75% of the state's total population" (*Oahu Travel & Vacation Guide*, 2006–2008, par. 4).
   B. In the 1700s, King Kamehameha I united the islands of Hawaii. However, it was not until the 1800s when King Kamehameha III "established his royal court in Honolulu" that Oahu became "the seat of power in Hawaii" (*Hawaii Visitors & Convention Bureau*, 2007). To date, Honolulu "is the eleventh largest city in the world" (*Oahu Travel & Vacation Guide*, 2006–2008).
   C. According to *Oahu Travel and Vacation Guide* (2007), the average temperature is between 68 and 85 degrees year round. People enjoy the warm ocean waters, which have an average of 76 to 78 degrees year round. (*Oahu Travel & Vacation Guide*, 2006–2008). I can tell you from personal experience that Oahu is the most beautiful place I have ever had the opportunity to visit.

Transition

Aside from the beautiful environment, let us discuss some of the foods native to Hawaiian culture.

II. The best place to go for an authentic Hawaiian meal is, of course, a luau.
   A. The one thing you are sure to find at a luau is Kalua pig. The word "kalua" indicates the imu (underground oven) in which the pig is cooked ("Luau Foods," 2008; Smith, 2008). First, the entire pig is seasoned with salt while the imu is prepared with "vegetation" and "hot rocks." Then, the pig is roasted inside the imu for five or more hours to give it a rich, smoky flavor (Smith, 2008).
   B. Another food commonly served at Hawaiian luaus is poi. Poi is a thick, purple colored paste made of pounded taro ("Luau Foods," 2008). Taro can only be cultivated by men and is named after the god Kane, provider of water and sun. There is to be no arguing or anger when poi is served; Polynesians brought poi to Hawaii back in 450 A.D. and it is considered "sacred" and significant in Hawaiian culture (Yuen Hernandez, 2008).
   C. Finally, it is nearly impossible to go anywhere on the island of Oahu without being served pineapple. From personal experience, I can tell you that pineapples aren't just served in tropical beverages. Pineapple can be served with any meal of the day, and it tastes just like candy! Perhaps you didn't know that the Delmonte and Dole Plantations are located on the island of Oahu ("Luau Foods," 2008). I took several photographs while driving passed both plantations. Did you know that only one pineapple grows on

one pineapple bush, and it can take up to two years to grow a single pineapple? According to resident Jaimi Dennis (2008), you can trick the pineapple into growing faster by covering the plant with a plastic bag and slipping an apple inside the tent. Gases emitted from the decomposition of the apple spur the growth of the pineapple.

Transitional Summary

While Hawaiian history and the food served at luaus is certainly worth learning about, Oahu is known for its array of tourist attractions.

III. Some of the tourist attractions on Oahu include Pearl Harbor, Diamond Head Mountain, and the North Shore.

    A. One of the most popular places to visit on Oahu is Pearl Harbor. Pearl Harbor, the only U.S. naval base that is a national monument, was bombed by the Japanese in 1941. It was the catalyst for the United States' involvement in WWII. The event killed and wounded approximately 2,390 men (*Hawaii Visitors & Convention Bureau*, 2007).

        1. The *U.S.S. Missouri* is the place where the U.S. and Japan signed their peace treaty (*Oahu Travel & Vacation Guide*, 2006–2008). General MacArthur "accepted the unconditional surrender" of Japan on the decks of this famous battleship (*Hawaii Visitors & Convention Bureau*, 2007, par. 6).

        2. The *U.S.S. Arizona* was sunk by the Japanese at eight o'clock in the morning on December 7, 1941 (*Hawaii Visitors & Convention Bureau*, 2007). There are approximately 300 bodies still trapped inside the ship, which is why they built the memorial (*Oahu Travel & Vacation Guide*, 2006–2008). Visitors can take a boat shuttle to the memorial to visit a shrine engraved with the names of all the men who lost their lives as a result of the bombing (*Hawaii Visitors & Convention Bureau*, 2007).

    B. Diamond Head is another popular place to visit. One of the world's biggest craters, Diamond Head Mountain is situated on the South Shore on the east side of Waikiki. It received its name in the 1820s after British sailors "noticed small sparkling calcite crystals in the beach sand nearby the crater" (*Oahu Travel & Vacation Guide*, 2006–2008). It used to be an active volcano, but it hasn't erupted in over 150,000 years. (*Oahu Travel & Vacation Guide*, 2006–2008). Visitors can hike 760 ft. to the top of the mountain (*Oahu Travel & Vacation Guide*, 2006–2008). Six years ago, my father and I climbed 99 stairs to the top of Diamond Head. The view is spectacular!

    C. In a personal interview with Hawaiian resident Jaimi Dennis (2008), I was informed that the North Shore is the most famous beach of all the Hawaiian islands.

        1. People visit this part of Oahu for laying out on the beach and boogie boarding, and many people sneak up there to visit the *Lost* set. But the North Shore is most famous for the Eddie Aikau Surfing Competition.

        2. Eddie Aikau Competition was inspired by surfer Eddie Aikau, who was famous for tackling 40′–50′ waves. No matter how high the waves were, "Eddie would go" (Burlingame, 1998, par. 15). This saying can be seen on t-shirts and bumper stickers all over the islands. Aikau was one of the crew members on a voyage from Hawaii to the Marquesan Islands (Burlingame, 1998). The canoe, Hokule'a, began flooding with water. Eddie went to get help and was never seen again (Burlingame, 1998). "The search for Aikau became the largest air-sea rescue effort in modern Hawaiian history" (Burlingame, 1998, par. 27). The Quiksilver In Memory of Eddie Aikau Big Wave International surf meet occurs only when the biggest waves descend howling upon Waimea Bay (Burlingame, 1998).

■ Conclusion

    I. Signpost/Restate thesis: In conclusion, today I have informed you about Hawaiian culture; more specifically, the beautiful island of Oahu, luau cuisine, and various tourist attractions.

    II. Tag ending/Audience appreciation: Thank you for your time. Or, as they would say in Hawaii, "Mahalo."

■ Key-Phrase Outline

While the intent of a full-sentence outline is to help you develop the ideas in your speech, the purpose of a key-phrase outline is to help you to prepare your delivery. The **key-phrase outline** is an abbreviated version of the full-sentence outline that is intended as a cue to each point in your presentation. Use it to practice your delivery.

Consider the following points as you develop this outline. First, convert the major points in your full-sentence outline from full sentences to key phrases. You may still need to include complete word-for-word quotes in your outline to ensure you communicate someone else's words accurately. Second, use standard outlining procedures: Roman numerals, capital letters, Arabic numbers. Third, space generously between the lines (key phrases) in your outline so that you can easily follow along during the delivery of your speech. It is easy to lose your place during the delivery when the outline is crowded or cluttered. Finally, insert directions or cues regarding delivery, such as *pause, slow down,* and *eye contact.* The necessity for these notes will become apparent as you practice your delivery.

Let's convert our full-sentence outline on Hawaii into a key-phrase outline we could use to practice our delivery.

■ Introduction

    I. Did you know that Honolulu, Hawaii, is the second cleanest place in the world? Hawaii is one of the most remote places in the world, located in the South Pacific equidistant from Japan and California. This remote paradise has some of the cleanest air in the world and consistently warm weather, and Hawaiian residents have a higher life expectancy than anywhere else in the nation According to *Hawaiian Health Trends,* "In 2000, the most recent year for which state estimates are available, people born in Hawai'i had a life expectancy of 80 years, three years longer than the U.S. average" ("Health Status," 1994–2008).

II. Today, I am going to inform you about Hawaiian culture; specifically, how the islands were united, luau cuisine, island creatures, and Oahu's tourist attractions.
(Slow down)

Signpost

I. First, I am going to give you some background information on the beautiful island of Oahu.

(Pause)

■ Body

I. History of Oahu
  A. "Oahu is the third largest island in the chain of eight major Hawaiian Islands, but it is home to 75 percent of the state's total population."
  B. How Oahu came to power
    1. King Kamehameha I united the islands of Hawaii.
    2. According to *Hawaii Visitors & Convention Bureau* (2007), in the 1800s Oahu became "the seat of power in Hawaii" by King Kamehameha III.
    3. Honolulu "is the eleventh largest city in the world."
  C. The island
    1. Climate
    2. South Pacific Ocean
    3. Beautiful scenery
       (Eye contact with the entire audience)

Transition

On to my next point
(Pause)

II. Luau cuisine
  A. Kalua pig
    1. The word *kalua* indicates the imu (underground oven) in which the pig is cooked.
    2. Seasoned with salt and roasted for five or more hours
  B. Poi
    1. Thick, purple paste made of pounded taro
    2. Can be cultivated only by men
    3. Named after the god Kane, provider of water and sun
    4. There is to be no arguing or anger when poi is served.
    5. According to Yuen Hernandez (2008), Polynesians brought it in 450 A.D. and is considered a "sacred," significant part of Hawaiian culture.

    C. Pineapple

        1. Delmonte and Dole Plantations are located on the island of Oahu.

        2. Pineapple grows on one pineapple bush, and it can take up to two years to grow a single pineapple. However, you can trick it into growing faster if you cover the plant with a plastic bag and put an apple inside.

Transitional Summary

Oahu history and cuisine discussed

III. Tourist attractions

    A. Pearl Harbor

        1. U.S. naval bombed by the Japanese in 1941. Approx. 2,390 men died.

        2. *U.S.S. Missouri*

            a. Place where the U.S. and Japan signed their peace treaty

            b. Gen. MacArthur "accepted the unconditional surrender" of Japan

        3. *U.S.S. Arizona*

            a. Sunk by the Japanese on December 7, 1941

            b. The reason for the memorial

            c. Visiting the shrine

    B. Diamond Head Mountain

        1. One of the world's biggest craters

        2. Situated on the South Shore on the east side of Waikiki

        3. Used to be an active volcano, but it hasn't erupted in over 150,000 years

        4. Visitors can hike 760 ft. to the top of the mountain.

    C. The North Shore

        1. In a personal interview with Oahu resident Jaimi Dennis (2008), I was informed the North Shore is the most famous Hawaiian beach.

            a. Laying out

            b. Boogie boarding

            c. Visiting the *Lost* set

        2. Eddie Aikau Competition

            a. Eddie's famous for tackling 40′–50′ waves.

            b. Died trying to save a sinking canoe, the Hokule'a

            c. According to Burlingame (1998), "The search for Aikau became the largest air-sea rescue effort in modern Hawaiian history."

            d. Quiksilver Eddie Aikau Big Wave International surf competition

Signpost

In conclusion,

■ Conclusion

    I. Informed you about Hawaiian culture; more specifically, the beautiful island of Oahu, luau cuisine and various tourist attractions.

    II. Thank you for your time, or as they would say in Hawaii, "Mahalo."

ETHICS in Communication
Organizing Your Speech

In the beginning of this chapter, we read about Adam and his informative speech to his classmates. Like all speakers, it is Adam's responsibility to make his presentation as easy as possible for his classmates to listen to, and he must communicate his ideas clearly so that they can be understood by the audience. A well-organized speech will help Adam be an effective and ethical speaker. Specifically, what does Adam need to do?

1. Why is an organizational pattern necessary?

2. How can a limited number of discrete main ideas help Adam?

3. What must Adam do in the introduction? In the conclusion?

4. Why are transitions so important to the overall organization of the speech?

5. What should Adam's outline look like?

6. How will you organize your ideas into an effective and ethical speech?

SUMMARY

This chapter provided discussions on the major parts of your speech and how to prepare a speech outline. The body is the main part of your speech. The ideas in that body often form patterns that provide a framework for arranging your speech more effectively; these patterns include causal order, problem/solution, spatial order, time order, and topic order.

The chapter also promoted outlining the body to help with your speech's development. Among the outlining principles discussed were the following: (1) An outline consists of coordinate and subordinate points, (2) each idea in an outline is discrete, and (3) the number of major ideas should be limited.

The introduction serves three purposes: to draw the audience's attention, to establish your credibility as a speaker, and to provide information about the topic. You can use a narrative, a startling statement, a rhetorical question, or a quotation to introduce your speech.

The conclusion signals the end of your speech. It also reinforces the central ideas in the speech and indicates what you would like the audience to do after the speech has ended. The conclusion can take various forms, including the summation, the challenge, and the call for action.

Transitions provide a link between the main parts of your speech. By previewing and summarizing ideas, they provide an additional opportunity for the audience to follow the speech. Signposts allow your audience to follow along with you as you proceed through the presentation.

Ideally, as a speaker you should use two outlines to prepare your speech. The first, a full-sentence outline, is meant to assist you in developing the ideas you wish to include in your speech. In preparing this outline, such principles as coordination and subordination, discreteness, labeling the parts of the speech, and a consistent symbol system are followed. The second outline, consisting of key phrases drawn from the full-sentence outline, is intended as an aid for the speech delivery (more about this in Chapter 14).

REVIEW QUESTIONS

1. Briefly describe the major parts of a speech.
2. Describe five ways to organize the ideas in the body of your speech.
3. What is the difference between coordinate and subordinate points?
4. Explain the three purposes of an introduction.
5. Identify the four different ways to introduce your speech.
6. Differentiate between a challenge and a call for action in the conclusion.
7. What is the primary purpose of a transition?
8. What are the benefits of preparing a full-sentence outline?
9. Why would you use a key-phrase outline?

KEY CONCEPTS

sequence
causal order
problem/solution order
spatial order
time order
topic order
coordinate points
subordinate points

discreteness
narrative
startling statement
rhetorical question
quotation
conclusion
summation
challenging the audience

call for action
transition
transitional preview
transitional summary
signposts
full-sentence outline
key-phrase outline

CHAPTER 14

Delivering Your Speech

AFTER STUDYING THIS CHAPTER, YOU SHOULD

understand

- the differences between oral and written communication.
- the four factors that help control speech anxiety.

be able to

- use the four types of delivery.
- enhance your speech delivery through spontaneity and sincerity.
- use your body to enhance your delivery.
- use your voice to improve speech delivery.

Professor Nancy Webber, director of the Women's Studies Department, has been invited to speak to the City Economic Council on job training for women. She is excited about the opportunity to talk about this topic because she has written several books about training women to rejoin the workforce.

She has lectured about this topic many times in her classes. However, preparing for this speech, she realizes that she will be speaking in a different situation and to a different kind of audience. For example, she won't know the members of the audience as she does when she lectures to her students. Also, the group will be larger than she is used to and the setting will be much more formal. Her lecture notes will not work in this speaking situation.

For the speech before the City Economic Council, Professor Webber decides to write her comments out word for word and to create several charts and graphs to use as presentational aids. Although the content may be the same as what she discusses with her students in class, Professor Webber's delivery will not.

■ ■ ■ ■ ■

There is no one right way to deliver a speech. Multiple types of delivery are possible depending on the audience, situation, and your own talents. It is best to find your own voice and the best approach for you and that situation, as Professor Webber has done. In this chapter, we will discuss the options you have for effectively delivering your speech. Effective speakers appreciate the different approaches to communication an audience brings to the interaction. Through thorough self- and audience analysis and practice, you can decide what is the best option for you.

Delivery is usually the most dreaded aspect of the speaking situation. Understandably, people feel self-conscious when they are standing in front of an audience. Fear of rejection is an overwhelming factor in public speaking; however, learning what to do in order to feel comfortable during speech delivery can lead to improved self-confidence. An audience views a composed public speaker as a confident communicator with a message worth listening to. Furthermore, the positive feedback received from the audience reinforces your self-confidence.

We are all afraid that we aren't "doing it right" and that the audience will reject us. It is essential that your delivery style be appropriate for your audience and the situation. Thorough analysis of your talents and skills and of the audience will help you to understand the diverse frames of reference you need to consider when delivering your speech. We begin this chapter with a discussion of the differences between oral and written communication. Many of us mistakenly believe that the speech is just an essay read aloud. To deliver your ideas effectively, you must understand the nature of oral and written communication.

ORAL AND WRITTEN COMMUNICATION

There are several aspects of oral communication that make it very different from written communication. Public communication is not just a message read aloud to an audience. First, the speech is a cooperative act between the speaker and the audience. Remember from Chapter 1 that all communication is an interdependent process. Your audience will be right with you and will provide immediate feedback to you. An effective speaker will adjust to the audience's feedback. Written communication does not allow for immediate feedback and does not allow the sender the opportunity to adjust to the audience's diverse approaches to the communication situation.

Second, the speaker's priority is to make it easy for the audience to hear the message. Remember in Chapter 3, we discussed how difficult it is to listen. You can help your audience listen by making your message simple, informal, personal, and vivid. In a written message, the writer has the luxury of using complex, formal messages, as the receiver can reread and review the message. Consequently, your audience will only listen to your message once. There is no opportunity to replay your speech.

Lastly, you must be concerned about all the intentional and unintentional nonverbal messages you send as well as the nonverbal feedback your audience will be giving you. In written communication, nonverbal messages are of little or no concern to the writer or the reader. Table 14.1 defines oral communication.

In the rest of this chapter, we will discuss specific ways to improve your delivery and to understand the interactive process of public communication. To that end, we will focus on the different types of delivery, sharing ideas, bodily action, and voice quality and control. Incorporating the techniques that are natural to your uniqueness will help you deliver your speech more effectively and, in turn, lead to greater confidence when you are giving a speech.

UNDERSTANDING SPEECH ANXIETY

Although most people like to talk in informal settings, many have a genuine fear of delivering a public speech. Personal concerns about how others perceive us are intensified when we speak in public. The internal tension is understandable; no one likes being rejected—the greatest fear associated with public speaking. Unlike

TABLE 14.1   Oral Communication

- Is a cooperative act between speaker and a diverse audience.

- Provides immediate feedback to the sender.

- Must be simple, informal, personal, and vivid.

- Contains both intentional and unintentional nonverbal messages.

SKILL BUILDING

Oral and Written Communication

Find an essay you have written for another class. Read it aloud.

1. How does it sound? Do you think an audience could easily listen to it?
2. How could you change the essay so that it could be delivered orally?
3. How might the diversity of the audience affect your delivery?

writing in a diary or turning in a project to an instructor, our public speeches are visible to an entire audience.

While there is no magic formula to dispel your fear of public speaking, you can take comfort in knowing that your nervousness can be significantly reduced by following a plan. This plan requires that you follow several of the points mentioned in Chapters 11, 12, and 13: Select an appropriate topic, analyze your audience, find supporting materials to incorporate in your speech, and organize your ideas and support into a logical presentation. As a result of doing this extensive preparation, you will know where your speech is going and what you are about. You will have become the expert on your topic and know how to relate your ideas to your diverse audience. All your hard work will pay off by translating into a feeling of confidence that you are well prepared and that you will not be caught off guard.

A few additional pointers can help you deliver your speech with less apprehension: Control excess tension, focus on the topic, remember that you are not alone, and develop a positive attitude.

■ Control Excess Tension

When told that they must deliver a speech, most people generally feel nervous. It's as if the word *speech* triggers an alarm. Nervousness often manifests itself in tension; it is possible, however, to use your body in a way that allows you to reduce the excess energy caused by tension. Merely taking a deep breath or a few steps away from the lectern may help free your body of extra energy. These small efforts will help you feel more relaxed when delivering your speech.

■ Focus on the Topic and Audience Feedback

Concentrating on what you are talking about, rather than thinking about the fact that you are standing in front of an audience, is an important step in reducing speech apprehension. Concentrating on your message helps reduce your anxiety because you stop focusing on your role and instead direct your energy toward the treatment of your topic. It is also important to remember that the audience is a vital part of the speech process and their feedback can help you succeed. If you engage in thorough audience analysis, you know what diverse approaches the audience has brought to your speech and you can adjust accordingly. Once you take the focus off yourself, you will be able to share your ideas with the audience. These ideas and the audience need to be the center of attention, not you! A second important factor, then, is to select a topic in which you are genuinely interested (see Chapter 11 for a more complete discussion of selecting a topic). Consider the following:

> Gale is a single mother of three young daughters and is working on a degree in prelaw at night. At least once a month, Gale volunteers at the local legal aid clinic. She strongly believes in giving back to her community and has seen how the clinic has helped her neighbors deal with inattentive landlords, resolve income tax issues, and other important legal matters. She decides to persuade her fellow classmates to also volunteer in their neighborhoods. Gale feels passionately about her topic and becomes very involved in the process of persuading her audience. Her audience gets caught up in Gale's enthusiasm and provides her with overwhelmingly positive nonverbal feedback by shaking their heads and smiling. As a result, Gale forgets about being nervous in front of her audience.

■ Remember That You Are Not Alone

Try to place the speech experience in its proper perspective. It is likely that several members of your audience have been in your shoes before, so they can empathize with your nervousness over speaking in public. People are basically kind. They do not want to see you fail. Perhaps this example will demonstrate our point: Have you ever been backstage in a theater when an actor forgot his or her lines? The audience did not laugh or ridicule the actor; instead, they remained quiet and probably empathized with the performer.

■ Develop a Positive Attitude

When you get up in front of your audience, it helps to remember that you have prepared something worthwhile to say to them. Since you are the person who has researched, developed, and organized your subject, no one will know your topic as well as you. In addition, the way you have decided to handle your topic probably depends on your values, attitudes, and past experiences. Even a simple assignment gives you an opportunity to bring your own rich background to the speaking experience. Condition yourself to think, "I have something interesting to share with others."

This positive attitude can carry over to your audience. Being involved in your presentation communicates a feeling of confidence to the audience. In turn, you should feel more comfortable because you will be able to observe the audience's involvement in your presentation. Remember that you are a unique individual who has something special to share with the audience. There is no one right way to deliver a speech. An understanding of your individual approach to the speaking situation and your appreciation for your audience's diverse approaches to the topic can only increase your confidence. Believe in your ability to share ideas. You do it all the time with your friends, work associates, and family.

COMMUNICATION IN ACTION

Speech Anxiety

Jackie is a student in your communication class. The thought of having to deliver a speech is so threatening to her that she is seriously thinking about dropping the class. In a small group, discuss the following:

1. In what ways can Jackie manage some of the anxiety she feels?
2. How can Jackie use her unique approach to communication to alleviate her anxiety?
3. What role does the audience play in helping Jackie feel more at ease?
4. What can you suggest from your own experiences to help Jackie cope with her fear?
5. How can learning how to manage your speech anxiety enhance your confidence as a communicator?

TYPES OF DELIVERY

Four methods of delivery can be used to share information in public. Each, of course, has its own place in a communication situation. However, certain methods appear to be more advantageous than others. Depending on your talents, the speaking situation, the topic, and your audience, one of these methods will be more effective. Described below are the different methods of delivery.

■ The Impromptu Speech

What is the usual response when someone is asked to deliver an impromptu speech? Panic comes to mind! An **impromptu speech** is delivered without advance preparation or practice. Although difficult for the student, the impromptu speech has its benefits. An instructor may want to give his or her students an opportunity to "think on their feet" and at the same time expose them to being in front of the class. The typical introductory speech on the first day of class helps fulfill this goal. In this context, the impromptu delivery represents a useful tool. On a more practical level, business seminars or meetings frequently give rise to impromptu speeches.

For example, the assistant director of the botanical garden asks Jerry to summarize his findings on the viability of instituting a continuing education program for the community. Although Jerry has no advance notice, he talks about the program to the staff members at the meeting. In this situation, the impromptu speech came about as a natural part of the meeting. Despite Jerry's success in the preceding example, the impromptu speech generally does little to bolster a speaker's confidence. After just a few minutes, the presentation commonly becomes repetitive, which causes the speaker to become self-conscious and nervous.

To give an impromptu speech simply because you have failed to prepare comments ahead of time communicates to your audience that you really did not care about your responsibility enough to adequately prepare for your talk. An ill-prepared speaker does not gain the respect of the audience. As a speaker, your credibility and confidence will be diminished if the audience perceives you as either unprepared or uncaring.

■ The Manuscript Speech

If you were in a position of authority, like the President of the United States, it would be appropriate for you to use a **manuscript speech**, one delivered from a prepared script. Consider former President Bush's delicate position after the September 11, 2001, attacks. When he spoke to the nation, the public was looking to the president for reassurances that everything was being done to catch the attackers and that the government was keeping our country safe. In addition, the world was watching to see what the United States's response would be to the attacks. The gravity of the situation required that Bush use a manuscript in which each word was painstakingly selected.

It is unlikely that you would find yourself in a situation of such magnitude; however, there are circumstances where a manuscript speech is appropriate, even desirable. If, for example, you are asked to explain new company procedures or describe the steps used in cardiopulmonary resuscitation (CPR), where accuracy is essential, a prepared manuscript is beneficial. The purpose of the manuscript is to keep you focused on your speech.

There are drawbacks, however. Because the manuscript speech is extremely precise, it is apt to be mechanical, lack spontaneity, and stifle interaction with the audience. It does not allow you to respond to the feedback you will receive from the audience. Some speakers even plan their gestures in advance. Indeed, it is a rare individual who can appear fresh when such minute details are orchestrated beforehand. If you must use a manuscript, make every effort to appear to be talking to your audience instead of reading lines to them. Remember from the beginning of this chapter, a speech is not the same as an essay. Consider the following:

> Myra Crandall is the newly elected president of the Southridge Elementary School Parent-Teacher Organization and a stepmother to two boys in first and third grades. As an administrative assistant to the plant manager at Rey Manufacturing, she does very little public speaking. Myra is nervous about the acceptance address she must deliver at her installation because she doubts her ability to speak in public. She writes out her entire speech ahead of time and essentially reads it to the group. When she looks at the audience, she sees people gazing around the room in a sure sign of boredom.

Manuscript delivery is undoubtedly difficult to master. Obviously, Myra's delivery was lacking in the preceding illustration. Successful delivery takes considerable time, practice, and familiarity with the types of situations that necessitate its use.

The Memorized Speech

The type of delivery that requires the greatest investment of time is the **memorized speech.** The speaker not only develops the complete manuscript, but he or she also spends additional time memorizing it word for word. When would a speaker choose to memorize a speech? Perhaps in these cases: when delivering a eulogy, making a sales pitch (especially if it has proven to be successful in the past), or toasting the bride and groom at a wedding. In each of these situations, considerable effort has gone into preparing the message and selecting appropriate words; the speaker wants to communicate his or her thoughts exactly as planned.

Delivering a memorized speech has its drawbacks, most notably the difficulty in maintaining spontaneity. As with the manuscript speech, it does not allow you to adjust to the audience feedback. There is an additional pitfall to the memorized presentation, one that most experienced instructors have seen snare the inexperienced speaker: Countless students forget a word or a phrase midway through their speech, lose their composure, and out of desperation return to the beginning of the speech to start again.

If you practice a speech sufficiently before giving it to your audience, a certain degree of familiarity results. Because you are now familiar with the ideas in your speech, you probably will not be shaken if a particular word or phrase escapes you during the pressure of the speaking situation. Unless your instructor asks you to memorize a speech for a specific assignment, try to avoid doing so.

Let us say that you need to memorize a phone number as part of a message you will later relay to a friend. Since you do not have a pencil and paper, you recite the numbers until they are committed to memory. While engaged in this task, you try your best to visualize the numbers. This seemingly simple task requires a great deal of concentration. When considered on these terms, the business of memorizing a speech suddenly becomes enormous. Nearly all the speaker's energy in this type of delivery is focused on remembering words, rather than on sharing ideas with an audience. The process of memorizing leaves little or no time for concentrating on how you deliver the speech to your audience.

The Extemporaneous Speech

The type of delivery that combines the best features of the preceding methods is the extemporaneous delivery. An **extemporaneous speech** is thoroughly prepared and practiced, but it is delivered in a conversational style. In an extemporaneous delivery, the emphasis is placed on sharing ideas that have been researched and analyzed. The speaker often uses note cards or an outline while delivering the talk and can enjoy some flexibility with the audience because he or she has prepared, organized, and practiced his or her thoughts in advance. This allows the speaker to respond to the feedback he or she receives from the audience.

Extemporaneous delivery implies that the speaker has a thorough knowledge and understanding of the topic and an intelligent plan to present it. It avoids the stilted, formal presentation inherent in the manuscript speech or memorized speech. In addition, it suggests to the audience that the speaker is trying to interact with them, because the speaker's language is more spontaneous and the response to

ETHICS in Communication
Delivering Your Presentation

Professor Nancy Webber has been invited to speak to the City Economic Council on job training for women in their community, a topic that Professor Webber knows a lot about. Thus, much of what she will present to the council is the same as the material she would present in one of her classes. But, the audience is different, and the situation is certainly different. How can she ensure that her delivery will be both effective and ethical when she speaks to the council?

1. How does the diverse nature of her audience impact her delivery?
2. How does the situation impact her delivery?
3. Why must Professor Webber pay close attention to audience feedback?
4. How can being herself and using her own style build her confidence as a speaker?
5. How will you effectively and ethically delivery your presentation?

audience feedback is more immediate. This feeling helps keep the audience involved because their diverse perspectives can be acknowledged. Consider the following:

> Harriet Gaynor teaches Economics 200, a required course for all liberal arts and sciences students at Western University. Over the years, Gaynor has developed a reputation on campus as a superior lecturer. She teaches multiple sections of this course. Much of her success is a result of the tremendous amount of time she spends preparing her material. She practices each lecture to become familiar with the ideas she wishes to present. Although she brings the same outline to each section of Economics 200, the words she delivers to each class differ. Her choice of words grows out of her relationship with each class. The humor, pace, and movement in each lecture depend on the feedback she receives from her class.

Professor Gaynor's ability to rely on the extemporaneous delivery has contributed to her success as a speaker and teacher. She is able to adapt to the different attributes, attitudes, and interests of her students. The flexibility and adaptability inherent in the extemporaneous delivery allow for a degree of give and take between speaker and audience. The four types of delivery are defined in Table 14.2.

TABLE 14.2   Types of Delivery

Impromptu	No advance preparation or practice
Manuscript	Delivered from a prepared script
Memorized	Manuscript committed to memory
Extemporaneous	Prepared, practiced, but conversational in style

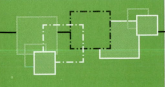

EMBRACING DIFFERENCE

Types of Delivery

Carlo has just listened to his professor discuss the different types of delivery used by speakers. His teacher reviewed the impromptu speech, the memorized speech, the manuscript speech, and the extemporaneous speech. In most instances, Carlo learned that the extemporaneous speech is the most effective type of delivery. However, he also knows that it is the speaking situation and the type of audience that must dictate the approach used by the speaker.

1. How does Carlo's delivery approach enhance his ability as a speaker?
2. To enhance your appreciation of difference, please complete the following activity.
   A. Identify a time when a speaker effectively used the following types of delivery. Describe the situation and the audience.
      1. Impromptu
      2. Manuscript
      3. Memorization
      4. Extemporaneous
3. How does this activity help you appreciate difference?
4. How does this activity enhance your ability as a public speaker?

SHARING IDEAS

Every speech delivery is enhanced by the speaker's ability to share ideas. The more a speaker can concentrate on the ideas in the speech rather than on himself or herself or the speaking situation, the more likely the receiver also will concentrate on those ideas. In other words, the speaker's goal is to get his or her audience just as involved in the subject as he or she is. This objective is possible only if the speaker is genuinely interested in the topic. A lukewarm attitude will not get the audience's attention. The individual who is able to concentrate on sharing his or her ideas will develop into a more confident, effective speaker. Several factors discussed in this section will aid the speaker in confidently communicating with the audience.

■ Spontaneity

Just as involvement leads to greater sharing of ideas, so too does a feeling of spontaneity with the audience. **Spontaneity** refers to a speaker's apparent natural behavior at the time of delivery. As a speaker's involvement with the topic increases and his or her concentration becomes focused on ideas and audience, he or she sends signals of spontaneity and immediacy that are absent from memorized and manuscript deliveries. Words chosen spontaneously convey to an audience that the sender both is interested in the topic and wants to share his or her ideas. Not only are the words more appropriate to the specific audience, but the accompanying vocal inflections also add to the interest, further capturing the attention of the audience.

The same is true of movements and gestures (see Chapter 5). The speaker may not be aware of facial expressions, gestures, or bodily movements, but when spontaneous, these reiterate the desire to share. For example, a preplanned gesture, such as mechanically pointing a finger when a certain word is said, can communicate an aura of superficiality. However, the same gesture made spontaneously will help draw the audience more completely into the presentation.

■ Sincerity

Another key component to sharing ideas is the incorporation of **sincerity** into the presentation; that is, a speaker wants to show the audience that he or she cares about the topic, its presentation, and the audience. By doing so, the speaker may capture the audience's interest in the topic. The speaker wants to start a chain reaction from speaker to audience. In turn, the positive feedback he or she gets from the audience will help the speaker feel more confident during the speech and in subsequent speeches as well. Audience support builds confidence.

For example, Tasha, who suffers from attention deficient disorder, wants to inform her audience about the disorder and how she copes with it everyday, especially as a student. Her sincerity affects the audience who respond with active nonverbal feedback like smiling and head nodding.

USING YOUR BODY

Effective use of your body is another way to enhance your speech. Your nonverbal communication can convey as much to the audience as the words in your speech. In fact, your bodily actions can reinforce the major ideas in the presentation. Becoming aware of some of the ways to use your body to increase audience involvement and understanding is highly desirable. Many components contribute to the role your body plays in delivering a speech, including gestures, facial expressions, walking transitions, appearance, posture, and eye contact (see Chapter 5 for a detailed discussion of nonverbal behavior).

■ Gestures

Hand movement in a speech delivery should be spontaneous; in other words, it should naturally stem from the speaker's involvement with the subject. Your hands can be used to emphasize or clarify your ideas.

Gestures are useful only as long as they remain natural. Adding gestures for the sake of incorporating movement into the delivery will detract from, not enhance, your presentation. Former President Bill Clinton, for example, would point his finger aggressively in an effort to drive home his points. This was very apparent during the Monica Lewinsky scandal. When confronted with allegations of a sexual affair, Clinton definitely pointed his finger at the press and said, "I did not have sexual relations with that woman, Monica Lewinsky" (January 26, 1998). His nonverbal message enhanced his verbal message and further emphasized his denial. The gesture appeared spontaneous and real.

■ Facial Expressions

Your face usually communicates your feelings, so use it to help communicate your message to the audience. As with gestures, your **facial expressions** should be spontaneous, arising naturally from your involvement with your topic. Allowing the audience to see your commitment to your topic also may elicit their interest; knowing that you have the audience's attention gives your confidence as a public speaker a welcome boost. Good technique obviously has its rewards.

We can look to the 2004 presidential primary race for an example of inappropriate use of facial expression. Former President George W. Bush was often criticized for his "smirk." Bush's facial expressions often gave the impression he was not serious or sincere. This hindered his ability to convey his credibility to the voters.

■ Walking Transitions

Foot movement can also be used to enhance your talk. More important, foot movement can help the speaker decrease the amount of physical distance between himself or herself and the audience. Foot movement has the benefit of reducing the speaker's dependency on the lectern. It also allows the speaker to divert some of his or her excess energy, thereby relieving the mental anxiety associated with talking before an audience. Taking a step or two forward to emphasize a point or turning slightly during a transition captures the group's attention and shows your involvement with the presentation.

When incorporating **walking transitions**, make sure that they grow out of your involvement with the presentation. They should not detract from your speech. If you have a reason to move about, you will avoid overuse. When you appear relaxed enough to move about in front of your audience, your efforts will contribute to a greater sense of confidence on your part.

■ Appearance

The speaker's **appearance** also communicates a message to the audience. The members of the audience see you before they hear you speak; consequently, their

A speaker's facial expressions can enhance or detract from his or her credibility.

Richard Nixon's appearance in his debate with John Kennedy in 1960 impacted the audience's overall impression of him.

first impression of you can be shaped by your appearance. In formal settings we see political speakers paying particular attention to their appearance. One memorable instance of the importance of appearance occurred during the 1960 presidential debate between John F. Kennedy and Richard M. Nixon. Nixon's suit was somewhat wrinkled, he had a five o'clock shadow on his face, and he was perspiring during the debate. On the other hand, Kennedy appeared presidential. After 50 years, scholars still point to this instance as a lesson for the importance of candidate appearance.

Although personal attire does not play a significant role in classroom speeches, you should make sure that your appearance does not draw the audience away from your intended message. For example, a wild hairdo will surely distract the audience. You do not want the audience to pay more attention to what you are wearing than to what you are saying to them. In fact, if your audience's attention is focused on your appearance, it is probably safe to say that your appearance is doing you a disservice. In deciding what to wear, consider both the audience and the nature of the speaking situation. For example, a talk with high school students about drug abuse would call for casual attire (no suits), while a presentation to a group of business managers would call for a suit (no jeans with sweaters). Both audiences would likely be uncomfortable if the speakers dressed differently. You should use your appearance to enhance your credibility, if possible. For example, if you were giving a speech on the importance of yearly veterinarian visits for pets, you might wear the uniform you wear as a veterinary assistant. Your uniform will communicate your expertise and will also help you feel more confident.

■ Posture

Good **posture** is one aspect of bodily action that commands the attention of your audience. When speaking in front of a group, avoid slouching or bending your knees; keep your spine straight, your shoulders back, and your feet a comfortable distance apart. You do not, however, want to look like a soldier standing at attention. Avoid a rigid stance because it communicates that you are tense and inhibits any other natural movement. Avoid, too, appearing so loose and casual that you find yourself leaning against the blackboard or sprawling over the lectern. Finally, avoid shifting your weight from foot to foot as you speak. Good posture can enhance your presentation because you will appear more confident and involved in the topic and the audience. You want the audience to concentrate on what you are sharing; proper posture will not detract from this goal. Instead, it will reinforce your image as a well-prepared, confident public speaker.

■ Eye Contact

Perhaps one of the most difficult skills for the public speaker to master is direct **eye contact.** As mentioned earlier, your eyes are one of your most revealing features; therefore, a conscious effort to establish direct eye contact acknowledges that you wish to draw the audience in. Understandably, many speakers feel anxious about this task. However, the rewards are gratifying: Your audience will feel more involved in your presentation, and you will be able to see it on their faces and in their eyes.

For many it is easier to establish direct eye contact with a small audience, because the size of the group is less threatening. Even with a small group, however, it is difficult to establish direct eye contact with every member of the audience; an attempt to do so will result in little more than scanning the audience. This is not direct eye contact; rather, it is a mechanical back-and-forth motion. Some speakers tend to look above the heads of those in the audience in an effort to appear to be looking at everyone. Still others simply stare out a window or keep their eyes glued to their notes. These techniques prohibit the speaker from responding to any feedback the audience sends.

What the speaker needs to do is establish direct eye contact with certain members of the audience. We suggest picking individuals who are scattered in different parts of the room. For your first speeches, try to include people with whom you feel comfortable or those whom you believe will be supportive. Doing so will make it easier for you to practice this technique and to respond to any feedback they might give you. As you gain experience and confidence, you will be able to gradually include members of the audience whom you do not know, as well as those who give negative feedback. You need to respond to both positive and negative feedback in order to make your speech more effective.

Serving Your COMMUNITY

Effective Delivery

The delivery of your message can have a great impact on the overall effectiveness of the message. Refer to the Serving Your Community activity in Chapter 13. Using the key-phrase outline you developed, do the following:

1. Schedule a meeting with the office of student government on your campus.

2. Ask if you and your partner can speak for a minute on the importance of volunteerism at the next meeting of the student government board.

3. As you deliver your one-minute presentation, use your body to communicate. Specifically try to incorporate:
   a. Gestures.
   b. Facial expressions.
   c. Walking transitions.
   d. Pausing.
   e. Eye contact.

4. As you deliver your speech try to use your voice to communicate your ideas. Specifically try to focus on:
   a. Volume.
   b. Rate.
   c. Inflection.
   d. Pause.
   e. Pronunciation.

5. After you each give the one-minute speech, review and discuss how your body and voice affected the speech.

6. How did this process help you appreciate difference?

In our culture, direct eye contact is extremely important because it communicates confidence and the appearance of a strong self-concept. In addition, it shows concern about communicating with others. An audience can sense when a speaker is in control and will respond favorably. Naturally, a boost to one's self-image will provide greater confidence for subsequent speeches. This "snowball" effect leads to growth and maturity for the public speaker.

Learning to use direct eye contact is like learning any other skill: practice is the key ingredient. At first, your attempts may seem mechanical. You may feel uncomfortable because you are self-conscious about your behavior. With time and practice, however, direct eye contact can become a natural part of your communication behavior. Know in advance that many people in the audience will be unable to establish direct eye contact with you; this does not mean that they are rejecting you.

USING YOUR VOICE

Your voice gives meaning to the words in your speech. As you may remember from Chapter 5, this is called paralanguage. Your voice can reflect the way you feel about your topic; therefore, you can use it to emphasize points. For example, a voice that quivers during the eulogy at a friend's funeral expresses the speaker's sorrow and pain. Likewise, a voice that grows louder reflects anger or passion about some issue, for example, a speaker's outrage over the number of homeless people in the United States and the lack of assistance governmental agencies provide. It is equally important that you pronounce words clearly and precisely so that the audience will understand your message. Several vocal aspects of delivery are discussed next, including volume, rate, inflection, pause, and pronunciation and articulation.

■ Volume

Volume refers to the loudness of a speaker's voice. Before the use of electronic devices, it was essential for an individual to speak in a loud and powerful voice. This holds true in the classroom as well, since it is not likely that you will have the opportunity to use a microphone. Consequently, you will find it necessary to adjust your voice so that all members of the audience will be able to hear your message. If your audience must strain to hear you, they will probably miss a large part of your message. In fact, you run the risk of losing them altogether as responsive members. Additionally, if you speak very softly, you may appear to lack confidence.

By the same token, you do not want to shout or scream at your audience in order to capture their attention. Shouting can be construed as overdramatization and may communicate to your audience that you are not sincere about the ideas you are sharing with them. Instead, it appears that you are acting a part in a play.

The level of your voice should correspond to the way you treat your topic. There will be times when you will want to raise or lower your voice based on your feelings about the subject. Let the volume of your voice change as a result of your enthusiasm for the topic. If possible, practice your speech in the same room in which you will be presenting it. Have classmates or friends sit in the back of the room during your practice session. Adjust your volume according to their feedback. You will then know how loudly to deliver your message when the time comes.

■ Rate

The **rate** of your speech is dependent on the number of words you deliver in a given amount of time. Most Americans deliver between 120 and 150 words per minute. Your rate should vary, depending on the speaking situation. The appropriate rate will grow out of the relationship among the audience, the message, and the speaker. Furthermore, the rate will fluctuate throughout the speech; there will be moments when you find it necessary to pick up the pace and other times when you find it more appropriate to slow down.

Although some beginning speakers talk too slowly, most novices experience the opposite problem: They tend to speak too rapidly. Anxiety usually causes this condition. When we get nervous, we tend to speak more rapidly owing to excess tension. The difficulty of the situation is compounded when the audience is unable to comprehend the message.

Special efforts are necessary first to identify and then to correct this problem. For instance, it is helpful to listen to your voice on a recorder. This gives you an opportunity to hear the speed at which you speak, thereby increasing your awareness of the problem. A friend or family member also can help by listening to you practice your speech. Ask that person to listen specifically to whether you deliver your speech too rapidly. Finally, indicate in italic print in your notes to slow down at particular points. Such reminders will keep you aware of your speaking rate during your delivery. For example:

> As part of his job as a sales representative, Patrick spends time engaged in public speaking. In order to enhance his presentational skills, he joined the local chapter of Toastmasters. Each month, members gather to give speeches and offer feedback to one another. In his first speech, the other members indicated that he spoke much too fast and that some of his important points were lost to them. In preparation for his second speech, Patrick has written *SLOW DOWN* at the top of his notecards to remind himself to speak at a normal pace.

■ Inflection

Think of how boring it is to listen to a speech delivered in a monotone voice. **Inflection** is the tone of your voice. Lack of variety in vocal inflection has been known to put more than one audience to sleep. The inflection of your voice can and should change as you move to different points in the speech. As you try to stir your audience, for example, the pitch of your voice should rise.

■ Pause

It is virtually impossible to deliver a speech without inserting some pauses. There are a few places in a speech where pauses can be very effective. First, a **pause** is helpful as you shift from one idea to the next. This gives your audience notice that you are about to move on to another point. Furthermore, it allows your audience time to assimilate new or complex ideas. Second, pauses are used effectively when you are striving for emphasis.

The technique of using well-placed pauses is developed with practice. As you become more adept at using pauses, you will achieve your goal of sustaining the audience's interest. An audience often responds to a pause by looking up at the speaker. They are waiting to hear more. You have their attention—now proceed.

Vocalized or verbal pauses such as *ah*, *um*, *like*, and *you know* should not be confused with well-placed silent pauses. In fact, these interjections can be interpreted as signs of nervousness or lack of adequate preparation and will detract from your effectiveness and credibility as a speaker.

■ Pronunciation and Articulation

If your audience is to understand the words in your speech, you must say them correctly **(pronunciation)** and clearly **(articulation)**. A common occurrence in speech is the mispronunciation of words. We have all done it at one time or another and have probably suffered a degree of embarrassment when the error was pointed out. For example, the following table illustrates four words that are frequently mispronounced:

Word	*Common Pronunciation*	*Correct Pronunciation*
February	Feb-u-ary	Feb-ru-ary
disastrous	di-sas-ter-ous	di-sas-trous
burglar	bur-ga-lar	bur-glar
athlete	ath-a-lete	ath-lete

To ensure that your delivery is free of mispronunciations, consult a dictionary for those words you have any doubt about. Also, practicing your delivery in front of a friend or family member may help catch errors.

Articulation refers to the clear or distinct pronunciation of words. It is not identical to pronunciation, for you can say a word crisply but still mispronounce it (for example, saying the *w* in *sword* or the *l* in *salmon* is a mistake in pronunciation). A few general pointers may give you more confidence over the question of articulation. Avoid the following when delivering your speech: (1) running words together, such as "wanna" for *want to* or "didja" for *did you*; (2) omitting word endings, such as "havin" for *having* or "runnin" for *running*.

PRACTICING YOUR SPEECH

We have discussed several steps that are designed to help you feel more confident when you are required to speak in public. It is important to remember that there is no one right way to deliver a speech. The appropriate delivery style will depend on you, your topic, the situation, and the audience. Implementing the skills in this chapter will help you feel more self-assured and in control. The finishing touches for your presentation are achieved through practice. Several steps to help you prepare to speak are discussed in the next section.

1. Begin to practice the speech aloud. There are several techniques you can use to become comfortable with your material. Try to become familiar with your ideas. This necessitates going through the speech completely several times. Even if you make a mistake, continue to go through the speech until you

reach its conclusion. This will help you to grasp the ideas and keep you focused on the ideas when you actually deliver the speech. You should know your message thoroughly so that you do not need your note cards—but have them handy just in case.

2. Once you become comfortable with the ideas, you need to refine your delivery. Begin to practice your delivery in front of a mirror. Take note of your movement, and keep in mind that any movement should reflect your involvement with the ideas. If you notice any annoying mannerisms, try to refrain from repeating them. You also may choose to use a recorder to check the quality of your voice. This can be especially helpful if you are having a difficult time with pronunciation. Finally, if a video camera and recorder are available to you, consider taping your delivery. Video equipment has the advantage of combining the techniques just mentioned in a single operation—you can both see and hear your delivery.

3. Once you have practiced your speech in front of the mirror or have taped your delivery, you may wish to elicit feedback from friends and family. While you are delivering your speech to the audience at home, practice establishing direct eye contact with them. This will help you to incorporate direct eye contact with members of your actual audience and help you practice adjusting your message to audience feedback.

4. Once you feel comfortable with your presentation at home, you also may wish to practice the speech in an empty classroom. Do so before the day that the speech is scheduled. This will give you an opportunity to become familiar with the setting of the speech. Also, practice with your presentational aids. It will take several practice runs for you to feel comfortable handling and presenting your presentational aids.

Keep in mind that each individual's background brings a uniqueness to any topic he or she chooses to share with an audience. Believing that you have something special to share will give you a tremendous boost in confidence. The speech is an interactive process between you and the audience. As a speaker, it is your goal to communicate your ideas in a way your audience can understand and appreciate them. Appreciating their different approaches to your message can go a long way in ensuring a successful speech.

DILBERT: © Scott Adams/Dist. by United Feature Syndicate, Inc. Reprinted by permission.

Communication and TECHNOLOGY
Effective Delivery and PowerPoint

PowerPoint is very rare at CEO conferences. Like Supreme Court justices, captains of industry like to see a speaker think, not watch him read (Stewart, 2001, p. 210).

The essence of any public presentation is the interaction between the speaker and the audience. The speaker must be able to continually adapt and adjust to audience feedback in order to effectively get his/her message across. For example, the speaker must be able to adjust voice quality, use walking transitions or other bodily movements to help the audience stay focused on the message.

With the advent of presentational software like PowerPoint by Microsoft, many speakers have forgotten the all important relationship between speaker and audience. PowerPoint and other presentational software have become a substitute for a "real" speaker.

Presentational software has become prevalent. In fact, 500 million people use PowerPoint in some way, according to Microsoft. Despite its millions of users, many businesses, conferences, and the military are beginning to ban the use of PowerPoint because it is interfering with, not helping, speakers communicate their messages clearly and effectively.

Many times speakers overuse or misuse presentational software. Specifically, PowerPoint limits the speaker's ability to creatively communicate ideas. According to Chip and Dan Heath, authors of *Made to Stick: Why Some Ideas Survive and Others Die*, "Business mangers seem to believe that once they've clicked through a PowerPoint . . . they've successfully communicated their ideas. What they've done is share data" (Ewers, 2007). In other words, public speaking is more than just data.

Second, and most important, PowerPoint detracts from the interaction between the speaker and the audience. According to Thomas Stewart, PowerPoint discourages questioning by the audience (2001). The speaker does not have a lot of freedom to pause, for example, in the middle of a slide presentation, to engage the audience's questions. Everyone, including the speaker, stares at the screen. Karen Friedman cautions, "These presenters are talking to their slides, not their audience. I see this every day, and I always tell my clients the same thing: Nobody came to see a slideshow, they came to see you" (Hill, 2003). The speaker's responsibility is to engage the audience and it seems that PowerPoint can hinder the interaction between the speaker and his/her audience.

If you decide to use PowerPoint or some other presentational software, there are some guidelines you can follow to ensure you creatively present your ideas and that you engage your audience. First, remember that more is less. Keep your slides simple and to the point. Don't put too much information on a single slide and don't have too many slides. Second, slides should be used to clarify ideas or help the audience visualize our main points. Charts, graphs, and photos, for example, are excellent tools that can be enhanced with the use of PowerPoint. Third, as you deliver your presentation, remember all the important aspects to effective delivery like eye contact (avoid reading your slides, talk to the audience), conversational quality, and spontaneity. Most of all, don't forget the audience is there and maintain constant contact with them through your delivery style. Lastly, technology fails. Be prepared to give your presentation if the computer or the PowerPoint files don't work. You need to flexible.

PowerPoint can be a useful tool if it is used properly. Just be sure that you remember the essence of any public presentation is the relationship and interaction between the speaker and the audience.

SUMMARY

This chapter provided information to help you deliver a more effective speech. There are distinct differences between oral and written communication. Oral communication is a cooperative act that includes immediate feedback from the audience. It requires the speaker to create a message that is easy for the audience to listen to. Unlike written communication, the sender must be concerned about the nonverbal messages of both the speaker and the audience. Stage fright is common to many people, but there are ways to cope with it. These include reducing excess tension, focusing on the topic, realizing that you are not alone, and developing a positive attitude. If you can remember to keep public speaking in its proper perspective, you will be less fearful of speaking in front of an audience.

There are four different types of speech delivery: impromptu, manuscript, memorized, and extemporaneous. Of these, the extemporaneous delivery has a major advantage: The speaker prepares the topic in advance, but the delivery is still flexible enough to allow the speaker to adapt to the audience.

There are several techniques you can learn to improve your ability to share ideas with an audience. Spontaneity and sincerity are two important aspects of delivery. In addition, you can use your body to its best advantage by incorporating the following into the delivery: natural gestures, facial expression, walking transitions, appropriate appearance, good posture, and direct eye contact. Still another way to enhance delivery involves the use of your voice. Volume, rate, inflection, appropriately placed pauses, and pronunciation and articulation are factors to consider when delivering your speech. Your confidence as a speaker will increase as you learn to effectively incorporate these techniques into your delivery.

Finally, the following suggestions may help when practicing your delivery. Once you feel comfortable with the material, begin practicing the speech aloud. Whether you do this in front of a mirror, a video camera, or your family, remember that you have something of value to share with the audience. Practicing your delivery should increase your confidence, because you will know that you have adequately prepared for your presentation.

REVIEW QUESTIONS

1. What are the differences between oral and written communication?
2. What steps can you take to help control speech anxiety?
3. Name the four methods of speech delivery and briefly describe each one.
4. Why is it important for your bodily movements to be spontaneous?
5. Why is it helpful for a speaker to establish direct eye contact with an audience?
6. What are the different ways in which you can use your voice to improve your delivery?
7. What steps can you use to practice your delivery?

KEY CONCEPTS

impromptu speech	gestures	volume
manuscript speech	facial expressions	rate
memorized speech	walking transitions	inflection
extemporaneous speech	appearance	pause
spontaneity	posture	pronunciation
sincerity	eye contact	articulation

The Informative Speech

AFTER STUDYING THIS CHAPTER, YOU SHOULD

understand

- the purpose of an informative speech.
- several appropriate informative speech topics.

be able to

- make a topic relevant to the audience.
- structure an effective informative speech.
- use the methods of narration, description, definition, and demonstration to present an informative speech.

I n his communication course, Melvin must research, write, and deliver an informative speech. One topic that he has always been interested in is illiteracy. Melvin's grandfather never learned to read, and he often told Melvin about his struggles at work and at home because he could not read. Melvin decided to find out about illiteracy in his community.

After interviewing several volunteers who teach adults to read at the high school, Melvin searches the library and the Internet for source material. He discovers that illiteracy is a problem that affects all ages and ethnic groups. In his community alone, over 12 percent of all adults cannot read at the eighth-grade level. Several factors contribute to illiteracy. These include family income, educational opportunities in the community, local crime rate, educational level of the family, and family support.

Melvin must decide how best to inform his audience about illiteracy. He could tell the story of his grandfather and describe all the struggles he went through because he could not read. Or he could use his speech to define illiteracy. But Melvin chooses to describe how illiteracy affects his community and what can be done to help those who are illiterate.

■ ■ ■ ■ ■

In this chapter, we will see that there are different types of informative speeches, and for each topic, there are several diverse approaches. Before we begin our discussion about the special qualities of this type of speech, it might be helpful to review how we got to this point. You will soon discover that all the necessary tools for preparing and delivering an informative speech were provided in the previous four chapters on public speaking.

Chapter 11 provided you with the foundation for public speaking and gave you direction; armed with a topic, a purpose, and a sense of your audience, you were ready for the next step in preparing a public speech—gathering materials. In Chapter 12 you discovered that your credibility as a speaker, and your topic itself, is possibly enhanced by supporting materials gathered from such sources as interviews, newspapers, periodicals, the Internet, and books. What did you do with this additional information? You incorporated it into the development of your speech. Chapter 13 demonstrated to you how, by ordering the ideas related to your topic, you could develop a logical, fluent speech. Outlining these ideas proved to be a systematic way to further develop your speech. At last you were ready for the delivery. Chapter 14 provided you with techniques for translating your written ideas into an effective oral presentation. Now let us put into practice all that you have learned, beginning with the informative speech.

THE NATURE OF THE INFORMATIVE SPEECH

The purpose of an informative speech is to educate an audience. "About what?" we might ask. Today we live in an information age that bombards us with new facts and ideas each day, yet we cannot possibly digest all this information, nor do we desire to. Rather, we make decisions about what interests us and our audiences and then we focus our attention on those issues and ideas. This becomes a key consideration when we select a topic for an informative speech and when we develop that topic.

Unlike the **persuasive speech,** whose purpose is to change an attitude or motivate to act, the overriding concern of the **informative speech** is to impart knowledge. Your appeal as a speaker is directed at the audience's desire for information that matters. In other words, you must operate on the premise that the members of your audience are eager to learn something new and that part of your function is to make the information relevant to them. How do you accomplish this?

Your first objective is to *engage* your audience. Ask yourself such questions as, "What do I know about the demographics of this audience?" and "What do I know about this group's attitudes and interests?" In other words, "What do you know about the frames of references of the audience members?" Remember, the audience brings diverse approaches to the communication process, and as the speaker, it is your responsibility to acknowledge and value these approaches, even if they are different from your own. You will likely be successful at drawing the audience's attention and establishing the relevance of your topic if you keep this in mind. For example:

> Artie is 33 years old and married, and he and his wife have three children. After receiving his bachelor's degree in finance, he went to work as a stockbroker. After several miserable years, Artie decided to go back to college and earn his teaching certificate, since he always wanted to be a high school social studies teacher. One requirement for his certificate is the completion of a basic communication course. When given his first speech assignment, to inform the audience, Artie struggles with what to teach the audience. His instructor suggests that he talk about his prior experience as a stockbroker, as he would have instant credibility. "That's boring and this audience of students who are 25 to 35 years old don't have any money to invest," said Artie. Artie's instructor suggests he focus on individual retirement accounts (IRAs) and the notion that the Social Security system will likely be bankrupt when his audience retires and that they need to prepare for their retirement. Artie agrees this would be appropriate for his audience, and he certainly knows a lot about the topic.

In this example, Artie has taken into consideration his interests and expertise and his audience's needs and interests to develop his informative speech topic.

This leads us to a second important quality of the informative speech—simplicity. If your audience is unfamiliar with your topic, yet you have succeeded in capturing their interest, it is crucial that you present your information so that it is easily digested. A sure way to lose an audience is to present information that is too complex or sophisticated for them to comprehend as you are speaking. This is not to say that the development of your topic should be simplistic; it should, however, be easy enough to follow. Clear understanding is essential to an informative speech. If the members of your audience cannot understand a point, they are apt to stop listening. When that happens, the relevance of your speech vanishes.

An informative speech with clear, easily understood ideas is made even better by the use of appropriate language. To a large degree, whether or not ideas are understood depends on the words you use. Concrete, descriptive terms help any audience to understand new ideas. It is therefore wise to limit the use of abstract language (review Chapter 4 for a discussion of abstract and concrete language).

Communication and TECHNOLOGY
Information Overload

"*Our poor brains are definitely suffering information overload. Technology is making quantum leaps, bombarding us with new things to focus on, but we have not been able to catch up and adapt. Our brains' attention levels are finite. When everything is screaming at us, we start withdrawing so that normal nice people become unempathetic,*" Felix Economakis, psychologist (Naish, 2009).

Do you feel overwhelmed by all the information you are confronted with each day? If so, you may suffer from information overload. This phenomenon has also been called data clutter, info glut, and info pollution. Marsha White and Steve Dorman argue that information overload "refers to the vast quantities of information speedily disseminated to a large and growing number of people" (2000, p. 160). According to a Yahoo! study, four of every five Internet users believe they suffer from information overload (Internet Stats Today, 2008). It is no wonder we feel this way. According to Andrea Coombes of Market Watch, a business-oriented website, "Every day, information workers in the U.S. are each bombarded with 1.6 gigabytes of information, on average, through emails, reports, blogs, text messages, calls and more" (2009). For example, at IBM, 400,000 employees send 12 million instant messages to each other per day (Coombes, 2009).

Information overload affects just about everyone. It can hinder learning and overall productivity. Some studies estimate that over $900 billion a year is lost in productivity (Coombes, 2009)! In addition, it can cause higher blood pressure, digestive disorders, lack of concentration, tension, less time with family and friends, longer days and shorter leisure time (White & Dorman, 2000, p. 160).

What can we do? Here are a few tips from several sources on how we can reduce our information overload:

1. Turn off the television. In the average U.S. household, the television is on for more than seven hours a day.

2. Turn off your mobile devices. These tend to control us rather than the reverse.

3. Say no to junk mail. Have your name removed from mailing lists that contribute little to your development.

4. Send less email and you will receive less.

5. Sort your inbox by sender so you can easily see the important messages from your supervisor, for example.

6. Turn off the "new mail" alerts. This will reduce the interruptions.

7. Learn efficient ways to search online. Adopt a search engine and learn its quirks so you develop expertise in using it.

8. Follow netiquette guidelines.

The remainder of this chapter is divided into three sections: (1) informative speech topics, (2) organizing the informative speech, and (3) methods for presenting an informative speech. At the end of the chapter you will find a sample informative speech, complete with commentary.

INFORMATIVE SPEECH TOPICS

As a speaker, you have the luxury of drawing from a vast body of potential topics for an informative speech. What you do with that topic determines whether your speech will be successful or unsuccessful. The key ingredient is discovering how to develop the topic to make it relevant to your audience. For example, a high school football team needs to listen to the coach's detailed strategy for Friday night's game, yet high school faculty interest would be limited. Similarly, an instructor would present different speeches about seeing eye dogs to an audience with a visual impairment and an audience with sight. For the first audience, the focus might be on instructing students how to use a guide dog; for the second audience, the focus might shift to working with students with visual impairments who use guide dogs. Whatever the topic, it must be adapted to the audience.

The bulk of informative speech topics fall into one of the following categories: recreation, concepts, places, objects, events, and people.

■ Recreation

One area that offers several topics for the informative speech is recreation. Activities such as sports, exercise, hobbies, and creative arts have a broad appeal. You can easily develop speeches that take a "how to" approach, such as how to play handball or croquet, how to carve a watermelon into a whale, or how to plan a cross-country biking trip. There are also all sorts of prospects for pointing out the benefits of recreational activities, as in this example:

> Cheryl works as a fitness instructor at the local YMCA. Her job is to develop and deliver workshops to the members about physical fitness, nutrition, and stress relief. Cheryl's supervisor has asked her to hold a workshop for the working mothers of the YMCA on how they can stay fit and relieve stress. After doing some research, Cheryl decides to focus her discussion on aerobic exercises and planning nutritious lunches that her audience can take to work with them.

Cheryl's effort to give her audience information that was related to their well-being helped reinforce the relevance of her speech.

■ Concepts

Topics for informative speeches can be drawn from concepts, that is, ideas, theories, or thoughts generally used to explain abstract subjects, such as democracy, supply-side economics, or bigotry. Because concepts are often abstract, your

Free speech and other abstract subjects can make excellent speech topics.

purpose will be in part to explain in more concrete language the ideas inherent in the topic. Your goal is to have the audience arrive at a better understanding of the concept by the speech's conclusion. Consider Juan's topic:

> Juan has come back to college after a two-year absence. He has been able to secure financial aid and can now complete his degree in political science. He hopes someday to go to law school and become a lawyer. One of Juan's passions has been to study the First Amendment to the United States Constitution and issues such as flag burning, freedom of the press, and the separation of church and state. For his informative speech, Juan decides to define and explain the concept of "free speech" to his classmates and to show how important this right is to democracy. To make the topic clear, Juan uses the case of a journalist who refused to reveal her sources in a story about a very important criminal case and was jailed.

Juan knows that for his speech to be effective, he must make the abstract topic of free speech concrete for his audience. He does this with the use of a true to life example.

■ Places

As the subject of informative speeches, places can include such things as institutions, historical sites, cities, geologic landforms, and buildings. Specific examples are Wrigley Field, the Lincoln Memorial, and Kilimanjaro. Consider the following:

Nell and her family have recently relocated to Georgia because of her husband's job. She is taking a few classes at the local community college in order to complete her associate's degree in nursing. As part of one of her nursing classes, Nell must talk about some aspect of herself and her experiences. She wants to tell her class of about the excitement of Chicago, where she grew up and lived until last year. In order to give them a flavor of what Chicago has to offer, she decides to talk about the Museum Campus. She describes the Field Museum of Natural History with its huge dinosaur exhibits, the Shedd Aquarium with its new Ocean-aquarium, and the Adler Planetarium's extensive telescope, all located within walking distance of one another. By the time she has completed this description, her audience is more than a little intrigued by these interesting places in the Windy City.

When you give a speech about a place you have visited, you have the opportunity to bring some of your own experiences to the topic. Your efforts are likely to maintain the audience's interest.

■ Objects

Our environment is filled with thousands of unique and interesting objects; many make ideal subjects for an informative speech. When speaking about an object, you might explain how its use has a special significance for your audience. A few objects you might choose to discuss include computers, digital cameras, or antique cars.

When you speak about an object, your purpose might be to explain its use, its appeal to a particular segment of the population, or its impact on society. For example:

Terri is a market research analyst for Toyota and a recent graduate with a bachelor's degree in marketing. She is scheduled to speak to a group of design engineers about how to increase sales for hybrid cars. Specifically, she plans to focus her comments on the specific features future car buyers will be looking for in a hybrid car. Terri's information is invaluable to the engineers because it gives them new ideas for the cars they will design over the next few years.

Terri's success in this example can be attributed to her efforts to tailor the information to the needs of her audience.

■ People

People represent a tremendous source for speech topics. You can easily develop a fascinating informative speech about an individual or a group of people, such as political leaders, steelworkers, or professional boxers. If you decide to speak about a person or group of people, try highlighting their unique qualities, contributions, or importance. For example, you might focus on the impact that Steven Spielberg has had on the motion picture industry, the contributions of Susan B. Anthony to the Women's Rights Movement, or Sarah Palin, the first Republican woman nominated for Vice President.

Sarah Palin, the first Republican woman nominated for Vice President, would be an interesting, informative topic.

■ Events

Exciting and important events take place in the world every day, and most would make interesting speech topics. Events you might talk about could be recent or historical. The Civil Rights movement during the 1960s and the Space Shuttle Challenger accident were important historical events in U.S. history. When speaking of an event, you might want to discuss the event in chronological or time order to ensure your audience can follow along as the event or events actually took place. Table 15.1 provides a summary of informative speech topics.

TABLE 15.1   Informative Speech Topics

Recreation	*Concepts*	*Places*
Swing dancing	Volunteerism	Colonial Williamsburg
Herb gardening	History of communism	Rain forest
Sky diving	Autism	U.S. national parks
Objects	*People*	*Events*
High-definition TVs	The Beatles	Assassination of Malcolm X
Shaker furniture	Sarah Palin	Barack Obama's Inauguration
Wii	Susan B. Anthony	Winter/Summer Olympics

ORGANIZING THE INFORMATIVE SPEECH

It may be helpful to review the material in Chapter 13 as you begin to structure your informative speech. There you will find a discussion about organizational patterns for the ideas in your topic; suggestions for developing the body, introduction, conclusion, and transitions; and outlining principles. Because you are working on an informative speech, you must always bear in mind that your purpose is to fill an information need of your audience. Your speech should first engage the audience's interest and then strive to present ideas that can be easily understood, always with the intent to maintain the relevance of your topic.

In the body of the speech, where you will focus your attention first, make sure to use an organizational structure that best fits the purpose of your speech. For instance, if your purpose is to describe the women's movement, you may first want to discuss many of the important leaders of the movement, such as Elizabeth Cady Stanton, Soujourner Truth, or Gloria Steinem, in a topical order. Another approach may be to discuss the problems women faced and then discuss the long-term effects the movement had on women's lives with a cause-and-effect organizational pattern. Similarly, if you want to explain how the movement developed over time, you could discuss the "first wave" (1878–1920), the "second wave" (1959–1979), and finally, the current "third wave" (1985–present) using a chronological pattern. The key is to identify the organizational pattern that best relates to the purpose of your speech.

As mentioned in Chapter 13, it is advisable to limit the number of points you plan to present in the body of an information speech. The audience will have an easier time absorbing the information in a speech that has a well-developed theme rather than one that is overburdened with minute facts. While facts are essential to the development of a topic, it is counterproductive to overwhelm the audience with excessive details.

When you construct an introduction, remember that your intent is to trigger a need in the audience. You want to demonstrate why it is important for them to listen to your presentation. Try to do this by highlighting ways in which the information is relevant to them. For instance, if you plan to inform the audience about ways to improve relationships, you might point out how this information will benefit their relationships. It is critical to encourage the audience to listen to you as you develop your ideas.

In the conclusion, summarize your ideas and suggest to the audience what it is you want them to walk away with after listening to your speech. If you have explained a new procedure to the audience, you will want to encourage them to be patient as they attempt this new task. Furthermore, you might suggest sources where they can gain additional information on the process you have just explained.

Finally, transitions should be used as a bridge between the major parts of the speech and to reinforce the points you present in the body. These transitions help your audience to retain the information you impart.

METHODS OF PRESENTING AN INFORMATIVE SPEECH

The effectiveness of an informative speech depends on the development of the topic and on your ability to narrate, describe, define, and demonstrate the ideas in your speech. These skills are discussed in the following section.

■ Narration

One way to present material in an informative speech is with a narrative. A **narrative** is a story or an account of an event told orally. The speaker can use a narrative to introduce a speech or to illustrate or clarify a point within a speech. In order to be effective, a narrative should evoke a feeling of "being there." When the members of an audience are able to visualize a point the speaker is trying to make, they develop a better understanding of the topic.

Narratives should use vivid language, should be easy to follow, and should avoid being too lengthy. You can create your own narrative for an informative speech, or you can quote the written or oral narratives of others. In a narrative, the speaker can use personal experience as the basis for a story.

For example, to illustrate his point about the need to help others, Christopher Reeve, in his commencement address at Ohio State University in 2003, said:

> It was not until I was immersed in my own rehabilitation that I realized an apparent tragedy had created a unique opportunity. Spinal cord patients like the ones I once dismissed were now in the next room traveling down the same hallways, and struggling right beside me in physical therapy. I came to know people of all ages and from all walks of life that I would otherwise never have met. For all our differences, what we had in common was our disability and the desire to find a reason to hope. I was inspired by so many and gradually discovered that I had been given a job that would create urgency and a new direction in my life: I could do something to help. (2003)

Source: From Christopher Reeve at his commencement address to Ohio State University on June 13, 2003. Reprinted with permission of the estates of Christopher and Dana Reeve.

Christopher Reeve effectively used a narrative about his rehabilitation to engage his audience.

Former Senator and now President Barack Obama uses effective description in his speeches.

This narrative is effective because it successfully transports the audience to Reeve's time in rehabilitation. We can picture him and his fellow spinal cord patients struggling to improve.

Description

A **description** is an image that is created verbally. In an informative speech, a description can be used to effectively communicate a speaker's ideas. How effectively depends on the language used. Descriptions that use **concrete terms,** where the language is detailed and specific, are easier for an audience to visualize than descriptions that use **abstract terms,** where the language is general or vague. A speaker might describe an object by telling about its shape, size, color, or texture. He or she uses words to paint a picture that the audience can visualize. Adjectives generally work best for this purpose, since by definition they act as descriptors. The following is a very effective description of the United States, according to former Senator and now President Barack Obama:

The pundits, the pundits like to slice and dice our country into Red States and Blue States; Red States for Republicans, Blue States for Democrats. But I've got news for them, too. We worship an "awesome God" in the Blue States, and we don't like federal agents poking around in our libraries in the Red States. We coach Little League in the Blue States and yes, we've got some gay friends in the Red States. There are patriots who

COMMUNICATION IN ACTION

Narration

1. Think about the topics you are considering for your informative speech. Choose one of those topics.

2. First, write down a personal experience that helps communicate your feelings about this subject.

3. Next, gather outside resources to help illustrate your feelings about the topic. Write down the information as a narrative.

4. Share both narratives with a classmate.

5. Use the feedback from your classmate to improve one of the narratives for your speech.

opposed the war in Iraq and there are patriots who supported the war in Iraq. We are one people, all of us pledging allegiance to the stars and stripes, all of us defending the United States of America. (2004)

The following description of the people of the United States pales by comparison: "We all live in the United States, regardless if we live in a Republican or Democratic state." An audience, after hearing this description, would have little sense of how much citizens of the United States have in common. The vague language used here fails to promote understanding.

■ Definition

Definition is a valuable form of support in the informative speech (see Chapter 12). Terms that are generally unfamiliar to an audience, however, need to be defined in language that the audience can easily understand. There are a number of ways to accomplish this, including the use of synonyms, antonyms, comparisons, and etymology. Sarah Palin, former Governor of Alaska and Vice Presidential Republican nominee, defined a hockey mom in her convention speech. She said, "I was just your average hockey mom and signed up for the PTA. I love those hockey moms. You know, they say the difference between a hockey mom and a pit bull: lipstick" (2008).

One way to define a term is by using synonyms. **Synonyms** are different words that have the same or nearly the same meaning. Substituting the word *customs* for *mores* or *drunkenness* for *insobriety* can help to clarify the definition of an idea in your speech.

A speaker also can use **antonyms,** words that have opposite meanings, to define a concept for the audience. *Despair* is an antonym for *hope*. For instance, a speaker might use the word *despair* as an antonym for hope and talk in terms of a "hopeful future in light of a despairing past."

It is sometimes desirable to define a concept or an idea by making **comparisons.** In his acceptance address at the 1984 Republican National Convention, Ronald Reagan attempted to illustrate the differences between the Democratic and Republican parties' views of America:

> The choices this year are not just between two different personalities, or between two political parties. They are between two different visions of the future, two fundamentally different ways of governing—their government of pessimism, fear, and limits, or ours of hope, confidence, and growth. Their government sees people only as members of groups. Ours serves all the people of America as individuals. Theirs lives in the past, seeking to apply the old and failed policies to an era that has passed them by. Ours learns from the past and strives to change by boldly charting a new course for the future. (1984, 706)

In this statement, Reagan attempted to define the differences between the two parties by characterizing his party as one of the future and the Democratic Party as one plagued by the past. His proffered future of hope, confidence, and growth was contrasted with a past defined by pessimism, fear, and limits.

SKILL BUILDING

Description

1. Pick one of the following topics:
   a. air travel
   b. hot tubs
   c. working overtime
   d. your favorite holiday
2. Using concrete language, describe the topic in as much detail as you can, making sure you define any terms the audience may not be familiar with.
3. With a partner, share your description and provide feedback on his or her description.

Still another way to define a term is to refer to its **etymology,** or origin. The etymology of a word is the history of its development or use in the language where it is found. For example, in a speech about three mayoral candidates, you might characterize one candidate as a liberal. To clarify what you mean by the term *liberal*, you refer to the word's etymology: *liberal* comes from the Latin *liber*, meaning "free, or liberated, befitting a freeman, generous" (Skeat, 1958, p. 293). One of the best reference sources for the etymology of words in the English language is the *Oxford English Dictionary*.

■ Demonstration

Demonstration is often an effective method for explaining a point or idea to an audience. In an effort to clearly explain a particular activity, such as cake decorating or operation of a video camera, you might show the audience the steps involved in

ETHICS in Communication
The Informative Speech

In the beginning of the chapter we met Melvin, who is preparing for his informative speech. Because of his grandfather's experiences, Melvin is interested in illiteracy. He decided to inform his audience about illiteracy and its effects on the community. How can Melvin ensure that his speech is ethical and effective?

1. Why must Melvin do a thorough audience analysis?

2. Melvin must do extensive research to find appropriate support material. Why can't he just rely on his grandfather's experiences?

3. Choosing an appropriate way to organize his ideas is essential to the overall success of Melvin's speech. Why?

4. What types of language should Melvin use: concrete or abstract? Why?

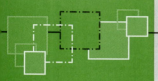

EMBRACING DIFFERENCE

The Informative Speech

In a group, brainstorm ideas for an informative speech. Choose one. Then, describe how each of the methods of presenting material can enhance your ability to inform your audience about this topic:

1. Narration
2. Description
3. Definition
4. Demonstration

1. How can this activity help you understand the diverse methods of presenting an informative speech?
2. How can your understanding of the different methods of presenting an informative speech help you understand the importance of embracing difference?

Serving Your COMMUNITY   Presenting Information

To understand the diverse methods of presenting an informative speech, complete the following:

1. Review the speech outline you were asked to develop on the importance of volunteerism in Chapters 13 and 14.
2. Use that outline to build an informative speech on volunteerism.
3. To enrich the development of the outline, please spend an additional two hours volunteering at the organization.
4. Choose two of the following methods of presenting an informative speech:
   a. Narrative.
   b. Definition.
   c. Demonstration.
   d. Description.
5. Compare and contrast how the different presentation methods can enhance your speech. Which one seems to work better? Why?
6. How did this process help you appreciate the different approaches to the informative speech?

the process. For example, Bill wants to explain the differences among various baseball pitches. To him the most logical and effective way to accomplish his goal is to demonstrate the different ways to grip the baseball for each type of pitch and to show the "follow through" motion for each pitch. His demonstration is accompanied by a verbal explanation.

SUMMARY

The purpose of an informative speech is to educate an audience. From the early stages of selecting a topic through the final stages of presenting that topic, the speaker must strive to make the information relevant to the audience. The speaker accomplishes this by engaging the audience's interest in the topic, by presenting ideas that can be easily digested, and by using appropriate language.

Informative speech topics generally fall into one of these categories: recreation, concepts, places, objects, or people. Whatever topic the speaker selects, it should be adapted to the audience in order to remain relevant. Determining what the audience wants to know is a major consideration for the speaker.

Once the topic is selected, work begins on developing the major and minor points. All this planning and outlining is done with one thing in mind: Every step of the way, give the audience information that will make a difference. The audience must come away from the speech having learned something worthwhile. Certain methods are especially effective in passing on new information. These include the narrative, education through a story or account; description, enlightenment through concrete, sharply focused language; definition, explanations of unfamiliar ideas by means of language that the audience already understands; and demonstration of a concept or process. All these parts add up to the speaker being a teacher, and the members of the audience being eager listeners.

REVIEW QUESTIONS

1. What is the primary concern when developing an informative speech objective?
2. List the six major categories for informative speech topics, and give an example of each.
3. When concluding an informative speech, what do you want to reinforce?
4. What are some resources you can use to create a narrative?
5. Why is it best to use concrete language when attempting to describe something in an informative speech?
6. Differentiate between the use of antonyms and the use of synonyms to define ideas in an informative speech.
7. When demonstrating something, why is it important to proceed slowly?

KEY CONCEPTS

persuasive speech
informative speech
narrative
description

concrete terms
abstract terms
definition
synonyms

antonyms
comparisons
etymology
demonstration

Sample Informative Student Speech

The Slow Food Movement

A famous journalist once said, "Pleasure is a way of being at one with yourself and others" (Pollan, 2003, p. 1). This journalist is referring to the importance of taking pleasure in something very simple: food! For those of you who don't know, this quotation was uttered by Carlo Petrini, the founder of what has become known today as the Slow Food Movement. As students, we eat fast food all the time because we are so busy. But your physical and mental health are important, and the Slow Food Movement can help us lead healthier lives. After researching the topic, I have come to appreciate the ideals concerning this slow-spreading phenomenon. Today, I am going to inform you about the Slow Food Movement; specifically, its origin, principles, and how it has evolved. To start off, I would like to discuss how the Slow Food Movement emerged.

The Slow Food Movement transpired 17 years ago when Italian journalist Carlo Petrini responded vehemently when a McDonald's was proposed to open on the steps of the Piazza di Spagna ("Best Food," 2008, par. 1; Hopkins, 2008; Pollan, 2003). He decided to use his ingenious public relations skills to encourage people to reject the "pervasiveness of fast, cheap, unhealthy, and processed foods" and opt for food that is fresh, prepared at home, and leisurely savored among friends and family ("Best Food," 2008, par. 6). Petrini became inspired by the ideal that "breaking bread" with friends and family is a "fundamental" part of our cultural "heritage" ("Best Food," 2008, par. 9–10). He remarks that taking time out of our days to enjoy delectable, home cooked meals while engaging in meaningful conversations is essential to our "health and psychological well being" ("Best Food," 2008, par. 10). The organization's mascot is a snail, which is signifies that pleasure is the primary principle of this "slow" movement; it is not intended to be political, nor should it be taken too seriously (Pollan, 2003; Hopkins, 2008). Members of Slow Food not only desire to reject the consumption of processed foods, but to improve the welfare of local food producers and raise awareness about endangered food plants and animals (Pollan, 2003). This brings me to my next point.

The first and most important principle of the Slow Food Movement is taking time to cook. According to Michael Pollan (2003) in his article "Cruising on the Ark of Taste," "pleasure is at the very heart" of the Slow Food Movement (p. 1). Imagine the kinds of food that are pleasing to your palate. Do you think of Grandma's homemade pot roast and mashed potatoes? Perhaps you're reminded of Mom's signature pasta dish or Dad's mouth-watering smoked turkey? While some people may be under the impression that the movement pertains solely to foods that are healthy and organic, the idea behind slow food is enjoying any kind of fresh food that is slowly prepared in your kitchen (Innes, 2008). One doesn't have to be partial to tofu and alfalfa sprouts to practice Slow Food ideals. The second principle pertains to eating meals with friends and family in a warm, welcoming environment ("Best Food," 2008). Rather than stopping at a fast-food restaurant to pick up a quick, greasy bite on your way home from work, set aside time to talk with family and friends over a tasty dish in order to keep old-fashioned traditions alive.

Importantly, the movement includes other principles aside from delighting in home cooked meals with friends and family. The third principle aims to help the economic hardships of local food industries (Pollan, 2003). One of the greatest criticisms the movement has suffered is its "elitist" implications ("Best Food," 2008, par. 10). Many argue that the principles are unrealistic in daily practice because organic foods and fresh produce are too expensive. However, consider the following data (show visual). In 1970, the percentage of a European family's annual income that went toward food and groceries was 32 percent ("Best Food," 2008, par. 11). To date, only 15 percent of a family's annual income goes toward food and groceries. According to Petrini (2007) in his book *Slow Food Nation*, organic foods and produce will be less costly if more people go to local farmers to purchase these foods. Slow Food uses the moniker "co-producer" to refer to consumers who help out the local food industries by buying healthy food at a reasonable price as opposed to the cheapest food on the shelves (Petrini, 2007).

The third principle directly correlates to the fourth, which seeks to assist small farmers and food producers. According to Jim Hopkins' (2008) article "'Slow Food' movement gathers momentum," rather than purchasing groceries from "industrial growers such as Tyson Foods or retail goliaths such as Wal-Mart," people need to shop at local venues (par. 3). As previously stated, if more people buy from local farm stands and grocers, organic and fresh food prices will decrease. Not only does the Slow Food Movement ameliorate the economy of local producers, it servers to increase awareness about endangered foods and how food is processed. According to Pollan (2003), "The Ark of Taste" includes a list of endangered food plants and animals. When certain foods are no longer available, it not only has biological effects on our ecosystem but threatens the "preservation" of certain practices that are embedded in different cultures, some of which are spiritual (Pollan, 2003, par. 6). Seemingly contradictory, the movement promotes the consumption of endangered foods so these do not become obsolete. In lieu of these five principles, the Slow Food movement adopts a "holistic approach" by joining producers and consumers as well as chefs, industries and academia ("Best Food," par. 14). Finally, I will explain how Slow Food has evolved since its origin.

Since the Slow Food Movement began, it has spread to 144 countries and is comprised of more than 86,000 members ("Best Food," 2008, par. 3–4; Hartz-Seeley, 2008). After Slow Food was founded in 1986 by Petrini, the movement spread to Paris, and three years later Slow Food International came to fruition (Innes, 2008). The Parisian philosophy of Slow Food pertains to enjoying "long lunches and good wine" and led to the creation of "conviviums," which are chapters of the movement including gourmet chefs and "high brow foodies" (Innes, 2008, par. 4).

Over time, the movement has developed chapters across the world, many of which embrace different ideals. Take the more liberal Tucson chapter, which emerged eight years after Slow Food came to light. They believe that Slow

The speaker uses a signpost.

Food isn't about being vegetarian or eating only organic foods; it is about eating foods that are fresh, clean, and not processed while paying a fair price to producers (Innes, 2008). The chapter's leaders organize "lectures, cooking demonstrations and meals at restaurants that support the slow-food movement" (Innes, 2008, par. 9).

What began as a trend in Italy spread to the United States, developed into five chapters by 1998, and evolved into approximately 160 chapters. According to Innes (2008), Slow Food is "one of the fastest-growing membership organizations in the United States" (par. 28). Recently, Slow Food USA coordinated an event in San Francisco aimed to raise awareness about "fair trade, sustainable farming practices and celebrating traditional foods" ("Slow Food Movement Picks Up," 2008). Slow Food USA is not only concerned about the obesity and diabetes epidemic in the U.S., but the detrimental effects that industrialized food corporations are having on the environment. According to Erika Lesser, Executive Director, these multinational corporations not only diminish natural resources, but are primarily responsible for the planet's pollution problems (Innes, 2008). Members of Slow Food USA adhere to Petrini's simple "mantra" of "Good, Clean, Fair" and believe that spending a little extra money on local foods will improve our health and the environment ("Best Food," 2008, par. 5; Pollan, 2003, p. 1; "Slow Food Movement Picks Up," 2008, par. 5). As Slow Food USA tends to take a more radical view of the movements, this organization creates a discourse for environmental and global issues ("Slow Food Movement Picks Up," 2008). One concern that has been raised concerns the carbon footprint that is created as processed foods are imported and sent from various manufacturing companies across the nation (Pollan, 2003). More eco-friendly members, such as "locavores," eat only fresh foods grown within a 100-mile radius of where they live (Hartz-Seeley, 2008). However, while taking such extreme measures to prevent pollution is certainly admirable, Carlo Petrini's vision centers upon pleasure in food, good conversation, and life, in general.

The speaker summarizes the main points.

In summation, I have informed you today about the origin, principles, and evolution of the Slow Food Movement. Aside from taking pleasure in homemade dishes, Slow Food explores "ethical and cultural" aspects of consumption in order to increase awareness of how food is processed, dining traditions, and the effect of large food corporations on small farmers and the environment (Hani, 2008, par. 7). I hope discussing this topic with you has helped raised your awareness of these important issues. Thank you for your time.

Lindsay Hingst
Purdue University Calumet
Spring 2009
Used by Permission

References

Best food. (2008, August 30). *Irish Times*. Retrieved from http://search.ebscohost.com/login.aspx?direct=true&db=nfh&AN=9FY1274925063&site=ehost-live

Hani, Yoko. (2008, February 29). Slow-food movement creeps to Japan. *Japan Times*. Retrieved, from http://search.ebscohost.com/login.aspx?direct=true&db=nfh& AN=2W62W6837927293&site=ehost-live

Hartz-Seeley, Deborah S. (2008, July 10). What prehistoric man ate: Forage through history and learn that the popular notion of eating local foods began when giant beasts roamed South Florida. *Sun-Sentinel*. Retrieved from http://search .ebscohost.com/login.aspx?direct=true&db=nfh&AN=2W62W62522120620&site = ehost-live

Hopkins, Jim. (2003, November 25). 'Slow Food Movement' gathers momentum. *USA Today*. Retrieved from http://www.usatoday.com/money/industries/food/ 2003-11-25-slowfood_x.htm?POE=click-refer

Innes, Stephanie. (2008, January 9) Slow food growing fast: International movement even has Tucson branch. *Arizona Daily Star*. Retrieved from http://search .ebscohost.com/login.aspx?direct=true&db=nfh&AN=2W62W6211706227& site=ehost-live

Petrini, Carlo. (2007). *Slow Food Nation: Why Our Food Should Be Good, Clean, and Fair*. Random House, Inc.

Pollan, Michael. (2003, May 01). Cruising on the ark of taste. *Mother Jones*. Retrieved from http://www.motherjones.com/news/feature/2003/05/ma_372_01.html

Schlosser, Eric. (2002). What's in the meat. In *Fast Food Nation* (pp. 194–222). New York: Houghton Mifflin Company.

Slow food movement picks up momentum in the USA. (2008, September 02). *Environmental New Network*. Organic Consumers' Corporation. 2008. Retrieved from http://www.enn.com/agriculture/article/38069

Spurlock, Morgan. (Morgan Spurlock). (2004). *Supersize me* [Motion picture]. Kathbur Pictures Incorporated.

Stapleton, John. (2008, August 04). Slow food movement provides shot in the arm for struggling farmers. *The Australian*. Retrieved from http://search.ebscohost.com/ login.aspx?direct=true&db=nfh&AN=200808041031272315&site=ehost-live/

CHAPTER
16

The Persuasive Speech

AFTER STUDYING THIS CHAPTER, YOU SHOULD

understand

- the definition of persuasion.
- the importance of making ethical statements.

be able to

- write a clear persuasive speech objective.
- organize an effective persuasive speech.
- increase your credibility.
- develop logical and emotional appeals in your speech.

Melvin's informative speech on illiteracy was very effective (see Chapter 15). Afterward, several students asked Melvin for more information on how they could help. He was more than happy to provide them with the information because after the process of researching and writing his speech, Melvin had become motivated to volunteer at the local high school literacy program. The program is in dire need of more people to help teach adults in the community to read.

Melvin's next speech assignment is to persuade his audience to take an action. He decides that he can use some of the same information from his first speech to persuade his audience to volunteer, as he does, at the local literacy program. Instead of focusing on describing the problem of illiteracy, Melvin will motivate his fellow students to help others.

He hopes to gain their attention by telling the story of his grandfather. He then will describe the extent of the problem of illiteracy in their community and the need for volunteers at the literacy program. Next, Melvin will explain to his audience how they can volunteer and that it will take only a few hours a week. Lastly, he will describe how great they will feel, as he does, by helping others in their community. He will strongly urge his audience to take this action by signing a pledge to volunteer three hours of time.

■ ■ ■ ■ ■

In this chapter, we will discuss the process of persuasion. Specifically, we will describe how to organize and present a persuasive speech that will motivate your audience to take action or change a belief, attitude, or value.

Although many of us may never seek election to a political office, we all participate in the persuasive process. We may try to persuade our employer that we deserve a raise; or we try to persuade our children that we know what is best for them by turning off the television; or convince our spouse that an expensive sofa would be perfect in the living room. In addition, we also encounter persuasive appeals on a daily basis; we read newspaper articles, watch television commercials, surf the Internet, and listen to the appeals of salespeople and candidates running for office.

Persuasion is the act of convincing an audience, through verbal and nonverbal communication, to adopt or change an attitude, belief, or value or to take an action. For example, a minister may try to persuade her congregants that they should annually contribute a certain percentage of their income to the church; a salesperson may try to persuade a customer that the red Ford Escape hybrid is the perfect vehicle for her; or a sports celebrity may try to persuade junior high school students to stay in school. In each of these cases, the speaker hopes that audience members will experience a change in their thinking as a result of his or her message and ultimately will take an action they may not normally have taken. Persuasion is often a complex process because the speaker must appeal to a group of unique individuals who each possesses a special frame of reference. As we discussed in all the previous chapters, it is essential that you, as the speaker, know and understand the diversity of your audience. Each audience member will bring his or her unique approach to the persuasive interaction. Ignoring your audience's diverse approaches will doom your presentation to failure. Thorough audience analysis is essential to persuading your audience.

DEVELOPING A PERSUASIVE SPEECH OBJECTIVE

When developing a persuasive speech, it is essential that you define your goal. What do you want the audience to do after listening to your speech? For example, do you want them to change their attitudes about allowing a tax credit to families whose children attend private schools, or do you want them to sign a petition to recall the mayor? In a persuasive speech, the speaker either calls for the audience to modify their beliefs or asks them to act on behalf of an issue or belief. As indicated in Chapter 11, developing a clear speech objective is essential in carrying out this process.

When calling on an audience to change a belief, use evidence to argue for or against a position. You are attempting to convince the members of your audience to alter their beliefs or behavior on a specific issue. To do this, you should use persuasive appeals (discussed later) to convince the audience of the value, morality, or advantage of your position.

Sometimes persuading your audience to alter an attitude is a question of degree. For example, if you wish to bring about a dramatic change in the audience's opinion, you might try to create a conflict for audience members to contemplate. After presenting your arguments, you hope the audience members will change their opinions. On the other hand, perhaps an audience is already sympathetic to a particular issue or policy; if so, you might try to reinforce or strengthen the audience's already positive feelings about the topic. For example:

> Skye, an African American student, has very strong feelings about the policy of racial profiling. She and several of her friends have been stopped by police because they "fit the description" of suspected criminals in her community. She wants this police practice stopped in her city. Her church is holding a rally against racial profiling next week and she has been asked to speak. Skye knows that her audience is already in favor of the proposal, so she wants to reinforce the audience's strong feelings against racial profiling. To make her points strong and clear, Skye will recount her encounters with local police and how she was a victim of racial profiling.

A second type of persuasive speech objective attempts to move the audience to immediate action. The speaker calls on audience members to adopt a specific behavior or to discontinue their present actions. For instance, you might call on audience members to fulfill their civic responsibility and vote in the next election. In this case, you are calling on the audience to act. Ted's speech is one example:

> Ted has returned to the local university to complete his degree in mechanical engineering. Ted has multiple sclerosis, a degenerative nerve disease, which forced him to leave his job as a construction worker. After a few weeks on campus, Ted has found it increasingly difficult to walk from one building to the next in the 10 minutes allotted. He is always late for his next class. As a member of student government, Ted proposed to his fellow senators that there should be more passing time between classes in order to make it easier for students with disabilities to get to their classes. His speech at the student government meeting urged his audience to take action by passing a resolution to increase the passing time and to begin discussions with the university's administrators.

TOPICS FOR A PERSUASIVE SPEECH

How do you decide what would make a good topic for a persuasive speech? The first thing you need to think about is your speech objective, which, as indicated earlier, grows out of what you are trying to accomplish with the audience. Obviously, some topics lend themselves to a persuasive speech better than others. Topics that are controversial or current are more appropriate for persuasive speeches than topics that are dated and no longer socially relevant. When choosing a topic, it is important to consider the things we discussed in Chapter 11: yourself, your audience, and the situation. Choose a topic that is important to you, relevant to the audience, and appropriate for the situation. Table 16.1 shows some examples of persuasive speech topics.

ORGANIZING YOUR PERSUASIVE SPEECH

In many ways, the organization of a persuasive speech follows the structure of an informative speech (see Chapter 13). First, you must engage the audience's attention; next, you attempt to appeal to a specific need or interest. The difference between

TABLE 16.1   Persuasive Speech Topics

Change a Belief/Value/Attitude	*Motivate to Act*
Everyone should protect themselves from AIDS.	Use a condom.
Global warming is destroying the environment.	Use alternative energy sources.
Being overweight can kill you.	Exercise regularly.
Americans don't participate in the democratic process.	Vote in the next election.

SKILL BUILDING

Developing Persuasive Speech Topics

In a group, brainstorm topics for your persuasive speech.

1. Which of the topics attempts to change an attitude, value, or belief?
2. Which of the topics attempts to motivate the audience to act?
3. Pick one topic and discuss how you might relate the topic to your audience.

persuasive and informative speeches, however, must be addressed at this point in the preparation process. As a speaker, you must decide whether you wish to educate your audience (the goal of an informative speech) or to do more, that is, change an attitude, belief, or value, or motivate them to action (the goal of a persuasive speech). If you choose the latter, the development of your speech body takes a slightly different focus. You must set out to "prove your case," or offer a solution to a problem. This section examines four organizational plans for doing just that: problem/solution, topical, comparative advantage, and Monroe's motivated sequence.

■ Problem/Solution

One way to organize your ideas is by using a **problem/solution** organizational pattern. The body of your speech first describes a problem that exists and then offers solutions to the problem. Many times, the solution you offer is the proposal you want the audience to believe or act on. For example, you could discuss the problems with parking at your school and then offer solutions such as a parking garage or more parking lots. This organizational pattern helps the audience to see clearly the connections between the existing situation (problem) and the future possibilities (solution). For her presentation before the hospital board, Tami, the head nurse in pediatrics, used a problem/solution plan:

> Tami needed to show the hospital administrators that more registered nurses are needed on each shift to properly care for the children. During the first part of her presentation, Tami discussed the large patient/nurse ratio, the long amount of time children had to wait for their medication, and the number of times each child needed to have his or her vitals taken (temperature, blood pressure, and pulse) during an eight-hour shift. She then discussed how having just one more nurse on each shift would solve these problems and would thus provide better care for the children in the pediatrics ward.

■ Topical Sequence

An important part of successful persuasion is providing good reasons for the belief you want the audience to hold or the action you want them to take. In the body of your speech, you can provide a detailed description of each of the reasons the audience should adopt your proposal. Using strong evidence and support, each of the reasons leads the audience to the conclusion you want them to reach. It is best to either put your strongest idea first or put your strongest ideas last. Either way, the audience will more likely hear your reason clearly. Never put your strongest reason in the middle of your speech. It will likely not be heard or will be forgotten by the audience. Let's see how Tami could have used a **topical sequence** instead of a problem/solution plan.

> Tami could begin the body of her presentation by discussing the reasons why another registered nurse is needed on each shift. Her strongest reason is an increase in the quality of patient care. With one more nurse, each patient could receive personalized attention from a nurse, thus ensuring that all doctors' orders are followed and the patient is comfortable. Another reason is that nurses could share the responsibility of answering and returning the calls from concerned parents, which is important in a pediatrics ward. Parents need to be more informed about their child's health and in a timely manner. Lastly, Tami could discuss the cost savings of having an additional nurse on each shift. Now, many nurses stay after their shift is over to care for especially sick children. When a nurse remains, she is paid time and a half for her overtime. An additional nurse would only have to be paid the normal rate per hour. Each of these ideas is a reason for adding an additional nurse to each shift.

■ Comparative Advantage

Often, the audience already understands the problem but is looking for the best solution. In this case, you might want to use a **comparative advantage plan.** This plan allows you to compare your solution to others and to show how your plan or proposal is superior. The body of your presentation, then, consists of descriptions of your proposal and that of others. Each of the main ideas emphasizes how your proposal is the best and emphasizes the weaknesses of the others. In Tami's presentation, she could discuss the merits of her proposal, adding one additional registered nurse to each shift, while discussing why instituting longer shifts or adding nonnursing personnel would not increase patient care.

■ Motivated Sequence

The **motivated sequence** design, advanced by Alan H. Monroe, focuses on creating a sense of need and then explaining how that need can be satisfied. If this sounds familiar to you, there is a good reason—the basic organizational pattern is that of problem/solution. There are five steps in this plan: (1) arousing attention, (2) showing a need, (3) satisfying the need, (4) visualizing the results, and (5) calling for action (see Table 16.2).

The first step in Monroe's motivated sequence—arousing the audience's interest in your subject—is basic to all types of public speeches, whether they are informative, entertaining, or persuasive. You cannot expect an audience to listen attentively

TABLE 16.2	Monroe's Motivated Sequence
1. Arousing attention	We attempt to capture the audience's attention with our opening remarks.
2. Showing a need	We determine the need or problem our topic suggests.
3. Satisfying the need	We argue how our proposal will meet the need or resolve the problem described earlier.
4. Visualizing the results	We create a visual image that projects what will happen if our proposal is embraced or rejected.
5. Calling for action	We urge the audience to demonstrate its support.

if you have not captured its attention. The techniques for drawing the audience's attention discussed in Chapter 13—using a narrative, a startling statement, a rhetorical question, or a quotation—apply to the persuasive speech. For instance, this opening statement is aimed at capturing the audience's interest. "According to the National Alliance to End Homelessness, over the course of a year, between 2.5 and 3.5 million people will live either on the streets or in an emergency shelter. In addition, about 600,000 families and 1.35 million children experience homelessness each year" (2007).

Step two, demonstrating a need, requires that you look closely at your topic in order to determine the need or problem that your topic suggests. For example, with the topic "homeless Americans," you might appeal to the audience's need for safety or shelter (refer to the discussion of Maslow's hierarchy of needs in Chapter 11) or establish the nature of the problem and its relevance to the audience. For example: "Our country is faced with a perplexing problem. A nation that takes pride in its high standard of living and considerable wealth must confront the mounting evidence that increasing numbers live without a roof over their heads and that the ranks of those who live in poverty are also on the rise."

In step three you begin to argue your case, to show how your proposal will either meet the need or solve the problem described earlier. This is the body of your speech, the place where you develop a well-reasoned logical appeal, a solid emotional appeal, or a combination of the two (discussed later in this chapter). You might propose, for instance, that "additional low-cost shelters must be made available for this growing segment of our population. In fact, this is in contrast to what is actually happening in our large cities, where low-cost housing is disappearing."

The purpose of the next step—visualizing the results—is to create a visual image that projects what will happen if your proposal is embraced or what will happen if it is rejected. It is also possible to show your audience both sides of the picture. In fact, by presenting the negative aspects first, followed by the positive, you can build a strong case for having your audience support the action you have proposed. In this part of your presentation, you want to increase your audience's identification with the problem. One of the most effective ways to do this is by describing the projected outcome in vivid language; the better your description, the better is the audience's conceptualization of the situation. If you choose to present a scenario that depicts the dangers the future holds should your proposal for increased low-cost housing be rejected, you might include this warning:

> Thousands of middle-class Americans are inching closer to joining the ranks of poor America. I've described what happens when unemployment becomes a way of life, when homes are repossessed by banks, when dejected individuals give up all hope and "check out" of life as they've known it. Expect to see more of these people on the streets in the future. They won't be able to afford a place to live if low-cost housing is replaced by parking lots, high-rise office buildings, and high-rent housing meant to lure prosperous people back to our cities. It's not only their sad plight—it's all of ours.

If the intent of your speech is to alter the audience's attitude, you can end on this note. If, however, you want your audience to actually demonstrate its support for your proposal, you would go one step further.

The call for action is the final step of the motivated sequence. In it you want to capitalize on the support you have attempted to win during the visualization step. For example, you might ask everyone to write their U.S. senators and representatives to urge them to vote for additional funds for housing for the poor and homeless or to volunteer at the local homeless shelter or to help build homes for Habitat for Humanity.

DEVELOPING PERSUASIVE APPEALS

Throughout your presentation, it is essential that you use several persuasive appeals. There are three types of appeals: credibility, logical, and emotional. Presentation of an effective persuasive speech rests on your ability to establish or enhance your credibility, as a speaker, as well as on your ability to develop sound logical or emotional appeals. Consider this point: If a speaker is not perceived by the audience to be a credible source, then even a well-constructed appeal will have little impact. Conversely, a well-reasoned argument can increase a speaker's credibility. The importance of each of these factors is discussed in the following section.

■ Speaker Credibility Appeals

A variable that plays a significant role in the persuasion process is the **credibility** of the speaker: Does the audience perceive the speaker as someone who is qualified to speak on a particular topic? For example, your experience as a swimming instructor would likely make you qualified to speak on the subject of water safety, yet it is unlikely that the same audience would perceive you as someone qualified to speak about the benefits of tax-deferred annuities. To a large degree, perception is a strong determinant in establishing your credibility as a speaker.

TABLE 16.3	Speaker Credibility
Competence	A demonstrated ability, quality, or special knowledge
Dynamism	Degree of excitement, energy, involvement in topic
Trustworthiness and ethics	Character and integrity perceived by the audience

Some audiences may see you as more qualified than other audiences. For example, an audience of persons who possess little information about a subject may see you as a credible speaker, whereas an audience of people whose background or experience is extensive may see you as less qualified. In addition to audience reaction, several other variables contribute to a speaker's credibility, including competence, dynamism, trustworthiness, and ethics (see Table 16.3).

Competence

Competence is a demonstrated ability or quality. In persuasion, competence is often a measure of a speaker's knowledge concerning a topic. Speakers may possess a special ability that qualifies them as experts. For example:

> Annie is a sixth-grade teacher and the girls' basketball coach. She has played basketball since she was five years old and even received a full athletic college scholarship. During Women's History Month, Annie was asked by a Girl Scout troop to discuss her experience as a student athlete at the high school and college levels and how athletics helped her become a better student. The goal of the presentation is to entice the young girls to play organized sports. Because of Annie's past experiences and her natural athletic ability, the Girl Scouts found her to be a credible speaker.

Classroom speakers, too, can achieve a degree of expertness because of the knowledge gained from personal experience.

> Luanne is very committed to MADD (Mothers Against Drunk Driving). She became involved in the organization six years ago when her son was killed by a drunk driver. That experience changed her life dramatically, but it gave her a special competence in mobilizing others to support the work of MADD. For her communication class, Luanne naturally wanted to address drunk driving, but more importantly, to persuade her classmates to join her as a volunteer for MADD. When she addressed her class about her experiences as a mother and volunteer, her fellow students listened attentively.

One of the best ways to demonstrate your knowledge or competence is to incorporate evidence in your speech. The use of supporting material can add substance to your ideas. For example, reference to a study by a leading cardiologist as reported in the *Journal of the American Medical Association* would add credibility to your speech's goal: "To persuade your audience that a high-fat diet can lead to heart disease." A thorough discussion of supporting materials can be found in Chapter 12. Being able to demonstrate your credibility increases the likelihood that your audience will listen to your presentation and support the position you are promoting.

Dynamism

Another dimension of credibility is dynamism. **Dynamism** is the degree of excitement that you bring to your presentation, often accomplished by demonstrating concern for and involvement in your topic. The dynamic speaker communicates that he or she is excited about the presentation, which in turn can elicit excitement on the part of the audience.

There are different levels of energy that can be demonstrated during a presentation. It is not necessary to scream and shout to show that you are a dynamic speaker; you can demonstrate involvement by being forceful, energetic, or sensitive—whatever is appropriate for your selected topic. How do you exhibit these qualities? By incorporating facial expressions, gestures, movement, and variety of vocal inflection into your speech. These behaviors were discussed in detail in Chapter 14.

Trustworthiness/Ethics

Trustworthiness refers to the kind of "character" you communicate to your audience. In other words, are you an ethical person? **Ethics,** the rules that govern moral behavior, must be considered as you develop your persuasive speech. The integrity

Competence is an essential part of speaker credibility.

you bring to your message affects both the way you interact with your audience and the way the audience assesses your credibility. People want to put their faith in someone of high moral character, someone who they believe is honest and reliable. Political leaders, for example, attempt to use their character or trustworthiness as a way to gain your support. Many times they may even support their "trustworthiness" with examples of past promises kept or by discussing their background. Or, candidates for office may have others speak to their character or trustworthiness.

For example, during the Republican National Convention, Democratic Senator Joseph Lieberman said:

> The sad truth is, today we are living through his [George Washington's] worst nightmare in the capital city that bears his name. And that brings me directly to why I'm here tonight. What, after all, is a Democrat like me doing at a Republican convention like this? Well, I'll tell you what. I'm here to support John McCain because country matters more than party. I am here tonight for a simple reason. John McCain is the best choice to bring our country together and lead America forward. And dear friends, I am here tonight because John McCain's whole life testifies to a great truth. Being a Democrat or a Republican is important, but it is nowhere near as important as being an American. (2008)

Many speakers have others describe their character and trustworthiness, as Joseph Lieberman (here) did for John McCain in the 2008 presidential campaign.

John McCain has established his character and trustworthiness without mentioning his own accomplishments because Joseph Lieberman has done it for him.

How do you convey your trustworthiness to an audience? If you are already familiar to an audience, your past behavior may speak for itself. However, how do you establish trust with an audience who has never heard or seen you before? You might try revealing a bit of your background as a way of introducing yourself. Often, mentioning how you are directly involved in your speech topic leads your audience to perceive you as sincere or committed, that is, trustworthy. A perception of the audience that you lack ethics or are not trustworthy can greatly diminish your credibility and decrease the believability of your propositions.

TECHNIQUES FOR ENHANCING YOUR CREDIBILITY

While the ability to persuade an audience depends on a speaker's competence, dynamism, and trustworthiness, you can employ specific techniques to enhance your credibility as a speaker.

■ Establish Common Ground with the Audience

One way to enhance your credibility is to establish **common ground** with the audience. Tell the audience how you are like them in some way. For example, you might try to share information about yourself that reflects a value system similar to the audience's. Another way to establish common ground is to include supporting material that your audience can identify with, preferably early in the speech. Consider the following:

> Pauline, a dietician, was invited to speak at a gathering of Weight
> Watchers, a group designed to help individuals to lose weight and eat

ETHICS in Communication

The Persuasive Speech

In the beginning of the chapter, we learned about Melvin and his attempt to persuade his classmates to volunteer their time to teach adults to read in their community. Melvin has done extensive audience analysis and understands the diversity of his audience. This will greatly improve his chances of persuading his audience because he can tailor his use of appeals to them. Melvin needs to also consider the ethical dimensions of the persuasive speech if he wants to be effective.

1. Explain why being honest with the audience is essential to Melvin and any persuasive speaker.

2. Using supporting material is essential. How can Melvin use research in an ethical and effective manner?

3. Some persuasive speakers are tempted to use name calling and other argument fallacies. Why is it important for Melvin to not include these in his persuasive speech?

4. We know that audiences believe speakers who they perceive as credible. How can Melvin establish his credibility?

healthier. At the beginning of her speech she related a story about herself and made reference to the fact she had once weighed 250 pounds and took the initiative to change her lifestyle by eating healthy and exercising regularly. After hearing this story, her audience was "with" her. Her effort to motivate the audience to begin an exercise program was successful, in part because of the shared experience she had with the audience.

■ Indicate Your Special Knowledge

Another technique that increases your credibility is to indicate that you have special credentials or knowledge that makes you uniquely qualified to speak on a topic. Without appearing to brag, tell the audience about your background and its special relationship to your topic. For example:

> The Parks and Recreation Department called a special meeting to respond to the community's outcry over the cancellation of a popular summer music camp for elementary school children. In an effort to justify the cancellation, the Parks and Recreation board members prefaced their remarks to the assembled parents by stating their qualifications as experts in recreation and child development. Dave, a concerned parent, was angered by what he considered to be their inept handling of the issue. He offered his own credentials, a Ph.D. in Music Education, and then spoke about the dire need for affordable musical instruction and experiences for children in the community and the effect the cancellation will have on the children already involved in the program. The effectiveness of his insightful remarks was reinforced by the positive response he received from the audience.

The person who introduces you to an audience can help reinforce your expertise. For example, the emcee at an American Association of Retired Persons luncheon introduced the keynote speaker in the following way:

> It is my sincere pleasure to introduce Dr. Clarice Fernandez to you. She is a clinical psychologist with an extensive background in the area of human sexuality. She is the author of two books, one which deals with sex after 60. Please join me in welcoming Dr. Fernandez, who will speak to you on improving intimate relationships in your senior years.

In this example, the introduction served to enhance the credibility of Dr. Fernandez. By highlighting her achievements, the emcee showed how Dr. Fernandez was uniquely qualified to speak on her topic. Clearly, it is essential to establish your credibility by discussing your qualifications to speak on the topics or to have someone else inform the audience of your qualifications.

■ Logical Appeals

The heart of a persuasive speech lies in the argument that the speaker constructs. There are a few ways to approach this argument; choosing the best one depends on such factors as (1) your speech objective, (2) the topic that you have selected,

COMMUNICATION IN ACTION

Identifying Credibility

1. Name a public speaker or speakers who possess each of the dimensions of credibility discussed above:
   a. Competence
   b. Dynamism
   c. Trustworthiness/ethics
2. Why does the speaker possess these dimensions of credibility, in your opinion?
3. What can you do to increase your own credibility based on the behavior of speaker(s)?
4. How can identifying ways to increase your credibility strengthen your confidence as a communicator?

(3) the audience to be addressed, and (4) how successfully you have established your credibility. Your assessment of these factors will help you to determine how you wish to build a logical argument.

A **logical argument** helps your audience understand your ideas, thereby increasing the likelihood that members will be persuaded by what you say. An argument means giving one or more "good" reasons for your plan or proposal. Two ways to develop logical appeals are through deductive reasoning and inductive reasoning.

Deductive reasoning follows a simple formula: It starts with a general premise, is followed by a minor premise, and ends by drawing a conclusion. In a persuasive speech, deductive reasoning can provide a clear development of your ideas and at the same time can assist the audience in following your thoughts. With deductive reasoning it is imperative that your premise, the proposition that serves as the basis for your argument, warrant the conclusion you are advocating. In the following example, your audience would probably accept the claims you are making because they are based on fact:

> *General premise:* One cause of skin cancer is exposure to the sun's ultraviolet rays.
> *Minor premise:* Those who sunbathe regularly expose themselves to ultraviolet rays.
> *Conclusion:* As a group, sunbathers are at a higher than normal risk for getting skin cancer.

Before constructing a persuasive speech using the deductive reasoning just provided, you should establish the relationship between your argument and your speech objective. In this case your speech objective might be "to persuade the classroom audience that sunbathing poses a risk to everyone's health." Beginning with your general premise, ask yourself whether or not the audience is likely to

Communication and TECHNOLOGY in Today's Society
Persuasion on the Internet

According to the *Pew Internet and American Life Project* (Raine, 2009), 74 percent of American adults use the Internet; 89 percent of those regularly use a search engine to find information. The Internet is an easy and fast way to find information about an almost unlimited array of subjects; daily online activities include searching for maps/directions, checking the weather, getting news/sports updates, looking for travel information, and doing research for school. Using any number of search engines, we can locate hundreds of sites for just about any topic. According to Browne, Freeman, and Williamson, "Information found on the Internet varies in its purpose: Web sites advocate causes, advertise products, entertain visitors and express opinions in addition to presenting scholarly research" (2001). Thus, most of the "stuff" on the Web is persuasion.

It is necessary for us to carefully evaluate any information found on the Web. Before using any information as support in our speeches, we must determine whether it is academic or scholarly research or propaganda or commercially driven information. Unfortunately, most of us are not as critical of website credibility as we should be, according to the Stanford Persuasive Technology Lab in its study titled, *How Do People Evaluate a Web Site's Credibility?* (Fogg, Sochoo, & Danielson, 2002) In fact, "nearly half of all consumers in the study assessed the credibility of sites based in part on the appeal of the overall visual design of a site, including layout, typography, font size and color schemes" (2002). In other words, consumers paid more attention to the color and design of a website than the identity of the author and his or her expertise.

Apparently, we can easily be fooled into thinking that a website offers credible information or advice. For example, when we do a search for "holocaust," hundreds of sites will appear. Among the legitimate scholarly sites, we will also find sites that appear scholarly, but use unsubstantiated and false information. One such site is sponsored by the Institute for Historical Review, which claims to be "an educational, public interest research and publishing center. It is non-partisan, non-ideological, and non-sectarian. . . . It is a vigorous defender of freedom of speech and freedom of historical inquiry." This sounds pretty legitimate, doesn't it? A closer examination shows that this site is dedicated to historical revisionism and tries to persuade viewers, using nonsense pseudoscience, that that the holocaust did not take place. Other examples of bogus sites that look legitimate include a site dedicated to Martin Luther King sponsored by a white supremacist group; SunSat Satellite Solutions Co., which looks exactly like a GPS mobile telephone tracking website, but actually features deceptive practices; and the National Motor Vehicle License Organization, which "offers a free searchable database of over 121 million United States driver's license photos," but is a hoax and scam.

Remember that written material is usually reviewed by others and is edited before publication. Anyone can put anything on a website. Thus, it is even more important that speakers check and double-check the information on the Internet. In Chapter 12, we discussed how to evaluate a website. Review those four questions (Who is the source? How old is the information? Is the information verifiable elsewhere? Is an email or other contact information provided?), and ask them of any website you find while researching and preparing your speech. The author(s) of the website may just be selling you something, or worse yet, advocating racist, sexist, or homophobic ideals while looking quite legitimate.

accept your statement without questioning its truthfulness. If you are in doubt, offer supporting evidence.

As a speaker, you need to realize the importance of building your arguments on a sound foundation. Lack of a sound premise spells disaster for the persuasive speech. Consider the following:

General premise: All college students watch MTV.

Minor premise: Catherine is a college student.

Conclusion: Catherine watches MTV.

The general premise in this example is faulty. Not all college students watch MTV. As a matter of fact, the average age of college students is steadily rising and the average age of the MTV viewer is between 12 and 18. Consequently, the incorrect premise means the conclusion is faulty.

Another type of reasoning you can use when developing a persuasive speech is **inductive reasoning**, in which one moves from specific instances to generalizations. For example, according to the U.S. Department of Justice,

Murder rates declined again in 2008.

Robbery rates declined again in 2008.

Assault rates declined again in 2008.

Speakers who use inductive reasoning need to be sure about the soundness of their ideas before making a generalization. Thus, we can argue that there are fewer

Logical appeals are enhanced by strong supporting material.

crimes committed and our society is safer than before. Faulty logic can trip you up if you are not careful, as in the following example:

> Susan had mechanical problems with her Pontiac after 25,000 miles.
>
> George had his Ford in for repairs at 23,000 miles.
>
> Valerie's Toyota has not required repairs. It now has 45,000 miles.
>
> *Conclusion:* Toyotas are superior cars.

In this example, the audience should be suspicious because the generalization is unwarranted. A larger and more representative sample is necessary to convince the careful listener of the validity of the generalization.

Supporting material in the form of statistics, research findings, or authoritative opinion can bring an added dimension to the logical appeal and can strengthen your argument, whether you have chosen to use deductive or inductive reasoning. For example, in the speech on crime, the citing of statistics (the number of reported cases of murder and assault for each of the last five years) or research findings would lend strength and credibility to the argument.

■ Fallacies

Fallacies are flawed arguments. The above example about cars clearly shows an overgeneralization, which is one type of argument fallacy. Such flaws as arguments ad hominem, assumptions of cause and effect, nonsequiturs, overgeneralizations, and faulty analogies can weaken persuasive speeches.

No doubt you have heard speakers attack the character of another person. This is called the fallacy of argument **ad hominem.** Sarah Palin, former Republican Vice Presidential nominee, used this type of argument against then-presidential candidate Barack Obama. She said, "We see America as the greatest force for good in this world. Our opponent though, is someone who sees America, it seems, as being so imperfect that he's palling around with terrorists who would target their own country" (2008). This ad hominem argument presented a negative image of Obama and portrayed him as being weak on national security. Instead of constructing well-reasoned arguments that protested Obama's proposed policies, Palin resorted to name-calling.

A second kind of argument fallacy is the **faulty cause-and-effect argument.** For example, the speaker who blames children's poor test scores on the teachers' strike earlier in the school year invites a challenge to his or her argument. There is no proof offered to show that one event caused the other to happen.

In a **nonsequitur,** the minor points are not related to the major points, or the conclusion does not logically follow the points that precede it. Look at this persuasive argument:

> We need to reverse the trend of teen gun violence in the United States.
>
> Television programs depict too much violence.
>
> Less violent television programs will help reduce the number of violent crimes annually.

"Your Honor, we're going to go with the prosecution's spin."

The conclusion drawn by this speaker does not logically follow the earlier points.

Overgeneralizations add a dramatic effect to your speech but are not logical. Be sure that your argument does not draw conclusions from a small sample or from just a few examples. Finally, a **faulty analogy** can hinder your persuasive efforts. In Chapter 12 *analogy* was defined as a form of support that compares the similar features in two seemingly different objects or situations. This definition implies that the comparison must be a valid one; when it is not, the analogy is flawed. The perceptive listener will be able to detect a faulty analogy, as in the following:

> Stephanie wants to persuade her history professor to use open book and open note exams. She doesn't think it's fair that she and her classmates should have to memorize all the facts and concepts learned in their history course. She says, "Doctors are allowed to look up difficult diagnoses in their medical textbooks, lawyers are allowed to look up case histories, so students should be able to look up tough test questions in their texts and notes."

■ Emotional Appeals

Emotional appeals are used to trigger the emotions or feelings of an audience: anger, fear, and pride. For instance, photographs of starving children in Third World countries can effectively stir our emotions. However, emotion should not be a substitute for reasoning; rather, the emotional appeal can serve as a supporter of a well-reasoned argument.

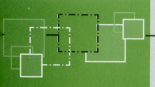

EMBRACING DIFFERENCE

The Persuasive Speech

Please read the speech at the end of the chapter. Identify examples for each of the following three types of persuasive appeals used by the speaker:

1. Logical appeals
2. Emotional appeals
3. Use of credibility

1. How can this activity help you understand the process of persuasion? How does it assist you in your attempt to persuade an audience?

2. How can your understanding of the different types of persuasive appeals help you understand the importance of embracing difference?

In constructing an emotional appeal, you can attempt to stir a wide variety of feelings. To a great extent your topic will dictate the type of emotional response you want your audience to exhibit. Do you want to anger them so they will be moved to take action? Do you want to appeal to their sense of pride or compassion? Or do you want to trigger their fears? Whatever your decision, there are specific ways to achieve the desired response.

One technique is to use emotionally charged language. This also serves as an indicator of your own involvement in the topic. The following examples help illustrate how language can play a significant role in generating an emotional appeal. This introductory statement is void of emotional language: "Statistics point to an alarming trend in this country. The rise in teenage suicides needs to be stopped." Now consider the treatment of the same topic using more powerful language:

> Your first reaction is to cry when you learn how this deadly disease is sweeping our society. It is like a cancer, spreading at a rapid pace, touching people from all walks of life. This cancer touches individuals in our rat-infested ghettos, as well as those in upper middle-class suburban ghettos. I am speaking about the epidemic of teenage suicides; the thousands of time bombs ticking away in today's adolescents.

In the second example note how much more of an impact the speaker's message would have on the audience. The language used by this speaker dramatically builds the case.

Another way to use the emotional appeal is to personalize your speech by telling a story. New York Governor Mario Cuomo shared part of his background

Serving Your COMMUNITY — Persuading Others

In Chapter 15 you were asked to develop an informative speech on volunteerism. Use your informative speech to build a persuasive speech that would motivate your fellow students to volunteer as you have done. In order to do this, engage in the following:

1. To enrich the development of the outline, please spend an additional two hours volunteering at the organization.

2. In order to build a persuasive speech, use Monroe's motivated sequence as your organizational pattern.

3. Present the speech to your classmates or to one of the many student organizations on campus. Ask for feedback from the audience. Were you persuasive? Why or why not?

4. How did this process help you appreciate the importance of connecting with your audience in a persuasive appeal?

in his Keynote Address at the 1984 Democratic National Convention. His words are intended to stir our national pride:

> That struggle to live with dignity is the real story of the shining city. It's a story I didn't read in a book, or learn in a classroom. I saw it, and lived it. Like many of you.
>
> I watched a small man with thick calluses on both hands work fifteen and sixteen hours a day. I saw him once literally bleed from the bottoms of his feet, a man who came here uneducated, alone, unable to speak the language, who taught me all I needed to know about faith and hard work by the simple eloquence of his example. I learned about our kind of democracy from my father; I learned about our obligation to each other from him and from my mother. They asked only for a chance to work and to make the world better for their children and to be protected in those moments when they would not be able to protect themselves. This nation and its government did that for them.
>
> And that they were able to build a family and live in dignity and see one of their children go from behind their little grocery store on the other side of the tracks in south Jamaica where he was born, to occupy the highest seat in the greatest state of the greatest nation in the only world we know, is an ineffably beautiful tribute to the democratic process. (1984, p. 649)

The success of Cuomo's appeal rests on his ability to make the audience feel as much gratitude toward his parents and as much pride in this country as he feels.

Emotional appeals alone will not persuade an audience. Your persuasive effort will be much more successful if you use emotional appeals in conjunction with your well-reasoned argument.

SUMMARY

Persuasion is the act of convincing an audience to alter or change an attitude, belief, or value, or to take an action. In a persuasive speech your objective is either to modify a belief or ask your audience to act on behalf of an issue or belief. With the speech objective and audience in mind, you begin to consider what would make a suitable topic. We discussed the fact that certain topics lend themselves to persuasive speeches, namely, those that are controversial or current. Choose a topic based on your extensive analysis of self, audience, and situation.

Once you have decided on your topic, your next decision involves choosing an effective organizational design. Four patterns were described in this chapter: problem/solution, topical, comparative advantages, and Monroe's motivated sequence. With the motivated sequence, the focus is on creating a sense of need and then explaining how that need can be satisfied. Each of the five steps in the motivated sequence was described: (1) arousing attention, (2) showing a need, (3) satisfying a need, (4) visualizing the results, and (5) calling for action.

There are three types of persuasive appeals. These include credibility, logical appeals, and emotional appeals. Credibility is the audience's perception of the speaker's competence, dynamism, and trustworthiness or ethics.

Also discussed were techniques for increasing your credibility, such as establishing common ground with the audience and demonstrating to the audience that you have special knowledge regarding your topic. Your efforts in both of these areas will help convince your audience—and yourself—that you are a credible speaker.

It is in the body of the speech that you develop your persuasive argument with the help of either a logical appeal or an emotional appeal. In this chapter we discussed how to develop a logical appeal by using either deductive or inductive reasoning. Deductive reasoning starts with a general premise, is followed by a minor premise, and ends by drawing a conclusion. Conversely, with inductive reasoning you move from specific instances to generalizations. While an argument should always be built on a strong logical base, it is sometimes appropriate to trigger the emotions of an audience. In an emotional appeal you can use emotionally charged language or attempt to personalize your speech in order to achieve the desired response from your audience. As your ability to develop convincing arguments increases, so too will your confidence as a public speaker.

REVIEW QUESTIONS

1. Identify the two different types of persuasive speech objectives.
2. Discuss why audience analysis is so important in choosing your persuasive speech topic.
3. Describe each of the persuasive organizational patterns.
4. Briefly describe the five steps in Monroe's motivated sequence.
5. What steps can a speaker take to increase his or her credibility?
6. How does the issue of trustworthiness and ethics enter into the development of a persuasive speech?

7. Differentiate between inductive and deductive reasoning. How can you use both types of reasoning in a persuasive speech?
8. What are argument fallacies?

9. What role does language play in a speaker's attempt to trigger the emotions of the audience?

KEY CONCEPTS

persuasion
problem/solution
topical sequence
comparative advantage plan
motivated sequence
credibility
competence

dynamism
trustworthiness
ethics
common ground
logical argument
deductive reasoning
inductive reasoning

fallacies
ad hominem
faulty cause-and-effect argument
nonsequitur
overgeneralizations
faulty analogy
emotional appeals

Sample Student Persuasive Speech

Join the Slow Food Movement

The speaker gains the attention of the audience.

The speaker uses a transition.

Approximately seventeen years ago, the proposal of building a McDonald's on the steps of Rome caused quite a stir ("Best Food," 2008). Italian journalist Carlo Petrini protested in anger, spawning the birth of the Slow Food Movement. This nonpolitical movement, which posits taking pleasure in eating fresh foods as its main principle, is a direct response to the fast-food epidemic (Petrini, 2007). Petrini was inspired by the idea that "breaking bread" with friends and family is a "fundamental" part of our cultural heritage, and the globalization of cheap, unhealthy foods threatens these traditions ("Best Food," 2008, par. 6). Take a moment to imagine the kinds of foods that are pleasing to your palate: do you think of Grandma's pot roast, Mom's signature pasta dish, or Dad's mouth-watering smoked turkey? Or do you think of a processed beef patty that includes meat from a dozen different cows? After reading many articles and perusing Petrini's book *Slow Food Nation*, I feel

The speaker establishes her credibility.

qualified to discuss with you the ensuing problems we face as the food industry threatens our nation. As students, we eat fast food all the time because we are so busy. But your physical and mental health are important and the Slow Food Movement can help us lead healthier lives. Today, I am here to persuade you to become part of the Slow Food Movement by illuminating problems of obesity, food processing, the downfall of small farmers, and the loss of cultural traditions. To begin with, I would like to discuss the first issue raised by the Slow Food Movement: obesity.

The speaker shows a need or problem.

According to Morgan Spurlock (2004), the director of *Supersize Me*, 60 percent of all Americans are considered obese. A major factor that contributes to obesity is the fact that fast food is convenient and affordable. In a nation where people are constantly "on the go" and don't have time to prepare a meal, fast food seems like the best option (Innes, 2008). However, the fact that fast food is readily accessible enables laziness, which further perpetuates obesity. According to John Fiscalini, "A lot of people don't like to cook.

The speaker uses an oral citation.

They like to nuke. We do live in a society where our time is so valuable that we don't sit and enjoy meals like our forefathers did" ("Slow Food Movement Picks," 2008, par. 7).

Another problem posed by the Slow Food Movement regards the processing industrialized food undergoes. For example, many of us enjoy sitting down with the family to chow down on turkey during the Thanksgiving holiday. However, have you ever stopped to wonder how that delicious meat is grown? According to Michael Pollan (2003), nowadays people commonly purchase what is referred to as "Broad Breasted White Turkey." "This turkey has been so thoroughly industrialized (to produce lots of white meat fast) that it can no longer fly, survive outdoors, or reproduce without help" (Pollan, 2003). These turkeys are ready for slaughter three to four months sooner than naturally grown turkeys, and their breasts are so huge due to growth hormones that they can only reproduce through artificial insemination (Pollan,

2003). Do you really want to be eating that? Even the freshness of produce is questionable. "The average distance food travels from farm to table is 1,500 miles. In the delay, sugars turn to starches, plant cells shrink and produce loses its vitality" (Hopkins, 2008). People who buy from local farmers get food that has only been sitting out for a day or two, whereas produce from Jewel or Strack and Van Til's that has been sitting on a "truck or supermarket shelf for a week" is less nutritious (Hopkins, 2008). And this is just the food that you buy at the supermarket. What about the food from fast-food restaurants?

"Every day in the United States, roughly 200,00 people are sickened by foodborne disease, 900 are hospitalized, and fourteen die," mainly children and the elderly (Schlosser, 2002, p. 195). The meat packing industry supplies beef from diseased cattle, causing foodborne illnesses such as the E. coli virus to infect unsuspecting consumers (Schlosser, 2002). Schlosser (2002) states, "A single fast food hamburger now contains meat from dozens or even hundreds of different cattle" and incompetent slaughterhouse inspectors are responsible for the distribution of "beef contaminated with fecal material, hair, insects, metal shavings, urine and vomit" (pp. 204–207).

Aside from obesity and food processing, "Slow Foodies" are concerned with the downfall of small farmers. Local economies suffer as a result of booming fast food industries and the low cost of processed foods found in the supermarket. According to Hopkins (2008), small farmers are a "vanishing breed" because their businesses are threatened by the increase of commercial industries, such as Tyson Foods and WalMart. "Crop fields, wildflower meadows and picturesque barns will survive only as long as farms are financially stable" (Hopkins, 2008). The current farm bill passed by Congress "favors industrial agriculture and undermines efforts to promote sustainable, organic and family-based farming" ("Slow Food Movement Picks," 2008, par. 11). The current farm bill is hurting the farming community, with more and more farmers becoming increasingly poor. The downfall of the American farmer will continue to be a problem if people do not fight for reforms and reject the "the industrialization of our food system" that has resulted in "an industrialization of eating" (Pollan, 2003).

Giant multinational food corporations are not only poisoning the nation with their processed foods, but they are also a threat to cultural identity and traditions. As stated by Pollan (2003) in his article "Cruising on the Ark of Taste," "What we eat is a marker of our cultural identity." He discusses how Native Americans, who have used Iroquois corn for culinary and spiritual purposes, are having difficulty preserving this vegetable. Hybrids of plants and animals are causing traditional foods to disappear, threatening biodiversity as well (Pollan, 2003). Activists are currently working to collect seeds from endangered food plants in order to preserve cultural heritage (Pollan, 2003). So what can be done to stop this problem from growing? Practice the ideals of the Slow Food Movement and educate others about it.

The first step is simple: stop eating fast food! Reject food items that are processed and reach for healthy alternatives: Fruits, vegetables, and whole-grain breads and pastas are delicious, give you more energy, and are better for

The speaker presents a solution to satisfy the need.

your body. Take time to savor the food you eat and slowly ingest it to avoid overeating.

The next step is to shop more sensibly. Take time each week to shop at local food markets to purchase items that are fresh and organic. It may cost a little bit more, but the money you will save on healthcare will be worth it in the long run. Also, if you buy foods from local food producers and farm stands it will "narrow the gap between producers and consumers" (Hani, 2008, par. 15). "By supporting local farms, you help ensure that there will be local farms tomorrow" (Hopkins, 2008). If you don't want to shop at local food markets, shop at places such as Trader Joe's and Whole Foods that offer a wide selection of organic food. If you must shop at a grocery chain, only shop in the outer aisles of the grocery store where fresh fruits, vegetables, meats and dairy products are available. If you find yourself browsing the inner aisles, always read the labels of food you are purchasing. If you are unable to pronounce an ingredient, you probably shouldn't be putting it into your body (Innes, 2008). Finally, educate others about Slow Food and the dangers of eating processed foods. Go online in search of local Slow Food chapters to find out about upcoming lectures, and bring a friend.

The speaker helps the audience visualize the results of taking the prescribed action.

Just imagine living in a nation where the majority of the population is at a healthy weight. Imagine only eating food that is "good, clean, and fair" (Petrini, 2007). If you join the Slow Food Movement, you will become healthier while taking pleasure in fresh, homemade foods. You can help local economies prosper and keep cultural traditions alive. If you don't embrace Slow Food ideals, industrialized food corporations will continue to control the masses and render local food producers obsolete. The average number of obese people will continue to rise, and thousands will continue to be adversely affected by processed foods.

The speaker uses a signpost ending.

The speaker calls the audience to act.

Appreciation to audience.

In summation, I strongly urge to abandon your fast-food lifestyle and make an effort to live by the pleasure-seeking ideals of Slow Food. Make a concerted effort to eat just one meal a day the slow food way. Buy fresh foods and take the time to prepare and enjoy a savory meal with family and friends. It will not only remind you of traditions that are important to our cultural heritage, but also will benefit your mind, body, and spirit ("Best Food," 2008). Thank you for your time.

Lindsay Hingst
Purdue University Calumet
Spring 2009
Used by Permission

References

Best food. (2008, August 30). *Irish Times*. Retrieved from http://search.ebscohost.com/login.aspx?direct=true&db=nfh&AN=9FY1274925063&site=ehost-live

Hani, Yoko. (2008, February 29). Slow-food movement creeps to Japan. *Japan Times*. Retrieved from http://search.ebscohost.com/login.aspx?direct=true&db=nfh&AN=2W62W6837927293&site=ehost-live

Hartz-Seeley, Deborah S. (2008, July 10). What prehistoric man ate: Forage through history and learn that the popular notion of eating local foods began when giant beasts roamed South Florida. *Sun-Sentinel*. Retrieved from http://search .ebscohost.com/login.aspx?direct=true&db=nfh&AN=2W62W62522120620& site=ehost-live

Hopkins, Jim. (2003, November 25). 'Slow Food Movement' gathers momentum. *USA Today*. Retrieved from http://www.usatoday.com/money/industries/food/ 2003-11-25-slowfood_x.htm?POE=click-refer

Innes, Stephanie. (2008, January 9). Slow food growing fast: International movement even has Tucson branch. *Arizona Daily Star*. Retrieved from http://search .ebscohost.com/login.aspx?direct=true&db=nfh&AN=2W62W6211706227& site=ehost-live

Petrini, Carlo. (2007). *Slow food nation: Why our food should be good, clean, and fair*. Random House, Inc.

Pollan, Michael. (2003, May 01). Cruising on the ark of taste. *Mother Jones*. Retrieved from http://www.motherjones.com/news/feature/2003/05/ma_372_01.html

Schlosser, Eric. (2002). What's in the meat. In *Fast Food Nation* (pp. 194–222). New York: Houghton Mifflin Company.

Slow food movement picks up momentum in the USA. (2008, September 02). *Environmental New Network*. Organic Consumers' Corporation. 2008. Retrieved from http://www.enn.com/agriculture/article/38069

Spurlock, Morgan. (Morgan Spurlock). (2004). *Supersize me* [Motion picture]. Kathbur Pictures Inc.

Stapleton, John. (2008, August 04). Slow food movement provides shot in the arm for struggling farmers. *The Australian*. Retrieved from http://search.ebscohost.com/ login.aspx?direct=true&db=nfh&AN=2008080410312723115&site=ehost-live/

Glossary

abdicrats   People who lack confidence and find it difficult to make decisions.

abstract terms   Language that is general or vague.

abstraction   The use of broad terms to explain ideas or concepts.

active listening   Listening with a sense of purpose.

ad hominem   An argument that attacks the speaker and does not address the issue.

adaptors   Nonverbal behaviors individuals use to adjust to or cope with uncomfortable communication situations.

affect displays   Nonverbal signs of our emotional state.

affection   The third interpersonal need identified by Schutz is the desire for intimacy.

agenda   An outline of the points to be discussed by a group.

aggression   Hostility; forcing a solution advantageous to ourselves.

allness stereotyping   We attribute a particular characteristic to a group of people for the purpose of this discussion.

ambiguous nonverbal messages   Nonverbal messages are ambiguous; it is difficult for anyone to accurately interpret the meaning of nonverbal communication.

analogy   Compares the similar features in two seemingly different objects or situations.

anecdotes   Brief narratives and stories to help personalize your ideas. They can help you make abstract ideas come alive for your audience.

antonyms   Words that have opposite meanings.

appearance   The speaker's appearance communicates a message to the audience. The audience sees you before you speak, thus their first impression of you can be shaped by your appearance.

arrangement   The physical placement of the members of a group.

articulation   If your audience is to understand the words in your speech, you must say them clearly.

attitude   A predetermined position regarding a person, event, concept, or object; affects the way we interpret data.

attribution   Involves assigning causation to our behavior and the behavior of others.

authoritative opinion   Words or ideas of individuals knowledgeable about a topic, similar or different ideas, facts, or concepts.

autocrat or autocratic leader   Person who dominates the communication process.

avoidance   We retreat from a problem in a relationship.

avoiding   The eighth stage of relational development; characterized by distancing.

bar graph   Primarily used to show the way different items compare and relate to one another.

blind quadrant   A window in the Johari window that represents the part of self that we either unconsciously reveal to others or are actually unaware of.

body   Main part of a speech.

bonding   The fifth stage of relational development; characterized by public expressions of commitment.

brainstorming   Encourages creativity and the free flow of ideas.

call for action   To inspire or motivate the audience to act.

causal order   Establishes the fact that certain events are linked to other events that have precipitated them.

certainty   The belief that others cannot possibly contribute new knowledge to the situation.

challenging the audience   Occurs when the speaker calls on the audience to think further about the topic.

channel   The vehicle by which the message is communicated from the source to the receiver.

chronemics   The study of how we use time.

circumscribing   The seventh stage of relational development; characterized by less communication and defense mechanisms.

closed survey   The respondent must select an answer from two or more choices.

closed questions   Designed to elicit specific feedback from the respondent.

closing   The final part of an interview.

closure   Filling in the gaps when parts are missing from stimuli.

coercive power   Derived from one's perceived ability to control another's behavior through negative reinforcement.

cohesiveness   Demonstrated sense of purpose within a group.

commitment   Motivation of members to meet the goals of the group; also plays a significant role in the outcome of small-group interactions.

committee   Small group of people assigned a task by a larger group.

common ground   One way to enhance your credibility is to establish common ground with the audience. For example, tell them you like them in some way.

communication   The interdependent process of sending, receiving, and understanding messages.

communication climate   State of mind brought to each communication situation.

comparative advantage plan   Often the audience already understands the problem but is looking for the best solution. In this case, you might want to use a comparative plan. This plan allows you to compare your solution to others' and to show how your plan or proposal is superior.

comparisons   Similarities and differences between ideas, facts, or concepts.

competence   Demonstrated ability or quality.

conclusion   The last section of a speech. It functions to draw the speech to an end, to reiterate the central theme of the presentation, and to indicate to the audience what you want them to do.

concrete terms   Language that is detailed and specific.

conflict phase   Ideas begin to surface regarding decision making, and disagreement and tension surface.

connotative meaning   Meaning determined by someone's experiences, values, and culture.

content message   The obvious message, words or language used.

context   The conditions surrounding communication with others are referred to as the context of the interaction.

control   Power or influence; a means of making the other party conform to our way of thinking.

control needs   Desire for power or influence.

coordinate points   Major ideas in a speech that grow out of the thesis statement.

cost-benefit theory   People choose to maintain or exit relationships based on the rewards they receive within those relationships.

cover letter   A short letter that introduces you to a prospective employer.

credibility   A variable that plays a significant role in the persuasion process. Does the audience perceive

the speaker as someone who is qualified to speak on a particular topic?

criteria   The minimum requirements a solution must have to be acceptable.

critical listening   Evaluating the speaker's message or intent.

culturally bound   Meaning derived from one's culture.

culture   The customary beliefs and attitudes of a racial, religious, or social group.

dating   The use of a specific time reference to clarify a message.

decision by consensus   Genuine agreement among members that an appropriate decision has been made.

decision by leader   The leader makes all decisions for the group.

decision by majority vote   Democracy in action.

decoding   The process of interpreting or attaching meaning to symbols.

deductive reasoning   Follows a simple formula: it starts with a general premise, is followed by a minor premise, and ends by drawing a conclusion.

defense mechanisms   Defensive communication is a person's reaction, either verbal or nonverbal, to a communication situation in which he or she feels personally threatened or uncomfortable.

defensive climate   Inhibits the interaction between people.

defensive communication   A reaction, either verbal or nonverbal, to a communication situation in which he or she feels personally threatened or uncomfortable.

definition   When your speech includes jargon (terminology of a specialized group or activity) or technical terms that the average audience has difficulty understanding, you should define those terms using language that is more appropriate for the audience.

democrat or democratic leader   Demonstrates his or her confidence in the group by involving group members in decision-making matters.

demographics   Easily identifiable characteristics such as age, sex, and ethnic/cultural/religious background.

demonstration   Method for explaining a point or idea to an audience.

denial   Refusal to acknowledge that a problem exists.

denotative meaning   Specific reference of a word; it is what we would find if we looked in a dictionary.

description   An image created verbally using concrete or abstract language.

descriptive language   Employs specific words that represent observable behavior or phenomena.

descriptiveness The ability to focus on observable behavior.

differentiating The sixth stage of relationship development; characterized by the need for independence and autonomy.

discreteness Quality of being separate.

distancing Keeping others away by acting cold, conceited, and aloof.

doublespeak Language used to misrepresent ideas or to mislead the listener.

dyadic communication The interaction between two people.

dynamism Degree of excitement that the speaker brings to the presentation.

emblems Body motions that take the place of words.

emergence phase Groups grow anxious to reach a decision.

emotional appeals Are used to trigger the emotions or feelings of an audience.

empathy The ability to understand what someone else is feeling, involves looking at a situation from the other person's perspective.

empowerment The ability to make choices.

encoding The process of putting thoughts, ideas, or feelings into meaningful symbols that another person can understand.

equality Treating others on a par with ourselves, represents a supportive climate.

esteem needs The desire for influence or status within the social structure.

ethics Rules that govern moral behavior.

etymology History of a word's development or use in the language where it is found.

euphemisms Words that substitute for other words because they are more pleasant.

evaluative behavior Judgmental; it attacks the individual rather than that person's actions.

examples Statements that attempt to illuminate the facts.

experimenting The second stage of relationship development; characterized by more in-depth topic discussion.

expert power One's superior knowledge in a particular field.

extemporaneous speech Speaker delivers the presentation from notes; spontaneous, yet prepared.

external noise Includes sounds or visual stimuli that draw our attention away from the intended message.

eye contact Perhaps one of the most difficult skills for the public speaker to master. Your eyes are one of the most revealing features; therefore, a conscious effort to establish direct eye contact acknowledges that you wish to draw the audience in.

facial expressions Your face communicates your feelings, so use it to help communicate your message to the audience. As with gestures, your facial expressions should be spontaneous, arising naturally from your involvement with the topic.

factual example Something that you have observed.

fallacies Flawed arguments.

family People who are related to you (parents, siblings, etc.).

faulty analogy Invalid comparison.

faulty cause-and-effect argument No proof offered to show that one event caused the other to happen.

feedback The receiver's response to the sender's message; it provides information about the way the message is being interpreted.

fillers or vocal interruptions Sounds used to fill in the gaps between the words that comprise our messages.

focus groups Used to discover what people are thinking and feeling and are primarily used by advertisers and marketers.

formula communication Safe, nonthreatening communication that involves little or no risk.

forum The group presents its ideas to an audience.

frame of reference Allows us to create and interpret messages; our unique view of the world and everything in it.

full-sentence outline Full sentences to list the major and minor points, as well as the different forms of support in the presentation.

functional perspective Leadership focuses on the kinds of leadership behaviors that any member of the group can exhibit, which collectively result in the group's making progress.

gatekeeper One who attempts to regulate the flow of communication within the group.

general purpose The overriding goal of a presentation is to inform, to persuade, or to entertain.

generalization The use of nonspecific language to describe objects, events, and feelings.

generic language We once agreed that "he" referred to any person, or that "man" referred to all people. This is called generic language.

gestures Hand movement in a speech delivery should be spontaneous; in other words, it should naturally stem from the speaker's involvement with the subject. Your hands can be used to emphasize or clarify your ideas, but are useful only as long as they remain natural.

graduated scale Also known as the Likert scale, gives individuals the opportunity to rank their feelings on a continuum.

groupthink The illusion of consensus among the group members.

halo and horns stereotyping Based on our observations of an individual in a particular situation or setting, we develop either a positive or negative perception about that person; we then allow our initial perception to transfer to other situations.

hearing One's physical ability to perceive sounds.

hidden quadrant One window in the Johari window; represents the part of self we keep to ourselves.

highly scheduled body Includes all the questions that the interviewer plans to ask.

hypothetical example Invites the audience to imagine a situation created expressly for the speech they are listening to.

ideal individuals People who feel comfortable with themselves and with others.

illustrators Nonverbal symbols that reinforce a verbal message.

impression management How we want others to perceive us.

impromptu speech Speaker delivers a presentation without preparation.

inclusion needs Desire to be part of a group.

indexing A technique that takes into account the individual differences among people, objects, and places.

individual roles The group member is more concerned with his or her own needs and recognition than of the overall group.

inductive reasoning One moves from specific instances to generalizations.

inflection The inflection of your voice can and should change as you move to different points in the speech. As you try to stir the audience, for example, the pitch of your voice should rise.

informational interview To acquire facts about a specific topic.

informational listening Allows you to focus on the content of the message in order to gain knowledge.

informative speech To impart knowledge.

initiating First stage of relationship development; characterized by small talk and the development of first impressions.

integrating The fourth stage of relationship development; characterized by coupling.

intensifying The third stage of relationship development; characterized by the expression of feelings for one another.

intentional communication Nonverbal messages conveyed by conscious decision.

interference Noise.

internal noise Thoughts or feelings that prevent us from processing a sender's message.

interpersonal communication The informal exchange that occurs between two or more people.

interpersonal conflict An expressed struggle between at least two interdependent parties who perceive incompatible goals, scarce rewards, and interference from the other parties in achieving their goals.

interpersonal needs theory William Schutz developed a theory based on the nature of our interpersonal needs. His theory argues that people have certain needs that affect their communication in interpersonal relationships: the need for inclusion, the need for control, and the need for affection.

interpreting To clarify the message and offer an alternative perception.

interpretation Occurs when we communicate our perceptions to others.

interview A planned and purposeful interaction between two parties in which questions are asked and answers are given.

interviewee The party who responds to questions from the interviewer.

interviewer The party who asks questions of an interviewee.

intimacy Sense of closeness and trust shared with others.

intimate distance That distance at which it is appropriate for highly personal communication encounters to occur.

intrapersonal communication communication with ourselves.

introduction The first part of a public presentation or interview.

jargon Terminology of a specialized group or activity.

Johari window Visual representation of self.

journals Contain research findings carried out in a particular field.

key-phrase outline Abbreviated version of the full-sentence outline that is intended as a cue to each point in the presentation.

kinesics The study of bodily movements.

knowledge-gaining groups Come together to learn or experience new things.

laissez-faire leader Gives minimal direction or instruction to group members; rather, members have complete freedom to make decisions.

language An arbitrary system of symbols that is governed by rules and conveys power.

leadership The ability to exert influence on a group by providing a sense of direction or vision.

leading questions Designed to move the interview in a specific direction.

legitimate power Derived from one's position of authority.

Likert scale Gives individuals the opportunity to rank their feelings on a continuum.

line graph Useful in demonstrating change over a period of time.

linear model The linear model argues that communication can only move in one direction, from the sender to the receiver.

listening More complex than hearing, it demands that we concentrate on what others say to us. To listen effectively, we must move the focus from ourselves and instead focus on the other person.

logical argument Giving one or more good reasons for a plan or proposal.

magazines Have a longer interval between issues than daily newspapers.

maintenance roles Deal with the relationships within the group.

manuscript speech Delivery of a speech word for word from a prepared statement.

Maslow's hierarchy of needs According to Abraham Maslow, people have the same basic needs, which are best understood when explained in terms of a hierarchy. These needs are classified as physiological, safety, belonging, esteem, and self-actualization.

mean The average of a set of numbers.

median The middle point of a set of numbers.

memorized speech Speaker delivers the presentation from memory; notes are used only as a reference.

message The thought, feeling, or action that is sent from the source to the receiver with the use of symbols.

message overload Attention to details instead of the main ideas of the message.

mode The number that occurs most frequently in a set of numbers.

moderately scheduled body The interviewer determines the primary questions ahead of time.

motivated sequence Design, advanced by Alan H. Monroe, that focuses on creating a sense of need and then explaining how that need can be satisfied.

multichanneled communication Use of body, voice, and, appearance to convey a message.

narrative Story or an account of an event told orally.

need to belong The desire to be part of a group.

needs Physical or emotional desires that grow out of circumstances in our immediate environment.

neutral One that does not "take sides."

neutral questions Questions that reveal nothing of the interviewer's biases, preferences, or expectations.

neutrality Indifference toward another individual.

newspapers An excellent source of supporting material for current topics is the newspaper. Topics tend to be brief but focused. Daily newspapers routinely include detailed accounts of events and reactions to those events, as well as factual and statistical information.

noise Often thought of as interference to the communication process.

nonscheduled body The interviewer works from an outline of topics, but no actual questions.

nonsequitur The minor points are not related to the major points, or the conclusion does not logically follow the points that precede it.

nonverbal communication Encompasses the broad spectrum of messages we send without verbalizing our thoughts or feelings.

norms Rules that dictate how group members ought to behave.

observation Helps us learn many things about audiences, such as sex, age, race, and how they react to what others say.

open quadrant A window in the Johari window that represents the aspect of our self we share with others.

opening The beginning of an interview.

open survey Gives respondents the opportunity to fully express their feelings.

open questions Nonrestrictive questions designed to give the respondent maximum latitude in formulating an answer.

oral citation Give credit orally to a source used in the presentation.

organization Another phase of the perception process; in other words, we perceive that certain items belong together, and therefore we tend to organize them that way.

orientation phase Beginning of a group discussion; members attempt to get to know one another.

outdoing others The need to constantly top the achievements of others.

overgeneralizations Add a dramatic effect to your speech, but are not logical.

overly critical communication Judging the behavior of others.

overpersonal individuals People who fear intimacy and who overcompensate by establishing many relationships.

oversocial individuals People who feel uncomfortable in social situations and overcompensate by excessive group participation.

panel Individuals attempt to solve problems or inform an audience about a topic.

paralanguage The vocal aspect of delivery that accompanies speech and other nonverbal utterances.

paraphrasing Restating another person's message in our own words.

passive aggression Subtle and covert aggression.

passive listening Only the sender is involved; no feedback is provided.

pause It is virtually impossible to deliver a speech without inserting some pauses. Pauses can be very effective and helpful as you shift from one idea to the next, giving your audience a sense that you are moving on to another point.

peers A group of significant others, also can profoundly influence our self-concept.

perception The process of assigning meaning to stimuli.

perception checking Using questions to clarify the understanding of the verbal and/or nonverbal message.

periodicals Written sources published at regular intervals (that is, weekly, monthly, quarterly, or semiannually).

personal constructs The characteristics we use to judge others.

personal distance The area most appropriate for interpersonal interactions dealing with personal matters, that is, approximately eighteen inches to four feet.

personal growth groups Focus on the individual and his or her personal well-being.

personal individuals People who feel comfortable with their ability to handle personal relationships.

personal space The area that exists between ourselves and others.

persuasion The act of convincing an audience through verbal and nonverbal communication.

persuasive speech Purpose is to change an attitude.

physiological needs The most basic needs, such as food, water, and air.

physical setting Such factors as seating arrangements, time of day, degree of privacy, room size, temperature, and lighting affect how people communicate with each other.

pie graph A pie shape divided into wedges, helpful in demonstrating to an audience the way something whole is divided into parts or the way one part of a whole relates proportionally to the other parts.

posture One aspect of bodily action that commands the attention of your audience. Avoid slouching or bending your knees; keep your spine straight, your shoulders back, and your feet a comfortable distance apart.

power Control, authority, or influence over others.

powerlessness Feeling not in control or having no power to make decisions.

presentational aids Visual or audio support for the verbal message.

primary questions Questions that introduce a major area of discussion to be guided by the interviewer.

primary sources Documents such as letters, manuscripts, or interviews.

problem orientation The parties involved realize that several people contribute to the problem and that adjustment of behavior is necessary on all fronts.

problem/solution order Approach to organizing a speech that involves identifying a conflict and then offering a potential course of action that will correct the problem.

problem-solving or task-oriented groups Come together to answer a question or provide a solution to a problem.

process-related leadership behaviors Those behaviors concerned with maintaining a positive climate within the group.

pronunciation If your audience is to understand the words in your speech, you must say them correctly.

prototypes Representatives of our ideal; we use this ideal as a means of comparison.

provisionalism A willingness to explore new ideas.

proxemics The study of physical space as it relates to human interaction.

proximity Closeness to one another; way to organize stimuli.

psychological climate The attitudes and feelings we have about ourselves and the other people involved in the communication.

psychological withdrawal We are forced to stay in a situation that makes us feel uncomfortable. We mentally escape from the situation.

public communication An individual shares information with a large group; the usual structure has a speaker presenting ideas to an audience.

public distance A distance exceeding twelve feet is most appropriate for public communication.

questioning Requesting additional information from the sender in order to help us understand the message.

question of fact The group argues whether or not a statement is true or false.

question of policy The group must decide if any specific action is in order.

question of value Morality is at issue.

quotation Someone else's words used as support in the presentation.

rate The rate of your speech is the number of words you deliver in a given amount of time. Your rate should vary depending on the speaking situation.

reaction formation We behave contrary to the way we really feel.

receiver The individual to whom the message is sent.

referent power Derived from one's feeling of identification with another.

reflective appraisals Also called the "looking glass self" because we see ourselves through other people's eyes.

regulative rules Unspoken rules that guide our use of language.

regulators Nonverbal behaviors used to control, or regulate, communication between people.

reinforcement phase Final phase of the decision-making process; consensus is achieved.

relational messages Sent nonverbally; hidden messages.

resume A short account of one's qualifications for a particular position.

reward power One's perceived ability to provide things like money, objects, or love.

rhetorical question Posed to the audience and later developed or answered in the talk.

roles A set of expected behaviors each member of the group must follow.

safety needs The second level on Maslow's hierarchy, which refers to our desire to feel secure.

sarcasm Biting sense of humor designed to keep people away and to maintain control of a situation.

secondary questions Designed to gain additional information from the interviewee.

secondary sources Interpretations of primary material.

selective attention The process of determining what we pay attention to and what we ignore.

self-actualization Perceiving that you are at the highest level of what you believe to be your potential.

self-concept Our perception of ourselves, or how we picture ourselves in a very broad sense.

self-disclosure The conscious decision to share personal information

self-esteem Our measure of self-worth; as such, it is the evaluative dimension of our self-concept.

self-fulfilling prophecy Our behavior matches someone else's expectations.

self-serving bias Occurs when we see ourselves in a positive light by blaming others or external forces for problems.

sequence Order of ideas in a presentation.

significant others Those individuals to whom we are emotionally close and whom we allow to influence our lives.

signposts Help the audience know where you are in the speech.

silence The absence of using your voice.

similarity Stimuli that resemble one another are commonly grouped together.

similes Like analogies, they compare two things; but unlike analogies, similes compare similar objects or situations using the words "like" or "as."

sincerity A key component to sharing ideas. As the speaker, you want to show the audience that you care about the topic, its presentation, and the audience.

situation A step in choosing an appropriate topic is analyzing the situation; consider the size of your audience, the time limit, and the size and shape of the room.

situational perspective Each group creates a new situation, and this situation dictates which style of leadership is most appropriate.

slang Used by a specific group; can be cultural, geographic, or generational.

small-group communication A small number of people who share a common goal or objective and interact face to face.

social distance Distance most appropriate for communication of a non-personal nature.

social groups Not to solve problems or accomplish specific tasks, but to interact.

social power Potential for changing attitudes, beliefs, and behaviors of others.

source The person who creates and sends a message.

spatial order Refers to organizing the parts of a topic according to the relationship of their positions.

specific purpose Takes into account the following factors: (1) what you hope to accomplish, (2) which aspect of the topic you will cover, by narrowing your topic, and (3) your intended audience.

spontaneity An open discussion of feelings

stagnating The eighth stage of relational development; characterized by little or no self-disclosure.

startling statement Shocks, arouses, or surprises an audience.

statistics Ideas presented in numerical terms; used as supporting material.

status Relative standing of one party in relation to another.

stereotyping Placing or categorizing people, places, objects, or events into groups based on generalized characteristics; also contributes to the way we perceive others.

strategy To manipulate interactions between people.

subordinate points Minor points that grow out of the major ideas.

summation Reinforces the main points in your speech.

superiority An attitude that an individual is better, more important, or more valuable than someone else.

suppression We acknowledge that a problem exists, but we attempt to minimize its importance.

supportive climate Encourages free and open interaction between people.

survey A set of questions used to gather information from an audience.

symbols Things, names for the objects around us.

symposium Small group of speakers who share a topic, but who discuss it individually, often focusing on a specific aspect of the topic.

synonyms Different words that have the same or nearly the same meaning.

task roles Used when concerned about meeting the group's goal or objective.

task-related leadership behaviors Those actions whose purpose is to keep the group focused on the problem or question.

technical language The specialized terms associated with a particular discipline, skill, or career.

terminating The last stage of relational development; characterized by the end of the relationship.

territory The space we stake out as our own.

thesis statement The major ideas of the speech; at the same time, it refines the specific purpose.

time order Ideas arranged in a chronological framework.

topic order Involves breaking down your main topic into smaller points that are pertinent to the main idea.

topical sequence An important part of a successful persuasion is providing good reasons for the belief you want the audience to hold or the action you want them to take. In the body of your speech, you can provide a detailed description of each of the reasons the audience should accept your proposal, putting your strongest ideas first or last.

touch A form of nonverbal communication that conveys a wide range of emotions.

trait perspective Certain individuals are "born leaders" because they possess such qualities as a forceful personality, marked intelligence, and dynamic communication skills.

transactional model Describes communication as an interdependent process where the speaker and receiver are simultaneously sending and receiving messages.

transition Provides a link between the main parts of your speech.

transitional preview Gives the audience an idea of what is to come.

transitional summary Recaps all the coordinate points.

trustworthiness Refers to the kind of "character" communicated to the audience by the speaker.

underpersonal individuals People who shy away from intimate relationships.

undersocial individuals People who find it difficult to participate in realtionships; those who have a lack of confidence.

unintentional communication Nonverbal messages conveyed without awareness or conscious decision.

unknown quadrant Window in the Johari window that represents to ourselves and others parts of our self we have yet to discover.

vague language Language that lacks directness and specificity; it is void of details.

value Determines the morality of an issue; that is, either something is good or bad, right or wrong.

volume The loudness of a speaker's voice.

walking transition Taking a small step to indicate the presentation is moving to another point.

References

Beaver, H. D. (2000, June). Visual aids: how much is too much? *ABA Banking Journal*, 92, 80.

Beebe, S. A., Masterson, J. T. (2006). *Communicating in small groups*, 7th ed. New York: Longman Press.

Beebe, S., Masterson, T. *Communicating in Small Groups: Principles and Practice*, eighth edition. Published by Allyn and Bacon, Boston, MA. Copyright © 2006 by Pearson Education. Reprinted by permission of the publisher.

Brilhart, J. K., Galanas, G. J., Adams, K. (2001). *Effective group discussion*, 10th ed. New York: McGraw Hill.

Browne, M. N., Freeman, K. E., Williamson, C. L. (2001) The importance of critical thinking for student use of the Internet. *College Student Journal* 34, 391–399.

Burlingame, Burl. (1998, March 6). Eddie: Riding on the Crest of the Myth. *Local Moco*. Retrieved October 21, 2008, from http://archives.starbulletin.com/1998/03/09/features/story1.html Honolulu Star Bulletin.

Burleson, B. R. (2003). Emotional support skills. In J. O. Greene & B. R. Burleson (Eds.), *Handbook of communication and social interaction skills* (pp. 551–594). Mahwah, NJ: Erlbaum. Retrieved from http://www.questia.com/read/104777811

Burrell, N. A., Koper, R. J. (1994). The efficacy of powerful/powerless language on persuasiveness/credibility: a meta-analytic review. In R.W. Preiss and M. Allen, (Eds.), *Prospects and precautions in the use of meta-analysis*. Dubuque, IA: Brown & Benchmark.

Bush, G. W. (2001a, September 20). Address to a joint session of congress and the American people. Retrieved from www.whitehouse.gov/news/releases/2001/09/20010920-8.html

Bush, G. W. (2001b, December 28). President, General Franks discuss war effort. Retrieved from whitehouse.gov/news/releases/2001/12/print/20011228-1html

Carmichael, S. (1969a). Stokely Carmichael explains black power to a black audience. In R. L. Scott and W. Brockreide, (Eds.), *The rhetoric of black power*. New York: Harper & Row.

Carmichael, S. (1969b). Stokely Carmichael explains black power to a white audience in Whitewater, Wisconsin. In R. L. Scott and W. Brockreide, (Eds.), *The rhetoric of black power*. New York: Harper & Row.

Centers for Disease Control and Prevention. (2007). Leading causes of death, females, 2004. Retrieved from http://www.cdc.gov/Women/lcod.htm

Centers for Disease Control and Prevention (2009). Colorectal (colon) cancer incidence rates. Retrieved from http://www.cdc.gov/features/dscolorectalcancer/

Cline, R. J. Welch. (1990, Spring). Detecting groupthink: methods for observing the illusion of unanimity. *Communication Quarterly*, 38, 112–126.

ComScore. (2008, January). *U.S. search engine rankings* [Data file]. Retrieved from http://www.comscore.com/Press_Events/Press_Releases/2008/02/Top_US_Search_Engines

Cooley, C. H. (1912). *Human nature and the social order*. New York: Scribner.

Coombes, A. (2009, May 18). Are we overwhelmed yet? MarketWatch. Retrieved from http://www.marketwatch.com/story/information-overload-deal-with-it

Cuomo, M. (1984, August 15). Keynote Address. *Vital Speeches of the Day*, p. 649. Reprinted by permission.

Diamond Head at a glance. (2006–2008). *Oahu Travel and Vacation Guide* Retrieved October 20, 2008, from http://www.to-hawaii.com/oahu/attractions/diamondhead.php Kanaimea Online Publishing.

Davich, J. (2001, March 22) E-mail explosion. *The Times*, pp. C1–C2.

Dennis, Jaimi. (2008). Personal Interview. Unpublished raw data.

Ekman, P., Friesen, W. V. (1969). The repertoire of nonverbal behavior: categories, origins, and coding. *Semiotica* 1, 49–98.

Ekman, P., Friesen, W. V. (1975). *Unmasking the face*. Englewood Cliffs, NJ: Prentice-Hall.

Ewers, J. (2007, January). "Making it stick." *U. S. News & World Report*. Retrieved from http://www.usnews.com/usnews/biztech/articles/070121/29estickiness_print.htm

Favorite Hawaii Quotations. (1999–2008). *Daily Celebrations* 1. Retrieved November 9, 2008, from http://www.dailycelebrations.com/hawaii_q2.htmCool Pup.

Fogg, B., Soohoo, C., Danielson, D. (2002). How do people evaluate Web site's credibility. Stanford Persuasive Technology Lab. Retrieved from www.consumerwebwatch.org/dynamic/web-credibility-reports-evaluate-abstract.cfm

Fox, A. (2006, January 12). Students able to put lectures on iPod. *The Western Herald*. Retrieved from www.westernherald.com/vnews/display.v?TARGET=printable&article_id=43c5c8d

Fox, S. (2008, August 6). Search engine use Pew Internet & American Life Project [Data file]. Retrieved from http://www.pewinternet.org/~/media/Files/Reports/2008/PIP_Search_Aug08.pdf.pdf

French, R. P., Raven, B. (1968). The bases of social power. In D. Cartwright and A. Zande, (Eds.), *Group dynamics*. New York: Harper & Row.

Frost, J. H., Wilmot, W. W. (1978). *Interpersonal conflict*. Dubuque, IA: William C. Brown.

Gibb, J. (1961). Defensive communication. *Journal of Communication* 11, 141–148.

Goett, J., Foote, K. (2000, March). Cultivating students research and study skills in Web-based learning environments. *Journal of Geography in Higher Education* 24, 92.

Goldbaum, E. (2007, October 5). Technology would help detect terrorists before they strike [University at Buffalo, State University of New York press release]. Retrieved from http://www.buffalo.edu/news/8879

Goss, K. (2000, May/June). Creating a generation of Internet worshipers. *Book Report* 19, 47.

Greenfield, J., Haugh, D. (2006, March 28). When what happens on MySpace doesn't stay on Myspace. *Chicago Tribune*; 159:87, p. 1.

Grob, L., Meyers, R., Schuh, R. (1997). Powerful/powerless language use in group interactions: sex differences or similarities? *Communication Quarterly* 45, 282–303.

Grossman, A. (2008, May 7). Your blog can be group therapy. *CNN*. Retrieved from http://www.cnn.com/2008/LIVING/personal/05/07/blog.therapy/index.html

Hadhazy, A. (2009, May 6). The final frontier: The science of *Star Trek*. *Scientific American*. Retrieved from http://www.scientificamerican.com/article.cfm?id=star-trek-movie-science&page=2

Hall, E. T. (1969). *The hidden dimension*. Garden City, NY: Anchor Books.

Hart, K. (2006, July 20). Portrait of a blogger: Under 30 and sociable. *The Washington Post*. D5. Retrieved from http://www.washingtonpost.com/wpdyn/content/article/2006/07/19/AR2006071901900.html

Health Status. (1994-2008). *Health Trends in Hawaii: A Profile of the Healthcare System* Retrieved November 18, 2008, from http://www.healthtrends.org/status_life_expect.aspx Hawaii Health Information Corporation.

Hill, Juliel. (2003, October). The attention deficit. *Presentations*, 17(10), 26–32.

Honolulu: World's Second Cleanest City. (2008). *Hawaii Travel Guide* Retrieved October 21, 2008, from http://www.hawaiilogue.com/honolulu-worlds-2nd-cleanest-city.html BootsnAll Travel Network.

Huffaker, D., Calvert, S. (2005). Gender, identity, and language use in teenage blogs. *Journal of Computer-Mediated Communication*, 10(2). Retrieved from www.jcmc.Indiana.edu/vol10/issue2/huffaker.html

Internet Stats Today. (2008, November 12). Information overload in Internet. Retrieved from http://internetstatstoday.com/?p=448

Jones, S. & Fox, S. (2009, January 28). Generations online 2009. Pew Internet and American Life Project. Retrieved from http://www.pewinternet.org/Reports/2009/Generations-Online-in-2009.aspx

Knapp, M., Vangelisti, A. L. (1992). *Interpersonal communication and human relationships*. Boston, MA: Allyn & Bacon.

Krebs, B. (2006, June 7). One-third of U.S. companies read employee e-mail [Web log message]. *Washington Post*. Retrieved from

Lenhart, A., Madden, M. Hitlin. P. (2005, July 27). Teens and technology. Pew Internet and American Life Project. Retrieved from http://www.pewinternet.org/

Lieberman, J. (2008, September 2). Speech before the Republican National Convention. Retrieved from http://www.npr.org/templates/story/story.php?storyId=94213979

Lipnack, J., Stamps, J. (2000). *Virtual teams: People working across boundaries with technology*, 2nd ed. John Wiley and Sons, Inc., Hoboken, NJ.

Luau Foods and Recipes. (2008). *Hawaiian Food Glossary* Retrieved October 20, 2008, from http://gohawaii.about.com/cs/luaurecipes/l/aa041902a.htm The New York Times Company.

Luft, J. (1970). *Group processes: an introduction to group dynamics*. Palo Alto, CA: Mayfield.

Lustig, M. & Koester, J. (2010). *Intercultural competence*. 6th ed. Boston: Allyn & Bacon.

Lutz, W. (1999). *Cut through the bull**** and get to the point!: Doublespeak defined*. New York: Harper Collins.

Maslow, A. (1970). *Motivation and personality*. New York: Harper & Row.

Muller, T. (2009, January 10). Apple's FY09 EPS estimate too low. *Financial Alchemist*. Retrieved from http://financialalchemist.blogspot.com

Naish, J. (2009, June 2). Warning: Brain overload. *Times ONLINE*. Retrieved from http://women.timesonline.co.uk/tol/life_and_style/women/the_way_we_live/article6409208.ece

National Alliance to End Homelessness. (2007, October 10). *Homelessness in the United States of America*. Retrieved from http://www.endhomelessness.org/content/article/detai1/1154

Oahu wasn't always the seat of power. (2007). *Hawaii: The Islands of Oahu* Retrieved October 20, 2008, from http://www.gohawaii.com/oahu/learn/history_culture Hawaii Visitors and Convention Bureau.

Oahu Travel and Vacation Guide. (2006–2008). Retrieved October 20, 2008, from http://www.to-hawaii.com/oahu/ Kanaimea Online Publishing.

Obama, B. (2004, July 27). The Audacity of Hope: 2004 Democratic National Convention Address. Retrieved from http://www.AmericanRhetoric.com

Obama, M. (2008, August 25). Democratic National Convention speech. Retrieved from http://www.npr.org/templates/story/story.php?storyId=93963863

Ogden, C. K., Richards, I. A. (1923). *The meaning of meaning*. New York: Harcourt Brace.

O'Grady, D. (2003, September). Meetings in America. Presented at the International Telework Advisory Group Annual Meeting. Retrieved from workingfromanywhere.org/

Osborn, A. (1979). *Applied imagination: principles and procedures of creative problem solving*, 3rd ed. New York: Scribner.

Palin, S. (2008, September 3) . Republican National Convention speech. Retrieved from http://blogs.suntimes.com/sweet/2008/09/sarah_palin_gop_convention_spe.html

Perez, M. (2008, June 10). Many tech workers would accept pay cut to telecommute. *InformationWeek*. Retrieved from http://www.informationweek.com/news/globalcio/trends/showArticle.jhtml?articleID=208403187

Plunkett Research, Ltd. (2009). *Telecommunications Industry Overview* [Data File]. Retrieved from http://www.plunkettresearch.com/Telecommunications/Telecommunications Statistics/tabid/96/Default.aspx

Rademacher, L. (2001). Effective note taking techniques. Unpublished manuscript.

Raine, L. (2009). *Trend data, December 2008*. Pew Internet and American Life Project. Retrieved from http://www.pewinternet.org

Reagan, R. (1984, September 15). Acceptance speech. *Vital Speeches of the Day*, p. 706.

Reardon, M. (2008, September 23). Text messaging explodes in America. *CBS News*. Retrieved from http://www.cbsnews.com/stories/2008/09/23/tech/cnettechnews/main4471183.shtml

Reeve, C. (2003, June 13). On Courage: The Ohio State University Commencement Address. Retrieved from http://www.christreevehomepage.com/spohio_uni_address2003.html

Rhodes, M. (2007, February 8). *Telework trending upward, survey says*. Retrieved from http://www.workingfromanywhere.org/news/pr020707.html

Rhodes, M. (2007, February 8). Telework trending upward, survey says [Press release]. Retrieved from http://www.workingfromanywhere.org/press.html

Rocca, M. (2008, April 6). My name is Mo R., and I am a nomophobe. *CBS News*. Retrieved from http://www.cbsnews.com/stories/2008/04/06/sunday/main3996583.shtml

Rosenbloom, S. (2008, January 3). Putting your best cyberface forward. *New York Times*. Retrieved from http://www.nytimes.com/2008/01/03/fashion/03impression.html

Samter, W. (1994). Unsupportive relationships: Deficiencies in support-giving skills of the lonely person's friends. In B. Burleson, T. L. Albrecht, and I. G. Sarason, (Eds.), *Communicating of social support: messages, interactions, relationships, and community*. Thousand Oaks, CA: Sage.

Sapir, E. (1921). *Language: an introduction to the study of speech*. New York: Harcourt, Brace & World.

Schantz, J. (1999, November 29). The limits of Internet research. *Community College Week* 12, 4.

Schutz, W. (1966). *The interpersonal world*. Palo Alto, CA: Science & Behavior Books.

Seabol, L. (2005, December 27). Online confessions. *Tuscaloosa News*. Retrieved from www.tuscaloosanews.com/apps/pbcs.dll/article?Date=20051227&Category=PULSE

Shrieves, L. (2006, January 12) Are electrontic devices making us antisocial? *Orlando Sentinel*,. from www.sun-sentinel.com/news/local/southflorida/sfl-19electronicdevices,0,1413613.story?coll=sfla-home-headlines.

Skeat, W. (1958). *A concise etymological dictionary of the English language*. Oxford: Clarendon.

Smith, S. E. (2003–2008). What is Kalua Pig?. *Wise Geek*. Retrieved October 26, 2008, from http://www.wisegeek.com/what-is-kalua-pig.htm Conjecture Corporation.

Snyder, B. (2003, May). Teams that span time zones face new work rules. *Stanford Business*. Retrieved from www.gsb.standford.edu/news/bmag/sbsm0305/feature_virtual_teams.shtml

Solomon, Charlene. (2001, June). Managing virtual teams. *Workforce, 80*(6), 60–65.

Starr, K. (2008, January 16). IPod backlash and the hidden costs of your portable security blanket. *Seattle Weekly*. Retrieved from http://www.seattleweekly.com/content/printversion/392887

Stelzner, M. A., Egland, K. L. (1995). Perceived understanding, nonverbal communication, relational satisfaction, and relational stage. Paper presented at the Annual Convention of the Western States Communication Association, Portland, OR.

Stewart, C. J. and Cash, W. B. (2008) *Interviewing: principles and practices*. New York, New York: McGraw-Hill.

Stewart, M. (2008, October 5). Palin hits Obama for terrorist connection. *CNN*. Retrieved from http://www.cnn.com/2008/POLITICS/l0/04/palin.obama/index.html

Stewart, T. (February 5, 2001) Ban it now! Friends don't let friends use PowerPoint. *Fortune*, p. 210.

Sullivan, H. S. (1953). *The interpersonal theory of psychology*. New York: Norton.

Thibaut, J. W., Kelley, H. H. (1959). *The social psychology of groups*. New York: John Wiley & Sons.

Turkle, S. (1995). *Life on the screen*. New York: Simon & Schuster.

U.S. Census Bureau. (2008a). Educational attainment by total money earnings in 2005 [Table]. Retrieved from http://www.census.gov/compendia/statab/2008/tables/08s0220.pdf

U.S. Census Bureau. (2008b, August). Income, poverty, and health insurance coverage in the United States: 2007. Retrieved from http://www.census.gov/prod/2008pubs/p60-235.pdf

U.S. Census Bureau. (2008c). Resident population by sex, race, and Hispanic-origin status: 2007 to 2007 [Table]. Retrieved from http://www.census.gov/compendia/statab/tables/09s0006.pdf

U.S. Department of Justice. (2009, June 1). Preliminary annual uniform crime report. Retrieved from http://www.fbi.gov/ucr/08aprelim/index.html

Verderber, R., Verderber, K. (1995). *Inter-Act: using interpersonal communication skills*. Belmont, CA: Wadsworth.

White, M. and Dorman, S. (2000, April). Confronting information overload. *Journal of School Health* 70, 160–161.

Whorf, B. (1956). The relation of habitual thought and behavior to language. In J. B. Carrol, (Ed.), *Language, thought, and reality*. New York: John Wiley & Sons.

Willer, L. (2001). Warning: welcome to your world baby, gender message enclosed. An analysis of gender messages in birth congratulation cards. *Women and language* 24, 16–23.

Yuen Hernandez, Stacey. (2004, July 30). What's There to Know About Poi?. *Poi to the World-Information about Hawaiian Poi*. Retrieved October 26, 2008, from http:// www.poico.com/artman/publish/article_4.php Craig W. Walsh.

Photo Credits

Page 1: Photos.com; p. 4: Getty Images, Inc.; p. 14: Michael Mancuso/Omni-Photo Communications, Inc.; p. 15: Alex Wong/Pool/MCT/Newscom; p. 20: Getty Images, Inc.; p. 23: Jupiter Unlimited; p. 32: Courtesy of Lisa J. Goodnight; p. 41: © Chuck Savage/CORBIS All Rights Reserved; p. 45: Spencer Grant/ PhotoEdit Inc.; p. 50: Doug Menuez/Getty Images, Inc.- Photodisc/Royalty Free; p. 58: Stock Boston; p. 64: Jupiter Unlimited; p. 68: Bill Bachmann/PhotoEdit Inc.; p. 80: Photodisc/Getty Images; p. 84: Fujifotos/K. Kai/The Image Works; p. 91: Larry Kolvoord/The Image Works; p. 93: Photos to Go; p. 99: Photos to Go; p. 102: Lori Adamski Peek/Stone/Getty Images; p. 109: James Wilson/Woodfin Camp & Associates, Inc.; p. 125: Jupiter Unlimited; p. 129: Paul Thomas/Image Bank/Getty Images; p. 133: Image Source/Corbis RF; p. 135: Tony Latham/Getty Images, Inc. — Stone Allstock; p. 145: Timothy Shonnard/Stone/Getty Images; p. 149: Rhoda Sidney/The Image Works; p. 154: Beaura Kathy Ringrose/Kathy Ringrose; p. 168: Stephen Agricola/The Image Works; p. 172: Photodisc/Getty Images; p. 176: Bruce Ayres/Stone/Getty Images; p. 183: Pearson Learning Photo Studio; p. 187: Sri Maiava Rusden/PacificStock.com; p. 190: Photos.com; p. 193: David Young-Wolff/PhotoEdit Inc.; p. 197: © F. Carter Smith/Bloomberg News/Landov; p. 202: John Neubauer/PhotoEdit Inc.; p. 204: Denis Poroy/AP Wide World Photos; p. 206: Bill Aron/PhotoEdit Inc.; p. 214: Spencer Grant/Photo Researchers, Inc.; p. 224: Spencer Grant/PhotoEdit Inc.; p. 233: © Google; p. 238: AFP PHOTO/Paul J. RICHARDS/Newscom; p. 245: Ron Frehm/AP Wide World Photos; p. 249: Richard Hutchings/PhotoEdit Inc.; p. 259: Lon C. Diehl/PhotoEdit Inc.; p. 260: Jose Gil/Shutterstock; p. 272: Gary Conner/PhotoEdit Inc.; p. 283: Eric Draper/AP Wide World Photos; p. 284: © CORBIS; p. 293: Mary Kate Denny/Stone/Getty Images; p. 298: Jana Birchum/The Image Works; p. 300: AFP PHOTO/Emmanuel DUNAND/Newscom; p. 302: Ron Edmonds/AP Wide World Photos; p. 303: GARY HERSHORN/CORBIS-NY; p. 312: Spencer Grant/PhotoEdit Inc.; p. 321: Joseph Rey Au/AP Wide World Photos; p. 322: Photoshot/Newscom; p. 327: Jupiter Unlimited

Index